Family Therapy

Family Therapy

A Systemic-Behavioral Approach

EDITOR
Joan D. Atwood, Ph.D., C.S.W.
Hofstra University

Nelson-Hall Publishers
Chicago

Cover painting: *New Year's Day III* by Robin McCloskey

Library of Congress Cataloging-in-Publication Data

Atwood, Joan D.
Family therapy : a systemic-behavioral approach / Joan D. Atwood.
p. cm.
Includes bibliographical references and index.
ISBN 0-8304-1300-6
1. Family psychotherapy. 2. Marital psychotherapy. 3. Cognitive therapy. I. Title.
RC488.5.A9 1992
616.89'156—dc20 91-42088
CIP

For information address Nelson-Hall Inc., Publishers, 111 North Canal Street, Chicago, Illinois 60606.

Manufactured in the United States of America

10 9 8 7 6 5 4 3 2 1

The paper used in this book meets the minimum requirements of American National Standard for Information Sciences—Permanence of Paper for Printed Library Materials, ANSI Z39.48-1984.

for my children,

Debby, Barbara, Lisa, Janine, and Brian

Contents in Brief

Contents

ACKNOWLEDGMENTS

This is always the last page I write when I'm finishing a book, and it usually poses a dilemma. It is either the easiest page to write or the most difficult or both. My style is generally to start out at a macro level of analysis and work my way to micro, so I'll try that here.

Thank you to my clients and students who have often taught me more than anyone else about creative and creating realities.

Thank you to my mentors for having exposed me to thinking about thinking and learning about learning.

- To Dr. Eugene Weinstein for social psychology, ethnomethodology, and symbolic interactionism—not to mention "alter ego." I miss you still.
- To Dr. John Gagnon for sociology, sexual scripting theory, and the idea that "we no longer seek truth, we seek relevance in that we construct our world rather than discover it."
- To Dr. Salvador Minuchin for pushing me over the edge when I said there was no cliff.

Thank you to my colleagues who contributed chapters to this project. Although we come from many different backgrounds and situations, we managed to achieve interdependence and autonomy.

A very special thank you to my friends who tolerated this "one more project."

- To Stellye and Mel Weinstein, who gave me pep talks over the phone at 8:30 A.M.
- To Gladys and Shelly Rothbell, who gave me pep talks at 8:45 A.M.
- To Robin Alloy, who gave me pep talks at 9:00 A.M. and occasionally at 11:00 P.M.
- To Bill Atwood, who said I'd better get off the phone if I wanted to get any work done.
- To Larry Maltin, who encouraged me throughout, who introduced me to Eastern philosophies, consciousness, unconsciousness, and who is my coauthor for a new book entitled *Relationships in the '90s*.
- To my graduate assistant Laurie Levine, who was instrumental in helping me end this project. I think I promise you won't have to type any more bibliographies.
- And finally to my family: Brian Atwood; Debra, Michael, Michael Jr., and Danielle Gibbons; Barbara, Steven, and Jessica Winnik; Lisa and Janine Quartararo; Stanley Pryor; Helen, Louis, and Anne Armagno; and Amy Flis. I love you all.

SECTION ONE

Introduction

There were two main goals in writing this book. The first was to present an integrated approach to family therapy—integrated in that the focus of the book is a combination of systemic and cognitive-behavioral theory. The diagnosis/assessment process is systemic, while the interventions are primarily cognitive-behavioral. The second goal was to present the material in the basic framework of a life cycle.

As the field of marital and family therapy expanded and scientific research accumulated, variations on systems theory emerged. Haley's strategic theory (1963), Bowen's multigenerational theory (1961), Minuchin's structural theory (1974), and MRI's communication theory (1959) provided various orientations that continue to expand the focus of the field from the more traditional individual therapies to encompass the family. These diversified theoretical orientations offered the premise that dysfunction within the marital or family system is represented by one (or more) member(s) as symptomatic behavior. In other words, using this approach, the locus of pathology and the focus of intervention are on the family system, or the context within which the individual is embedded, rather than on the individual him/herself. This, of course, represents what most theoreticians call a paradigmatic shift, à la Kuhn.

It is important to note, though, that these theoretical orientations in the field of marital and family therapy, although mainly based on systems theory, are comprised of distinctly different and sometimes contradictory components. Much of this diversity centers around treatment approaches, case management, and the role and function of the therapist. As a result, the field of marriage and family therapy needs a theoretical synthesis, based on responsible scientific research. What is necessary now is an integration of the basic concepts and unique techniques of the various theories to form a more comprehensive, unified theoretical framework. In doing so, it is wise to include considered and thought-through aspects of various individual approaches to psychotherapy, so that the baby is not thrown out with the bathwater.

Cognitive-behavioral therapy has many useful implications in the theory and practice of systemic marriage and family therapy, in developing a more comprehensive theory, and in establishing a cohesive approach in which graduate students can be trained. In this way, competing theoretical orientations can begin to be unified. Training institutions and graduate schools can then provide their students with a generically based systemic approach that incorporates specific concepts and practical contributions of existing individual psychotherapeutic theories. This cohesive model will not only provide beginning and postgraduate students with a strong theoretical basis, but it will also supply them with comprehensive skills for assessment, treatment planning, case management, and therapeutic change. In this manner, beginning and advanced students of marriage and family programs can gain an understanding of the more typical presenting problems. This will enable them to successfully develop and apply appropriate therapeutic techniques with their clients. In sum, this book attempts to unify various aspects of systemic family theories and to expand the focus of cognitive-behavioral theory to include the family. Thus, it is a beginning, an attempt to form an integrated theoretical orientation for the field of marriage and family therapy.

Clinicians and students can see how assessment, generation of hypotheses, hypotheses testing, treatment planning, interventions, and therapeutic techniques can be derived from this therapeutic approach. In addition, they can see how to use cognitive-behavioral techniques to create systemic change.

Although this book is comprehensive in its treatment of the subjects identified in the table of contents, not all topics relevant to families could be included. The topics selected were those the author believed most students and clinicians would experience in their professional lives. For example, sexual issues in marriage counseling and the remarried family are included because of their high incidence in the counseling situation.

The proposed audience for this book includes graduate students in marriage and family counseling, counseling psychologists, psychiatric nurses, social workers, and family psychologists. In addition, this book will acquaint the beginning practitioner and reacquaint the seasoned practitioner with the theoretical components of the marital and family situations most commonly encountered in practice.

For the most part this book will impart technical knowledge in nontechnical language. It is based on many years of experience. The issues and problems presented are indicative of the family's struggle to maintain itself by changing and adapting to changing conditions. The treatment strategies and interviewing techniques described are those the practitioner would use while working with families. All case material is real but disguised, originating from the authors' clinical practices. The book not only teaches interventive strategies relevant to treating the specific issue, but also reviews current theories, research, and therapy relevant to treating each specific problem. In so doing, it bridges the gap between cognitive-behavioral techniques on the one hand and systemic theory on the other. The cognitive-behavioral view provides a practical, concrete foundation for marital and family systems that in many ways helps to foster rapid change. However, it sometimes overlooks the family systems dynamic. This deeper understanding of the family system is provided by systemic interpretations.

The first section is comprised of four chapters. The first, "The Historical Aspects of Marriage and Family Therapy," written by Joan D. Atwood, describes the development of the field of family therapy, illustrating the interdisciplinary contributions to the field. There is a discussion of the macrosociological influences on the family, depicting the family, embedded in the larger social structure, influencing and being influenced by the larger social system. There is also reference to the changing roles in the family, along with an examination of how changes in role sets have in many ways increased the family's socioemotive functions. The author suggests this as a contributing factor to the increase of psychological conflict around social role issues. Multidisciplinary contributions to the field of marriage and family therapy are explored, along with the contributions of its founding fathers, and the author ends with a brief presentation of key terms used in family systems therapy.

Chapter 2, "The Field Today," also by Joan D. Atwood, presents key concepts from five major theoretical approaches. A brief overview of a family therapy model demonstrates the various foci and contributions of this interdisciplinary movement. There follows an exploration of the contributions of the fields of sociology and social psychology to family therapy theory, and the chapter ends with a presentation of the new physics and its broad implications for theory construction and therapy.

Chapter 3, "Gender Issues in Couples Therapy," contributed by Barrie Zucal, discusses gender issues in marriage and family therapy. She presents a thorough literature review showing the development of feminist family therapy. The chapter is rich with case illustrations, highlighting many important considerations for the family therapist.

Chapter 4, "The Role of 'Fun' in Family Therapy," by Ethan Roberts, explores the use of humor in family therapy. He shows how humor can be an important adjunct to therapy, preventing therapist burnout and assisting structural family change. Regardless of the therapist's theoretical orientation, though, Roberts insists on the therapist's responsibility to instill hope in the client. In addition, he includes practical suggestions for families and therapists and a discussion of the traps and pitfalls that can make family therapists "crazy."

CHAPTER ONE

THE HISTORICAL ASPECTS OF MARRIAGE AND FAMILY THERAPY

Joan D. Atwood, Ph.D., C.S.W.

Thomas Kuhn (1962), in *The Structure of Scientific Revolutions,* set out to scientifically study and challenge commonly held assumptions about the way in which science changes. He stated that most theorists believe that science advances in a cumulative manner, each advance building on all that preceded it. In other words, science achieved its present state by slow and steady increments. Kuhn, however, believes that important changes in science arise not from accumulation, but from revolution. He posits five stages in the process of paradigmatic revolution. They are: (1) paradigm, (2) normal science, (3) anomalies, (4) crisis stage, and (5) revolution.

A paradigm, according to Kuhn, is a fundamental image of the science's subject matter. Normal science requires a period of accumulation of knowledge in which scientists work and expand the reigning paradigm. Such research and data accumulation creates anomalies, things which eventually may produce a revolution. A revolution occurs when the reigning paradigm is overthrown and a new one is born. It is the purpose of this chapter to examine family therapy in a historical light, to explore the possibility that it represents a distinct break with the reigning paradigm—that of the individual approach—in psychotherapy.

Most individual therapies deal with the transference relationship between the patient and the therapist and ignore the actual interactional processes between the patient and the social environment, the family. Thus, individual psychotherapy focuses on insight, fantasies, history, and the client-therapist relationship. In contrast, family therapy focuses on the communication processes, power balances and imbalances, influence processes, structures for conflict resolution, and the current functioning of the family system *as a system*. The goal of family therapy is not to effect change in an individual within the family *per se,* but rather to effect change in the structure of the family and the sequences of behavior among its members.

The assumptions of the family therapist are, therefore, that the individual with the symptom belongs to a larger system; that the larger system is an essential ingredient, in terms of diagnostic focus, in assessing the etiology of the complaint; and that the treatment plan must include strategies aimed at modifying or altering the behaviors and structure of the entire family system. In addition, the family is seen as a small, boundary-maintaining, natural group wherein the behaviors of any one member affect the behaviors of all other members. Thus, the family is more than an interaction of personalities. The family develops a conception of itself. When this conception of familial relations is recognized by the community, the family acquires an institutional character. This is what is meant by the family as a social institution. A family with no conception of its role in the community or of the responsibilities of its individual members, would not be an institution, might not even be family. The family is embedded in the larger social system, and as such is affected by and affects the macro system.

This chapter briefly explores the historical environment conducive to the development of the field of family therapy. Its purpose is to give the reader an introduction to key concepts used in family therapy and to the history and development of the field, in order to familiarize the reader with its multidisciplinary background and founding members. Its secondary purpose is to consider the effect of changing roles in the family. In so doing, it explores the notion that family therapy represents a distinct break, a paradigmatic shift, from the traditional psychotherapeutic methods and assumptions.

The Family as a Social Institution

In small primitive societies, the family is largely self-sufficient, providing for most of its members' needs. The entire family cooperates to make tools, build shelters, hunt, gather, or grow food. In modern complex societies, the family has fewer functions. Schools and teachers are largely responsible for formal education, churches and synagogues for religion, government and police for social control. The family continues, however, to be an essential part of advanced societies, especially in providing socialization, affection, and companionship. In other words, the modern family is responsible for fulfilling its members' socioemotive needs.

The study of family structure and function, with all its ramifications, is an enormously broad field, drawing on the disciplines of cultural anthropology, political science, economics, theology, genetics, psychology, social work, and sociology. The U.S. Census Bureau defines a family as a group of two or more persons related by blood, marriage, or adoption. While two spouses or two siblings may constitute a family, the term usually implies the presence of children. Taking into account the enormous number of single-parent households, Broderick and Schrader (1981) define a family as consisting of at least one child and one adult who live together and make emotional claims on each other. Regardless of whether a family includes one or two parents, the care, protection, and socialization of children is a central focus. The human infant is dependent on adult care for its survival. And unlike many lower animals who can survive without parents within a relatively short time after birth, human parents in industrial societies must be available and receptive to offspring for sixteen or more years. Just as there are various types of marriages, there are also many types of families. Today the economically self-sufficient family is almost nonexistent. Processed and packaged foods come from the supermarket freezer rather than from the family vegetable garden. Mother's homemade soup has been replaced for the most part by canned soups. The clothes the family wears are now mass-produced and bought from large department stores. As a result, family members usually produce very little. The family is now a consumer unit rather than a producing unit.

With the demise of the farm-based family, the educational, religious, and protective functions of the family also became less important. Schools and religious institutions now provide the bulk of formal learning experiences about life and religion. Law enforcement agencies have virtually taken over the protective function of the family. Police and military forces help protect us from criminal and foreign assault.

But no other institution has taken over the basic function of the family: emotional bonding. Providing love and care for its members is the family's specialty.

The Changing Roles in the Family

Any consideration of the family necessitates a discussion of how the larger social system impinges on family roles. This macrosystem affects the roles within the family system. Traditionally, highly structured roles very clearly specified the division of labor according to gender.

The increasing industrialization of the early 1800s tended to create changes in the female role, which eventually resulted in changes in the male role. Machinery too large to be housed in the barn stimulated the development of the factory system. The ability to work in a factory originally appeared as freedom for women whose homes had been the setting for all their work. Industrialization created the need for increased mobilization, as families moved to the cities to be nearer the factories. For many, this increased mobilization led to a shift from the extended to the nuclear family, since many in the extended family system chose to remain on farms.

Whereas the preindustrial family performed a variety of tasks, the contemporary, mass society family specializes in child rearing. Thus, as the family lost its economic, protective, and educational functions, it came to specialize increasingly in providing emotional services. As postindustrial society grew increasingly mobile and competitive and the importance of the extended family declined, the nuclear family became a refuge from the competitive pressures of the marketplace. It also equipped the young with the resources necessary for reacting to those pressures. The preindustrial family required women as well as men to engage in instrumental (economically productive) roles and required men as well as women to take part in expressive (child-rearing) roles. As the postindustrial family focused increasingly on child-rearing functions, however, women specialized in expressive roles while men specialized in instrumental roles.

As the family shifted from a unit of production to a unit of consumption and children became economic liabilities rather than assets, there were far-reaching and complex demographic effects. The large families (seven to eight children) of the nineteenth century gave way to the smaller families (one to three children) of the twentieth century. Concurrently, women became relatively isolated in middle class households as men left to go to work. In consequence, children had fewer siblings and relatively isolated mothers, and small children were largely removed from the socializing influence of adults outside their immediate families. Gender roles polarized, leading to dependence on the mother as the sole expressive figure in life, with the father relatively remote. This changed the nature of family interaction. Whereas the preindustrial family interacted in terms of family functions (occupational training, religious training, etc.), family members in contemporary society interact chiefly in terms of parallel activity, conversation, or play.

As late as 1850, a woman's personal property legally belonged to her husband, she could not vote, and she had little access to formal education (Richmond-Abbott, 1979). With few exceptions, her role was to manage her household and her children. Industrialization and the shift to the nuclear family decreased her contact with extended family adults as tension-releasing outlets. Thus, as the primary responsibility for the occupational, educational, or religious training of the children was replaced by social institutions, the nuclear family became a tightly knit unit responsible for fulfilling almost all of the socioemotive needs of its members.

The woman's rights movement, which began in 1848, issued a declaration of objectives for women. The specific goals set down at this early meeting have largely been achieved: Women may now own their own businesses and attend prestigious women's and coeducational schools. In this process, the status of children also changed. During the colonial period, children were economic assets, providing an invaluable work force for the economically self-sufficient family. Today, children are an economic drain and must be wanted and loved for reasons other than the work they can perform. Modern-day parents are psychologically rewarded by their children and see life as more fulfilling because of them (Richmond-Abbott 1979).

In summary, the transition of marriage and the family from colonial times to contemporary America can be described as a weakening of extended family ties and a lessening of specifically family functions, balanced by a greater focus on individual psychological growth and more egalitarian relationships between spouses. While the causes of transition are many and diffuse, the changes from an agricultural to an industrial economy and from a rural to an urban society are the prime factors. Thus, when industrialization moved economically productive work from the household to other specialized secondary institutions, a change occurred in masculine and feminine roles. This change affected not only sex role behavior, but also family demography and family role interaction.

Sociologically and psychologically, contemporary men and women are in a state of conflict. Studies indicate that roles are becoming more complex. Women are expanding traditional roles by claiming more power in economic planning and spending and increased decision making in important family matters. At the same time, they are pursuing careers outside the home. These changes are being accomplished through the expansion of their work hours in order to maintain both home and career. As the dual-career family becomes typical, men are forced into more of the caretaking role. The implications are far-reaching. First, both parents must function at a very high energy level, which leads to an increase of heart disease and stress-related illness. Second, as women continue to move up the career ladder, it is likely that they will not spend as much time in the traditional role of socializing their youngsters. This could lead to a relaxing of the parental socializing process. This may create a more androgynous socialization process for youngsters, but it could also lead to a higher incidence of latchkey children and/or juvenile delinquency. In addition, both men and women may experience increased pressures around and dissonance within the changing roles. It is often these socially determined psychological family problems that therapists encounter.

The perspective of this book is that the larger macrosystem, the economic system, determines the belief systems of social male and female roles within family systems. What it means to be male or female in this society is learned. Thus, gender is an additional organizing unit of the family. In this view, gender is a historical construct which each society shapes according to its economic and ideological needs.

Traditional Psychotherapeutic Approaches

Socially determined psychological conflict has traditionally been approached from an individual psychological perspective. Historically, traditional psychotherapeutic approaches have focused mainly on the influence on adult behavior of early parent-child interactions, emphasizing how these interactions determine the ways we perceive reality as adults. Therapy involves regression to those early experiences, reliving the emotionality associated with them, and then working forward to the next stage or the next area of conflict. The role of the therapist in this model is to direct and guide the client and to help the client discover how early conflicts are relived in present interactions with others.

Although psychoanalytic thinkers have often been criticized for not considering the individual in a social context, I believe that these representatives of traditional psychotherapy have a clear theoretical understanding of the family system as an interlocking network of relationships, and of the influence of that network on individual personality development. Their emphasis is on perceptions of early interactions as determinants of intrapersonal and interpersonal variables throughout all phases of the family life cycle. The focus is not on the emergence of new properties and principles characteristic of the evolving relationship system. Intervention is therefore directed to individuals, and the techniques for producing change involve seeing one member in psychoanalysis, excluding the rest of the family, and ignoring changes in the system that result from changes in the individual.

In fact, family systems theory and associated therapy can be considered a logical step in the development of the work of Sigmund Freud. Before Freud, mental illness was considered a product of organic brain pathology for which treatments—the few that there were—were medical. Freud introduced a new dimension of functional illness, the concept that mental illness could be the product of a disturbance in brain functioning rather than an organic or structural defect. He conceptualized this functional disturbance as the product of a disturbed parent-child relationship during the patient's early years. That emotional illness developed in relationship to others was a new paradigm.

After Freud came the discovery that focusing on the mother-child symbiosis revealed only a fragment of the larger family emotional system. By the early 1950s there were ever-increasing efforts to involve the family in the therapy of the patient. It has been recognized for some time that the success of the patient's therapy was in some way tied to the support and reactions of his or her family. Most therapists had seen cured patients leave the hospital, return to their families, and promptly regress into old symptoms. Many early efforts with families were attempts to deal with this problem.

The family movement in psychiatry began in the late 1940s and early 1950s, with several investigators working independently from the clinical or theoretical notion that family was important. The shifting focus from individual to family confronted these investigators with the dilemma of describing and conceptualizing a family relationship system.

Thus, family therapy theory began in the early 1950s—in the field of schizophrenia. Therapists observed that many schizophrenic patients had a striking number of relatives who seemed psychotic. Some investigators began to study the families of schizophrenics. Many of these early investigators were psychoanalysts, including Murray Bowen, Don Jackson, Lyman Wynne, Theodore Lidz, and Stephen Fleck. They hypothesized that schizophrenia might be an adaptation to a disorganizing and confusing familial environment on which the present or future schizophrenic was dependent and from which she/he could not escape.

Just as Freud's study of the clinical phenomenon of hysteria contributed to the development of new knowledge about the mind and its relationship to behavior and to a new treatment (psychoanalysis), the investigation of schizophrenia facilitated new understanding of the link between behavior and the social environment and led to the development of family therapy.

The History of Family Therapy

These early investigations of the family shaped the course of family therapy for the next several decades. For example, conceptualization of the identified patient as the family scapegoat and awareness of the effects of reinforcement of that role by means of the label "sick" have inclined family therapists away from a medical model (with its role assignments of "healer" and "defective"). A new generation of family therapists emerged, motivated to treat families in which the identified patient was less severely disturbed than a schizophrenic and more likely to be treated successfully. These factors helped remove family therapists from the hospital setting and from the most seriously disturbed patients. The splitting of family therapy from general psychiatry occurred almost simultaneously with the advent of new and effective pharmocologic agents for many psychiatric disorders, beginning with chlorpromazine and reserpine in the early 1950s and soon including tricyclics, MAOIs, and lithium carbonate. Family therapy, now dominated by antimedical, antipsychoanalytic, and antidisease biases, kept the focus off the hospitalized patient and often off any serious consideration of individual psychopathology. General psychiatry at this time emphasized disease entities, courses of illness, and medication responses that could be measured for specific biologic interventions.

The new discipline isolated itself in order to develop and perfect its unique methodologies. The adolescence of family therapy in the 1960s and 1970s was dominated by a surface idealization, hero worship, separatism, and tendencies toward radical denial of both illness and professional expertise. Underneath this, though, was the healthy development of a genuine advance in skills and a consolidation of identity that has enabled family therapists to move on to a more integrative stage and to return to the most disturbed patients, who most need their skills. In order to understand the field today, it is important to examine the movement in more detail.

As Gurman and Kniskern (1981, 1991) point out, marriage and family therapy developed from many different professions which dealt with relationships among family members. However, it began as at least seven largely independent movements: (1) The Marriage Counseling Movement, (2) The Social Work Movement, (3) The Development of Social Psychiatry, (4) The Early Sexologists, (5) The Family Life Education Movement, (6) Cybernetics, and (7) The Family Therapy Movement.

The Marriage Counseling Movement

The Marriage Counseling Movement differs from the others inasmuch as it developed as a part-time second profession for psychoanalysts, physicians, ministers, psychologists, sociologists, lawyers, social workers, and educators who became involved in people's marital problems as a spin-off from their primary vocations.

The Social Work Movement

Social historians date the beginning of social work in this country from the founding of the first citywide charity organization in Buffalo, New York, in 1877. Adopting the British model, these early organizations were concerned with the poor. However, they believed that the proper unit of concern was not the single client, but the family. Some names associated with this movement are: **Robert Paine,** president of the Boston Association of Charities ("Each one of the 7,716 cases reported is a human family with human lives, cases and woes," Paine said); **Zilpha Smith,** an early (1890) pioneer in the conversion of voluntary service into a profession requiring advanced training; and **Mary Richmond,** originally the general secretary of the Baltimore charity and a leading national organizer. Richmond's book *A Real Story of a Real Family* set a new standard of family-oriented case-record keeping among social workers. She wrote another book, *Social Diagnosis,* stating that therapy should not be confined to the patient alone, but should also include those with whom she/he lives. At that time, however, marriage and family therapy did not take hold in the social work profession, for at least two reasons. First, the importance of family seems to have been so taken for granted that it did not need to be written about or discussed. Second and more important, psychiatry—with its focus on the individual—had a powerful impact on social work from the 1920s on. The orthopsychiatric team of social worker, psychologist, and psychiatrist all but submerged any interest in family therapy that had been evident earlier. Thus, social work as a profession did not take the lead in the marriage and family therapy movements. It is only recently that social workers are showing an interest in marriage and family therapy and electing to pursue advanced training in the field.

The Development of Social Psychiatry

The psychiatric community represents a much later and originally quite separate movement toward joint marital therapy.

Adler

While Freud recognized that the familial relationship was crucial in shaping the personality, Adler, in 1910, felt that Freud underemphasized social influences on personality. He believed that the driving dynamics of life lay in the deeply internalized sense of inferiority we all acquire from having been born small and helpless. Rather than by the sexual drive, as Freud postulated, Adler believed that we are motivated by a compulsion to achieve feelings of adequacy and power. In this struggle we follow one of two paths. We might flee into illness from which we dominate and manipulate those around us through weakness (a strategy later theorists called metacomplementarity [see Watzlawick, Beavin, and Jackson 1967]). Or we might engage those around us in a more open struggle for power. In the second option, Adler foreshadowed the theories of most contemporary family therapists who also explain individual pathology as a by-product of family conflict.

Adler was instrumental in the creation of child guidance clinics in which the whole family was involved. Teachers and schools were another focus of his efforts, and he was an active lecturer who sought to help schools provide equal opportunity and to help children overcome feelings of inferiority.

Jung

Jung lived to see the emergence of both psychoanalysis and family therapy. Although he is generally associated more with psychoanalysis, his basic concepts clearly transcended the mechanistic models of classical psychology, coming much closer to the conceptual framework of modern physics (Capra 1983). Jung was concerned with wholeness and the totality of the psyche relative to its wider environment. He spoke of a dialectical framework characterized by fluctuations between opposite poles and of a movement toward integration or synthesis of both.

In 1910 Jung also broke with Freud. He spoke of the persona (or mask) which each of us assumes in social situations in order to meet the expectations of others. This concept is very much like those developed by social psychologists Mead and Cooley. Here, Jung is talking about the role of social expectations. These ideas are somewhat similar to those of systems thinkers and family therapists.

Rank

In the 1920s Rank introduced innovations in style which were more appropriate to family therapy than traditional techniques had been. He focused more on what was happening during the session itself and less on what had happened years before. He introduced his own personality and feelings into sessions instead of remaining detached and fostering idealization. He set a definite time limit on treatment.

AS HITLER FORCED ANALYSTS TO LEAVE Europe in the 1930s, a strong community of analysts developed in America, bringing their knowledge of the work of Adler, Jung, and Rank. They took the work of anthropologists and sociologists into account. Among the most influential were Frieda Fromm-Reichman and Harry Stack Sullivan. Fromm-Reichman emphasized the interaction between man and society. Her emphasis on the development of individuality foreshadowed the work of Bowen and others on the importance of differentiation from the family. Sullivan focused on the role of interpersonal relationships in psychological development, the basic foundation of contemporary family theory.

Fromm-Reichman

Beginning in 1935, Frieda Fromm-Reichman worked near Washington,

D.C., at Chestnut Lodge, a private long-term hospital for schizophrenics and other seriously disturbed patients. In a short paper in 1941, she summarized some recent advances in psychoanalytic therapy, emphasizing a shift from the mental realm—with its focus on unconscious wishes and fantasies—to the social sphere and to concern with the person's real relationships.

In 1948, Fromm-Reichman coined the term *schizophrenogenic mother* to describe the type of mother capable of inducing schizophrenia in her children. Such mothers were characterized as cold, domineering, rejecting, yet overprotective. The father, meanwhile, was faulted for his passivity in not interfering in the pernicious mother-child relationship. Thus, Fromm-Reichman argued that schizophrenia evolves in the context of the mother-child relationship, and she believed as did Sullivan that there is no developmental period when the individual exists outside the realm of interpersonal relatedness. It is unfortunate that it was usually the mother who was made to feel most responsible for the family's distress. This is problematic for the field of psychotherapy in general and family therapy in particular.

Sullivan

The work of Harry Stack Sullivan and his followers during the 1940s, principally with schizophrenics, set the stage for the emergence of family therapy a decade later. Influenced by sociologists and anthropologists, Sullivan's work emphasized social factors and came to be known as the *New Interpersonal Theory of Psychiatry* (1953).

Sullivan (1965) published a report on his outstanding work with hospitalized schizophrenics. That report had definite family implications. Observing the transactions between hospital personnel (physicians, nurses, and aides) and patients, Sullivan noted that the patients improved when staff members responded to them in ways different from those they had come to expect as a result of their experience in their families of origin. Patients, according to Sullivan, perceived the staff as an extension of the family and reacted to and dealt with staff as they did with their families. The "hospital family," therefore, was seen by Sullivan as possessing important potential for aiding the patient's improvement.

Sullivan was the most interpersonally oriented of all the American analysts. He was most influenced by the social psychologists Mead and Cooley. One of his central ideas is that before a child has learned to communicate in symbols, she/he experiences his/her mother's emotions through empathy. Maternal anger or disapproval appears in the child as insecurity or anxiety. The concept of self is shaped by the parts of one's behavior that others respond to positively or negatively. He used the term "reflected appraisals" to indicate much the same process as Cooley's "looking glass self" or Mead's "generalized other." His theory of child development viewed the child as growing in response to shifting social situations as she/he matures. He was one of the first to assert and demonstrate that schizophrenia could be treated by psychotherapy. Some of the founders of family therapy (Bowen and Jackson) were initially engaged in a Sullivanian approach to schizophrenia. Like Whitaker, Sullivan was first and foremost a clinician rather than a theorist; he refused to be impressed by any theory that could not be demonstrated in practical work with patients. His emphasis was on trusting one's own experience, not the reigning dogma.

Sullivan was influenced by both sociologists and anthropologists. His personality theory is an interpersonal framework in which he challenges the "illusion of personal individual personality." According to Sullivan, personality is inseparable from interpersonal relationships, and in fact, it consists mainly of interpersonal behavior. People are the products of interpersonal situations. Consistent with this model, in the 1920s he created a treatment program for schizophrenics that focused on altering the patient's social environment. He also suggested that a therapist was not an observer, but a participant in an interpersonal situation, foreshadowing the findings of the New Physics and the "New Family Therapy" (see chapters 2 and 20).

Following Sullivan, more recent social psychiatrists, such as Horney (1937, 1939) and Thompson (1951), were aware of and had a greater understanding of the relationship between a patient's behavior and his/her familial experiences and interactions (Gurman and Kniskern 1981, 1991).

The Early Sexologists

Next on the scene were the sex therapists who led up to the work of Masters and Johnson (1966). Two men, Havelock Ellis of Great Britain and Magnus Hirschfield of Germany, were the important forerunners in this field.

Havelock Ellis

Havelock Ellis was a medical doctor who was raised in Victorian prudery. He vowed to do all in his power to spare others the ignorance and discomfort about sexual matters which he had experienced as a young man. He developed his own version of non-demand pleasuring, which later influenced Masters and Johnson.

Magnus Hirschfield

Magnus Hirschfield founded the Institute of Sexual Science in Berlin in 1918, and together with Ellis founded the World League for Sexual Reform. He instituted the first German Marriage Consultation Bureau. He influenced his colleagues to set up the first publicly funded Center for Sexual Advice in Vienna. By 1932 there were hundreds of these centers throughout Germany, Austria, and Switzerland. Their main function was to give counseling on contraception, but psychological and relationship matters were routinely discussed. When Hitler came to power, he destroyed the centers and converted them to Health and Racial Hygiene Bureaus. Their revised function was to screen individuals who wanted to marry to make sure they were intellectually, physically, and emotionally fit. The concept Hirschfield developed, however, survived in America where at the same time another movement was taking place that would eventually pave the way to clinical sex therapy (Gurman and Kniskern 1981, 1991).

The Family Life Education Movement

In 1883, parent groups began meeting to discuss the best parenting methods. In 1908, at the American Home Economics Convention, courses were instituted in home economics "to improve American homemaking." The emphasis was initially on cooking, sewing, etc., but later other aspects of the woman's role were emphasized. In 1914 and 1917 the Smith-Lever Act and the Smith-Hughes Act were passed, providing federal grants to establish and maintain county home demonstrations and vocational home economics instruction in high schools throughout the country. In 1923 Vassar College introduced the first preparation for parenthood course at the college level. In 1924 a similar course was offered at Boston University, along with a noncredit course on marriage. In 1930 Paul Popenoe set up a series of workshops all over California: "Love Before Marriage," "Love in Early Married Life," "Love After 40," and "The Family in a Changing Social Situation." In 1936 Ernest Groves instituted the first functional marriage and family relations course for college credit. In 1948 marriage and family relations courses were taught at 632 colleges by home economists who expanded the definition of their profession, by nontraditional sociologists who identified themselves with a nontraditional approach to the family, and by psychologists. In 1938, a professional association called the National Council of Family Relations (NCFR) was founded by Paul Savre, and in 1939 a professional journal called *Marriage and Family Life* was established. The field was coming into its own (see Gurman and Kniskern 1981, 1991).

Cybernetics

The seeds of the family therapy movement were sown by a disparate group of researchers and theorists from a variety of disciplines. Some were early explorers in the field of cybernetics. Included in this group were mathematicians Norbert Wiener, John von Neuman, and Walter Pitts; physician Julian Bigelow; physiologists Warren McCulloch and Lorente de No; psychologist Kurt Lewin; anthropologists Gregory Bateson and Margaret Mead; economist Oskar Morganstern; as well as others from the fields of anatomy, engineering, neurophysiology, psychology, and sociology (Wiener 1948).

In what has since been recognized as a major departure in the way we study and come to know our world, the science of cybernetics concerned itself with organization, pattern, and process rather than with matter, material, and content. In the words of Ashby (1956, p. 1), another pioneer, cybernetics "treats, not things but ways of behaving. It does not ask 'what does it do.' . . . It is thus essentially functional and behavioristic." The field of cybernetics dates from approximately 1942, and Norbert Wiener is usually given credit for naming the science.

Norbert Wiener

Norbert Wiener (1948, 1954), an M.I.T. mathematician who had worked on computer technology during the war, wrote about the "Second Industrial Revolution." He coined the word "cybernetics," meaning a circular and reflexive system of information flow in which information and control are linked together. This is an important forerunner of the way some systems therapists later began to look at human communication and systems interactions. More recently Watzlawick's *How Real is Real?* (1977) delineates some of the same issues in anecdotal form. Cybernetics, called systems theory in the United States, is the basic underlying theory of most major schools of family therapy.

The Family Therapy Movement

The family therapy movement, as we know it today, grew primarily out of the field of psychiatry. It first appeared as a separate discipline with a series of papers emphasizing the importance of family in the etiology and management of serious emotional difficulties. In 1921 Flugel published the *Psychoanalytic Study of the Family*. In the 1930s and 1940s, Moreno's work with group psychodrama included work with married couples and other family members. In 1938 Ackerman published an article entitled "The Unity of the Family." In 1945 Richardson's book, *Patients Have Families,* was published. In 1949 in England, John Bowlby published an article, "The Study and Reduction of Group Tension in the Family," in which he described conjoint family interviews used as an adjunct to individual interviews at the Tavistock Child Guidance Clinic. In 1949 and 1951 in the United States, Rudolf Dreikurs of the Community Child Guidance Center of Chicago developed a similar program to the one at Tavistock.

Family therapy was founded between 1952 and 1961. It began simultaneously, among independent therapists and researchers, in many parts of the United States. By the end of the 1950s, it emerged as a connected movement whose members exchanged correspondence and visits and began to cite one another in footnotes. In 1952 a number of pioneers took major steps toward establishing conjoint family therapy as an approach to treatment. Then, in 1961 nearly all of them met to prepare the way for the first state-of-the-art joint handout and to found a common journal, *Family Process,* which first appeared in 1962 (Gurman and Kniskern 1981, 1991).

Some Founding Members

John Elderkin Bell. John Bell is a rarely mentioned founder of family therapy. Although he is associated with family group therapy, his early work with families is often overlooked because he did not begin publishing until the 1960s. Unlike other founders of family therapy, he had few students and did not establish an important clinical center, develop a training program, or train well-known followers.

However, Bell was one of the first to see families conjointly, although his initial decision to do so was based on a serendipitous experience during a visit to England. At the time, Bell, a professor of psychology at Clark University in Worcester, Massachusetts, was visiting the medical director of London's Tavistock Clinic, Dr. John Sutherland. Sutherland was describing to Bell the work of a psychiatrist on his staff, Dr. John Bowlby. He mentioned that Bowlby had begun having the whole family come in with the patient.

On his way home, Bell began thinking about seeing whole families, and once back in the United States, he was presented with a case that seemed adaptable to that approach. By the second session, Bell was convinced that the *family* had the problem, not the thirteen-year-old son, the original patient. Only years later did he learn that Bowlby had not been seeing whole families together, but had been treating each member of the family on an individual basis and occasionally calling them together for group conferences.

Bell had stumbled onto family treatment, however, and had found it a viable option, so he created an approach based on the theory of group dynamics and group psychotherapy. In 1961 he published *Family Group Therapy,* one of the classics in the field. John Elderkin Bell is often thought of as the Father of Family Therapy.

Other clinicians/researchers also noticed contextually shifting behaviors, (e.g., when another family member became ill as the patient improved in functioning). As a result they began to ask new types of questions: What processes caused people to shift their basic behaviors, to change their attitudes and logic when they were put in different contexts and/or with different combinations of people? How does changing the attitudes and functioning of one member influence others to change their behavior? How did the presence of family members make a difference in therapy? What was this system of checks and balances in behavior? Several other voices in the field began to question the traditional focus on individuals and its effectiveness in dealing with mental illness.

Nathan Ackerman. Throughout its early years, the family therapy movement was divided along ideological lines between those who leaned toward an intrapsychic approach and those who espoused a systemic orientation. Nathan Ackerman was the outstanding proponent of the former position. He combined psychodynamics with the notion of an individual's social role to understand the ongoing interaction between heredity and environment to maintain homeostasis within and between the person, the family, and ultimately, society. However, he emphasized the intrapsychic effects of families on individuals more than the effects of behavioral sequences, communication, and interaction that later systems-oriented family therapists stressed.

Ackerman became convinced that emotional problems could be generated by the immediate environment as well as by the dynamics of the psyche. He joined the psychiatric staff at Southard School, a facility for disturbed children associated with the Menninger Clinic in Topeka, Kansas. By 1937 he was the chief psychiatrist at the Child Guidance Clinic. He adopted the prevailing orthopsychiatric practice whereby the psychiatrist saw the patient and the social worker saw the mother. But by the mid-1940s, he noted a growing flexibility in the field, so that a single therapist would sometimes see both mother and child. He experimented in his private practice and conducted seminars on the relationship between the child's illness and the mothering and fathering the child received. He began to see the family as the proper unit of diagnosis and treatment, so he began to send his staff on home visits to study the family.

For the clinical world, he provided the primary bridge between the intrapsychic and the systemic approaches to therapy. His article "The Family as a Social Unit" appeared in 1937 and is credited as the earliest publication in the field. Indeed, Ackerman is considered by some (Nichols 1984) to be the "Grandfather of Family Therapy." Thus, while much other work with families was an outgrowth of research into schizophrenia, Ackerman believed that undue emphasis on this obscured family therapy's true origins "in the study of nonpsychotic disorders in children as related to the family environment" (Ackerman, 1967). In 1955 he organized and led the first session of family diagnosis and treatment at the American Orthopsychiatry Association meeting in New York City (Nichols 1984). Two years later he opened the Family Mental Health Clinic at Jewish Family Services in New York City, which led to the founding of the Family Institute. His *Psychodynamics of Everyday Life* (1958) was the first full-length study combining theory and practice, and in it he emphasized the importance of role relations within the family (Nichols 1984).

In 1962, two years after he opened the Family Institute, he joined Don Jackson of Palo Alto and began publishing what is today one of the most influential journals in the field, *Family Process,* with Jay Haley as the first editor. During this period Ackerman was a professor of psychology at the Columbia University College of

Physicians and Surgeons, and from 1964 to 1967 he also served as a consultant to the family studies section at the Albert Einstein College of Medicine. Soon after his death in 1971, the Family Institute was renamed the Ackerman Family Institute in his honor.

Even though Ackerman's contributions should not be underestimated, they are focused more on the shift from individual to interpersonal interactions and on clinical expertise than on theory construction. Ackerman approached the family mainly through children. He believed that when a child had problems, the rest of the family was involved in the problems, and a family diagnosis and family treatment were needed. Ackerman's work with families as organic systems was psychodynamically oriented—drawn from psychoanalysis.

Ackerman was also interested in group psychotherapy and the work of Moreno. Initially, he hated the routine chore of going to visit a patient's family. This attitude was sharply revised when he became involved in an extensive study of mental health problems among the unemployed in a depression-struck mining town in Western Pennsylvania (Ackerman 1958). Seeing how the configuration of family life was radically altered by the miners' inability to fulfill their habitual roles as providers showed Ackerman the relationship between family ties and health.

With Ackerman's death some tension between ideological camps lessened, and family therapists in general tended to move toward a systems perspective. However, others in the first generation of family therapists also had intrapsychic training, and their work with families continued to be flavored by this initial orientation.

Christian Midelfort. Christian Midelfort was relatively isolated from the developing movement. His autonomy, like Bell's, seemed to be a function of his isolation from a particular school or training center in the early days of the family therapy movement, rather than of the value of his work or the timing of his entry into the field. Midelfort's introduction to family therapy came through observing his father's techniques in the latter's medical practice. Midelfort's own experiments were some of the earliest and most innovative in family therapy.

Midelfort was a psychoanalyst who received his training at the Payne-Whitney and Henry Phipps psychiatric clinics. He then went into practice at the Lutheran Hospital in La Crosse, Wisconsin. In 1952 he delivered a paper on the use of family therapy techniques at the meeting of the American Psychiatric Association (APA). His *The Family in Psychotherapy* (1957) was one of the first books on the subject. In it he describes some practices used at his hospital. There, relatives of psychiatric patients acted as nurses' aides and companions, in constant attendance to supervise occupational, recreational, and insulin therapies, to minimize suicidal risk, fear, aggression, and insecurity, and to take part in therapeutic interviews with patient and psychiatrist. Under his guidance family treatment for all types of mental illness was also extended to the outpatient department (Midelfort 1957, pp. v–vi). Despite his innovations and orientations, Midelfort was outside the mainstream, and his potential as an early contributor to family therapy was never fully realized. Because he was so isolated, his influence has been minimal, and few contemporary family therapists are aware of his contributions.

The research on and treatment of

schizophrenia were the focus of study for two other original individuals in family therapy development: Theodore Lidz and Lyman Wynne. However, both of them are more like Bowen (see chapter 2) in terms of their initial psychodynamic orientations, and both are usually identified more with specific conceptual contributions than with comprehensive models of their own creation. Further, Wynne is the only pioneer who continues his research with schizophrenics up to the present (Nichols 1984).

Theodore Lidz. After receiving his M.D. from Columbia University in 1936, Lidz studied neurology at London's National Hospital. He returned to the United States and from 1938 to 1941 was a resident in psychiatry at Johns Hopkins University. During his final year as a resident, Lidz initiated his examination of the characteristics of schizophrenics' families, concluding that the influence of fathers could be at least as important as that of mothers (Lidz 1949).

Lidz was a faculty member at Johns Hopkins from 1942 to 1946. From 1942 to 1951, he also trained at the Baltimore Institute of Psychoanalysis, although from 1946 to 1951 he served as a lieutenant in the U.S. Army. During this period, he also undertook a longitudinal study of sixteen middle- and upper-middle-class families of schizophrenics. He became concerned with the failure of these families to develop adequate boundaries and with the intense symbiosis derived from a parent's need for and inability to differentiate himself/herself (usually defined as herself) from the patient.

As in his earlier study, Lidz consistently found patterns of severe dysfunction and pathology in these families; ultimately, he challenged some major beliefs in the field. He rejected the Freudian notion that fixation in the oral stage, followed by stress-induced regression in young adulthood, caused schizophrenia. Based on his research, he also refuted the belief, proposed by Frieda Fromm-Reichman and John Rosen, that schizophrenia is caused by maternal rejection. In addition, Lidz widened his focus to include both the entire maturation period (not just infancy) and the role of fathers along with that of mothers. He must be given credit for recognizing the crucial role of fathers in child development and family life—they do more than simply offset destructive mothers.

Following completion of both his military service and his training in psychoanalysis, Lidz moved to New Haven, Connecticut, and continued to study the relationship between schizophrenia and the family. *Marital schism* and *marital skew* are two concepts that grew out of his research. He found the first condition to be hardest for males, the second for females.

Lidz (1973) claims that many schizophrenic children come from families that fall into one of two categories: *The schismatic family,* in which parental discord has divided the family into opposing factions, and *the skewed family,* which remains reasonably calm only because one spouse is totally dominated by the pathology of the other. Marital schism features open conflict between the parents, who attempt to control each other through various power plays. These parents are two antagonistic and competing factions. Spouses unable to achieve role reciprocity or complementarity of purpose are characteristic of marital schism. Each may attempt to coerce the other into meeting his or her expectations, may distrust the other's motivations, and may undermine the other's position, particularly with respect to parenting.

By contrast, one strong and one weak spouse are characteristic of marital skew. In marital skew, the dominant partner is seriously disturbed, and the spouse passively submits to the disturbed partner's will. Since the strong one allows the weak one to dominate, conflict is masked and no discrepancy between what is felt and what is admitted is openly acknowledged (Simon, Stierlin, and Wynne 1985). In both situations, the child is denied the emotional support necessary for a sense of security and self-worth, necessary ingredients for emotional growth. Disruption of generational boundaries embroiling marital partners in competition for their children's loyalties is one major symptom observed in disturbed families.

Lidz developed a relational focus and a holistic perspective that included more than the symptom-bearing patient. Indeed, the significance of his work lies in his early emphasis on the importance of family communication patterns and role relationships, along with a focus on individual developmental processes which create the context within which schizophrenia emerges. He therefore moved away from a concentration on individual pathology to an emphasis on family dysfunction as the matrix out of which pathology arises. This concept is one of the fundamental building blocks of family therapy. The clinical research of both Bowen and Wynne followed upon Lidz's research on the role of the family in the etiology and treatment of schizophrenic disorders. In 1961, he was one of the early pioneers who agreed to be consulting editor of *Family Process*.

Lyman Wynne. Lyman Wynne and his colleagues described both *pseudomutuality* in the family relations of schizophrenics, and the *rubber fence*—the sudden rebound back into the family by the pathological patient who appeared to be leaving that emotional field.

Wynne graduated from Harvard Medical School in 1948. Trained originally as a psychiatrist, in 1952 he obtained a doctorate in social psychology at Harvard, where he was influenced by the family system ideas of Talcott Parsons, especially Parsons's ideas about personality as a subsystem within the larger family system. Early in his career Wynne worked at Massachusetts General Hospital with Eric Lindeman, the pioneering student of grief reactions among family members. Wynne first worked with families, instead of just with individuals, in 1947. Influenced by Parsonian social psychology, Wynne concentrated primarily on role relationships and communication disturbances in families with a schizophrenic member. He and his associates developed a number of concepts, including those of alignments and splits in families, pseudomutuality, the rubber fence, and others that were published primarily in book chapters and a series of papers (Singer and Wynne 1963; Singer and Wynne 1965a, 1965b; Wynne 1961; Wynne et al. 1958; Wynne and Singer 1963). In 1971 Wynne moved to the University of Rochester, where he continues to be a prolific publisher of articles on family relationships and on research into the treatment of schizophrenia. He is one of the few researchers who has continued to study the area of family and schizophrenia.

Like Lidz, Lyman Wynne concluded from his studies on schizophrenia that the significance of the family could not be underestimated. He also believed that role relationships are crucial and that the understanding of pathology requires a consideration of communication patterns. His concepts have proven instrumental in helping people who work with families to understand them at the level of process rather than of content.

When Murray Bowen came to the National Institute of Mental Health (NIMH) in 1954, he and Wynne began to share their thoughts and concerns on issues related to mental illness and family treatment. Wynne began research on the families of schizophrenics in 1954. At the 1956 and 1957 meetings of the American Psychiatric Association, he and Bowen opened dialogues with Ackerman, Jackson, and Lidz. In 1956, when Bowen left for Georgetown University, Wynne became chief of the family research section.

By 1958 Wynne had introduced the concept of pseudomutuality, a predominant absorption with fitting together at the expense of the differentiation of identities of the persons in the relationship (Wynne et al. 1958, p. 207). That is, affirmation of a member's identity is a threat to the family, whereas in well-functioning families there is a more appropriate balance between separateness and togetherness. In pseudomutuality there is a lack of humor and spontaneity, roles are rigidly assigned and maintained, and family members insist on the desirability and appropriateness of this rigid role structure.

Families characterized by a pseudomutual pattern are totally focused on the whole. Such family centeredness is maintained by a flexible but nonstable boundary that Wynne referred to as the rubber fence. The rules comprising this boundary are in continual flux as the family opens to let in what it considers acceptable and closes unpredictably to exclude what is not acceptable. Communication, individual perceptions, and identity formation are all problematic in this confused and enmeshed context.

Thus, according to Wynne, the behavior of the schizophrenic is a symptom of family dysfunction rather than an example of individual pathology or of inappropriate, schizophrenic parenting. Togetherness in such families is valued above all else, and significant relationships outside the family are not tolerated. The acting-out characteristic of schizophrenic behavior may be needed to achieve recognition of individual difference. Having succeeded in attaining this recognition, however, the now-separate individual is labeled "schizophrenic" and is ejected from the family. Once the schizophrenic is ejected, the family's pseudomutuality is restored.

On the other hand, *pseudohostility* is a superficial alienation of family members that masks both the members' needs for intimacy and affection and also the deeper levels of chronic conflict and alienation. Like its counterpart, pseudomutuality, pseudohostility reflects a distortion of communication whereby rational thinking about relationships is obstructed. Both patterns focus on descriptions of family alignments and splits that define the emotional system of which the schizophrenic is a part.

During Wynne's twenty years at NIMH, he and his colleagues wrote many articles detailing the results of their research and therapy with schizophrenics, revising and updating their earlier theorizing. This emphasis on keeping theory consonant with practice continues at the present. An active researcher and practitioner, Wynne continues to add to our knowledge of communication deviance in the families of schizophrenics.

Wynne also spoke of the feeling of going crazy himself, of being drawn into the quicksand of the family's interior. He spoke of the need to have a cotherapist in the room. This was unheard of in the world of dynamic psychoanalytic psychiatry, where all was confidential, hush-hush, and private. Wynne and his team's need for co-therapists was essentially a need to have someone "sane" to talk to, for the communication patterns of the schizophrenic patients and their families consisted of strange usages and meanings in sequences which deviated greatly from the expected norm. Wynne and Margaret Thaler-Singer began then, and continue to study families of this type, constructing—both together and separately—many hypotheses about the crazy-making quality of schizophrenic family communication (e.g., Singer and Wynne 1965, 1966; Wynne and Singer 1963; Singer 1967; Wynne 1977).

Gerald Zuk. Zuk, who in the fall of 1964 organized the first national meeting of experienced family therapists in the United States, has contributed a half-dozen concepts from his work in therapy, most of which have been tested through research (Garrigan and Bambrick 1973, 1977a, 1977b, 1979). His best-known concepts are the *go-between role,* the *celebrant role, and the side-taking of the therapist*. He is the founding editor of the *International Journal of Family Therapy*.

J. L. Moreno. In describing the base from which family therapy arose, Jackson and Satir (1961) referred to important developments in the 1920s and 1930s in the work of Moreno, Sullivan, and Beaglehole. J. L. Moreno and others made important contributions to group therapy. They began to use group therapy with hospitalized patients in 1920, analyzing interaction between individuals in the group and interpreting the interaction in terms of motivation.

Gregory Bateson. Gregory Bateson was an anthropologist and philosopher on the faculty of Stanford University. He was interested in general systems theory, in hierarchies of classification, and also in hierarchies of logical types that produced such paradoxical statements as the classic, "I am lying." It is true only if it is false and false only if it is true—and the harder one thinks about it, the more disoriented one feels. Using the theory of logical types, however, it became clear that the paradox consists of two contradictory statements which elude comparison because they are at different logical levels. There is the evident content of the statement, "I am lying," and there is also the framing statement (or meta-statement, as it came to be called) which is not explicitly spelled out but is inherent. When the meta-message is made explicit, the original statement loses some of its mind-boggling paradoxical qualities and assumes the qualities of a mere pair of contradictory statements (A is true/A is not true).

Bateson had been formally introduced to the world of hypnosis and to the ideas of Milton Erickson at conferences in New York City in 1941 and 1942. Through both the earlier conference and joint writings, he helped introduce the work of hypnotist Erickson. Bateson's goal was to find a framework for the behavioral sciences more appropriate than those currently in use. He corresponded with physiologist Warren C. McCullicock, who shared his interests; psychologist Lawrence Kubie also played an important role.

During World War II Bateson, then an American resident, was assigned to an intelligence team in the Pacific, because he had studied several cultures in that part of the world. His job with the team was to transmit messages which would confuse or mislead the Japanese.

During the 1946–1947 academic year, Bateson was a visiting professor at the New School for Social Research in New York City; he spent the next academic year as a visiting professor at Harvard University, then joined the Department of Psychiatry at the University of California Medical School as a research associate. He worked there for two years, and says (1977, p. 332), "In those two years, my beginnings as well as the premises of *Steps to an Ecology of Mind* (1972) were established."

In 1946, the Macy Conference was the first of ten small conferences devoted to Circular Causal and Feedback Mechanisms in Biological and Social Systems. This title was later changed to Cybernetics. Whereas the term "cybernetics" was widely adopted in Europe, in the United States it was called systems theory, after Ludwig von Bertalanffy's use of general systems theory. At the 1946 conference, Bateson spoke on his search for an adequate framework for the social sciences and on the limitations of learning theory for describing stability mechanisms in various cultures. He began to play a vital role in connecting the physical and behavioral sciences via his relationships with Wiener and Von Neumann.

In 1952 Bateson received a grant from the Rockefeller Foundation to research the role of the paradoxes of abstraction in communication. This study examined levels of communication in terms of the theory of logical types. Jay Haley and John Weakland became part of Bateson's research team in early 1953, and were joined later that year by William Fry. Haley was a communication specialist, Weakland a chemical engineer turned cultural anthropologist, and Fry a psychiatrist interested in studying humor. The focus was on levels of communication and, more important, on conflicts between these levels. In this process the researchers studied the language of schizophrenics (Nichols 1984).

The original team of researchers was soon joined by psychiatrist Don D. Jackson. He became their clinical consultant and supervised the therapy with schizophrenic patients. The goal of the research project was to outline a theory of communication that would explain both schizophrenia in general and schizophrenia in the family context in particular. In 1956 the team's landmark paper "Toward a Theory of Schizophrenia" was published.

Each of these early theorists made major conceptual innovations in studying family processes and describing pathological phenomena and agreed upon such concepts as ego fusion, blurred boundaries, cross-generational coalitions, difficulty in individuating, and ambiguous, bizarre communication patterns. However, no convincing evidence supports the view that the basic problem of schizophrenia arises as an adaptation to the family or as a result of malignant family processes. Furthermore, although family communication certainly plays a part in the manifestation of symptomatic behavior, in terms of etiology, family therapy has not been able to reverse the basic schizophrenic disease process. For our purposes, what is relevant is that this research on schizophrenia led ultimately to the development of family therapy.

Bateson is considered one of the most important figures in the development of family therapy theory, especially the philosophical framework underlying this movement. His translation of concepts underlying engineering and mathematics into the language of the behavioral sciences was crucial. Yet Bateson himself was neither an engineer, a mathematician, nor a family therapist. Rather, he was an anthropologist and/or ethnologist, and his ultimate contributions were to the realm of epistemology.

The major contribution of his work was its delineation of the theory of logical types, with mathematical proofs of the inevitability of self-reference and paradox in all formal systems, due to a discontinuity between a class and the members of that class.

Applying these notions in the context of a cybernetic perspective, by the 1940s Wiener had already begun to see such constructs as Freud's id and unconscious and Jung's archetypes as informational processes. For Bateson the importance of such insights cannot be overestimated. For him, cybernetics resolved the ancient problem posed by dualistic thinking about mind and body. Mind could now be described as immanent rather than transcendent, in systems. Bateson now set about translating the practice of psychiatry into a theory of human communication.

Following Wiener's pioneering 1948 description of cybernetics as the science of pattern and organization, Bateson, in 1951, was the first to conceptualize the family as a cybernetic system. In 1956 von Bertalanffy, a biologist, outlined the principles of general systems theory, upon which first-order cybernetic family theories are based. His theory focused on the tendencies of organized systems (machines, living organisms, etc.) to maintain their organizations through feedback and homeostasis. Systems theorists, based on a first cybernetic stance, see behavior as circularly organized within a system with rules of operation. Chapter 20 discusses the "second cybernetics," which deemphasizes the family as a social system with predictable regulatory mechanisms, and instead presents the family as a creator of its own reality.

Social Systems

In language very similar to that of Eastern philosophers and new physicists, systems theorists, based on the work of von Bertalanffy (1965), define systems as organic wholes composed of interacting and interdependent parts. Although the various components of a system are interrelated, they are neither in balance nor proportionate to one another in a systematic way. There are imbalances, tensions, and conflicts in the system. Where there are imbalances, stability-promoting processes (morphostasis—that which maintains the status quo), and change-promoting processes (morphogenesis—that which changes the status quo) serve as integrators or adaptor variables to increase or decrease the system's maintenance or change.

In complex systems, the parts work in tandem, in coordinated opposition to each other, to regulate and balance the system. Over time, systems reveal a fundamental pattern of oscillation, or cyclical change, among the various parts; the influence of each element moves into temporary ascendency, in response to input from the larger environment, and then is overcome by its opposite. Also, systems can be maintained by discontinuous change. In other words, chaos in a system may reflect yet another view of stability.

Briefly, living systems exhibit stability and order by being dynamic in nature. The very quality that allows living systems to remain systems, with continuity of structure and function over time, is the constant change and adaptation between each system and its environment. This fundamental fact presents us with the metapolarity of living systems: change and no-change. The Eastern philosophy of Taoism also suggests that harmony arises from a balanced integration of what appear to be opposing forces.

Systems theorists study persons in context. They examine reciprocity, complementarity, and symmetry in communication and behavior as these patterns are reflected in the family. Chapter 2 explores the process (experiential, communication school of family therapy) through which dysfunctional communication patterns maintain (through homeostasis or morphostasis) the family system. Currently, the New Family Therapists are examining the socially constructed use of meaning (through language) as the object of intervention in the family (see chapter 20). Others (structural family therapy) look at the dysfunctional structure of the family as determined by the family's hierarchy, patterns, and rules and the way these maintain the system (through homeostasis or morphostasis). For the most part, family therapy theory based on systems theory has not yet examined (specifically) how discontinuous change occurs (through morphogenic processes), although it has been discussed by Papp, 1982; Hoffman, 1981; and Watzlawick, 1976. Perhaps the theorists need to move to a new model—one that incorporates the ordering of change in the system. (For a discussion of the underlying historical processes of change in the role of women, see Atwood and Weinstein, 1989).

These early explorers—trained in psychology, psychiatry, social work, anthropology, or sociology—were in new territory. Psychoanalysis could not explain family phenomena. Psychologists knew that behaviorist theories of stimulus-response did not fully account for the behavior of individuals in context, nor did operant conditioning explain switches in behavior and in the meaning of language in response to switched contexts. Neither psychiatry nor psychology had any full theory to deal with multipersonal or interpersonal behavior, phenomena, communication, and interactions. It is not surprising, then, that these early explorers began to look beyond their own disciplines for answers.

Key Terms

Boundaries: Refers to an individual's identity within the family, in relation to self and to other family members, and to the family's identity as a unit in itself and in relation to the larger social system.

Change: May be first order change or second order change. *First order change* occurs within the system, according to the rules of that system. *Second order change* involves a change in the rules of the system, and thus in the system itself.

Disengaged: Describes relationships that are distant and rigid.

Enmeshed: Describes relationships that are close and diffuse.

Entropy and negentropy: *Entropy* is a tendency toward maximum disorder and disintegration. If a balance between openness and restrictiveness is appropriate, being too open or too restrictive will lead to dysfunction in the system. This occurs when a system is *entropic*. By contrast, when the appropriate balance between openness and restrictiveness is maintained, the system is in a state of negative entropy (*negentropy*) tending toward maximum order.

Equifinality: The results of interactions among the parts of the system.

Family communications: The process and manner by which family rules and regulations are implemented.

Family structure: Rules and regulations for control and maintenance of the family system.

Family system: A dynamic order of people (with their intellectual, emotional, and behavioral processes) in mutual interaction.

Family subsystem: May be a piece of the family system: i.e., the sibling subsystem has its own structure and communication process.

Feedback: The interactional process among the parts of the system. Feedback maintains the system's functioning and refers to the ways the elements of the system relate to one another.

Genogram: A three-generational map of the family which allows both therapist and family to examine the family in its intergenerational context.

Hierarchy: The structure of levels of authority negotiated by the family.

Homeostasis: The ability of the system to maintain itself; the dynamic balance of the system. Homeostasis implies a relative constancy in the internal environment—a constancy maintained by a continuous interplay of dynamic forces.

Morphogenesis: Change-promoting processes; processes that change the status quo of the system.

Morphostasis: Stability-promoting processes; processes that maintain the status quo within the system.

Openness and closedness: The extent to which a system screens out or lets in new information.

Organizational structure: A system composed of a set of interdependent parts. A change in one part of the system will affect change in other parts of the system. The system itself has basic needs to adapt, survive, and maintain itself, and it therefore takes action and behaves.

Paradox: Redefines the context, thus changing the meaning of a situation and opening up new behavioral alternatives. Prescribing the symptom is a classic example of a paradox.

Recursion: The mutual influence and mutual interaction of people and symptoms.

Reframing: A change in perception. It takes in a situation, lifts it out of its context, and places it in a new context which defines it equally well. For example, the smother mother becomes the mother who loves too much.

Rules: The characteristic relationship patterns within the system. These rules express the values of the system as well as the roles appropriate to behavior within the system.

Triangulation: A situation in which two people unable to relate to each other use a third person, usually a child, to reestablish contact and restore some kind of homeostatic balance.

Wholeness: The relationship between the total system and its parts.

References

Ackerman, N. (1937) "The family as a social and emotional unit," *Bulletin of the Kansas Mental Hygiene Society* 12 (2).

——— (1958) "The emergence of family diagnosis and treatment: A personal view," *Psychotherapy* 4: 125–29.

Ashby, W. (1960) *Design for the Brain*. London: Chapman Hall Science Paperbacks.

Atwood, J. D., and E. Weinstein (1989) "Socially determined psychological conflict in women," *New York Journal of Mental Health* 3 (2) 23–32.

Bateson, G. (1972) *Steps to an Ecology of Mind*. New York: Ballantine Books.

——— (1977) "The birth of a matrix, or double bind and epistemology," in M. Berger, ed., *Beyond the Double Bind*. New York: Brunner/Mazel.

Bell, J. (1961) "Family group therapy," *Public Health Monograph No. 64*. Washington, D.C.: U.S. Government Printing Office.

Broderick, C., and S. Schrader (1981) "The history of professional marriage and family therapy," in A. Gurman and D. Kniskern, eds., *Handbook of Family Therapy*. New York: Brunner/Mazel.

Capra, F. (1983) *The Tao of Physics*. New York: Bantam Books.

Gerrigan, J., and A. Bambrick (1975) "Short-term family therapy with emotionally disturbed children," *Journal of Marriage and Family Counseling* 1: 379–85.

——— (1977a) "Family therapy for disturbed children: Some experimental results in special education," *Journal of Marriage and Family Counseling* 3: 83–93.

——— (1977b) "Introducing novice therapists to 'go-between' techniques of family therapy," *Family Process* 16: 237–46.

Gurman, A.S., and D.P. Kniskern (1981) *Handbook of Family Therapy*. New York: Brunner-Mazel.

——— (1991) *Handbook of Family Therapy*, vol. 2. New York: Brunner-Mazel.

Horney, K., (1937) *The Neurotic Personality of Our Time*. New York: W. W. Norton.

——— (1939) *New Ways in Psychoanalysis*. New York: W. W. Norton.

Hoffman, L. (1981) *Foundations of Family Therapy*. New York: Guilford Press.

Jackson, D., and V. Satir (1961) "Family diagnosis and family therapy," in N. Ackerman, ed., *Exploring the Basis for Family Therapy*. New York: Family Service Association.

Kuhn, T. (1962) *The Structure of Scientific Revolution*. Chicago: University of Chicago Press.

Lidz, R. and T. Lidz (1949) "The family environment of schizophrenic patients," *American Journal of Psychiatry* 14: 241–48.

Lidz, T. (1973) *The Origin and Treatment of Schizophrenic Disorders*. New York: Basic Books.

Masters, W., and V. Johnson (1966) *Human Sexual Response*. Boston: Little, Brown.

Nichols, W. (1984) *Family Therapy: Concepts and Methods*. New York: Gardner Press.

Papp, P. (1982) *The Process of Change*. New York: Guilford Press.

Richmond-Abbott, M. (1979) *The American Woman: Her Past, Her Present, Her Future*. New York: Holt, Rinehart and Winston.

Simon, F., H. Stierlin, and L. Wynne (1985) *The Language of Family Therapy: A Systemic Vocabulary and Sourcebook*. New York: Family Process Press.

Singer, M., and L. Wynne (1963) "Differentiation characteristics of parents of childhood schizophrenics, childhood neurotics, and young adult schizophrenics," *American Journal of Psychiatry* 120: 234–43.

——— (1965a) "Thought disorder and family relations of schizophrenics: III. Methodology using projective techniques," *Archives of General Psychiatry* 12: 187–200.

——— (1965b) "Thought disorder and family relations of schizophrenics: IV. Results and implications," *Archives of General Psychiatry* 12: 201–212.

——— (1966) "Principles of scoring communication defects and deviances in parents of schizophrenics: Rorschach and TAT scoring manuals," *Psychiatry* 29: 260–88.

Sullivan, H. (1953) *The Interpersonal Theory of Psychiatry*. New York: W. W. Norton.

——— (1965) *Personal Psychopathology: Early Formulations*. New York: W. W. Norton.

Thompson, C. (1951) *Psychoanalysis: Evolution and Development*. New York: Hermitage House.

Watzlawick, P. (1976) *How Real Is Real?* New York: Random House.

Watzlawick, P., J. Beavin, and D. Jackson (1967) *Pragmatics of Human Communication*. New York: W. W. Norton.

Wiener, N. (1948) "Cybernetics," *Scientific American* 179: 14–18.

——— (1954) *The Human Use of Human Beings*. New York: Anchor Press.

Wynne, L. (1961) "The study of intrafamilial splits and alignments in exploratory family therapy," in N. Ackerman, ed., *Ex-*

ploring the Base for Family Therapy. New York: Family Service Association of America.

——— (1977) "Schizophrenics and their families: Research in parental communication," in J. Tanner, ed., *Developments in Psychiatric Research*. London: Hoddler and Stroughton.

Wynne, L., et al. (1958) "Pseudomutuality in the family relationships of schizophrenics," *Psychiatry* 21: 191–206.

Wynne, L., and M. Singer (1963) "Thought disorder and family relations of schizophrenics, I and II," *Archives of General Psychiatry:* 191–206.

CHAPTER TWO

THE FIELD TODAY

Joan D. Atwood Ph.D., C.S.W.

In traditional psychotherapy the individual is the unit of analysis. The focus of treatment is on individual psychopathology. Family therapy, however, presents a theoretical system with a therapeutic method that works toward improving the family system. Therefore, the unit of analysis—the focus of treatment—is the family. Family systems theory offers a rationale for the orderly coordination of what at first glance appear to be competing and even incompatible methods. However, these different approaches need not be mutually exclusive. Therapists use many of the same basic psychoanalytic core concepts in both types of therapy: unconscious, resistance, transference, multiple psychic determinism, narcissism, object relations, and structural theory, probing for unconscious meanings, interpretation of resistance and transference, demonstration of regression, confrontation of defenses, working through, analysis of dreams, slips of the tongue, errors, symptomatic behavior, and the like. What is different in family systems treatment is that the focus for change is on the family system.

The five evolving models of family therapy in this chapter are all embedded in the larger social system, in that the constructs used are more meaningful in Western cultures.

Psychodynamic Object Relations Theory and Intergenerational Relationships

In psychodynamic approaches to family therapy, there is a mixture of psychodynamic, or analytic, psychology and systemic thinking. Sometimes these therapies are referred to as transgenerational or extended family therapies. They are typified by the object relations approach, Bowen's theory, and the work of Ivan Boszormenyi-Nagy.

Many object relations theorists have developed their own idiosyncratic object-relations theories, that stem basically from Freudian psychoanalysis. However, from the perspective of psychoanalysis, there is greater emphasis on the internal world of fantasized objects, while in the case of family therapy, there is greater emphasis on the external world and on the objects about which such fantasies are created.

Psychodynamic/psychoanalytic family therapy assumes that resolving problems in relationships in the clients' current families or in their current lives calls for intrapsychic exploration and resolution of problematic unconscious object relationships internalized from early parent-child relationships. These early influences affect and explain the nature of present interpersonal difficulties.

Object relations theory can be applied to relationships across generations. For example, children may be unconsciously perceived by a parent as projections of that parent's own split-off traits. Children, in turn, may subtly conform to these projections and act out the parent's introjects. For example, one child may be unconsciously chosen as the "promiscuous one," to act out the impulsive sexual behavior that his or her parent has internalized as a bad object and then projected onto the child. Another child may act as "feelings" of a highly rational parent. The role of each family member, according to Brody (1959), "allows the internal conflict of each member to be acted out within the family, rather than within the self . . . (p. 392)." For a detailed explanation of contemporary object relations family therapy, see Scharf and Scharf 1987; and Slipp 1991.

Murray Bowen

Murray Bowen's theory clearly illustrates the psychodynamic approach to family therapy. Bowen joined the staff at the Menninger Clinic in Topeka, Kansas, in 1946, and remained until 1954. Originally trained in neurosurgery, he switched to psychiatry and was among those influenced by Joseph Rosen's work with schizophrenics and their families. However, by 1950 Bowen had begun to focus on mother/child symbiosis, assuming schizophrenia was the result of an unresolved tie with the mother (Hoffman 1981, p. 29). Here we see Bowen's tendency to overimplicate the mother and to minimize the father's role. In 1951 he instituted a treatment plan at Menninger in which mothers and their schizophrenic children resided together for several months in cottages on the clinic grounds. In 1954 Bowen went to NIMH, where he instituted and directed the classic study in which whole families of schizophrenic patients were hospitalized for observation and research. He studied seven such families between 1954 and 1959. Initially he used separate therapists for each family member, but he soon began using family therapy as the sole therapeutic treatment for families coming into the hospital. Bowen presented reports of his research in the spring of 1957, at two national professional meetings which some family therapists regard as the symbolic beginning of the family therapy movement.

In that same year, Bowen was part of a panel on family research at the meeting of the American Orthopsychiatric Association. This significant event marked the first public acknowledgment at the national level of studies previously unrecognized and somewhat underground. The panel, organized by John Speigel, included Theodore Lidz of Yale University and David Mendel of Houston, Texas. Bowen, along with Lidz and Don Jackson, was part of the family research panel for which Nathan Ackerman served as secretary at the 1957 APCA meeting in Chicago.

At the time of these meetings, Bowen, who had left NIMH in 1956, was a faculty member in the Department of Psychiatry at Georgetown University Medical School. His plans to take the family research project with him did not materialize, for the department chairperson who had hired him died shortly after Bowen arrived. However, at Georgetown, Bowen developed his comprehensive theory of family therapy. Inspired by an entire generation of students, he became an internationally renowned leader of the family therapy movement. Indeed, Bowenian family therapy has made many important contributions in terms of such concepts as triangulation, intergenerational transmission, level of differentiation of self, and undifferentiated family ego mass.

Bowen's ideas and development are spelled out in a series of papers published as *Family Therapy in Clinical Practice* (Bowen 1978). His major concepts include the nuclear family emotional process, the family projection process, the scale of differentiation, triangles, multigenerational transmission process, and societal regression (Kerr 1981). One hallmark of Bowen's therapy has been his emphasis on the role of therapist as "coach." In that approach, the therapist is not only a role model for individuals in the process of their differentiation from their families of origin, but is also a facilitator of their efforts to go back home in person in order to differentiate themselves. To Bowen the family is an emotional system—the nuclear family, all those living in a household, and the extended family, living or dead, regardless of where they reside. This approach contrasts with that of family therapists who encourage or require clients to bring their parents and siblings in for a few family-of-origin sessions. Both approaches are, of course, aimed at resolving the problems individuals have carried from their original family relationships into their present lives.

Murray Bowen hospitalized entire families that contained a schizophrenic member. In his study of them, he developed an intergenerational schema showing children with low differentiation of self trapped in *triangling*—or serving to stabilize—immature parental marriages. Such absorption of parental immaturity comes at the cost of further failure of self-differentiation. According to Bowen, these children were destined to marry equally undifferentiated offspring of similar marriages, and to require their own offspring to triangle their even more immature marriage. By this descent into ego fusion or even lower levels of differentiation, the theory argued, a schizophrenic is eventually formed.

In studying these schizophrenic families, Bowen noticed a striking lack of ego boundaries between the schizophrenic patient and at least one other family member (usually the mother). Often one person would speak for the other, and anxiety was easily transmitted from one member to the other.

Bowen's observations led to theoretical concepts that attempted to explain schizophrenia and other disorders in terms of family dynamics. The health of each family member, Bowen contends, is based on the degree of his/her *level of differentiation*. The higher the level of one's self-differentiation the more distinguishable his/her emotional and intellectual system. That is, a differentiated person can participate emotionally without fear of becoming fused in the undifferentiated *family ego mass,* or emotional oneness. For Bowen, there are two aspects of the differentiation process: (1) The differentiation of self from others, and (2) the differentiation of feeling processes from intellectual processes. The theory distinguishes between people who are fused and those who are differentiated.

The preferred characteristic is differentiation, by which individuals can transcend not only their own emotions but also those of the family system. People with high levels of differentiation are flexible, goal-directed, adaptable, and self-sufficient. Undifferentiated individuals are more rigid, seek love and approval, and are more emotionally dependent on others for their well-being. In effect, differentiated persons feel their own feelings, and while aware of the feelings of others around them, can maintain a degree of objectivity and emotional distance. Thus, differentiated persons have a conscious (intellectual) awareness of the emotional dynamics around them and can transcend this level of interaction. (It is interesting to note that Bowen's system values the qualities for which men are socialized and devalues those for which women are socialized.)

A critical goal of therapy, then, is to help family members differentiate from the family's emotional togetherness. Bowen believes that when one person differentiates, a ripple effect occurs throughout the family.

Projection of problems onto one or more family member(s) describes another of Bowen's concepts: *triangulation*. Bowen believes that the triangle is the basic building block of the family emotional system. The dyad, or two-person system, is stable as long as it is calm. If stress in the system is transitory or not chronic, the dyad remains relatively stable. The degree of anxiety or stress needed to destabilize the system is somewhat related to the degree of undifferentiation in the spouses. When anxiety between two family members increases, a vulnerable third person may be drawn into the emotional issue. This "triangling in" of the third person reduces the anxiety level. Continued undifferentiation of the family may result in marital conflict, dysfunction in one spouse, or impairment of one or more children.

Bowen (1978) contends that this impairment of undifferentiation may be transmitted across multiple generations as the most undifferentiated offspring marry partners with similar levels of undifferentiation. It is through this *family projection process* that parents transmit their lack of differentiation to their children. Emotional fusion between spouses produces anxiety evidenced by marital conflict and tension. The projection process involves parents who attempt to seek stability and assurance from the child, who needs stability and assurance from the parents. In the more typical pattern of triangulation, the child resonates with the mother's instability and lack of confidence in herself as mother, which the mother interprets as a problem in the child. Mother increases her attention to and overprotectiveness of the child, who becomes more impaired. The father's role, as the third leg of the triangle, is to calm the mother and support her in dealing with the child. The couple colludes and stabilizes around the child's problem and the triangle becomes a stable field (Singleton 1982). The eventual result, according to Bowen, is a schizophrenic offspring.

This transmission of the emotional process is called *multigenerational transmission process*. In other words, the level of differentiation/undifferentiation transmitted across generations is not constant. Rather, each subsequent generation moves toward a lower level of differentiation (Singleton 1982), so that there is increasing lack of differentiation and increasing emotional fusion with each subsequent generation. Emotional problems, the base of interpersonal problems, are the result of a multigenerational sequence in which all members are actors and reactors (Nichols 1984). The multigenerational transmission process continues until unresolved emotional attachments and cutoffs are successfully dealt with.

Bowen also distinguishes between *solid self* and the *pseudoself*. This distinction is closely tied to valuing the transcendence of the intellectual over the emotional. That is, the person with a solid self operates on the basis of clearly defined beliefs, opinions, convictions, and life principles developed through intellectual reasoning and the consideration of alternatives. On the other hand, the pseudoself, consistent with emotional fusion, is characteristic of the person who makes choices based on emotional pressures rather than reasoned principles. The decisions and choices these individuals make at different times may be inconsistent, but they do not see this inconsistency.

People who leave their families of origin with a pseudoself or are fused to their families of origin often marry others to whom they may also become fused. Thus, two undifferentiated people tend to find each other. The result can be an *emotional cutoff* from the family of origin and the subsequent fusion of spouses. In addition, the unproductive family processes of the previous generation pass on to the next generation through such a marriage.

In a marriage of fused spouses, each pseudoself relies on the pseudoself of the other for stability and emotional distance, for the differentiation that each lacks. In effect, two undifferentiated people are pretending to be differentiated, and each is looking to the other for cues on how to respond emotionally and what choices to make. This is an unstable field: The husband looks to the wife, who looks to the husband, who looks to the wife, etc.

This instability can lead to (1) reactive emotional distances between spouses, as each fails to find stability in the other; (2) physical or emotional dysfunction in one of the spouses; (3) overt marital conflict; or (4) projection of the problem onto one or more of the children. The extent of the lack of differentiation is related to the severity of the problems, the degree of emotional cutoff from families of origin, and the level of stress in the family (Nichols 1984).

In sum, emotional cutoff is one way people handle their attachments to their parents or their families of origin at the point of separation. In the fused family, triangulation is common, and being in a triangle implies some level of undifferentiation. The greater the triangulation, the lower the level of differentiation, the more intense the involvement with the family of origin, and the more challenging the separation process. Bowen refers to the lack of differentiation at the point of departure from the family of origin as unresolved emotional attachments. These may be handled through either denial or isolation of self and development of a pseudoself—all forms of emotional cutoff. The undifferentiated individual may therefore choose to live close to the parents, move far from the parents, isolate emotionally from the parents, or combine emotional isolation with physical distancing.

Ivan Boszormenyi-Nagy

Boszormenyi-Nagy, a Hungarian psychiatrist with psychoanalytic training, emigrated to the United States in 1948. In the mid-1950s he teamed with Geraldine Spark, whose background was in psychiatric social work and psychoanalysis and whose previous experience was in a child guidance clinic. Over the years they devised a theory of families that focused on the impact of intergenerational processes.

Boszormenyi-Nagy founded the Eastern Pennsylvania Psychiatric Institute (EPPI) in Philadelphia in 1957 and served as director of the family therapy project there while occupying other positions as a psychiatrist. In the early years of EPPI's study of schizophrenia and the family, he was joined by such key figures as James Framo, David Rubenstein, Albert Scheflen, Geraldine Spark, and Ray Speck. Gerald Zuk joined EPPI in 1961.

Boszormenyi-Nagy became more intensely interested in the importance of transgenerational relationships and their possibilities for working with patients. His book *Invisible Loyalties: Reciprocity in Intergenerational Family Therapy* (Boszormenyi-Nagy and Spark 1973) remains one of the more important sources for transgenerational approaches to therapy. His orientation, currently labeled Contextual Family Therapy (Boszormenyi-Nagy and Ulrich 1981), represents one of today's major schools of family therapy.

Ivan Boszormenyi-Nagy and his colleagues emphasized the importance of *transgenerational entitlements* and *indebtedness* in the formation of symptoms within the family. He believes that invisible, often unconscious, loyalties or bonds across generations greatly influence present behavior. A scapegoated child's misbehavior may be his/her version of loyalty, acting out the parent's need for a focus of anger (a cycle that may connect to behavioral sequences begun generations ago). Such loyalties arise from the basic human concern for fairness and lead to creation of unconscious *ledgers* of what has been given and what is owed. One accumulates merit to the extent that she/he balances the ledger. Ledgers are a statement of entitlement and indebtedness for each individual in the family. However, the parent-child relationship is asymmetrical: the child's entitlement naturally exceeds his/her indebtedness.

One of Boszormenyi-Nagy's most significant contributions was the introduction of a moral dimension to therapy (Nichols 1984). He believes that trust and loyalty are the crucial dimensions in relationships, and that family ledgers must be balanced in this area. His therapy involves discovering the ways in which loyalties to parents and grandparents keep people stuck in patterns that limit their capacities as parents and spouses. The goal of therapy is the "ethical redefinition of the relational context" (Boszormenyi-Nagy 1966), so that trustworthiness will be mutually valued and concern for future generations will provide the impetus to seek family health.

He believes in intensive family therapy based on psychoanalytic principles and aims at reconstructive change in individuals and family groups. His supportive therapy attempts to clarify communication, alter interaction patterns, and facilitate the family's ability to cope with concrete stress situations.

James Framo

Framo, who started seeing families and couples in 1958, has worked primarily with couples. Family of origin sessions, in which he sees adults with their parents and siblings as an integral part of therapy, have become a salient feature of his work. He has also been instrumental in bringing Fairbairn's (1952) object relations theory and its marital therapy applications developed by Dicks (1967) to the widespread attention of therapists in the United States. His theory of symptoms is based largely on their subject-relations concepts. Framo's selected papers have been published under the title *Explorations in Marital and Family Therapy* (1982).

Framo believes in a primary relationship between intrapsychic and transactional influences. He emphasizes transgenerational projective identification, in which children subtly collude in identifying and acting out the projected "introjects" (i.e., bad objects) of their parents.

Boszormenyi-Nagy and Framo edited *Intensive Family Therapy* (1965), which quickly became one of the more important books in the field. In it, fifteen authors, including Ackerman, Bowen, Whitaker, Wynne, Warkentin, and Zuk, reflected on the field as they saw it at the time.

William Fairbairn

Fairbairn (1952) contended that the development of satisfying object relationships is a fundamental human motivation. To him, this meant that individuals may seek to resolve a childhood conflict by internalizing a simultaneously loved and hated parent image, thereby mastering and controlling that ambivalent image in his/her own psyche. These internalized images tend to split into good and bad objects, resulting in "introjects"—psychological representations of those objects which unconsciously influence the individual's relationships.

Harry Dicks

Dicks (1963, 1967) was one of the first to apply Fairbairn's (1952) object relations concepts to marriage. Dicks stated that distressed marriages are characterized by "mutual attribution and projection, with each spouse perceived to some degree as an internal object" (p. 126). Dicks's conceptualizations are useful in understanding why many "cat and dog" marriages stay together but seem impervious to change. Each spouse's ego identity (which includes both good and bad objects) is, in effect, preserved by having one or more bad objects split off onto his/her partner. In other words, each spouse disowns his/her own bad object introjects, and needs the other to accept their projections. Each begins to conform subtly to the inner role model of the other. Dicks (1963) believed that this collusive process continues because both spouses hope to integrate lost introjects by finding them in each other.

This results in unconscious bargains (Sager 1976) which may take many forms (e.g., "You be my courage, and I will be your support"; "You be tender, and I will be strong.") The distressed marriage, then, adds up to a total personality. (For a description of object-relations marital therapy, see also Crisp 1988; Scharff and Scharff 1987 and 1991; and Slipp 1988. For an example of the collusive patterns in couples, see Willi 1979; Hendrix 1988.)

Norman Paul

Paul (1977) believes that family members most tenaciously withhold feelings associated with grief. His major contribution involves treatment procedures derived from his contention that a direct relationship exists between family members' maladaptive responses to the deaths of loved ones and the subsequent rigidity of family patterns. Paul believes that a family turns to a "pathological stable equilibrium" when grief is not appropriately expressed. The family scapegoat generally maintains this state, serving the symbiotic function of turning the family's attention away from recognition of its grief.

Donald Williamson

Donald Williamson (1981) hypothesizes that a family life cycle stage occurs in about the fourth decade of life. The goal of this stage is to terminate the hierarchical power structures governing the relationships between an adult and his/her older parents and to redistribute power between the two generations.

The family of origin therapies of Bowen (1978), Framo (1976), and Williamson (1981, 1982a, 1982b) either explicitly or implicitly acknowledge the potential risks of parental projections, and attempt to weaken their hold by helping adult clients renegotiate their relationships with their aging parents. Framo (1976) contends that "dealing with the real, external figures loosens the grip of the internal representatives of these figures and exposes them to current realities" (p. 194).

Experiential Family Therapists

Rather than focus on internal psychodynamics, communication theorists assume that one can learn about the family system by studying verbal and nonverbal communication. Their focus is therefore on observable current interactions (relationships) within the family system, not on historical analyses of the individual family members. Communication theorists make these basic assumptions:

1. All behavior is communicative.
2. Every communication has a content/report and a relational/command aspect. The latter classifies the former and is, therefore, a metacommunication. The metacommunication is the nonverbal message. It is that aspect of the message that places a demand on the recipient.
3. Relationships are defined by command messages and are dependent upon the punctuation of the communication sequences between the communications. Each individual punctuates his/her reality in different ways; that is, behavioral sequences are understood and meaning is experienced relative to the epistemology of the observer.
4. Human beings communicate both digitally (verbally) and analogically (nonverbally).
5. All communicational interchanges are either symmetrical (equal and parallel, in which either participant can lead) or complementary (in which one participant leads and the other follows).
6. Problems are maintained within a context of recursive feedback loops of recurrent patterns of communication. The core concept of communication theory is that relationships can be understood by analyzing the communicational and metacommunicational aspects of their interactions.

Virginia Satir, Carl Whitaker, and the Palo Alto Group are representative of this approach.

Virginia Satir

Virginia Satir entered the field of family therapy via education and social work. She termed her approach a "process model" in which the therapist and the family join forces to promote wellness. This model's premise is that families are balanced, rule-governed systems through which the basic components of communication and self-esteem provide a context for growth and development.

Satir believed that individuals are innately good and have the capacity to develop to their full potential, that all individuals possess all the resources necessary for positive growth and development. In her model, there is mutual influence and shared responsibility—everything and everyone has an impact on and responds to the impact of everything and everyone else. Therefore, there can be no blame, only multiple stimuli and multiple effects. Therapy for Satir is a process of interaction between clients and therapist. The therapist may take the lead in helping to facilitate growth, but each individual is in charge of him/herself.

When this development of potential is blocked or hindered, a pathology occurs. The concept of maturation is central to Satir's viewpoint. She believes that mature people can take full charge of themselves and assume responsibility for their own choices and decisions. Choices and decisions that lead to growth are based on people's accurate perceptions of themselves and others, and on their finding affirmation of their perceptions within their environments. To develop this maturity, it is important to be able to separate oneself from one's family, to become a differentiated self. The mature individual is characterized by (1) the ability to be in touch with his or her own feelings; (2) the ability to communicate clearly with others; (3) the ability to accept others as different from oneself; and (4) the willingness to see difference and differentiation as a source of growth and learning, rather than as a threat.

Satir's other core concept is *self-esteem*. One cannot be mature without a feeling of self-worth. She believes that the emotional system of the family is expressed through communications. Thus, the essence, the substance of communications lies in the feeling dimension. Dysfunction occurs when communications are incongruent, by which Satir means that the communicational and metacommunicational aspects of the message do not correspond. She describes four types of dysfunctional communication that occur when people fear rejection, judgment, or exposure of weakness, when people's self-esteem is shaky and vulnerable:

1. **Blaming**—defining the problem as being in others.
2. **Placating**—acting apologetic, agreeable, and often ingratiating, seeking approval from others.
3. **Distracting**—chattering irrelevantly.
4. **Superreasonable**—assuming a rigid computer-like posture devoid of feelings, appearing extremely logical and intellectual, at least outwardly.

People who communicate in any of these styles not only reflect low self-esteem, but also communicate nonacceptance of the other person or persons.

Satir assesses whether or not family members are to express what they see or hear, identifies family members to whom one can talk, assesses the degree of freedom to disagree or disapprove, and observes how one asks questions when one does not understand.

The emphasis of Satir's therapy is on improving communication by correcting discrepancies between the literal (report) message and the metacommunicational (command) message.

Carl Whitaker

Carl Whitaker, noted for his pioneering work with schizophrenic patients and their families, has also worked with children in a child guidance format and with delinquent adolescents in a residential facility in Louisville, Kentucky. In the early 1940s, he moved to Oak Ridge, Tennessee, where, with John Warkentin, he began introducing family members into therapeutic sessions for cotherapy. Whitaker and Warkentin moved to Emory University in Atlanta, Georgia, in 1946, and Thomas Malone joined them in 1948. From 1945 to 1965, Whitaker treated schizophrenics with aggressive play therapy. He and his group experimented with various ways to treat such patients and their families.

Whitaker's background was in obstetrics and gynecology, not in psychoanalysis. Exposed to Rankian influences during his Louisville years, he developed an approach known as Existential Psychotherapy or Symbolic Experiential Family Therapy. His approach has been widely demonstrated in workshops and conferences around the United States and elsewhere. Whitaker's contributions are reflected in *From Psyche to System* (Neill and Kniskern 1982).

Whitaker and associates, together with professionals from Philadelphia including John Rosen, conducted a series of four-day conferences on the treatment of schizophrenia. The tenth conference, held at Sea Island, Georgia, included Gregory Bateson and Don D. Jackson (1955). Whitaker also published one of the first significant papers on conjoint marital therapy (1958), and was among the first to team teach with others and begin sharing techniques and discoveries in the growing family therapy field (Guerin 1976). The Whitaker group left Emory in 1955 and went into private practice in Atlanta. Whitaker moved to the University of Wisconsin in 1965, and stayed there until his retirement.

Whitaker believes that theories are useful only for beginners. When therapists develop courage based on their abilities, they can give up theories. Because of his atheoretical approach, his model is hard to understand and almost impossible to duplicate. He believes that therapy is an art and recommends substituting faith in one's own abilities for theory.

In this sense, therapy is a growth process from which both therapist and client share and benefit. It is an intimate, interactive, parallel experience in which each becomes equally vulnerable and neither takes responsibility for the other. It is intuitive; it aims at increasing anxiety within a caring environment. It is experiential, intrapsychic, and paradoxical. The aim of Whitaker's therapy is to help individuals grow in the context of their families. The family is an integrated whole, and from a sense of belonging to the whole comes the freedom to individuate and separate. The family is the key to individual growth and development.

Whitaker believes that the basic goal of therapy is to balance and facilitate both individual autonomy and a sense of togetherness. This goal is achieved by enhancing creativity, or "craziness," within the family so that all are free to grow and change. Therapy occurs in three phases—engagement, involvement, and disengagement. The therapist increases, in a caring way, the anxiety with which both she/he and the family approach therapy. Using paradox, the therapist escalates the pressure to produce a psychotic-like episode, so that the client must reintegrate in a new and more meaningful way. During this process the therapist both belongs to and separates from the family, moving in and out of an intense, sane and crazy, symbiotic relationship in which intrapsychic responses are shared and roles are often reversed. As the client reconciles the sane and crazy elements within him/herself, to enjoy his/her own and the family's creativity, she/

he achieves individuation and rebirth until she/he can establish an independent peer relationship with the therapist, who now becomes a consultant to the family.

Whitaker defines seven therapeutic techniques important to the therapeutic process: (1) Redefining symptoms as efforts toward growth; (2) modeling fantasy alternatives to real life stress; (3) separating interpersonal stress from intrapersonal stress; (4) adding practical interventions; (5) augmenting the despair of a family member; (6) generating affective confrontation; and (7) treating children like children and not like peers (Whitaker and Keith 1981).

The Palo Alto Group (MRI)

The founders of family therapy laid the groundwork for family therapy theory by positing many of its concepts around schizophrenia. The Palo Alto group—Bateson, Jackson, Weakland, and Haley—extrapolated from Bateson's observations on animal play, and posited the *double bind,* an intense disorganizing pattern of communication in which the person at risk for schizophrenia receives conflicting injunctions at different logical levels, together with an injunction not to leave the field.

The Palo Alto group emerged from a different background than the other early researchers. In 1952, Gregory Bateson, a catalyst for the early Palo Alto work, received a foundation grant in connection with the Veterans Administration Hospital in Menlo Park, California, to study patterns and paradoxes in communication. By appointing Jay Haley and John Weakland to work with him, Bateson sought the support of their backgrounds in communication and anthropology, respectively. William Fry, who had just finished his psychiatric residency, was added a few months later. The project lasted until 1954; Don Jackson, John Weakland, and Paul Watzlawick represent the contemporary theorists who worked on this project.

Don D. Jackson

Narrowing their focus, this group began to study schizophrenia. Don D. Jackson, who in 1954 had just completed his psychiatric residency at Chestnut Lodge in Maryland, had been influenced by the late Harry Stack Sullivan and other interpersonalists; he was brought into the project as a consultant on the treatment of schizophrenia. Jackson reported on the schizophrenia project at a 1957 national psychiatric meeting, at which he met Ackerman, Bowen, Lidz, and Wynne. It was here that the Palo Alto Group came upon the family therapy movement, almost accidentally, since they had not been aware that family therapy was being used elsewhere.

Jackson's major contributions deal with the organization of human interaction. In addition to his role in developing the double-bind concept, he is also responsible for introducing the notion of homeostasis. Jackson hypothesized that families develop recurring patterns of interaction which maintain the stability of the family, especially in times of stress. He described families as rule-governed systems.

According to Jackson, a system operates with three kinds of rules. These include covert norms, overt values, and metarules—rules for changing the norms and values. The process of defining rules is called *calibration,* or the range of behaviors considered acceptable. A family experiencing symptoms indicates a need for recalibration and a need for a rule to change the rules.

At the beginning of the Palo Alto Group's work, the two major concepts used were the double bind and family homeostasis (Jackson and Weakland 1959). In a classic paper entitled "Toward a Theory of Schizophrenia," Bateson, Jackson, Haley, and Weakland (1956) introduced the concept of the double bind, which consisted of a parent sending messages at two different levels, with one message disqualified by the other. Theoretically, a double bind requires six ingredients: (1) two or more processes in operation; (2) repeated experiences; (3) a primary negative injunction; (4) a secondary injunction, conflicting with the first on a more abstract level; (5) a tertiary negative injunction prohibiting the victim from leaving the field; and (6) a victim who perceives the world in double-bound positions. Widely hailed in the early years as the etiological factor in schizophrenia, the double bind theory is today recognized as not peculiar to families producing schizophrenics, and thus not necessarily an etiological factor in schizophrenia. In 1962, when the schizophrenia project ended, the group agreed that in schizophrenia the double bind is a necessary but not sufficient condition to explain etiology, and conversely, is an inevitable by-product of schizophrenic communication. Both the double bind and homeostasis continued to be of major significance in the Palo Alto Group's family work (Watzlawick and Weakland 1977).

In 1959, backed by private finances, Jackson founded the Mental Health Research Institute (MRI) as a division of the Palo Alto Medical Research Foundation. Virginia Satir and Jules Riskin joined Jackson. In 1961 Jackson published a paper arguing that conjoint family therapy was superior to therapy with individual family members (Jackson 1961) and continued as a consultant to the Bateson project. Jackson and Ackerman, from New York's Family Institute, then began to sponsor a new journal, *Family Process,* with Jay Haley as its first editor, in 1962. When the Bateson project closed that year, Haley and Weakland moved to MRI. Meanwhile, from 1961 to 1966, Satir trained therapists at MRI. Her book *Conjoint Family Therapy* (1964) and the workshops and demonstrations she conducted, both there and at the Esalen Institute in Big Sur, California, were instrumental in popularizing the Palo Alto version of family therapy and making Satir its best known exponent. Today MRI continues as a significant center for treatment and for the study of family therapy. The early emphasis on communication was subsequently supplemented by the opening of the Brief Therapy Center in 1967.

During the 1960s, Jackson and his MRI associates wrote many articles describing communicational strategies as devices for establishing or escaping definitions of intrafamilial relationships (Hoffman 1981, p. 23). Strategic family work evolved largely from this work at the MRI. It was also influenced by Milton Erickson's emphasis on hypnosis and paradoxical therapeutic strategies. Haley, who also worked at MRI and was a biographer of Erickson, continues to influence the growth and direction of strategic family therapy today.

The MRI group operates from a process rather than an organizational model. Issues of hierarchy and power are not as important as those of interactional sequence. The family's sequence of behavior around its attempted solution is assumed to maintain the presenting problem (Watzlawick, Weakland, and Fisch 1974). The MRI therapist tracks this cycle of behavior within the family by asking questions, then assigns homework (either direct or paradoxical) designed to break up the existing sequence of behavior.

John H. Weakland

John Weakland received his academic degrees in chemistry and chemical engineering. After six years of working in these fields, he became interested in sociology and anthropology, and in 1953 moved to California to participate in Bateson's Palo Alto study of human communication. There he studied hypnosis and therapeutic practice with Milton Erickson.

Building on the concept of family homeostasis, he began a study of schizophrenics and their families. His viewpoint in the Palo Alto Group was interactional, his orientation anthropological. Families were seen as a particular culture, and the group's goal was to describe both normal and abnormal behavior patterns within this culture. Even though therapy was not part of the original plan, the team members developed an interest in alleviating stress and solving problems. The outcome of this concern was the development of the concept of Brief Therapy (Watzlawick and Weakland 1977).

According to the assumptions of the Brief Family Therapy Model, only issues defined by the family should be targeted for change. Such problems are to be specified in behavioral terms, as are the desired outcomes of therapy. After discovering the communicational patterns that maintain the problem behavior, the therapist seeks to interdict these patterns through paradox. Sessions are kept to a maximum of ten, and family progress is evaluated during a follow-up study several months after termination of therapy. In 1974, Watzlawick, Weakland, and Fisch outlined the basics of this model, including a delineation of first- and second-order change in their book *Change*.

Paul Watzlawick

Paul Watzlawick is a native of Austria. He studied philosophy and modern language in Italy (1949) and psychotherapy at the Jung Institute. In 1960, frustrated with the results of traditional therapy methods, he became a research associate and investigator at MRI.

There he investigated behavioral change, with a focus on interpersonal communication and its disturbances within families. Not only did the Brief Therapy approach solve the client's presenting problems, this resolution often led to positive changes in other areas of the family.

The basic premise of Watzlawick's theory of communication is that no phenomenon can be completely understood without examination of its context. Thus, relationships manifested through communication are the appropriate subjects of study (Watzlawick, Beavin, and Jackson 1967). The goal of therapy with the behavioral effects of communication is problem resolution. Problems are situational, arising from difficulties in interaction. Resolving problems requires altering the client's perception of reality by changing the language employed to communicate about the problem.

According to Watzlawick (1978), the language of change is the analogic mode, a function of the right hemisphere of the brain. The therapist gains access to the right hemisphere by using homonyms, synonyms, ambiguities, and puns to block the brain's logical left hemisphere. He uses paradox, reframing, and requests for the client's worst fantasies. Facilitation of second-order change is achieved through making the covert overt, advertising instead of concealing, and using resistance (Watzlawick, Weakland, and Fisch 1974). In each case changing the rules of the system—altering the context by providing information from outside the system—is the way to problem resolution. Watzlawick (1978) believes that therapists cannot *not* influence. They are active, and they are responsible for the moral judgments they make.

Strategic Family Therapy

Strategic family therapy and structural family therapy were born on opposite coasts of the United States. Strategic family therapy is rooted in the Palo Alto research group of the early 1950s. As part of his research on family communication, Gregory Bateson began to look at schizophrenia as a discrepancy between levels of communication. When the Bateson project published "Toward a Theory of Schizophrenia," they helped therapists throughout the country examine the double-binding communications of family members. In so doing, strategic family therapy came of age.

Strategic family therapy is characterized by its use of specific strategies for addressing family problems (Madanes and Haley 1977). Therapy is geared toward changing the presenting complaint and is typically accomplished by the therapist first assessing the cycle of family interaction, then breaking that cycle through straightforward or paradoxical directives. Therapy is not growth- but change-oriented, and the therapist is responsible for successful therapeutic outcomes. The therapist focuses on present interaction; she/he does not interpret family members' behavior or explore the past. Therapy is terminated when the presenting problems have ceased. Strategic Family Therapy is represented by Jay Haley and the Milan Group.

Jay Haley

Jay Haley is acknowledged as a pioneer in the field of family therapy. He began his career by studying schizophrenia with Gregory Bateson. In 1967 he became director of family therapy research at the Philadelphia Child Guidance Clinic, where he worked with Salvadore Minuchin, Braulio Montalvo, and Bernice Rosman until 1976. In 1976, Haley founded the Family Therapy Institute of Washington, D.C., with his wife, Cloe Madanes.

Haley focuses on sequences of behavior, communication patterns, and the here-and-now. He uses directives and action plans to change behavior and creates strategies to fit the uniqueness of the family. His approach to therapy is method-oriented and problem-focused, with little or no attempt to instill insight. He also uses the concepts of power and control in his description of family patterns, for he sees communication sequences and symptoms as attempts to control or influence. According to Haley, people inevitably engage in reciprocal attempts, through digital and analogic communication, to control the nature of their relationships. Symptoms are behaviors beyond one's control. They are, on the other hand, very controlling in terms of the alternatives available to anyone who has a relationship with the symptom bearer. The nonsymptomatic person in the relationship is relatively powerless since it is not appropriate to try to make someone stop doing what she/he cannot help doing. Haley therefore defines certain symptoms as tactics to maintain a particular arrangement in a relationship or a family.

Haley agrees with Minuchin that problems are maintained by a faulty family hierarchy. One goal of therapy, therefore, is to alter the family's interactions, thereby changing the hierarchical structure. Also, he contends that the presenting problem is often a metaphor for the actual problem (Haley 1976; Madanes 1981).

Haley often aligns himself with the parental generation in dealing with child-focused problems (Haley 1980). Bringing parents together to work on a child's problem can realign problematic hierarchies and strengthen the couple's relationship. Haley and Madanes alter malfunctioning triangles (Haley 1976, 1980) and incongruent hierarchies (Madanes 1980, 1981) through such diverse interventions as paradox, reframing, ordeals, "pretending," and unbalancing through creating alternative coalitions.

In his therapy Haley does not believe that asking why a problem exists is useful. The key question is, what is maintaining the problem? Telling people what they are doing wrong is not only not useful, it often initiates resistance. Further, like the behaviorists, Haley believes that changing behavior leads to changes in feelings and not vice versa, as the object relations theorists believe.

His general therapy strategy is to intervene so that the covert hierarchical structure reflected in repeated sequences of behavior cannot be maintained. In addition he seeks to change symptomatic metaphors to allow more adaptive ones to emerge. Directives are very important. While directives are generally viewed as assignments for the family to perform outside therapy, Haley suggests that all therapist behavior in the session is a directive. Directives serve three purposes: (1) they facilitate change; (2) they involve the therapist in the therapy by keeping him/her figuratively in the family during the week; and (3) they offer a stimulus, reactions to which give the therapist information about family structure, rules, boundaries, and interactions.

Going beyond the behavior paradox that one cannot not behave and the communication paradox that one cannot not communicate, Haley adds that one cannot *not* attempt to influence the definition or nature of relationships. He is convinced that whole families should be treated. Only one therapist is to see the family, in order to direct the therapy more immediately and to establish control. A second therapist or team observes the family from behind a one-way mirror. There may be flexibility in the techniques used, but there is no flexibility about the first interview. It should accomplish (1) the social engagement of the family, (2) the definition of the problem, (3) the interaction stage at which the family members discuss the problem among themselves, (4) the definition of the desired changes in terms of solving the presenting problem as specified in behavioral terms, and (5) the ending of the interview with directives and the scheduling of the next appointment.

According to Haley some, but not all, directives are paradoxical in the sense of prescribing the symptom or prescribing resistance. In either case the therapist maintains control by anticipating family members' responses to therapy. Another form of directive is the *metaphoric task*. During the session the therapist might use a metaphor to symbolize a problem or issue that the family does not discuss. The therapist thus indirectly plants the seeds of possible change. Another directive used by Haley (1984) is *ordeal therapy*. Here the therapist prescribes an ordeal equal to or greater than the distress of the symptom itself, so the symptom becomes harder to keep up than to abandon. It is essential to select an ordeal that is good for the client, such as dieting or exercise. The ordeal must also be something the client can do and cannot legitimately object to doing. Further, it cannot harm the person or anyone else. For example, for people who suffer from insomnia, Haley might prescribe that they scrub the kitchen floor with a toothbrush whenever they wake up in the middle of the night.

Haley feels that in order for change to occur in the client, the style of interaction in the social unit of which the client is a member must also change.

The Milan Group

Systemic family therapy as practiced by the Milan Associates (Selvini-Palazzoli et al. 1978) shares similar roots with both the MRI and the Haley versions of strategic family therapy—all were influenced by the work of Gregory Bateson. This led all three groups to view problems as being maintained by behavioral sequences. However, MRI and Haley were further influenced by the work of Milton Erickson, while the Milan group held true to Bateson's original work.

The first major publication of the Milan Group was *Paradox and Counterparadox* (Selvini-Palazzoli et al. 1978). This book recounts a series of trial and error encounters with dysfunctional families, focusing on a search for the "pathological nodal point" (Tomm 1984, p. 115), the point which, when changed, would allow the family to evolve into a new form. In 1980 the group split into two pairs: Palazzoli and Prata have studied the effects of a single sustained and invariant intervention, while Boscolo and Cecchin have concentrated on developing new training methods (Tomm 1984).

The Milan group focused on overcoming the tyranny of linguistics, which they believe keeps therapists and clients thinking in an intrapsychic linear manner. They forced a different language on themselves, in order to understand families in different ways, in the process substituting the verbs "to seem" and "to show" for the verb "to be." Families were described as paradoxical, in the sense that they came to therapy to change, yet each member of the system sought to prevent change. The group devised interventions to break the impasse imposed by the family's paradoxical request for both stability and change. Such interventions took the form of the *counterparadox,* which effectively overwhelmed the paradox posed by the family: "We think that you should not change, because it is a good thing that. . . ." They would give a positive connotation to all behaviors in the homeostatic pattern and prescribe no change in the context of change (therapy), putting the family in a therapeutic double bind.

Bateson's *Steps to an Ecology of the Mind* helped them view systems as always evolving, even while appearing to be stuck. The process of the Milan Group builds on systems theory/cybernetics and information theory. They see the world primarily in terms of patterns and information, rather than of mass and energy. Theirs is a recursive approach in that theory and clinical practice respond to feedback derived from the therapy. They participate in and are a part of the families they see.

They believe that mental problems reflect problems in social interaction. Therapy is directed toward inferred patterns of interaction, rather than toward individuals or intrapsychic problems. Their model is built on a circular epistemology in which the observer focuses on recursiveness in the interactions of the family and on holistic patterns. The members of a family seem caught in this recursive pattern and are viewed more with compassion than with condemnation.

The Milan Associates explain their in-session behavior in terms of three themes: *hypothesizing, circularity,* and *neutrality* (Selvini-Palazzoli et al. 1980). The therapist is constantly generating hypotheses about why the family behaves as it does. These hypotheses create a map from which questions can be directed to the family and interventions made. All hypotheses, including those developed by the family, are considered equally valid.

Circularity describes the way the therapist conducts the session. Throughout, she/he uses triadic or circular questions, in which one family member is asked to comment on the interactional behaviors of two others. In this way the therapist develops a systemic picture of the family's behavior (Penn 1982) and new information is introduced allowing family members to experience themselves in a new context. Palozzoli et al. (1980) contend that sometimes simply conducting a session using circular questions will introduce enough new information to produce change.

Therapist neutrality is the glue that holds this process together. By avoiding issues of hierarchy, power, and side-taking, the therapist is free to experience the system in its entirety. This facilitates the generation of new hypotheses and allows the family to develop at its own pace in its own way. Within this neutral zone, the family is free to decide whether or not it wishes to change (Tomm 1984).

Structural Family Therapy

While communication theorists tend to emphasize the "how" of family interaction, the "bits and pieces" of communication, structural theorists tend to emphasize the dynamic orderings of the system itself, the actual structure within which elements of communication take place.

Salvador Minuchin

Salvador Minuchin is the person most frequently associated with the development of the structural school. In the 1960s he and his colleagues were working at the Wiltwyck School for boys, serving a population primarily from New York's inner city. They found long-term psychoanalytic, passive, growth-oriented therapy extremely ineffective with these children, whose issues were immediate and survival-based. These therapists experimented with a more active approach to therapy in which they worked with the boys and their families together (Aponte and VanDeusen 1981). *Families of the Slums* (Minuchin et al. 1967) was written about the Wiltwyck School experiences and is the first book to present the structural approach in therapy. The other theorists who contributed to its development are Montalvo, Umbarger, Aponte, Walters, Fishman, and Greenstein.

Starting with this work with low-socioeconomic-status families, structural family therapy is a problem-solving approach to a dysfunctional family context. Although Minuchin's work with psychosomatic families is well known (Minuchin, Rosman, and Baker 1978), he has broadened his theoretical base and applied this approach to patients of varying socioeconomic classes with a variety of presenting problems (Minuchin and Fishman 1981). In this sense Minuchin is one of the first family therapists who considered the larger sociopolitical system as a major influence on family organization and structure (see also Elizur and Minuchin 1989).

He believes that the structure of the family is "an open sociocultural system in transformation" (Minuchin 1974, p. 14). Family structure is sociocultural in that it integrates the demands of society with those of the internal family system to shape the individual. Because Minuchin was one of the first family therapists to recognize and examine larger sociocultural influences on the family system, it would be most illuminating to read an analysis by him of the organizing role of gender. Minuchin is well aware of the gender inequities in contemporary society, and this, combined with his knowledge of macrosociological theory, makes him the natural theorist to integrate the role of gender into structural family therapy theory.

Minuchin describes four types of stress: (1) stressful contact of one family member with extrafamilial forces, (2) stressful contact of the whole family with extrafamilial forces, (3) stress at transition points in a family, (4) stress around idiosyncratic problems. In each of these situations, the key to successful adaptation is the transformation of structure through boundary negotiation.

Structural family therapy focuses on patterns of interaction within the family which give clue to the basic structure and organization of the system. For Minuchin (1974) structure refers to the invisible set of demands that organizes the way the family interacts, or the consistent, repetitive, organized, and predictable modes of family behavior which allow us to consider the family as "structured" in a functional sense. Thus, observations of patterns of family interactions provide information about how the family is organized to maintain itself. A family operates through repeated transactional patterns which regulate the behavior of its members. These patterns include how, when, and to whom family members relate. The concepts of *patterns* and *structure* imply a set of covert rules of which family members may not be consciously aware, but which consistently characterize and define their interactions.

For structural theorists, diagnosis is directed toward, and treatment is predicated upon, a system's organizational dynamics. They believe that *boundaries* are critically important. Boundaries are the rules and regulations that separate the system from its environment. They may be a manifestation of the system's rules and regulations. A boundary can be highly permeable, so that thoughts and feelings are easily exchanged, or highly impermeable, so that thoughts and feelings are either not exchanged at all or are exchanged only with difficulty. The clarity of the boundaries is determined by how well lines of responsibility have been thought out and how clearly designation of authority has been defined. Minuchin postulates three types of boundaries: (1) enmeshed boundaries, where relationships are diffuse and close; (2) disengaged boundaries, where relationships are inappropriately rigid and distant; and (3) clear boundaries, where relationships are within the "normal" range. The extremes of disengagement and enmeshment indicate the potential for symptom formation.

Structural theory defines three subsystems: the spouse subsystem, the parental subsystem, and the sibling subsystem. The rule among these subsystems in the functional family is hierarchy. Structural theory insists on appropriate boundaries between generations.

Minuchin charges the therapist with three major tasks: To join the family as a leader, to unearth and evaluate the underlying family structure, and to create circumstances to allow the transformation of this structure. The therapist's tasks are to form the therapeutic system and to restructure the family system. There are at least seven strategies for facilitating change: actualizing transactional patterns; marking boundaries; escalating stress; assigning tasks; utilizing symptoms; manipulating moods; and providing support, education, and guidance.

The family developmental tasks in this process require modification of the family structure. This structural modification is accomplished through boundary negotiation and modification. Minuchin believes that there are generic and idiosyncratic constraints on this process. The generic constraints are so called because they are "universal rules governing family organization" (Minuchin 1974, p. 52). For example, in any family system with children, there must be a power hierarchy. The idiosyncratic constraints are composed of unique individual expectations and intentions of each family member. Through universal rules the patterns are explicitly or implicitly formed.

The goals of structural therapy are somewhat idiosyncratic, although some general patterns and structures do recur within a given cultural context. These general goals therefore guide the structural therapist:

1. There must be effective hierarchical structure. The parent(s) must be in charge. There must be a generation gap based on parental/executive authority.
2. There must be a parental/executive coalition. The parents must support and accommodate each other, to provide a united front to their children.
3. As the parental/executive coalition forms, the sibling subsystem becomes a system of peers.
4. If the family is disengaged, the goal is to increase the frequency of interaction and move toward clear, rather than rigid, boundaries. This shift brings an increase in nurture and support to complement the previous independence and autonomy characteristic of families with rigid boundaries.
5. If the family is enmeshed, the general goal is to foster differentiation of individuals and subsystems. This reflects a respect for differences in developmental stages of the children and permission for age-appropriate experimentation with independent activity.
6. There must be a spouse subsystem established as an entity distinct from the parental subsystem.

Structural family therapy focuses on two kinds of live, here-and-now activities: *enactments* and *spontaneous behavioral sequences*. When a therapist asks for an enactment, she/he seeks a demonstration of the way a family deals with a specific kind of problem in order to observe the sequence. This gives the therapist clues to the family structure. Spontaneous behavior sequences are transactions in the family as natural parts of its pattern. If the therapist successfully joins the family, the family will begin to reveal pieces of its structure through transactions.

Behavioral Therapy

The procedures for behavioral therapy parallel the procedures for the scientific study of behavior consistent with the logical positivist-empirical tradition of research. Behavior therapy uses any number of specific techniques, employing psychological (especially learning) principles to deal with maladaptive human behavior. The term "behavior" is interpreted broadly as encompassing covert responses (for example, emotions and implicit verbalizations), when these responses can be clearly specified, in addition to overt responses. Among the techniques included in this school are systematic desensitization, assertiveness training, modeling, operant conditioning, extinction, and aversive conditioning (Rimm and Masters 1974).

Behavior therapy can be traced back to Pliny the Elder's use of aversive conditioning in the treatment of alcoholism (Franks 1963); the son of a Chinese emperor's operant conditioning of the royal cavalry in order to cause the assassination of his father (Kreuger 1961); and the application of procedures similar to reciprocal inhibition reported in Paris (case described in Stewart 1961) of a patient suffering from debilitating obsessions. Early behavioral treatment involved having the patient engage in competing responses (reciting songs), with food contingent on his/her responses.

While these examples are of historical interest, they are not the major antecedents of modern behavior therapy. Vastly more influential were the writings of Pavlov (1927), a major precursor of what is now called "classical conditioning," and the writings and experiments of Watson and his associates (Jones 1924; Watson 1914; Watson and Rayner 1920), which pointed to the application of Pavlovian or classical conditioning principles to human psychological disorders.

Two books were of paramount importance in establishing the foundations of this new discipline, Skinner's (1953) *Science and Human Behavior* and Wolpe's (1958) *Psychotherapy by Reciprocal Inhibition*. Skinner provided a basis for the belief that much human behavior can be understood in terms of operant conditioning, and Wolpe conceived of human neurosis in terms of Pavlovian and Hullian learning principles. Far more important, he outlined specific therapy techniques (for example, systematic desensitization and assertiveness training) aimed at dealing with what was then called neurotic behavior. Wolpe also provided impressive case-history outcome data to support his so-called reciprocal inhibition techniques. Another significant contribution was Eysenck's (1960) *Behavior Therapy and the Neuroses*. In 1963 Eysenck founded the first behavior therapy journal, *Behavior Research and Therapy*. Recent years have witnessed numerous behavior therapy conferences and the development of such professional organizations as the Association for the Advancement of Behavior Therapy and the Behavior Research and Therapy Society.

Bandura's (1969) social learning theory emphasized vicarious learning (modeling), symbolic/cognitive processes, and self-regulation, concepts very relevant to marital and family therapy. This theory emphasizes cognitive processes in the form of mediation variables (Mahoney 1988; Beck 1976; Meichenbaum 1977). In addition, Bandura's (1982) "reciprocal determinism" is useful in describing the dynamics of relationships. Along this same line, social psychologists Thibaut and Kelley's (1959) theory of social exchange helps the behavior therapist focus on family interactions. The social exchange perspective analyzes interactions in terms of the relative amounts of supposed reward and cost to the people in the relationship. The assumption is that people in relationships seek to maximize rewards and minimize costs. Over time, a reciprocity is achieved and an equilibrium is established. Thus, positive behaviors beget positive behaviors and negative behaviors beget negative behaviors.

Assumptions of Behavior Therapy

1. Relative to psychotherapy, behavior therapy concentrates on the maladaptive behavior itself, rather than on its presumed underlying cause.
2. Behavior therapy assumes that maladaptive behaviors are to a considerable degree acquired through learning in the same way that adaptive behavior is learned.
3. Behavioral therapy assumes that psychological principles, especially learning principles, can be extremely effective in modifying maladaptive behavior.
4. Behavior therapy involves setting specific, clearly defined treatment goals.
5. The behavior therapist adapts his/her method of treatment to the client's problem.
6. Behavior therapy concentrates on the here and now.
7. It is assumed that any techniques subsumed under the label *behavior therapy* have been subjected to empirical tests and have been found to be relatively effective.

Behavioral therapy has been applied to parent skills training (Miller 1979; Walker 1976; Gordon and Davidson 1981; Hansen and L'Abate 1982), marital therapy (Jacobson and Gorman 1986; Stuart 1980), and sexual therapy (Masters and Johnson 1970; Kaplan 1974; Heiman, LoPiccolo, and LoPiccolo 1981).

Using the behavioral model, assessment and intervention are informed by behavioral principles. There is an emphasis on identifying current controlling conditions. Labeling is deemphasized. Observable, countable responses, along with positive, not punitive, change methods, are emphasized. There is a focus on measurements of effects. Special causative factors related to "problematic" behavior are rejected. For a detailed examination of behavior modification principles, please refer to Gambrill (1978).

Overview of Family Therapy

There are two general sources of behavior: (1) early childhood socialization and (2) ongoing socialization, or socialization after childhood (see Brimm and Wheeler 1966).

The individual's perceptions of early childhood interactions are the concern of psychoanalysts and object relations family therapists. Traditional psychodynamic approaches (Freudian and neo-Freudian) address change through understanding individuals' perceptions of their early childhood experiences, and how these early experiences are manifest in the individual's present life situation. This therapy aims to create a corrective experience for the individual's early traumatic experiences. Through analysis of the transference and by providing the client with a "good enough" mothering experience (via the therapist), the therapist frees the client to change and grow psychologically.

Early childhood socialization factors help individuals define their behavior by helping to create belief systems. Ongoing, here-and-now socialization processes determine how these belief systems are maintained and how they function in individuals' current lives—how they define situations (Thomas 1976). Social psychologists explore this level of analysis. Gergen and Gergen (1983) used the term "self-narratives" to describe the social psychological process whereby individuals tell stories about themselves to themselves and others. Self-narratives are the means by which individuals establish coherent connections among their life events. These narratives, or belief systems, are originally created and maintained by interactions with significant others. The process begins at birth and continues until death. A person will seek out events and persons consistent with his/her belief system. These belief systems in turn lead to belief states—emotional reactions to belief systems—and belief behaviors—behaviors consistent with the belief system. Change occurs when inconsistency is introduced.

This school was originally influenced by the early social psychologists, Mead (1934) and Cooley (1904), who looked at the development of the self in relation to others. Thibaut and Kelley (1959) are more contemporary social theorists who represent the social exchange model. Exchange relationships involve reciprocal returns or rewards, based either on money or goods or on more subjective emotional rewards. Change occurs, according to these theorists, when the costs of a behavior outweigh its rewards.

The way individuals define situations (their belief systems) often determines how they behave. And the way individuals behave is studied by the behaviorists. Since learning theorists believe that all behavior is learned, they study how individuals learn things. According to these theorists, behaviors occur and are maintained because they are reinforced. Reinforcement increases the probability that a behavior will recur. Punishment, or withdrawal of a reinforcement, decreases the probability that a behavior will recur.

The feedback or the consequences of behaviors, which learning theorists study, determines if individuals' definitions of situations or belief systems will be maintained. For example, if a behavior is reinforced, the person is more likely to define the behavior as positive and to continue the behavior in order to receive the reinforcement. If the behavior is punished, the person is likely to define the behavior as negative and to decrease the behavior. Although learning theory can be very complicated, these are its fundamental principles. More recently, cognitive psychology has studied how individuals' thoughts affect their behavior. These theorists look at people's thoughts or their self-talk. The focus of change is on changing negative self-talk—e.g., saying "I can," instead of "I can't."

Given the assumptions of both the cognitive-behavioral and the systemic schools of thought, the format of this book maintains systemic level of analysis throughout; whereas cognitive-behavior techniques and strategies are utilized and considered in increasing the possibility of systemic change. As far as assessment, systemic analysis is utilized, while cognitive-behavioral techniques are often employed in creating systemic change.

Systems theory and cognitive-behavioral psychology have many similarities. Neither, for the most part, looks at why a behavior is learned in the first place, only at what is maintaining the behavior. Neither is interested in history-taking, although some (Bowen 1978) spend a great deal of time using the genogram and examining multigenerational transmission processes. Both focus on the here-and-now:

behavior is functional for the individual or the system at the time it occurs. The major difference lies in the systems theorists' belief that all behavior is interpersonal and their focus on the interpersonal; whereas cognitive-behavior psychologists look at the reinforcements and punishments which maintain individual behaviors.

The Neglected Role of Sociology and Social Psychology

It should be obvious by now that the influences on and precursors to the family therapy movement are multidisciplinary. The obvious stimuli are philosophy, communication theory, physics, and especially the often underestimated sociology and social psychology.

Some family therapists address the influence of social structure, among them the feminist family therapists (Goldner 1985; Greenspan 1983; Hare-Mustin 1987; McGoldrick, Anderson, and Walsh 1989; and Perelberg and Miller 1990), who identify the social structure organizing gender role definitions and expectations. For the most part, however, references to sociological analysis are ignored by family therapists. The major exception is, of course, Minuchin. The influence of sociological thinking is always evident in his work, from his structural analysis of the family system (Minuchin 1974) to his later works that explore the foster care system, and in which his analysis becomes even more macrosociological. Elizur and Minuchin's (1989) latest book, *Institutionalizing Madness: Families, Therapy, and Society,* examines the macrostructure and its role in social service agencies.

Sociologists have a long history of examining the role of the larger system in maintaining economically deprived classes (Coser and Rosenberg 1976) and the role of ethnicity in family life (Jenks 1972). Yet family therapy theorists write as though these sociologists did not exist. The family life cycle has long been described by social psychologists (Brim and Wheeler 1966; Gagnon 1974), yet they are rarely cited in the family life cycle literature. The role of social psychological theory in the development of constructivism (see chapter 20), the "new" family therapy theory, cannot be overemphasized. For example, it was sociologist W. I. Thomas who stated that if people define situations as real, they are real in their consequences. These theorists have a long tradition of examining the social construction of reality (see Berger and Luckman 1966; Gergen and Gergen 1983; Reiss 1981). Watzlawick (1984), taking Thomas's thesis as the basis for his theory of change, carries Thomas's idea one step further. He argues that since beliefs can provoke real consequences, it is possible to decide in advance what consequences we seek, and then choose the beliefs—constructs of reality, or definitions of the situation—which promise the desired consequence. Yet only a footnote in Watzlawick's book credits Thomas's work.

Sociologists have long studied the systemic processes leading to social stability and the processes leading to social change. They (Durkheim 1933; Coser and Rosenberg 1976) have long pondered Lynn Hoffmann's (1981) question, "How does one disrupt an arrangement that in some ways promotes family stability (morphostasis) and instead help the family achieve a transformation that will represent a more complex integration (morphogenesis)?" (p. 167). It is puzzling that in light of the long-standing sociological inquiry into macrosystemic morphostatic and morphogenetic processes at a social level, family therapy theorists have instead looked to biologists Marturana and Varela (1980) and to physicist von Foerster (1981) to understand these processes. As Bateson (1972) points out, "We might expect to find the same sort of laws at work in the structure of a crystal as in the structure of society . . . the development of an evolutionary model for social change that so closely parallels laws for change from the world of chemistry and physics seems to offer a hope that this prophecy might one day be fulfilled." In addition to physics and biology, though, it seems not only logical and plausible but mandatory that family therapy theory begin to appreciate the sociological level of inquiry.

The New Physics and the Implications for Therapy

Most theorists would agree that family therapy represents a radical paradigmatic departure, from the more traditional psychotherapies' emphasis on the individual. Recently, evidence has been accumulating that the basis of our perceptual reality may be changing.

Eastern Philosophy

Direct mystical experience is at the core of all Eastern philosophies. Contrary to Western traditions, Eastern philosophers do not see the intellect as their source of knowledge, but use it only to analyze and interpret personal mystical experience. Thus, direct experience comes from direct insight, which lies outside the realm of the intellect and is obtained by watching rather than thinking; by looking inside oneself; by observation (Bucke 1989; Grof 1988a, 1988b; Prophet 1986). Western psychology has not really addressed the spiritual side of man's/woman's nature, choosing either to ignore its existence or to label it pathological (Atwood and Maltin 1991). Yet recent developments in physics indicate that it may be time to consider a link between Eastern and Western psychology.

For the Eastern philosopher all things and events perceived by the senses are interrelated and connected, only different aspects or manifestations of the same ultimate reality. Their highest aim is to become aware of the unity and mutual interrelation of all things, to transcend the notion of the isolated individual self, and to identify with the ultimate reality. The emergence of this awareness—enlightenment—is not only an intellectual act but also an experience which involves the whole person and is religious in its ultimate value. In the Eastern view the division of nature into separate objects is illusory, and such objects have a fluid and ever-changing character. The Eastern view is essentially dynamic; time and change are essential features. The cosmos is one inseparable reality—forever in motion, alive, organic—spiritual and material at the same time. The two basic themes of this conception are the unity and interrelation of all phenomena and the intrinsically dynamic nature of the universe.

Western Physics

Our earliest scientific traditions led to the belief that the world is divided into space and matter, with discrete particles that constitute the building blocks of nature. Matter was considered solid and immutable; space was experienced as emptiness. As a result models of the world were erected based on formulas of force, motion, mass, and energy which were of immeasurable help in manipulating the environment. The Newtonian formulation of the laws of motion, mass, and force was such a model.

Less than one hundred years later, a new physical reality was discovered which made the limitations of the Newtonian model apparent: Faraday and Maxwell (in Capra 1982) proposed the theory of electromagnetism. Forces themselves became the primary units of investigation. They replaced the concept of a force with that of a force field, and in so doing were the first to go beyond Newtonian physics. However, soon after, in his paper on the special theory of relativity, Einstein (Capra 1982) demonstrated that the discrete entities of time, space, matter, and energy were bound together in a four-dimensional continuum. This led him to a number of conclusions. First, there is no universal flow of time, which means that the same event can be perceived as occurring in different sequences depending on the relative position of the observer. Second, mass is a form of energy at rest. Third, space is affected by mass in the form of curvature; one can no longer think of empty space in which mass rests. Energy, mass, time, and space are a continuum which is almost impossible to experience at our normal level of conscious functioning. With the development of Heisenberg's (Capra 1984) Uncertainty Principle, the reality of matter was called into question. The Uncertainty Principle suggests that at the subatomic level, matter does not exist with certainty—it has a tendency to exist. (For a detailed description of the new physics, see Capra 1982, 1984; Zukav 1979).

What are the implications? It is possible that every part of the universe is affecting every other part in an interconnecting web. The whole is determining the particulars. The particulars are connected to the whole in ways not obvious to ordinary conscious experience. The universe appears fundamentally interconnected, interdependent, and inseparable. Thus, in attempting to penetrate basic substrata of the fundamental entity of our material world—the atom—one finds processes, not things, or basic building blocks of nature. These processes are interconnected; each affects the other. The world thus appears as a complicated tissue in which connections of different kinds alternate or overlap or combine, to determine the texture of the whole. Human beings are part of this web.

AS A RESULT OF THESE DEVELOPMENTS in multidisciplinary areas, the outstanding feature of the last quarter of the twentieth century is likely to be the collapse of the materialistic paradigm that dominated world thought for many centuries. With the impact of the new physics, systems theory, and many other conceptual revolutions, old structures have begun to crumble. Solid matter dissolves into waves of probability, and the new physics seems to be approaching the mystic vision of which seers and sages of all traditions have spoken.

Out of this understanding of the new physics we can perhaps begin to relate intellectually to what Eastern mystics have been trying to communicate for years. The physical vacuum, as it is called in field theory, contains the potential for all forms of the particle world. These forms, as Capra (1982) points out, are not independent physical entities, but merely transient manifestations of the underlying void which is pulsating in endless rhythms of creation and destruction. In the same way each object in the world is not merely itself but involves every other object, indeed everything else.

The new physics and systems theory challenge fundamental assumptions in the logical positivist-empirical science derived from classical physics. The assumptions of contemporary psychotherapy, too, are faced with challenges:

1. Reality may exist independent of us, but we cannot know that reality.
2. The reality that exists for us, the reality we can observe, is relative to the theory we use as a metaphor for that reality.
3. What we can observe is a function of the means (tools, instruments, and machines) we use to measure phenomena of interest (phenomena that exist and are meaningful) and of our theories which suggest whether or not anything is "out there" and, if so, what it might be,
4. Reality is a dynamic, evolving, changing entity.
5. To observe a phenomenon is to change the nature of the phenomenon observed.
6. Phenomena observed take on characteristics of the theory or model used to guide and systematize the observations.
7. The appropriate unit of analysis is not elementary parts, but relationships, the basis of all definitions.

Thus, it appears that the choice of a set of explanations of a phenomenon depends not on "facts," but on a consensus of reality among the researchers in a common field (Kuhn 1962). As researchers, we no longer seek "truth," we seek relevance. We therefore construct our world rather than discover it. These assumptions are exactly those presently being examined by the constructivists in family therapy (see chapter 20). Essential to this new direction in physics is the understanding of the nature of order, and since the perception of order, as Capra (1982) points out, is the fundamental aspect of the rational mind, there is a crucial link between the material and the mental worlds. What we observe are virtual aspects of an underlying interconnected reality which links everything in an instantly connected pattern with everything else, in ways which are not ordinarily consciously observable to us.

At this crucial evolutionary crossroads, human beings, who are part of this interconnected reality, are groping for a new model, a new philosophy, a new paradigm, a new consciousness to replace the old. Any movement toward a new consciousness must relate to an individual search for inner peace. We must move toward a realization of the truth at the core of our being, and toward the higher consciousness that is the birthright of each of us. Our traditional Western psychotherapies do not generally lead us along this path.

With the collapse of the old paradigms, we are witnessing a movement in the West, in physics and in social systems theory, toward a general theory development—that of expanded consciousness toward a psychological awareness of the interrelatedness of all things.

References

Aponte, H., and J. Van Deusen (1981) "Structural family therapy," in A. Gurman and D. Kniskern, eds., *Handbook of Family Therapy*. New York: Brunner/Mazel.

Atwood, J.D., and L. Maltin (1991) "Putting Eastern Philosophies in Western Psychotherapies," *The American Journal of Psychotherapy* 45 (2): 1–15.

Bandura, A. (1982) "The psychology of chance encounters and life paths," *American Psychologist* 37: 747–55.

——— (1969) *Principles of Behavior Modification*. New York: Holt, Rinehart and Winston.

Bateson, G., et al. (1956) "Toward a theory of schizophrenia," *Behavioral Science* 1: 251–64.

——— (1972) *Steps to an Ecology of Mind*. New York: Ballantine Books.

Beck, A. (1976) *Cognitive Therapy and the Emotional Disorders*. New York: International University Press.

Berger, B., and T. Luckman (1966) *The Social Construction of Reality*. New York: Doubleday.

Bertallanfy, L. von (1969) *General Systems Theory*. New York: George Braziller.

Boszormenyi-Nagy, I. (1965) "A theory of relationships: Experience and Transaction," in I. Boszormenyi-Nagy and J. Framo, eds., *Intensive Family Therapy: Theoretical and Practical Aspects*. New York: Harper and Row.

Boszormenyi-Nagy, I., and G. Spark (1973) *Invisible Loyalties: Reciprocity in Intergenerational Family Therapy*. New York: Harper and Row.

Boszormenyi-Nagy, I., and D. Ulrich (1981) "Contextual Family Therapy," in Gurman and Kniskern, *Handbook*.

Bowen, M. (1966) "The use of family therapy in clinical practice," *Comprehensive Psychiatry* 7: 345–74.

——— (1976) "Theory in the practice of psychotherapy," in P. J. Guerin, ed., *Family Therapy: Theory and Practice*. New York: Gardner Press.

——— (1978) *Family Therapy in Clinical Practice*. New York: Jason Aronson.

Brody, W. (1959) "Some family operations and schizophrenia," *Archives of General Psychiatry* 1: 379–402.

Brim, O., and S. Wheeler (1966) *Socialization After Childhood: Two Essays*. New York: John Wiley.

Bucke, R. (1989) *Cosmic Consciousness: A Study in the Evolution of Human Kind*. New York: Citadel Press.

Capra, F. (1982). *The Turning Point*. New York: Bantam Books.

——— (1984) *The Tao of Physics*. New York: Bantam Books.

Cooley, C. (1902) *Human Nature and the Social Order*. New York: Scribner's.

Coser, L., and B. Rosenberg (1976) *Sociological Theory: A Book of Readings*, 4th ed. New York: Macmillan.

Crisp, P. (1988) "Projective identification: Clarification in relation to object choice," *Psychoanalytic Psychotherapy* 5 (4): 389–402.

Dicks, H. (1967) *Marital Transitions*. New York: Basic Books.

Durkheim, E. (1933). *The Division of Labor in Society*. New York: Free Press.

Elizur, J., and S. Minuchin (1989) *Institutionalizing Madness: Families, Therapy, and Society*. New York: Basic Books.

Eysenck, H. (1960) *Behavioral Therapy and the Neuroses*. Oxford: Pergamon Press.

Fairbairn, W. (1952) *An Object Relations Theory of the Personality*. New York: Basic Books.

Ferber, A., M. Mendelsohn, and A. Napier, eds. (1972) *The Book of Family Therapy*. New York: Science House.

Foerester, H. von (1981) *Observing Systems*. Seaside, Calif.: Intersystems.

Framo, J. (1976) "Family of origin as a therapeutic resource for adults in marital and family therapy," *Family Process* 15: 193–210.

——— (1982) *Explorations in Marital and Family Therapy: Selected Papers of James L. Framo*. New York: Springer-Verlag.

Franks, C. (1969) *Behavior Therapy: Appraisal and Status*. New York: McGraw-Hill.

Gagnon, J. H. (1974) "Scripts and the coordination of sexual conduct," in J. K. Cole and R. Deinstbier, eds., *Nebraska Symposium on Motivation*. Lincoln: University of Nebraska Press.

Gambrill, E. (1978) *Behavioral Modification: Handbook of Assessment, Intervention and Evaluation*. San Francisco: Jossey-Bass.

Gergen, K. J., and M. M. Gergen (1983) "The Social Construction of Narrative Accounts," in K. J. Gergen and M. M. Gergen, eds., *Historical Social Psychology*. Hillsdale, N.J.: Eribaum.

Goldner, V. (1985) "Feminism and Family Therapy," in *Family Process* 24: 31–47.

Gordon, S., and N. Davidson (1981) "Behavioral Parent Training," in Gurman and Kniskern, *Handbook*.

Greenspan, M. (1983) *A New Approach to Women and Therapy*. New York: McGraw-Hill.

Grof, S. (1988a) *Beyond the Brain*. Albany: State University of New York Press.

——— (1988b)*The Adventure of Self-Discovery*. Albany: State University of New York Press.

Guerin, P. J., ed. (1976) *Family Therapy: Theory and Practice*. New York: Gardner Press.

Guerin, P. J., and E. Pendagast (1976) "Evaluation of family system and genogram," in Guerin, *Family Therapy*.

Gurman, A. S., and D. P. Kniskern (1981) *Handbook of Family Therapy*. New York: Brunner-Mazel.

——— (1991) *Handbook of Family Therapy* vol. 2. New York: Brunner-Mazel.

Haley, J. (1976) *Problem-Solving Therapy*. San Francisco: Jossey-Bass.

——— (1980) *Leaving Home*. New York: McGraw-Hill.

Hansen, J., and L. L'Abate (1982). *Approaches to Family Therapy*. New York: Macmillan.

Hare-Mustin, R. (1987) "The Problem of Gender in Family Therapy," *Family Process* 26 (1): 15–28.

Heiman, J., L. LoPiccolo, and J. LoPiccolo (1981) "The treatment of sexual dysfunction," in Gurman and Kniskern, *Handbook*.

Hendrix, H. (1990) *How to Get the Love You Want*. New York: Brunner/Mazel.

Hoffman, L. (1981) *Foundations of Family Therapy: A Conceptual Framework for Systems Change*. New York: Basic Books.

Jacobson, N., and S. Gurman (1986) *Clinical Handbook of Marital Therapy*. New York: Guilford Press.

Jenks, C. (1972) *Inequality: A Reassessment of the Effect of Family and Schooling in America*. New York: Harper and Row.

Jones, M. (1974) "The elimination of children's fears," *Journal of Experimental Psychology* 7: 383–90.

Kaplan, H. (1974) *The New Sex Therapy*. New York: Brunner/Mazel.

Kerr, M. (1981) "Family systems and therapy," in Gurman and Kniskern, *Handbook*.

Krueger, J. (1961) "An early instance of conditioning from the Chinese dynastic histories," *Psychological Reports* 9 (9): 117.

Kuhn, T. (1962) *The Structure of Scientific Revolution*. Chicago: University of Chicago Press.

Madanes, C. (1980) "Protection, paradox and pretending," *Family Process 19:* 73–85.

——— (1981) *Strategic Family Therapy*. San Francisco: Jossey-Bass.

Madanes, C., and J. Haley (1977) "Dimensions of family therapy," *Journal of Nervous and Mental Disease* 165.

Mahoney, M. (1988) *Human Change Processes: Notes on Facilitation of Personal Development*. Hillsdale, N.J.: Eribaum.

Masters, W., and V. Johnson (1970) *Human Sexual Inadequacy*. Boston: Little, Brown.

Maturana, U., and F. Varela (1987) *The Tree of Knowledge: The Biological Roots of Human Understanding*. Boston: New Science Library.

McGoldrick, M., C. Anderson, and F. Walsh (1989) *Women in Families: A Framework for Feminist Family Therapy*. New York: W. W. Norton.

Mead, G. (1934) *Mind, Self, and Society from the Standpoint of a Social Behavioralist*. Chicago: University of Chicago Press.

Meichenbaum, D. (1987) *Cognitive Behavior*

Modification: An Integrative Approach. New York: Plenum Press.
Miller, C. (1979) *Louisville Behavior Checklist*. Los Angeles: Western Psychological Services.
Minuchin, S. (1974) *Families and Family Therapy*. Cambridge, Mass.: Harvard University Press.
Minuchin, S., and H. Fishman (1981) *Family Therapy Techniques*. Cambridge, Mass.: Harvard University Press.
Minuchin, S., et al. (1967) *Families of the Slums*. New York: Basic Books.
Minuchin, S., B. Rosman, and L. Baker (1978) *Psychosomatic Families: Anorexia Nervosa in Context*. Cambridge, Mass.: Harvard University Press.
Neill, J., and D. Kniskern (1982) *From Psyche to System: The Evolving Therapy of Carl Whitaker*. New York: Guilford Press.
Nichols, M. (1984) *Family Therapy: Concepts and Methods*. New York: Gardner Press.
Pavlov, I. (1927) *Conditioned Reflexes,* G. V. Anrip, trans. New York: Liveright.
Paul, N. (1976) "Cross-confrontation," in Guerin, *Family Therapy*.
Penn, P. (1982) "Circular questioning," *Family Process* 21 (3): 267–80.
Perelberg, R., and A. Miller (1990) *Gender and Power in Families*. New York: Tavistock/Routledge.
Prophet, M. (1986) *Cosmic Consciousness*. Livingston, Mont.: Summit University Press.
Reiss, D. (1981) *The Family's Construction of Reality*. Cambridge, Mass.: Harvard University Press.
Rimm, D., and J. Masters (1974) *Behavior Therapy: Techniques and Empirical Findings*. New York: John Wiley.
Sager, C. (1976) *Marriage Contracts and Couple Therapy*. New York: Brunner/Mazel.
Satir, V. (1964) *Conjoint Family Therapy*. Palo Alto, Calif.: Science and Behavior Books.
Scharf, D., and J. Scharf (1987) *Object Relations Family Therapy*. Northvale, N.J.: Jason Aronson.
——— (1991) *Object Relations Couple Therapy*. Northvale, N.J.: Jason Aronson.
Selvini-Palazzoli, M., et al. (1978). *Paradox and Counterparadox*. New York: Jason Aronson.
——— (1980) "Hypothesizing-circularity-neutrality: Three guidelines for the conductor of the session," *Family Process* 19: 3–12.
Singleton, G. (1982) "Bowen family systems theory," in A. Horne and M. Ohlsen, eds., *Family Counseling and Therapy*. Itasca, Ill.: F. E. Peacock.
Skinner, B. F. (1953) *Science and Human Behavior*. New York: Macmillan.
Slipp, S. (1988) *The Technique and Practice of Object Relations Family Therapy*. Northvale, N.J.: Jason Aronson.
Stewart, M. (1961) "Psychotherapy by reciprocal inhibition," *American Journal of Psychiatry* 118: 175–77.
Stuart, R. (1980) *Helping Couples Change*. New York: Guilford Press.
Thibaut, J., and H. Kelley (1959) *The Social Psychology of Groups*. New York: John Wiley.
Thomas, W. I. (1976) "The definition of the situation," in Coser and Rosenberg, *Sociological Theory*.
Tomm, K. (1984) "One perspective on the Milan systemic approach: Part II," *Journal of Marital and Family Therapy* 10: 253–71.
Walker, H. (1976) *Walker Problem Behavior Checklist*. Los Angeles: Western Psychological Services.
Watson, J. (1916) "The place of the conditioned emotional response in psychology," *Psychological Review* 23: 89–116.
——— (1914) *Psychology from the Standpoint of a Behaviorist*. Philadelphia, Pa.: Lippincott.
Watson, J., and R. Rayner (1920) "Conditioned emotional reactions," *Journal of Experimental Psychology* 3.
Watzlawick, P. (1978) *The Language of Change*. New York: Basic Books.

——— (1984) *The Invented Reality*. New York: W. W. Norton.

Watzlawick, P., J. Beavin, and D. Jackson (1967) *Pragmatics of Human Communications: A Study of Interactional Patterns, Pathologies, and Paradoxes*. New York: W. W. Norton.

Watzlawick, P., and J. Weakland, eds. (1977) *The Interactional View: Studies at the Mental Research Institute, 1963–1974*. New York: W. W. Norton.

Watzlawick, P., J. Weakland, and R. Fisch (1974) *Change: Principles of Problem Formation and Problem Resolution*. New York: W. W. Norton.

Whitaker, L., and D. Keith (1981) "Symbolic-experiential family therapy," in Gurman and Kniskern, *Handbook*.

Willi, J. (1979) *Couples in Collusion*. San Francisco: Jossey-Bass.

Williamson, D. S. (1981) "Personal authority via termination of the intergenerational hierarchical boundaries," *Journal of Marital and Family Therapy* 7: 441–52.

——— (1982a) "Personal authority in family experience via termination of the intergenerational hierarchical boundary: Part II," *Journal of Marital and Family Therapy* 8: 23–37.

——— (1982b) "Personal authority in family experience via termination of the intergenerational hierarchical boundary: Part III," *Journal of Marital and Family Therapy* 8: 309–323.

Wolpe, J. (1958) *Psychotherapy by Reciprocal Inhibition*. Stanford, Calif.: Stanford University Press.

Zukav, G. (1979) *Dancing with Wu Li Masters*. New York: William Morrow.

CHAPTER THREE

GENDER ISSUES IN COUPLES THERAPY

Barrie Zucal, M.S.

Abstract

This paper explores feminist challenges to family therapy in terms of the impact of gender on family therapy theory and practice. Gender role socialization has an impact on each partner in a couple relationship and also on the therapist. Some conflict between partners results from gender role stereotyping, which polarizes partners and becomes the basis for inequities and power differentials. Treatment suggestions are included.

Jane: He's very good, really. He helps me do things around the house. I really appreciate it.

Dick: Yeah, she makes me lists.

Therapist to Jane: You both work a forty-hour-plus week. It seems that you are the one responsible for getting the housework done.

Jane: Oh, no. We share.

Therapist to Jane: It seems that he is good at "helping" and following through on your delegation of tasks, but you are delegating. You are taking the responsibility for being aware of what needs to be done, dividing the tasks between the two of you, and doing your share. Do you follow up to see that he's done his job?

Dick: Yeah, and she reminds me and reminds me and reminds me if it isn't done when she wants and exactly how she wants it.

Therapist to Jane: So you are also in charge of follow-up and motivation. You are responsible for getting the housework done. He is your helper.

Jane: I never thought of it that way.

Therapist to Dick and Jane: How did this happen? How did Jane become the partner responsible for getting the housework done?

This dialogue presents a microcosmic look at gender issues in couples therapy. It is an approximation of a session conversation, but the content is real and so is the situation the couple describes. We know the conversation is real because we have heard variations on this theme hundreds of times. But have we heard it as a gender issue? Perhaps we have simply judged her as overfunctioning and him as underfunctioning.

That's a popular assessment these days, but we must realize that that assessment itself is probably rooted in our gender expectations of appropriate functioning for males and females in the family domain.

It is primarily feminist family therapists who are challenging the field of family therapy to acknowledge gender as a basic organizing principle in culture, large systems (government, etc.), family systems, and the individual thinking of family therapists. This paper will explore feminist thinking about the relationship of gender-role socialization to conflict in heterosexual couples. The literature review presents feminist thinking that challenges some basic tenets of family therapy. The second section of the paper will suggest clinical implications and applications of this information.

Literature Review

A feminist look at family therapy was offered by Rachel Hare-Mustin when she published "A Feminist Approach to Family Therapy" in 1978. She used a feminist framework to challenge what she called "unquestioned reinforcement of stereotyped sex roles" in family therapy. She defined a *feminist framework* as one which recognized the importance of the social context in its impact on the family and acknowledged that "sex roles and status prescribed by society for females and males disadvantage women."

Ten years later Goodrich et al. (1988) defined feminism as "a philosophy which recognizes that men and women have different experiences of self, of other, and of life and that men's experience has been widely articulated while women's has been ignored or misrepresented." Walters et al. (1989) view feminism as "a humanistic framework or world view concerned with the roles, rules, and functions that organize male-female interaction."

These authors and others (Lerner 1985; Goldner 1985; Braverman 1988) agree that our society is patriarchal, in that women are oppressed and men are elevated.

Avis (1988), quoting Jagger and Rothberg (1984), defines feminism as a comprehensive analysis of the nature and causes of women's oppression and a correlated set of proposals for ending it. She continued to categorize feminist thinking. Liberal feminists believe that oppression of women is rooted in larger systems (legal government) that set social policies and norms. Social feminists offer Marxist theories about inequities in class society as the basis for the conflicts between men and women. They expand the Marxist concept of production to include reproduction—sexuality, bearing and raising children—and show how the lower classes produce less and reproduce more, thus remaining lower class. Radical feminists contend that women's oppression is fundamental, has always existed "across time, culture, and class and is embedded in every aspect of life including language and is, therefore, the hardest form of oppression to eradicate." (Avis 1988).

In 1990 feminists would question the term "sex-role stereotyping" as Hare-Mustin used it in 1978. They would say that the term suggests a biologically based evolution of thinking and behavior. Now feminist family therapists (Walters et al., 1988; Lerner, 1985; Goodrich et al., 1988) accept that assignment of tasks or traits to one sex or the other is based on gender, which is a social construct. This is an important difference, because the term "sex roles" seems to assign a biological base behavior, a base closer to nature and a natural order. According to current feminist authors, culture, not nature, determines appropriate masculine and feminine behavior. This behavior is learned. (Braverman 1988; Avis 1988; Kantor and Okun 1989).

Gender is "a central organizing principle of knowledge and culture," according to Virginia Goldner (1989). She asserts that family therapy theory and practice is conspicuous for its lack of attention to power differentials based on gender. She believes that families are organized around gender hierarchies to the same degree that they are organized around generational hierarchy. She repeatedly cites Haley as an example of a major influence on family therapy, one who has raised the issue of generational power differentials but continues to ignore gender.

Feminist Family Therapy

Feminist family therapists see gender inequities embedded in our culture and in the historic model of the family over time: ". . . . the overinvolved mother and the peripheral father of the archetypal family case emerge as products of a historical process two hundred years in the making" (Goldner 1985). In fact, this archetype spans cultures from the earliest history (Zucal 1984). Separate domains—woman's the family and man's the outside world—have generally dominated in our culture. Exceptions were allowed when the dominant male culture determined that women should step outside the home for a specific purpose—such as during World War II when women joined the outside work force to produce war materiel needed by fighting men. More recently, the economy has forced women into the outside labor force. Gender issues must be addressed in the context of the culture which perpetuates them and in terms of contemporary historical social arrangements.

The need to address gender in cultural context leads to the criticism that family therapy is isolationist: the family is usually seen in a vacuum, as a system unto itself apart from the interaction of the family with larger systems (Lerner 1989; Walters et al. 1988). Walsh and Scheinkman (1989) criticize Jackson's work for focusing on the interior of the family and for suggesting that genuine understanding can be achieved out of context. Avis (1988) questions the reliance of family therapy on systems theory as the single organizing framework for conceptualizing and intervening in the family. Goldner (1985) wonders why family therapists have had so little interest in feminist literature.

Feminists want family therapists to widen their scope of vision and to address the power differentials between males and females, husbands and wives, mothers and fathers. They are concerned that lack of attention to gender issues has led family therapy theory and practice to reflect the values of the patriarchal society. In practice, this means that the concerns of women are minimized and the female can appear pathological measured against a male model of wellness (Walsh 1989; Walsh and Scheinkman 1989; Hare-Mustin 1989). This model of wellness includes the skills and characteristics that emotionally healthy men are socialized to achieve.

Bowen's Differentiation of Self Scale is one measure of wellness predicated on the male model (Braverman 1988; Walsh 1989). Here the top of the scale, reflecting health, includes the male values of autonomy, separateness, being for self, rationality, and logic. Toward the bottom of the scale, approaching more pathological behavior, are the traditionally female characteristics of being intuitive, being emotional, and being for others. Bowen's concept of an undifferentiated ego mass describes enmeshment, which is considered unhealthy. To be differentiated and separate is to be healthy. Bowen does speak of reconnecting after differentiating, but practitioners of Bowenian therapy usually emphasize the traditional male value of differentiation without promoting the traditionally female value of togetherness. Minuchin is also criticized for reinforcing gender stereotypes and dysfunction by taking the position of a distant paternalistic authority figure (Walsh and Scheinkman 1989).

Family therapy is criticized for perpetuating power differentials because of its lack of attention to differences between male and female socialization. Males are socialized to become part of the dominant male culture—to be rational, problem-solving, goal-directed, achievement-oriented, and for themselves (Kantor and Okun 1989). Lerner (1989) says the dominant culture sets the rules of appropriate behavior for the subordinant culture. She believes that women are socialized to be complementary to men—dependent, accommodating, nurturing, valuing connection and affiliation. Woman is then in a bind, unhealthy if she becomes "intensely involved" (Walters et al. 1989) with her child. She is unflatteringly labeled "over-involved," "enmeshed," or "fused;" she is *enabling* if she takes care of her alcoholic husband and *too much in love* if she gives much of herself to nourish a relationship with an uninvolved and self-serving man.

These socialized differences can cause partners to become polarized in their expectations. She seeks profound connectedness, while he fears losing his separate sense of self. Males come to marriage with a birthright of perceived power. Women struggle for power and then are uncomfortable about using it (Kantor and Okun 1989). Family therapists must acknowledge these socialized differences, because they are the soil from which power differences grow and are replanted in the next generation.

The differences are restrictive and constraining for both partners. They perpetuate the myth of male superiority and female inferiority. These socialization processes now separate, rather than connect, partners. Separate socialization forces each partner to deny or repress some parts of him/herself (Hare-Mustin 1989).

Feminists refute the concepts of circularity, neutrality, and complementarity, each of which supports the myth of equal power and equal responsibility for partners and for family members. Circularity implies that all members engage in a never-ending repetitive pattern of mutually reinforcing behavior. In this view, children or women could be provocative to their abusers. In reality, however, a child cannot be construed as having equal power with which to resist an adult or equal responsibility for perpetuating a pattern of abuse. Nor can a woman—typically younger, smaller, and with fewer resources than the male who batters her—be blamed equally for the crime perpetuated against her. Goldner (1985) believes the family concept of reciprocity "blames the victim and maintains the status quo." Maintaining a neutral stance toward the victim and the abuser, as the Milan Group advocates (Walsh and Scheinkman 1989), subtly removes a portion of responsibility from the man and places it on the woman, making her equally responsible. The concepts of neutrality, circularity, and complementarity render invisible the differences in power and influence among family members.

Clinical Considerations

The Couple's Relationship

Most clinical implications of feminist family therapy literature call for enlarging the therapists' perspective on gender. The clinician must recognize gender as a main structural variable around which behavior and relationships are organized (Goldner 1985). Gender will be relevant in recognizing both cultural themes affecting the couple's perception of its problem and power differentials reflecting the inequities of the larger culture. Gendered thinking resulting from socialization will arise in all discussion topics: money, sex, parenting, and task assignment inside and outside the family (Boss and Thorne 1989).

Gendered socialization leads to the evolution of structure in the couple's relationship. In a complementary relationship, she learns to complement him. In everyday terms tasks are divided, and she gets to do whatever he doesn't. True, this relationship doesn't promote competition, but it usually does promote an overload of domestic and child care responsibility for the wife—on top of work, if she works outside the home. In a more symmetrical structure, more responsibilities are shared—perhaps he does more nurturing and she takes more financial responsibility. The symmetrical structure supports competition over who will be taken care of (Papp 1989).

Traditional socialization may also polarize partners in their expectations of each other. Based on his sense of himself as logical, he may see her expressed emotions as overreactions. Based on her ability to intuit his needs, she may feel neglected because he does not intuit hers. Socialized reinforcement of gendered differences makes it difficult for partners to appreciate each other's values and to be empathic with each other.

Consider, as most feminists do, that women are more unhappy in their marriages than are their husbands. Why? Women usually take more responsibility for the quality of the relationship than do their husbands, and women generally have less access to social and economic resources. They also face an unavoidable conflict between childbearing and childrearing and the other things they would like to do.

When a feminist therapist meets with a married couple, she/he must also understand each partner and the relationship in its larger context—their current family, their families of origin, their work systems, the family itself from a historic perspective, and the dilemmas of each partner in present-day culture. A therapist helping a woman consider divorce needs to know that her income will probably take a 40 percent nosedive the first year that she is separated (Walters et al. 1989). How does a female therapist understand a man's reaction to finding out that being a good provider isn't enough, unless she understands that providing has been part of his role definition since our earliest history? He has not been taught to express his feelings. He has been taught that he should make money. Gender issues must be seen in a larger context.

The Gender of the Therapist

Feminists remind us that not only couples but also therapists are affected by gendered socialization. They urge us to know ourselves in the context of our own genders. Lerner (1988), quoting Carter (1985), tells us, "Our only choice is to be conscious or unconscious of our value system." Walters et al. (1989) tells us "there is no such thing as neutrality. A neutral therapist is one who leaves the prevailing patriarchal assumption unchallenged and in its place."

Kantor and Okun (1989) challenge us to be aware of our gender-related blind spots. If we are women, they ask us whether we get overly involved, taking too much responsibility for the quality of the relationship? They ask us to what extent our socialization has an impact on our thoughts, beliefs, attitudes and actual behavior during sessions. We must assess whether our appreciation of connectedness or our fear of separation affect our ability to help couples deal with conflict in their relationships. Our role as soothers and smoothers of the water may affect our ability to tolerate anger—our own or that of our clients. Does this same role cause us to interfere in the process, to rescue a client or a couple from uncomfortable feelings? Women therapists socialized in a male-dominated culture may fear men's power and let power plays go unchallenged in the couple's work. Have we learned to see men as vulnerable, and to fear hurting them? Are we protecting them from their wives? How does being working women ourselves, operating in the traditionally male sphere outside the home, affect our ability to relate to a woman who is involved in a more traditional role? Our tendency to nurture may interfere with our ability to set boundaries, plan rationally, and use the expert skills that are traditionally male.

If you are a male therapist, your tendency to distance may interfere with your ability to come close and be empathic. Are you concerned that you may be perceived as less than masculine if you are empathic? Being raised to be an authority can affect your ability to collaborate. Must you be the expert at all times? Does being goal-directed cause you to interfere in or take over a client's process to get to the point? You may overlook the power of your position because you are so used to it. You may be more comfortable with action methods than with teaching the process of relating. Does your comfort with separateness have an impact on your judgment of a partner's need for closeness? Will you find such a need appropriate or inappropriate? Men often need to appear competent in a way that affects their ability to take risks and to be creative in ways which would benefit the couples they work with. Does your need to appear competent make it harder for you to acknowledge your gender biases (Kantor and Okun 1989)?

Kantor and Okun (1989) tell us that women therapists may have an easier time than men in acting as couples' therapists. Women have been acculturated in two systems: the male dominant and the female subsystems. They have been raised in and learned to work in the dominant one and have "neutrality and emphatically identified with other females and shared attachments and long-life subordinate experiences." They have learned the language of both sexes. They may also be more sensitive to males because they have been acculturated in the dominant system. It is harder for males to learn the language of the female subsystem. They may not have easy access, and they may find it difficult to tolerate a woman's anger related to her subordinate position (Kantor and Okun 1989).

It is my observation that male therapists are expected to be more competent simply because they are male. Most women are acculturated to expect authority and competence from men, not from other women. It is my observation that a woman tends to devalue her own experience and competence because it is different from a man's. Women often believe that men are more competent because they function outside the home in the seats of power. If in fact this gender bias does exist, male therapists, competent or not, would naturally be perceived as more competent simply because they are male.

Women are also questioned by feminist therapists about our expectations of our couples-clients based on our own gender expectations. Specifically, we may look to the female to initiate change because we see her culturally as more accommodating and as valuing the relationship more than her husband does. Do we appreciate minimal change from men because we accept that relationships are not their domain? Our own gendered thinking affects our expectations for change and our ability to support the couple in its efforts to build a mutually satisfying relationship. We must address the almost archetypical image of "the angry, demanding bitch" and not be put off by her anger or minimize her demands. Instead, we must understand her sense of injustice and teach her to use her anger to effect change (Lerner 1985). We must not blame individual men for their lack of involvement or for their privileged position. Instead, we must teach them to cultivate the parts of themselves they so often deny, to experience both the satisfaction of letting go of their rigid role definitions and the comfort of closeness. Examining our own gender-based expectations of clients will help us to help them explore and set goals for themselves.

Whether male or female, we as therapists must recognize our power and authority over clients (Kantor and Okun 1989). We are the specialists. If we are not aware of our own power and authority, we cannot appreciate its ramifications on the gendered process we are engaged in with our clients. For example, female clients may overcomply to please a male therapist. Males clients may want to "buddy" with a male therapist; with a female therapist they may resent directness, be flirtatious, or play the little boy. Clearly, gender has implications for the therapeutic process.

Each of us must learn the indicators of our own blind spots (Kantor and Okun 1989; Braverman 1988). We must learn to work through those blind spots for our own senses of comfort and to incorporate the best of what is traditionally male and female in ourselves and provide the most unbiased services for our clients.

For Systems Therapists

According to feminist family therapists (Walters et al. 1989), feminists believe that "fusion and distance are opposite sides of the same coin." They are concerned that systems therapists too often apply the pejorative terms *enmeshed* and *fused* only to close relationships involving women, thus discrediting the values of intimacy and involvement. They offer the traditional pursuer-distancer process as an example of inappropriately labeling a woman's efforts to do what she has been socialized to do—to make connections. If she initiates conversation about the problems that interfere with her connection to her husband, she may be labeled overly concerned or overfunctioning. She may be told to back off and be shamed and blamed for carrying out her "socially mandated tasks." This traditional treatment is not helpful to her partner either, because it suggests that he cannot be challenged or confronted for fear he will flee or collapse.

The Woman's Project in Family Therapy (Walters et al. 1988) also challenges the concepts of complementarity and boundaries as discriminating against women. "Systems theory discriminates against women by seeking balance and equilibrium for the family system without addressing the unequal access of each individual to choice of role." (Walters et al. 1989). The concept of boundaries, which addresses appropriate separateness between individuals and generations, does not acknowledge the female concept of relatedness, which allows more closeness than the male view may deem appropriate.

The concept of triangles—conflict between two people detoured through a third—is pejorative. The term allows no room for gender-related behavior which most often places women on the fused side of the triangle and men in the distant position. Triangles also define the problem as inside of the family alone. Walters et al. (1989) are concerned that too often interventions to break triangles are undertaken in ways that diminish women's self-esteem. They use a case to illustrate:

> If there is a triangle including a wife, her husband, and the husband's mother, and the conflict is seen between an overly responsible wife fighting with her husband's mother for privacy and/or a mother who can't let go, the intervention may damage the women. If instead the conflict is seen as two women trying to carry out their responsibilities in the face of the man's withdrawal, the challenge can be for the husband to be more involved with both women.

Finally, these authors question the function of the symptom in the family. Systems thinkers usually consider the symptom as a way of regulating the system. They believe that there is a tendency to blame the wife/mother for perpetuating the symptom, when in fact she is simply perpetuating her gender role, which may or may not perpetuate the symptom.

Treatment Considerations

Avis (1988) states that therapists, in actually working with a couple, should reduce the hierarchy between the couple and the therapist. They should try to focus on strengths and to give the clients more control over the therapy. Hare-Mustin (1978) suggests beginning the therapy by defining mutual accountability in the contract.

Walters et al. (1988) say we must work on two levels. On a behavioral level, we can examine the "repetitious patterns and reoccurring cycles of interaction around which the presenting problem is organized." On the ideational level, she elicits attitudes, beliefs, expectations, and assumptions that maintain the cycles. Because men and women are not aware of these ingrained beliefs, she urges us to listen carefully to their metaphors and fantasies. She advocates working to create empathy and equity rather than complementarity or symmetry, in couples' relationships.

In doing so, we must listen to women's anger and help them own it rather than project it onto their partners (Lerner, 1985). We need to recognize ineffective anger that lets the partner off the hook and actually maintains the status quo. Therapists must help men verbalize feelings other than anger as a way of building bridges to their partners and of becoming more fully human themselves. *Learned helplessness*, which contributes to frustration, lack of momentum, and anger, needs to be acknowledged as *learned*.

Healthy use of boundaries and reciprocity should be encouraged, with both concepts grounded in everyday interaction. Is it all right for a woman sometimes to say no to nurturing? Will the man sometimes nurture? If so, is he filling in for what is really her responsibility? How is it decided who does what? Remember the couple in the beginning of the paper. Do they both feel satisfied that they have a reciprocal agreement? What would a day in the life of their relationship look like if they did?

Guilt related to not fulfilling gender role expectations must be recognized. When guilt appears in one partner, it is a good time to enlarge the frame and include the part socialization plays in creating nearly insoluble dilemmas for women, men, and couples who try to establish new ways of relating and connecting.

The communication process should be scrutinized. Threats of physical violence must be addressed and dealt with immediately. Obvious verbal abuse—blaming, name-calling, shaming, accusations, and judgments of the other as "stupid"—must be addressed not only because of their obvious effect on self-esteem, but also because these tactics are covert power plays. They are also related to gender, in that men often resort to physical threats—I'm bigger than you, I can control you—or threats of abandonment or separation, because they are more comfortable with these concepts than women are. Women may use their acknowledged role as relationship specialists in the family to label men inadequate or incompetent. Both manipulations fit the socialized means of achieving power in the relationship.

However, most couples are more subtle in their efforts to achieve power through communication. For example, one partner may minimize the importance of what the other is saying with phrases such as "Do we really need to discuss this?" and "Why are you making this such a big deal?" If one partner labels another as overreacting or unfeeling, the issue becomes the partner's inappropriate behavior rather than the problem at hand. Such an assessment creates a diversion through a power play, and one partner sits in judgment of the other.

The therapist should discuss these *as* power plays, so that power is the issue. Then the therapist should help each partner strive for personal clarity in his/her perception of power in the relationship. Incongruence between stated bargains and actual behavior should be challenged.

Reframing is a powerful tool used to show women's gendered learning as strength. A woman's anger can be reframed as protective or as an indicator of her concern. Her efforts to connect can be so framed rather than presented as efforts to pursue, entrap, or change her partner. Displays of emotion can be framed as serious efforts to communicate.

Contextualizing can involve relating current behavior, process, and themes to a historical context, to another generation of family context, or to a cultural context. Walters et al. (1988) gives us an example of a couple who believed the cultural concept that "a woman has a sexual problem if she does not want to meet a man's needs." Walters's use of fantasy and metaphor are techniques to equalize the partners as they work jointly out of socially prescribed ways of communicating. Both are involved in right brain activity—a similar activity for each even though their fantasies will be different. Similarities can be acknowledged, since they build bridges more obviously than do differences.

It is also possible to examine family rituals from a gender perspective, to make the couple aware of their arrangements. Who prepares? Whose responsibility is the ritual? Is ritual life solely the woman's responsibility? Within rituals lie hidden assumptions about men and women's positions in the family (Black 1989).

The use of stories in therapy is an interesting technique. Clients' stories or remembrances are examined in the context of the time period when they originated, the possibilities for men and women at the time, their aspirations and disappointments, how women were restrained, and how the stories perpetuate gender myths. Clients are asked to choose among possible interpretations and to consider their own lives as narratives in construction (Laird 1989).

Concluding Thoughts

The contributions of feminism and feminist thinking to a critique of family therapy are enormous. The perspectives of feminists raise our consciousness and help us as therapists add one more base from which to examine our theory, personal beliefs, and in-session work. They call much-needed attention to the inequities of our marriages, our families, our systems, and our culture. Their thinking can enlarge our perspectives, affect our choice of interventions, and help us see women in a more positive light.

However, in relation to our clinical work I find some feminist thinking disturbing. The word "feminist" derives from females and the emphasis of the feminist literature is surely to empower women. That in itself is a fine goal. I believe that feminists would say that powerful women would balance the equation with already powerful men. Perhaps that is the reason there is only token reference to men as individuals in the feminist family therapy literature. Walters et al. (1989) say that individual men should not be blamed, but in general the literature abounds with references to distant patriarchs whose influence has kept women from controlling their own lives.

If men as a group are blamed, won't this thinking affect the way a therapist views an individual male in a couple's relationship? I don't see sensitivity to the individual male in the feminist literature, although I have heard it from Walters in person (1990). If there is heightened sensitivity to the individual woman and to women in general, aren't the feminists creating a kind of countermovement to male-dominated thinking? Such thinking can becomes just as exclusive and one-sided as male thinking is accused of being.

Hoffman (1990) refers to Gilligan (1982) as "putting forward a third view, which is that both men and women need to be able to choose the different voice that has been derogatively assigned to women. She is talking about a more balanced cultural repertoire for both genders." She prefers the term "gender sensitive" to "feminist." For her, this term avoids defining the problem of the family or the couple in female terms, "while remaining faithful to an ideal of justice."

I like the term "gender sensitive" better than "feminist." It implies a knowledge of and sensitivity to gender issues without aligning me with one gender or the other. I feel that to connect with one gender may be to separate myself from the other. This is not a good position for a couples' therapist. The term *feminist* suggests a stationary loyalty, rather than involvement in a process to create justice for all.

References

Ault-Riche, M. (1988) "Teaching an integrated model of family therapy: Women as students, women as supervisors," in L. Braverman, ed., *A Guide to Feminist Family Therapy*. New York: Harrington Park.

Avis, J. (1988) "Deepening awareness: A private study guide to feminism and family therapy," in Braverman, *Guide to Feminist Family Therapy*.

Bepko, C., and J. Krestan (1985) *The Responsibility Trap*. New York: Free Press.

Black, E. I. (1989) "Rituals of stabilization and change in women's lives," in M. McGoldrick, C. Anderson, and F. Walsh, eds., *Women in Families*. New York: W. W. Norton, 451–69.

Bograd, M. (1988) "Enmeshed, fusion, or relatedness? A conceptual analysis," in Braverman, *Guide to Feminist Family Therapy*.

Boss, P., and B. Thorne (1989) "Family sociology and family therapy: A feminist linkage," in McGoldrick et al., *Women in Families*.

Braverman, L. (1988) "Feminism and family therapy: Friends or foes?" in Braverman, *Guide to Feminist Family Therapy*.

Braverman, L., ed. (1988) *A Guide to Feminist Family Therapy*. New York: Harrington Park.

Gilligan, C. (1982) *In a Different Voice*. Cambridge, Mass.: Harvard University Press.

Goldner, V. (1985) "Feminism and family therapy," *Family Process* 24: 31–48.

——— (1989) "Generation and gender", in McGoldrick et al., *Women in Families*.

Goodrich, T., et al. (1988) *Feminist Family Therapy*. New York: W. W. Norton.

Hare-Mustin, R. T. (1978) "A feminist approach to family therapy," *Family Process* 17: 181–94.

——— (1989) "The problem of gender in family therapy theory," in McGoldrick et al., *Women in Families*.

Hesse-Biber, S., and J. Williamson (1984) "Resource theory and power in families: Life cycle considerations," *Family Process* 23 (2): 261–78.

Hoffman, L. (1990) "Constructing realities: An art of lenses," *Family Process* 29 (1): 1–12.

Jagger, A. M., and P. S. Rothenberg (1984) *Feminist Frameworks: Alternative Theoretical Accounts of the Relations between Women and Men,* 2nd ed. New York: McGraw-Hill.

Kantor, D., and B. Okun (1989) *Intimate Environments*. New York: Guilford Press.

Laird, J. (1989) "Women's stories: Restoring women's self-constructions," in McGoldrick et al., *Women in Families*.

Lerner, H. G. (1985) *The Dance of Anger*. New York: Harper & Row.

——— (1988) "Is family systems theory really systemic? A feminist communication," in Braverman, *Guide to Feminist Family Therapy,* 47–60.

Luepnitz, D. (1988) *The Family Interpreted*. New York: Basic Books.

McGoldrick, M., C. Anderson, and F. Walsh, eds. (1989) *Women in Families*. New York: W. W. Norton.

McGoldrick, M., C. Anderson, and F. Walsh (1989) "Women in families and in family therapy," in *Women in Families*.

Napier, G. (1988) *The Fragile Bond*. New York: Harper & Row.

Walsh, F., and M. Scheinkman (1989) "(Fe)-male: The hidden gender dimension in models of family therapy," in McGoldrick et al., *Women in Families*."

Walsh, F. (1989) "Reconsidering gender in the marital *quid pro pro*," in McGoldrick et al., *Women in Families*.

Walters, M. (1990) *The Co-Dependent Cinderella Fights Back*. Presentation at Family Therapy Networker Conference, Washington, D.C., March.

Walters, M., et al. (1988) *The Invisible Web*. New York: Guilford Press.

Warburton, J., A. Newberry, and J. Alexander (1989) "Women as therapists, trainees, and supervisors," in McGoldrick et al., *Women in Families*.

Watzlawick, P. (1978) *The Language of Change*. New York: Basic Books.

Zucal, B. *The Evolution of Sexual Hierarchy* (1984) Unpublished paper, part of master's thesis, University of Maryland, College Park, Md.

Chapter Four

THE ROLE OF "FUN" IN FAMILY THERAPY

Ethan Roberts, M.A.

A Definition of Fun and Its Application to Family Therapy

The concept of fun as an integral part of family therapy has not received much emphasis in the past, perhaps because the field has been more concerned with techniques for symptom reduction and second-order change. In fact, the whole idea that therapy could or should be fun is probably abhorrent to many therapists, including those family therapists more accustomed to working with serious, somber issues.

However, family therapy has flourished because of its ability to see the serious as absurd, the destructive battle as the "dance," the manipulation as the "game."

Within this framework it is entirely valid to create a therapy that is enjoyable for both the therapist and the family. Fun can be introduced as an alternative to systems which present as angry, depressed, or hopeless.

Webster's New Collegiate Dictionary (1979) defines fun as "providing entertainment, amusement, or enjoyment; playful, often boisterous, action or speech." Using this definition, it is easy to see how family therapy naturally lends itself to fun. Tasks which incorporate entertainment as a reward for positive behaviors in the family are frequently assigned to members between sessions. The anecdotes that families relate in sessions are frequently *amusing* or even *absurd*, if one goes beyond their painfully detailed manner of presentation. Finally, what could be more *boisterous* than the interactions of family members in sessions?

Families devoid of fun usually manifest themselves as disengaged, rigid, or severely conflicted. When families take themselves too seriously, they cannot help but maintain their rigidity, violence, addictions, apathy, etc. The therapist who attempts to change these families without introducing fun into the sessions will probably fail simply by trying too hard.

The family therapist must intervene, must interject whatever fun is available or congruent with the family's interests. Fun can be introduced through assignments, interventions, use of humor, or through the therapist's presence. Any intervention which creates an enjoyable experience for the family while it also creates new realities in awareness, communication, or role expectations among members can be considered fun.

Playing with Serious Families

There are several therapeutic games regularly advertised in family therapy journals which are useful for eliciting thoughts and feelings from nonverbal children, overly serious families, and families with limited positive interactions. Sometimes the games work in unexpected ways.

The author recently worked with a family in which the presenting problem was the withdrawn behavior of the ten-year-old son. Because this family had three young boys, ages twelve, ten, and eight, it seemed a good idea to help them through the use of one of the more popular therapeutic games (Boardman and Boardman 1983).

Although the game was great fun and the other boys expressed themselves very well, the ten-year-old remained sullen, even sulking when he realized that he wasn't going to win (despite the noncompetitiveness of the game). He then enacted the presenting problem beautifully by sprawling face down on a couch and hiding his head under a pillow.

The therapist decided to use this melodrama as the basis for an intervention. He asked the father, who has been quite peripheral in the family, to coax the boy to discuss what was bothering him. The father failed miserably, and the boy's embarrassment increased his already sullen demeanor.

To engender cohesiveness between father and son while decreasing the attention paid to the boy's dysfunctional behavior, the therapist took the rest of the family out of the room, leaving the father and ten-year-old alone to work things out.

Ten minutes later, the therapist reentered the room to find the boy sitting up and laughing with his father, who proudly announced that the two of them had found a solution to the problem: the boy could call himself "first runner-up."

This was the beginning of several interventions designed to help the father feel more confident in his dealings with the children. As his competence and his outlook improved, the boy's involvement with the family improved metaphorically, and his withdrawn behavior declined.

What is significant about this case is that the intervention of family play was the catalyst for change. Previous attempts at helping the family by talking had not been nearly as effective. A follow-up one year later found the father still taking an active parenting role and the ten-year-old son asymptomatic.

Other therapists have succeeded by asking family members to put on a play during a session (Ariel, Carel, and Tyano 1985). They found that this helps engage the family in enactment, uses metaphors that children understand, and is inherently paradoxical because it asks the family to pretend to have the symptom (Madanes 1981). The therapeutic goals of the play are to change the family's self-image, frame of reference, emotional atmosphere, and structure, thereby enhancing positive functioning and coping skills.

The therapist's role during the performance of such a play is like that of a news reporter, adding commentary as needed. In addition, the therapist may reinforce selected aspects of the play, provoke certain reactions, and direct the action.

The Use of Humor

The role of humor in family therapy sessions is extremely important, because without humor dysfunctional families become draining and stressful to the therapist. The use of humor allows the therapist to counteract the family's dramatic pull and to resist buying into their hopeless state (Bergman 1985).

Bergman also believes that using humor helps the therapist regain control of a session when it slips away because of prevailing despair. If the family is too serious, Bergman urges the therapist to become lighthearted and humorous. Conversely, if the family is too glib about serious matters, the therapist must become more somber.

Humor helps the family relax and is an important part of the joining process. Dysfunctional families usually arrive for their first session wearing the look of dental patients with abscessed teeth. Adding humor to the first session can help the family trust the therapist with their pain.

Humor also helps the therapist feel more positive about the family. This increases his/her motivation to become creative and productive. Carl Whitaker (Simon 1985) maintains that if a therapy session is satisfying and alive for the therapist, the client automatically benefits. (Contrast this with the usual therapeutic notion that if the client has a productive session, the therapist will feel good.) Indeed, if Whitaker does not get something out of the interview for himself, he is left feeling very unsatisfied.

This idea is reconfirmed by Bergman (1985), who notes:

> As far as I know, there is no commandment that says a therapist must endure suffering and sometimes abuse in a treatment session directed at helping others. When I am in a treatment session I am, of course, focused on helping a family change, but I am also out to have some fun. . . . I'm doing this for me, but I suspect there are also clinical spin-offs that work therapeutically towards change. (p. 184)

Humor can also be employed paradoxically to exaggerate the absurdity of the client's dilemma. Allen Fay (1978) utilizes paradoxical humor by answering his clients' irrational statements with more of the same:

> *Patient:* I am afraid that you may dislike me if I tell you something.
>
> *Therapist:* I dislike everyone, so there's no problem. (p. 56)

Fay also coaches clients to use paradoxical humor with family members when their usual methods of offering support or reassurance prove fruitless. For example, Fay worked with a couple in which the forty-three-year-old husband was depressed and felt like a failure, following the bankruptcy of his business. After months of trying to reassure him of his worth, the wife was convinced that her efforts were not making him feel any better.

Fay instructed the wife to respond paradoxically to the husband's self-despair in this way:

> *Husband:* I am a total failure, a worthless person; my life has no meaning.
>
> *Wife:* You certainly are a failure. You are a disgrace to me and to the children and to our friends and neighbors. You are a failure not only in business, but as a father, as a husband, as a lover. You have never functioned in your life, have never amounted to anything, and never will. (p. 39)

After this, the husband stopped making self-defeating statements, and the destructive interactional game ended.

Thus, humor can be a powerful tool for changing repetitive, dysfunctional interactions. Humor helps families see their endless feedback loops as absurd and funny, freeing them from the belief that those customary patterns are their only possible ways to interact.

One cautionary note: humor should never be used in an insulting or denigrating way, and family therapists must walk a very fine line between the use of humor and the application of thinly veiled sarcasm or anger.

The Use of Metaphors

A metaphor is a statement about how one thing resembles something else (Haley 1987). Metaphors are indirect, frequently symbolic images that are very useful in helping families see or experience new realities within their situation. Metaphors in therapy have been described as linguistic interpretations vividly linked to concrete experiences (Simon, Stierlin, and Wynne 1985).

Using metaphors in a session makes the therapy process more enjoyable because it reframes rigid or dysfunctional patterns in playful ways. Images come alive in metaphors as ordinary people are transformed into kings and queens, knights on white horses, fairy godmothers, or various well-known characters—Don Quixote, Archie Bunker, Scarlett O'Hara, etc.

Metaphors can also describe the actions of family members by saying, for instance, that parents are sinking into quicksand, or seem trapped like prisoners of love. The only restrictions on metaphors are the limits of the therapist's imagination. Even then, families seem quite adept at creating their own images once the therapist introduces metaphors as a regular part of the therapeutic language.

Therefore, if the family uses a metaphor to complain about or scapegoat the identified patient, it offers the therapist a wonderful opportunity to carry the same metaphor one step further in a way that will promote change. If the family complains that the teenaged son acts "like he's the king and we're his slaves," the therapist might respond, "Perhaps, then, it is time for the slaves to revolt!"

The therapist can also utilize this technique with families who use clichés or adages to maintain homeostasis and resist directives. If parents lament that they cannot agree on discipline because "if I say black, he says white," the therapist can respond with, "Let's see what it would take to make things look gray."

When a family hears its own words positively reframed or relabeled through the use of metaphor, it perturbs its systemic comfort by creating the possibility of change. Yet because metaphors are indirect suggestions, they usually provoke less systemic resistance than direct requests.

The use of therapeutic metaphors also adds a creative element to the therapy which can be fun for both the family and therapist. As Bergman (1985) states, "For me, metaphor is the music in life where words are the lyrics. It's three-dimensional, connected to emotions, and always connotes powerful messages" (p. 188).

Bergman complies his own list of metaphors to describe various clients. "Tanks" are noisy people who bulldoze their way through life. "Submarines" are people with low self-esteem. "Barracudas" are therapist killers. "Radar" is what the identified patient demonstrates by detecting family problems and then becoming symptomatic as a protective response. Using metaphors like these helps the therapist add some playfulness to otherwise serious, emotionally draining families.

The author worked with a family in which the thirteen-year-old daughter had become very powerful after her attempted suicide a few months earlier. In the first session the mother complained that she was afraid to discipline or even challenge her daughter on any level, for fear that the girl would make another attempt on her own life. "We're all walking on eggshells right now," she sighed. The father agreed somewhat sheepishly with his wife, and the sixteen-year-old sister added that the younger girl was always trying to be her boss.

The author observed that in this family there was an obvious reversal of hierarchy, with the youngest daughter treated like a queen and the rest of the family acting subservient. The intervention was a paradoxical ritual, metaphorically employing the family's situation. The author asked the other family members to make a "royal crown and robe" out of ordinary materials. The younger daughter was asked to wear these clothes and to parade around the house "like a queen" for half an hour every day for a week. During that time the family should (within reason) cater to the "queen's" every whim.

Through the use of ritualized metaphor, this intervention demonstrated the excessive and ridiculous power this young girl held over her family. The results were quite dramatic: After the family made the garments, the daughter tried them on but refused to continue the ritual. This prompted the normally complacent father to take charge and to insist that the daughter follow the therapist's instructions. Within a few weeks, the daughter was no longer in charge of the family, and there were no further suicide attempts.

The author developed another metaphorical technique—*sign labeling*—as a playful response to rigid family behavioral patterns. When the family begins to label someone in a pejorative way, the next question is directed toward the labeled person: "Do you agree with that label?"

If the labeled person disagrees, the differing viewpoints are explored. However, if the labeled one agrees with the designation, the next question is, "How long have you been acting this way?" Usually the response is either "all my life" or "for a long time."

At that point the therapist shows the family a small, but heavy piece of smooth wood. Covering the wood is a sheet of construction paper, and at the top are two small screws attached to a loop of soft yarn. The descriptive label is then written in bold letters on the paper to make a sign. The labeled person is then asked to wear the sign around his/her neck for the remainder of the session.

This use of metaphor usually takes the family by surprise and elicits some welcome laughter. Frequently the labeled person is asked, "Does your label feel like a heavy weight around your neck?" The therapist reinforces the metaphor by explaining that labels carried around through life are even more burdensome.

This intervention has a dramatic and often paradoxical effect on both the labeled person (who is not necessarily the identified patient) and the other family members. Any embarrassment the labeled person may experience from this intervention is slight compared to the humiliation of carrying the burden of labels like "lazy," "underachiever," "no good," "sick," "hyper" around for a lifetime.

Sign-labeling is an example of using objects as metaphors. Objects can be quite effective at capturing and holding a family's interest. Objects as diverse as puppets, song lyrics, photographs, straws, games, and empty chairs have been very effective techniques for creating metaphors in family therapy (Sherman and Fredman, 1986).

Even the family therapist can be thought of in metaphorical terms. Jeffrey Kottler (1986) describes the therapist as a "family detective," always searching for clues to the family mystery. The good detective asks such questions as:

- Why this particular symptom?
- Why does it emerge now?
- What secrets are being kept which are metaphors for the symptom?
- What do family maneuvers (e.g., changing appointments, trying to form alliances with the therapist) indicate?

Since the family likes to be mysterious, we should respect that by being mysterious ourselves or by intriguing when assigning tasks or reframing the family dilemma.

Similarly, Bergman (1985) advocates looking for adventure, intrigue, mystery, mischievousness, surprise, outrageousness, and humor in sessions. He believes that the first session should always be exciting for the therapist.

Thus, through the use of metaphors the family therapist can add fun to the sessions, creating a more enjoyable experience for all. Metaphors capture the family's attention and help the therapist feel more creative and satisfied.

Increasing Family Therapy Enjoyment

I propose a four-part method for increasing total enjoyment of family therapy. This method need not be used in sequential order, but instead ought to become a simultaneous process incorporated into one's work. By and large this method transcends theoretical orientation, so that family therapists of almost every persuasion can use those techniques without sacrificing their theoretical positions.

The four-part method includes:

1. The use of self
2. Taking therapeutic risks
3. Taking control of the therapy
4. Reducing stress-creating circumstances

The Use of Self in Family Therapy

All therapists, whether directive or nondirective, use themselves in therapy. Just as it is impossible not to communicate, it is also impossible for a therapist not to use him- or herself. However, it is the manner in which the family therapist uses the self that is important.

For example, structural family therapy for the most part developed from the use of self techniques created by Salvador Minuchin (1974; Minuchin and Fishman 1981).

Minuchin uses himself to the fullest extent in sessions, kneeling on the floor to play with a small child, moving himself to sit next to parents, sharing an ashtray, etc.

By contrast a therapist such as Maurizio Andolfi (1979) uses himself to stir up family anxiety, purposely creating dramatic tension in order to change rigid interactional sequences.

The late Virginia Satir was another fine example of a therapist who utilized herself in sessions, sometimes by giving a hug, at other times by using her magical ropes to show how people were psychologically bound together.

The use of self should also include allowing oneself to feel and even share feelings with the family at different times. This might seem to conflict with the idea of neutrality, but in fact it frequently keeps the therapist from being pulled into the family's emotional system. For example, the therapist might comment to the family, "I'm feeling a great deal of anxiety in the room right now. Besides myself, who is probably the most anxious right now?"

Even the emphasized neutrality of the Milan method (Boscolo et al. 1987) employs use of self at times—such as when saying to the family, "I don't know what's going on,"—thus using confusion as a tool for generating information.

Thus, the use of self leads to increased joining, reduction of therapeutic enmeshment in the system, and a more dramatic impact on the stuck system.

Taking Therapeutic Risks

Therapeutic risks make sessions come alive and help families achieve maximum growth and fulfillment. Constantly playing it safe in therapy is a metaphor for family homeostasis, which keeps members locked in stale, repetitive roles. When therapists take risks, they send messages that the world outside the family is a flexible place.

By contrast family therapy without risks quickly becomes stagnant and boring. This generally occurs during the middle stages of therapy, after some first-order change has already been realized. Families (and even therapists) may become complacent at this time, relieved of the anguish of the symptom but unwilling to take further steps toward changing what seems comfortable.

Therapeutic risks in family therapy may include mild confrontation, humor, paradoxical messages, dramatic interventions (e.g., rituals), or the use of self.

Taking a therapeutic risk involves putting oneself on the line and overcoming one's own fears. Typically, therapists fear taking a risk because they

1. Feel it might hurt the family.
2. Do not want the family to reject them.
3. Worry that the family will terminate the therapy.
4. Feel risk-taking is contrary to what therapists should do.
5. Fear putting themselves on the line.
6. Fear they may be going against the policies of the agency for which they work.

But if the therapist has taken the time to formulate a plan which includes the risk and is based on sound theoretical premises, these fears are unnecessary.

Before any therapeutic risk is undertaken, that risk should

1. Have some therapeutic purpose.
2. Be in the family's best interest.
3. Not be done merely for self-aggrandizement.
4. Involve unbalancing of a rigid system or prodding a stuck therapy.

Risk-taking simultaneously frees both the family and the therapist. The family is temporarily unbalanced from rigid, dysfunctional patterns, and the therapist is extricated from entanglement with that system.

Taking Control of the Therapy

The importance of control in family therapy cannot be overstated. If the therapist does not control the therapy from the start and maintain that control, she/he will ultimately have less success and enjoyment, will work harder, and will suffer more frustration. Ironically, Bergman (1985) calls the jockeying for control between the therapist and family prior to onset of treatment "fun and games."

When the family controls the therapy, its game is to stabilize and to thwart any efforts aimed at systemic change. Those "helpful" family members who call between sessions to suggest that the therapist could really get at the truth by seeing so-and-so individually are more interested in homeostasis than in cooperation.

Taking control of the therapy means that the therapist decides which family members attend sessions, how often they meet, how long the sessions are, etc. If the family shows up for a session without certain key members, the therapist must decide how to respond.

Possible responses include refusing to see the family, sending a paradoxical letter to the absent member(s) (Weeks and L'Abate 1982), or sending the family home to insist that the absent person(s) attend. One should never proceed with the philosophy of "I'll take what I can get."

Within the session the therapist may need to control chaotic sequences of redundant, angry interactions which escalate tensions between family members. Allowing such sequences to continue is destructive and leaves everyone feeling defeated and hopeless.

The therapist must also take control when one member insists on being the cotherapist, trying to establish a controlling alliance with the therapist. In such cases the therapist can support other family members' efforts to help the therapy or tactfully dissuade the overly helpful person from his/her efforts.

Taking control of the therapy increases the therapist's enjoyment of the work, because she/he feels more in charge of the therapy's direction and can increase the productivity of sessions.

Reducing Stress-Creating Circumstances

To become more effective at family therapy while enjoying the work more, one should minimize work-related stress whenever possible. One way to do this is by making deliberate efforts to reduce stress-creating circumstances, both in and out of therapy sessions.

Bergman (1985) believes in the general rule that the therapist should never work harder than the family. Not only does this rule reduce unnecessary pressure on the therapist, it also helps families develop autonomously.

Bergman also identifies families metaphorically as either ripe or unripe fruit (i.e., ready or not ready to change), and suggests that the therapist not waste time working with the unripe variety. Essentially, the difference between the two is that anxiety is greater in ripe families, while resistance is greater in the unripe families. Families will change only when their anxiety is greater than their resistance.

Another good rule for avoiding stress-creating circumstances is to refrain from working with families similar to others that proved cumbersome in the past. Some therapists agree to see any family that comes along. This approach probably addresses the therapist's need for economic or emotional fulfillment, but it leads to increased stress and anxiety in the long run.

Instead, each therapist should have a personal list of family types which for him/her are untouchable. Of course, the types will vary from therapist to therapist, but untouchable families are best referred to someone else who does not mind working with them.

This does not automatically preclude working with families that are inherently difficult or stressful, such as families with abusive or violent behavior, families of substance abusers, or families affected by suicide, mental illness, or criminal behavior. Much should depend on the family's motivation for change. A few suggestions follow, which may help decrease therapeutic stress while working with violent or alcoholic families.

When working with violent or potentially violent families, take a firm approach from the onset. Ideally, insist that the family agree to a written nonviolence contract in the very first session. Tell the family that under no circumstances will violence of any kind be tolerated in the therapy session. Ask family members to agree to phone a friend or a hotline for help if tensions escalate at home. Inform them of your legal responsibility to inform Child Protective Services if you suspect or become aware of any form of child abuse.

If the family will not comply with these requests, do not agree to work with them. Otherwise, the stress on the therapist from trying to keep the peace will be overwhelming, and the family will make little progress toward resolving disputes without force.

When working with alcoholic family systems, refuse to continue if any family members come to the session intoxicated. Urge the drinker to attend A.A. and the other family members to attend Al-Anon, Alateen, or other such groups. If they continually refuse, terminate the therapy with the knowledge that little can be done to help them on a permanent basis. This also holds true for families with drug-addicted members.

Whenever possible, schedule sessions flexibly without adhering to a set time allotment. However, try to keep the session from going overtime unless productive change is actually occurring.

Allow intervals of two or three weeks between sessions, to give the family time to do their assignments and to allow shifts in the systemic organization to occur. The more the family gains between sessions, the more optimistic they will become about making future gains. Families that feel good about themselves bring more enjoyment to the sessions.

Bergman (1985) offers several suggestions for reducing therapeutic exhaustion when working under stressful circumstances:

1. Invite a cotherapist or team to observe a session.
2. Maximize leverage for change by working with as many family members as possible.
3. Invite the grandparents in to reduce the threat of family violence.
4. Make future sessions contingent upon the family doing the assigned homework. This is called *reverse treatment*, because instead of the family seeking therapy in order to change,

the family must change in order to stay in treatment.
5. Do not feel obligated to fill an hour with a boring or unmotivated family.

Thus, to create more fun in therapy, one must first eliminate the stress-creating circumstances which increase therapeutic anxiety and impede positive regard for the work. When positive feelings for the work diminish, the usual outcome is that little demon called burnout.

What Is Burnout?

Burnout is a mental and physical condition which may be characterized by apathy, depression, anxiety, fatigue, or psychosomatic disorders (Kramer 1980). It often occurs when therapists have excessive caseloads, work too intensely, or become too emotionally involved with their clients over a long period of time. Usually, the therapist is working harder or feeling more anxious than the family, and therefore suffers more.

Other factors may include caseloads which lack variety, severely dysfunctional clients, and extreme job demands which transcend normal work hours and impinge on one's personal life.

Kottler (1986) includes boredom, demoralization, dissatisfaction, restlessness, and weariness as less severe forms of burnout. He finds that the highs and lows of helping clients make burnout the single most common personal consequence of practicing therapy.

When burnout occurs, the family therapist may experience feelings of insecurity about families whom she/he has previously helped or with whom she/he is working now. The therapist may begin to say things like, "I really don't know what I did to change this family," or "All of a sudden I feel stuck with several of my families, and I don't know what to do."

Kottler cites four causes of burnout in therapists:

1. Unrealistic expectations
2. Excessive need to control
3. Bureaucratic constraints/power struggles at work
4. Emotional stress

Ironically, many family therapists seem to develop the very behaviors which may lead to burnout if they are not careful. Directive therapy often serves as a showcase for the therapists' own needs to control, fix, lead, and intensify. If left untempered, these needs frequently create power struggles with families and trigger emotional stress in the therapist.

Recognizing Burnout

It is vital for the family therapist to recognize the early signs of burnout before it becomes severe. Kottler (1986) has identified many of these, including feelings of helplessness, reluctance to go to work or to see particular clients, excessive daydreaming, lack of enthusiasm, use of stress-reducing drugs or alcohol, and general unwillingness to discuss work in social or family circles.

Charles Kramer (1980) developed six categories of indicators for therapeutic burnout:

1. **Acting out:** Lateness, forgetting appointments, ending sessions early, frequent errors, premature termination, constant client turnover.
2. **Emotional over/underresponsiveness:** Irritability, no fun, frustration,

boredom, sleepiness, sympathy, anger, depression, lack of interest or anticipation, anxiety, lack of humor, impatience.
3. **Physical reactions** (before, during, or after sessions): headaches, rapid heartbeat, gastrointestinal reactions, tenseness, fatigue, flushing.
4. **Fantasy reactions:** Day or night dreaming about a family.
5. **Technical reactions:** Being too directive, nondirective, reassuring, arbitrary, superficial, intellectual, or clichéd. Fixed focus of discussion with primary attention on the identified patient or non-present scapegoat.
6. **External signs:** Bringing client problems home, or bringing home problems into sessions.

I disagree slightly on one point: Fantasy reactions are very common in well-functioning therapists who work with severely dysfunctional, stuck families. Fantasy can be considered an adaptive response for therapists, helping them cope with the stress of working with crazy-making families. As Luigi Boscolo (1987) notes: "When you are seeing a stuck family you begin to have fantasies about changing your job, fantasies of changing your wife. Fantasies of giving up this family and finding a new one. You start to have physical symptoms—you begin to be sleepy during sessions" (p. 124).

Beginning family therapists can take heart from the knowledge that no one in the field is entirely immune from burnout, and that it is an ever-present shadow endemic to the profession. Even the most famous therapists have grappled with burnout at one time or another.

Reflecting on the beginning of his own career, Carl Whitaker (Simon, 1985) recalls that: "When I first took over at Emory (University) at thirty-four, I knew nothing whatever about families and I was in the state of psychosomatic collapse. Once every few weeks, I would break out in cold sweats and vomiting and go home and crawl in bed and pull the covers over my head and put myself back together" (p. 71).

Overcoming and Preventing Burnout

The first step towards overcoming or preventing burnout is to recognize either that you already have it or that you are headed in that direction. Kramer (1980) offers several suggestions for reducing burnout:

1. Try different approaches or techniques.
2. Read about what others do.
3. Teach others what you know.
4. Look for feedback from coworkers.
5. Watch carefully for self-reactions, telltale signs of burnout.
6. Review your notes frequently, compare case outcomes.
7. Start a peer supervision/consultation group.
8. Write up what you do—present a workshop or conference paper.
9. Go into personal therapy.
10. Pace yourself, limit the number of disturbing family cases or meetings you have per week.
11. Take a vacation or time out.
12. Every once in a while, play with the idea of giving up this field!

Kottler (1986) adds a few more suggestions to this list:

1. Take more responsibility for your own growth.

2. Use multiple measures of success in your work.
3. Set limits with demanding clients/colleagues.
4. Develop outside interests.
5. Confront the sources of stress.
6. Exercise your mind and body.

Kottler also feels that the cure for boredom (i.e., mild burnout) is to focus on the uniqueness of each case/client and the opportunity for growth in every encounter. In his view, clients respond to deliberate shifts in the therapist's concentration by becoming more alive or exciting.

Whitaker (Simon 1985) seems, over the years, to have changed his philosophy about working with families in order to avoid burnout. He states, "I want it to be very clear that I'm not in a panic about their life. . . . I don't care if they change or not." He further elaborates on the actual damage that families can do to the therapist's emotional state: "Most therapists have the idea that when the family shows up, you should give them your left breast. If they bite that, give them the right one. I think that's crazy" (p. 29).

Whitaker seems to advocate a more detached, objective, and neutral approach. While on the surface he may seem somewhat cold or lacking empathy, in many ways his approach is more a prescription for survival in family therapy. Perhaps Whitaker feels it is better to seem aloof than to be burned out.

The importance of neutrality as a tool for preventing burnout cannot be overemphasized. Maintaining neutrality fosters curiosity (Cecchin, 1987), promotes systemic thinking, and helps the therapist avoid forming stressful alliances with the family.

Thinking systemically also helps create a more enjoyable therapy because it opens up new ways of seeing the family problem, so that new possibilities for second-order change can emerge. Ultimately, watching second-order change take place makes doing family therapy more fun and worthwhile.

Twenty Suggestions for Having More Fun in Family Therapy

The following is a practical list of suggestions which the therapist can use to increase the fun and enjoyment of working with families:

1. Decorate the office attractively (plants, fish, mobiles, blackboard, calendars), to create a positive environment for the family.
2. Leave adequate space between appointments.
3. Leave your work at the office. Never take your clients to bed, not even in your thoughts!
4. Cancel your appointments when you feel ill.
5. Share your feelings with coworkers on a regular basis. Use supports when necessary.
6. Use a genogram to see the three generations that have created the current family dilemma.
7. Watch for patterns more than for content.
8. Always remain *meta* to the family system; strive for neutrality at all times.
9. Learn to laugh at yourself and at what you do.
10. Use as much humor in your therapy as the family can tolerate.
11. Let parents parent their children. Therapists should not take on the par-

enting role, even if the parents pressure him/her to do just that.

12. Whenever possible, especially with difficult cases, work with a therapeutic team or cotherapist.
13. Ask family members to talk directly to one another, rather than talking through you. Refuse to be a sponge for their intensity!
14. Videotape difficult families and ask a colleague to watch the videotape and offer helpful feedback.
15. Utilize a consultant or supervisor when you feel stuck.
16. Always look for strengths in individual family members and in the family system as a whole.
17. Use objects (toys, props, food, music, art, etc.) for symbolic effect in the therapy.
18. Formulate and assign families tasks that match the level of absurdity in their situation.
19. Keep the number of severely dysfunctional clients in your caseload down to a workable minimum.
20. Accept that you cannot help everybody.

Twenty Suggestions for Having No Fun in Family Therapy

Believe it or not, some therapists do not like to have fun while they work. They prefer to work long hours for very little satisfaction, risking occasional burnout to convince their loved ones that they really do deserve a medal. This next list is for them:

1. Take on numerous tough cases just for "the challenge."
2. Blame yourself when families relapse or struggle.
3. Schedule sessions one after another, so that you can maximize your earnings and help as many people as possible.
4. Take work home with you and think about your clients all night. Tell your family that this is part of your job.
5. Have lengthy, confronting arguments with resistant clients.
6. Every so often, allow yourself to be drawn into family alliances to see if you can change things from within.
7. Take over for inept parents; lecture their children. Show them the correct way to parent.
8. Allow sessions to extend beyond the allotted time (even if another client is waiting) in order to learn something new about the family or to "fix" something which won't wait until the next appointment.
9. Avoid doing your paperwork until it piles up, then do it all late one night after your last session is over.
10. If an attempted solution fails, keep trying it. Maybe the family is just being resistant.
11. Try to force reluctant family members to attend therapy sessions, or try to do effective therapy with half a family.
12. Give the family your home or personal phone number, just in case they have an emergency late at night.
13. Try to reason with irrational family members, especially if they are substance abusers, violent, or obsessive.
14. Let family members express all their feelings, no matter how long it takes.
15. Hold long phone conversations with distraught parents between sessions. Let them lean on you for support.
16. Fight with your colleagues over whose orientation works the best. If you still cannot convince them that

your methods are better, write an article or book to back up your claims.

17. Never vary your working style, techniques, or caseload type. People will respect your consistency.
18. Let the family dictate its own therapy process and pace.
19. Refuse to terminate treatment until every one of the family's problems has been solved. If none are left, ask more questions about the past until you uncover the hidden "excess baggage" which remains.
20. Try to solve your own family problems by using family therapy techniques on your loved ones. Then deny that you are doing so.

Fun Tasks

Most therapists have one or two preferred tasks which they enjoy assigning to families because these tasks have a high success rate. Yet even the most successful task may be resisted by families because they seem arduous or require them to switch roles or alliances. Sometimes after doing the task, they are quite surprised to find that they are actually having fun. This is an added benefit, and the therapist can be pleased when this occurs.

Certain tasks seem more enjoyable than others by nature, because an element of fun is already built into the assignment. Among these "fun tasks," Madanes (1981) developed a paradoxical technique called "pretending," in which the symptomatic person is asked to "pretend" to have the symptom at a structured time during the day. For example, a depressed man is asked to pretend to his wife (without disclosing if he is pretending or not) that he is feeling depressed. Madanes theorizes that the act of pretending removes the power from the symptom, and changes the usual interactions around the symptom.

A variation of this task assigns one family member to ask the symptomatic member to pretend to have the symptom. This often leads to a quick reduction of the symptom, because it changes the nature of the power between the family members.

Pretend tasks are fun because the family has such a hard time doing them that they frequently end up laughing together when they try. This reduces the hostility or resentment around the symptom and demonstrates the absurdity of the situation.

Another fun task (Madanes 1984) usually given to couples is called "Create a Special Memory". The couple is sent off to create their own special memory in whatever way they choose without the therapist's imposed structure.

One couple to whom the author gave this task decided to have dinner together—in Curaçao! Another couple, married for fifteen years, spent a romantic evening at home wearing their wedding clothes. The fun of this task resides in the imaginative ways in which couples can respond.

Reversal tasks (Papp 1983) are given to one particular member of a family without the others' knowledge, in order to create a change in that other part of the system. One member is asked to reverse the usual way she/he behaves in order to paradoxically initiate a reversal in what the others do.

An example would be asking an adult whose parents call constantly to call their parents ten times a day, until the parents respond paradoxically by suggesting a reduction in the number of calls. Another example asks a family member whom everyone relies on excessively to suddenly become helpless and dependent.

Reversal tasks are fun to give and fun for the client to do because they ask people to pretend, to act, and to behave in uncustomary ways. There is a certain element of mischievousness inherent in the task, as one member is asked to "put one over" on another member.

Tasks with fun already built in can be given to families, so that they must have fun in order to complete the task. Some examples are asking a disengaged married couple to go out on a date once a week, renting a videotape relevant to the family problem, gift-giving (Sherman and Fredman 1986), sending someone on vacation, or sending a couple to a weekend retreat. Children have even been made responsible for their parents' happiness (Madanes 1984), as a paradoxical method of getting the parents to take charge of their own lives.

An excellent way to motivate families to complete future tasks is to make sure that the very first task given is fun. If their first experience is positive, they will be more inclined to carry out other, more difficult tasks.

Traps and Pitfalls That Make Family Therapists Crazy

Family therapist, beware! There are snakes, dragons, and demons everywhere, just waiting for an unsuspecting therapist to come along. Lurking in dark shadows, they creep up on the therapists and grab them when they are most unsuspecting. They can make anyone crazy, and eventually cause even the heartiest to feel burned out.

Who are these snakes, dragons, and demons? Why, they are just ordinary families, plain folks with only one thing in common: they do NOT want to change. They will go to almost any length to avoid changing, including setting traps for the therapist.

The following quotes, all taken from the author's personal experience, should give the reader a good idea of what these potential traps look like. To preserve sanity and diminish frustration, be prepared to step carefully around these traps at all times. Certainly, each therapist can create his/her own list of favorite one-liners:

1. Who referred us? Well, nobody; we just sort of heard about you.
2. I don't remember our last therapist's name.
3. Can I talk with you privately?
4. My husband doesn't know I'm calling you.
5. I'm sure my son would open up if you'd just see him alone.
6. My wife has to work late (said on the telephone ten minutes prior to the session). Should the rest of us come?
7. If my father/mother comes here, then I'm not coming!
8. (To spouse) You see, he agrees with ME!
9. My son feels uncomfortable with the videotaping.
10. Oh, did you give us a task last week?
11. My husband is an alcoholic. He'll never agree to come.
12. Our appointment was yesterday? I thought it was next week.
13. I was hoping that you (the therapist) could talk some sense into him, because I can't.
14. The last three therapists we saw did things differently.
15. When YOU get married/have children of your own/get to be our age, you'll understand.
16. I'm not what you'd call abusive or anything, but there are times when

you just have to give him a crack across the face when he's fresh! Don't you agree?

17. Can I call you at home if there's an emergency?
18. Don't you think it would be better to put him/her someplace?
19. I just thought I'd give you a call to tell you something else about my husband/wife which didn't come out last session. Do you have a moment?
20. (With hands reaching for the doorknob to leave) Oh, did I mention before that my mother was diagnosed paranoid/schizophrenic?

When Having Fun Is More Difficult

It is not the aim of this chapter to suggest that every family therapy session can be fun. There will be sessions of rediscovered grief and anguish, confrontations between irresponsible teenagers and their beleaguered parents, threats of suicide, divorce, violence, and abandonment.

Family therapy deals with issues of life and death, illness, abuse, and catastrophes. It is not always neat, nor pretty, nor as easy as it looks on the videotapes by the "masters." At times the therapist may forget what having fun is all about.

However, one of the primary responsibilities of the family therapist is to try always to convey a sense of hope to the family, no matter how arduous the journey it faces. We can do this by using humor and our own experiences and by redefining crises in ways which highlight the silver lining of each cloud. When all else fails, give the family a reward ("With all that you have been through, Mr. and Mrs. Jones, now is the time to do something nice for yourselves").

The family therapist should keep in mind that she/he cannot force humor into an inappropriate moment. Such an attempt would make the therapist seem like the mascot in an alcoholic family system, or would show lack of sensitivity to the family's pain. If it seems impossible at a particular moment to have fun with a family, wait until a better opportunity presents itself.

Unfortunately, difficult sessions can be as hard on the therapist as on the family. Bergman (1985) urges on the family therapist the general philosophy of not taking too many things seriously, of staying "meta" to the family's seriousness, and of seeing family provocations as maneuvers. In this way, one can avoid being fooled or upset.

Some therapists refuse even to work with certain families because of violence, abuse, suicide attempts, alcoholism, etc. From past experience these therapists believe that some families are not worth the effort. Even Whitaker (Simon, 1985) has noted: "Over the years, I've become more and more convinced that there are a few people whom I can make good contact with and may be useful to, and there'll be several untreated families left in the world after I die, so why struggle with the ones who society has destroyed, and now wants me to fix? I don't intend to be a victim of society's demands" (p. 74).

However, due to agency policies or economic realities, not all family therapists have this same choice. When it is either impossible or unethical to refuse one of these families, the therapist must be aware of the increased risk of stress and burnout. With this realization, the therapist can use the methods described earlier to prevent burnout.

One must also resist thinking that even the most dysfunctional families can be saved from themselves, for this thinking is unrealistic. Additionally, this philosophy may set up between the therapist and the family a symmetrical battle which is almost impossible to win. Finally, to think along these lines is to invite an increase in frustration when things do not work out according to plan.

Applying Fun across Different Modalities

The application of fun to family therapy is not restricted to any particular modality. Every approach can be modified to incorporate the elements of fun previously discussed here. Several theoretical bases already employ some of these ideas.

Structural family therapy emphasizes considerable use of self to make changes in the family organization. Strategic therapists are likely to take therapeutic risks, to become less involved in the family emotional system, and to be creative in their interventions. Multigenerational therapists use genograms to broaden the scope of the family's vision and decrease the intensity level of the problematic here and now. Systemic therapists work in teams and seem always to be experimenting with new therapy models. They are also adept at remaining in control of the therapy at all times, even with severely dysfunctional families. Eclectic therapists borrow different ideas from the different schools; they may benefit the most from the suggestions in this chapter.

The best idea is to be as creative as possible, because creativity helps generate solutions. Kottler (1986) notes that creativity is often resisted because it may involve breaking rules and taking risks. Yet family therapy began as a creative effort, frequently breaking the established rules of more traditional, linear-oriented therapies.

The continual evolution of family therapy demands that we occasionally break away from our own established norms and rules, moving toward new (and, we hope, more fun) ways of working with families. As Kottler states, "The process of doing therapy awakens in us the sense of ourselves as explorers." As explorers we are compelled to move forward to seek better methods of helping our families and ourselves.

Summary

Despite the proven effectiveness of family therapy, it has frequently been a serious and arduous undertaking for both the family in treatment and the therapist who works with them. This chapter's aim has been to provide the family therapist with some suggestions for making sessions more fun and less stressful for all involved.

Having fun in family therapy is not always possible, because some difficult cases involve violence, divorce, and substance abuse. However, even in such cases, the therapist can do much to alleviate stress, avoid traps which pull the therapist into the family system, and introduce some degree of enjoyment.

Our responsibility to the family is to create hope by whatever means possible. Therefore, our responsibility to ourselves as family therapists is to stay creative, alive, and vibrant. The best way to do this is to go have some fun.

References

Andolfi, M. (1979) *Family Therapy: An Interactional Approach*. New York: Plenum Press.

Ariel, S., C. Carel, and S. Tyano (1985) "Uses

of children's make-believe play in family therapy: Theory and clinical examples," *Journal of Marital and Family Therapy* 11: 47–60.

Bergman, J. S. (1985) *Fishing for Barracuda: Pragmatics of Brief Systemic Therapy*. New York: W. W. Norton.

Boardman, R., and L. Boardman (1983) *Family Happenings* [a game]. Kids in Progress, Inc.

Boscolo, L., et al. (1987) *Milan Systemic Family Therapy*. New York: Basic Books.

Cecchin, G. (1987) "Hypothesizing, circularity, and neutrality revisited: An invitation to curiosity," *Family Process* 26: 405–413.

Fay, A. (1978) *Making Things Better by Making Them Worse*. New York: Hawthorne Books.

Haley, J. (1987) *Problem Solving Therapy*, 2nd ed. San Francisco: Jossey-Bass.

Kottler, J. A. (1985) *On Being a Therapist*. San Francisco: Jossey-Bass.

Kramer, C. (1980) *Becoming A Family Therapist*. New York: Human Sciences Press.

Madanes, C. (1981) *Strategic Family Therapy*. San Francisco: Jossey-Bass.

——— (1984) *Behind the One-Way Mirror: Advances in the Practice of Strategic Therapy*. San Francisco: Jossey-Bass.

Minuchin, S. (1974) *Families and Family Therapy*. Cambridge, Mass.: Harvard University Press.

Minuchin, S., and H. Fishman (1986) *Family Therapy Techniques*. Cambridge, Mass.: Harvard University Press.

Papp, P. (1983) *The Process of Change*. New York: Guilford Press.

Sherman, R., and N. Fredman (1986) *Handbook of Structured Techniques in Marriage and Family Therapy*. New York: Brunner/Mazel.

Simon, F. B., H. Stierlin, and L. C. Wynne (1985) *The Language of Family Therapy: A Systemic Vocabulary and Sourcebook*. New York: Family Process Press.

Simon, R. (1985) "Take it or leave it: An interview with Carl Whittaker," *Family Therapy Networker* 9 (5): 26–41.

Webster's New Collegiate Dictionary (1979) Springfield, Mass.: Merriam.

Weeks, G. R., and L. L'Abate (1982) *Paradoxical Psychotherapy: Theory and Practice with Individuals, Couples, and Families*. New York: Brunner/Mazel.

SECTION TWO

Adolescence

Perhaps no other stage in the family life cycle presents such opportunity for change and growth as does adolescence. This section, comprised of four chapters, addresses issues and areas that are specific to adolescent concerns and development: the home, the school, and the self. Each chapter, written from a systemic point of view, integrates a cognitive-behavioral theoretical framework. In addition to a comprehensive examination of their subjects, the authors focus on the practical issues facing the adolescent and discuss related adjustment problems and diagnostic, assessment, and treatment issues.

Chapter 5, "Adolescents and Their Families: Systemic Considerations," by Frank Genovese, explores this life cycle stage and its most common treatment issues. He discusses horizontal and vertical life stressors, illustrating the need for system transformation at adolescence. Along with the developmental tasks involved in the adolescent's life, parents are usually also immersed in their own crisis—the mid-life one—at this time. In keeping with a three-generation orientation, there is also a transition between the parental and grandparental subsystems, since the grandparents are either dying or becoming older and possibly more dependent on their children. After a review of individuation and the three generations, Dr. Genovese presents implications for system transformation, along with an exploration of various treatment approaches.

Chapter 6, "Family Therapy with Adolescents in a School Situation," by Vita Bollman and Richard Shearman, centers on the adolescent who has remained in special education through elementary school and into high school. This is often a hostile, school-resistant adolescent whose parents feel and react in a similar fashion. The authors describe an integrated and in-depth Focused Family Counseling approach which they developed to address a wide range of adolescent school-related problems. Common problem areas—such as truancy, behavioral difficulties, and incomplete homework—for students in regular and special education classes are outlined. Operating within an integrated framework including behavioral, cognitive, dynamic, and systems approaches, the authors describe a multisystem model for concentrating the collective efforts and concern of clinicians, teachers, and parents on helping the student. In addition, they discuss methods for dealing with homeostatic resistance, setting up the model within a school system, and delivering intervention strategies, illustrated by a case presentation.

Chapter 7, "Treating the Family with an Adolescent with Family Art Therapy," by Shirley Riley, illustrates the dual challenge of dealing with a family that not only has an adolescent-centered problem, but is also arrested in its development as a whole. The family as a unit, along with all its individual members, are developmentally delayed and, consequently, are all behaving as though they were adolescents. These "adolescent families" are often headed by a single parent. Riley focuses on the major life cycle task confronting adolescents: individuating themselves from the family while at the same time maintaining healthy, supportive relationships with each member. When the parents are acting like adolescents themselves, problematic issues may arise which resemble issues also seen in alcoholic and violent families. Riley supplies a list of possible areas in which to intervene and appropriate strategies to use in treatment.

Chapter 8, "Family Therapy and Adolescent Sexuality," by Estelle Weinstein and Efrem Rosen, discusses how the adolescent's experience markedly affects his or her future capacity for sexual intimacy and the maintenance of interpersonal relationships. They present a two-stage model of adolescent sexuality; the development of sexual intimacy and the changes in the meaning of sexual behavior and intimate relationships; and the influence of the adolescent's peer group, family, sociocultural factors, and religious orientation. The authors also describe psychological implications, problems (e.g., sexual abuse, masturbation, sexual orientation issues, adolescent pregnancy, and sexually transmitted diseases), and issues (e.g., redefinition of parenting roles), along with the more typical reactions of the adolescent's parent to these changes and preventative strategies or therapeutic interventions that may be employed. The author's approach to this topic emphasizes a developmental, psychoeducational perspective.

CHAPTER FIVE

ADOLESCENTS AND THEIR FAMILIES: SYSTEMIC CONSIDERATIONS

Frank Genovese, Ph.D.

It would be difficult to raise a serious objection to Braulio Montalvo's (1988) assertion that,

> For the first half of this century our concept of adolescent problems pertained to inner hydraulics in disarray, or to social upheaval generated within a context of peers. Therapy for disturbed adolescents focused on individual dynamics or group treatment, and for the most part, did not take into serious consideration adolescents in relation to their families. Adolescent problems were regarded as due mostly to the internal difficulties inherent in the stage of life, and the family was seen mainly as a backdrop to the vicissitudes of personal development.

A survey of some of the handbooks and textbooks on adolescent psychology that were written before the ascendancy of the systemic paradigm supports Montalvo's position.

Of the four chapters in *Normal Adolescence* (Settlage 1968), published by the Committee on Adolescence of the Group for the Advancement of Psychiatry, none deal with systemic issues. *Adolescence: Psychology, Psychopathology, and Psychotherapy* (Miller 1974), *The Psychology of Adolescence: Essential Readings* (Esman 1975), and the *Handbook of Adolescent Psychology* (Adelson 1980) contain 20, 26, and 18 chapters, respectively. None directly address family issues.

Miller (1974), citing Blos, writes that "Adolescence can best be defined as a 'process of adaptation to puberty.' " Esman (1975) takes the position that "the scientific study of the psychology of adolescence is distinctly a product of the twentieth century, and can be said to coincide with the growth of psychoanalysis as a method of investigation and as a theoretical system." Addison (1980), in describing his work, states, "We begin with a group of conceptual essays, chapters devoted to adumbrating some of the important current perspectives in adolescent psychology—the historical, longitudinal, psychodynamic and biological approaches."

The relative paucity of theoretical essays and of papers which systemically describe therapeutic interventions with families of adolescents is not surprising. No one is prepared to pinpoint the birthday of family therapy, but many (e.g., Hoffman 1981; Nichols 1984) trace the beginnings of systemic thinking to the 1950s. The field is very young.

Of the various approaches which have gained legitimacy within the general family therapy paradigm, life cycle theory most easily accommodates itself to a systemic discussion of adolescence.

The concept that both families and individuals develop through a predictable series of stages was first suggested by Haley (1973) and Solomon (1973). Carter and McGoldrick (1980, 1988) have presented a highly articulated family life cycle paradigm, which posits that symptoms are most likely to occur when two sources of stress impact simultaneously on a system.

Carter and McGoldrick (1988) understand the term "family" to include the emotional system of at least three generations. A nuclear family and the individuals who comprise that family are heirs to family patterns, myths, secrets, and legacies. Stressors from this source are referred to as vertical ones because their impact is seen as echoing down through the generations.

Horizontal stressors are those which accompany the normative developmental demand placed on a system as it matures, and other, unexpected ones. Firings, deaths, and serious illnesses are examples of unexpected stressors.

If horizontal and vertical stressors intersect, the probability of the appearance of symptoms within the family increases. Carter and McGoldrick (1988) suggest that the birth of a child can be a stressful horizontal developmental task which will be made infinitely more difficult by the added impact of a vertical legacy that illuminates child-raising with a negative light.

Family Life Cycle: Implications for System Transformation in Adolescence

A family must undergo a fundamental transformation at adolescence (Carter and McGoldrick 1988). Parents (the second generation) can no longer expect to maintain complete autonomy over their children (the first generation). The boundary between the parental and adolescent subsystems becomes more permeable as the nature of the communication between these subsystems changes. The boundary around the entire nuclear family also becomes less rigid as the adolescents "open the family to a whole array of new values as they bring friends and new ideals into the family arena" (Preto 1988). Ideal boundaries are flexible enough to allow adolescents to move in and out, to experiment with their increasing independence. Even such an ideal developmental transition puts strain on the family system.

Mid-Life Crisis

Carter and McGoldrick (1988) point out that the emancipation of children is not the only developmental issue at work in most family systems during adolescence. They write, "The central event in the marital relationship is usually the 'midlife crisis' of one or both spouses, with an exploration of personal, career and marital satisfactions."

The recognition that the parental subsystem may be highly stressed at this time serves the clinician well. Presenting "adolescent" problems may represent a triangulation of the child in an attempt to detoxify the couple's issues. The authors are unambiguous in this regard: "There is usually an intense renegotiation of the marriage, and sometimes a decision to divorce. A focus on parent-adolescent complaints by either the family or the therapist may mask an affair or a secretly pondered divorce, or may prevent the marital problems from coming to the surface."

Parents and Grandparents

In keeping with their three-generation orientation, Carter and McGoldrick (1988) speak of the transition which commonly occurs at this time between the parental and grandparental subsystems. Typically, the grandparents are becoming frail. They are facing or have faced retirement, old age, illness, or death. The boundaries between the parental and grandparental subsystems must become flexible enough to allow the beginning of the shift toward "joint caring for the older generation."

Williamson (1983) describes the process by which the parental and grandparental subsystems become peers in his article "Coming of Age in the Fourth Decade." The similarities between the development tasks required of "coming of age" and those typically assigned to the adolescent-parental subsystems are substantial. Each appears to be a bench mark in the processes of separation-individuation (Mahler et al. 1975).

Williamson (1983) suggests that the second and third generations in a three-generation system are often collusively and reciprocally involved in the avoidance of "facing and renegotiating inter-generational politics."

Structurally, this collusion allows the grandparental subsystem to maintain inappropriate power with respect to the parental subsystem. As a result of this "very widespread" structural pattern, people in their forties still relate to a "Mommy and Daddy." The process permits both generations to deny the aging and approaching death of the grandparents. Denial serves an anxiety-reducing function for both generations.

A successful renegotiation of this hierarchical boundary leads to the establishment of peerhood between parents and grandparents and of "personal authority" for the members of both generations. By "personal authority" Williamson (1988) implies the ability to be intimate or not, more or less at will.

Individuation and Three Generations

Echoing a line of thinking that is gaining acceptance within the family therapy community, Williamson (1983) writes,

> Obviously, the purpose of intergenerational consultation includes helping clients to be and increasingly become different from their parents. However, it is also intended to enable clients to be comfortable with being the same as their parents, since this sameness is now chosen and, thus, authentic within the new self . . . *Experience suggests that a life lived in total commitment to differentiation of self will end in disappointment and despair. Differentiation of self as a way to self-fulfillment is inherently contradictory . . . Once an adult posture has been taken on the intergenerational stage it is not possible for the client ever again to talk to parents as a child . . . It may be that, because there is no way back, most people are fearful of taking the step forward.* (Emphasis mine.)

The remarkable similarities between the second-order, fundamental, and permanent change described here by Williamson, and that required for a successful transition at adolescence between the second and first generation, is mirrored by the common pitfall they share. Carter and McGoldrick (1988) write, "Families that become derailed at this stage (adolescence) may be rather closed to new values and threatened by them and they are frequently stuck in an earlier view of their children." At the time of adolescence, then, the three generations may be reciprocally reinforcing unrealistic conceptions of each other. Perhaps the confusion characteristic of the mid-life crisis is a reflection of another confusion: the one engendered as adults attempt to redefine boundaries, power hierarchies, roles, and rules with both their children and their own parents.

Preto (1988) reminds therapists that "All transformations threaten previous attachments," and "All change implies the acceptance of loss." From a life cycle perspective, then, any depressive reactions associated with the mid-life crisis may involve the loss of the previous relationship with both the first and third generations, as well as the loss of the parents' youth. While the potential for growth at mid-life is great, there is much to be mourned.

In her article Preto (1988) underscores the three-generational view of transformation. She writes,

> Adolescence demands structural shifts and renegotiation of roles in families involving at least three generations of relatives. Adolescent demands for more autonomy and independence tend to precipitate shifts in relationships across generations. . . . In families with adolescents, triangles generally involve the following players: the adolescent, the father, and the mother; the adolescent, a parent, and a grandparent; the adolescent, a parent, and a sibling; the adolescent, a parent, and the adolescent's friends.

Developmental Tasks

The primary developmental tasks of adolescence involve transformations around the issues of sexuality, identity, autonomy, and separation.

Changes brought on by the onset of puberty signal not only physical but also psychological development (Preto, 1988). Adolescents' self-concepts change with sexual maturity. This maturity also radically alters the way in which they are perceived by others. Preto suggests, "Coping with this upsurge in sexual thoughts, feelings and behaviors is a major task for all family members." Parents tend to worry about their daughters and wish to protect them from sexual exploration, rape, and unwanted pregnancy. They tend to be worried that their sons' increasing sexuality will distract them from their studies.

Preto (1988) reports, not surprisingly, that parents who are comfortable with their own sexuality are more comfortable with their adolescents' heightened sexuality, and are also better able to communicate this acceptance than those who are not. Open communication about sexual issues and the setting of appropriate limits increase the likelihood of the development of a positive sexual self-image. This probability is greatly decreased if the adolescents' sexuality is denied, ignored, or rejected.

An increase in incestuous impulses between the child and the opposite-sex parent is likely during adolescence. Preto (1988) suggests that some adolescent "obnoxious" behavior and some parental "difficult" behavior may be in the service of distancing and desexualizing the relationship.

In addition, struggles between adolescents and same-gender parents take on an increasingly competitive coloration. The heart of these conflicts lies in conflicting beliefs concerning what comprises appropriate gender roles. After repeating the often-cited research that, more than any other group, adolescents assume stereotypical sex-type behaviors, Preto (1988) writes, ". . . it seems natural that they (adolescents) would confront and challenge parental behavior that does not conform to their expectations."

Preto (1988) refers to the transformation of the self through the adoption of a new self-concept as the second major task of adolescence. She writes, "This self-structure undergoes its greatest transformation during adolescence . . ."

The author sees traditional developmental theories as incomplete, in that they are primarily based on studies of men. Preto (1988) supports the notion that females define their identity "more on the relationships and connections they make and maintain whereas males place the emphasis on separation and individuation." This creates a double bind for women in that society's depiction of the "ideal adult" is more similar to its depiction of the "ideal male" than to that of the "ideal female." Preto mentions a point sometimes overlooked by other theorists concerned with gender issues when she writes, "Male adolescents who do not have strong sex-typed identities may also experience more difficulty than their more 'masculine' counterparts."

This writer very strongly agrees with Preto's observation. He would add that he has observed in boys a very wide range along the affiliation-differentiation continuum.

Within the context of a caring, nonjudgmental relationship, a therapist may often find an "Alan Alda" effectively hidden by the public persona of "John Wayne." The Jungian concept of animus-anima is real and powerful.

McGoldrick (1988) makes a strong argument against sex-role typing. She writes, "For some reason there appear to be certain phases in development, including preschool and adolescence, when children seem to hold more rigidly to sex-role stereotypes—even more than their parents and teachers. It is important not to encourage this stereotyping, but to encourage girls especially to develop their own opinions, values, aspirations and interests."

Boys, too, must be free to develop without the restraints of stereotyping. Parenting should foster in both sexes the sort of "personal authority" (Williamson, 1983) which allows the freedom to be at some times more affiliative, and at others more differentiated.

In their 1985 article, Preto and Travis describe the third major developmental task of adolescence, the establishment of autonomy and separation. The authors begin the account with a repetition of the position that growth implies loss:

> Separation always involves some element of grieving. As children enter adolescence, their membership status in the family alters radically. As they increase and strengthen their alliances outside, their participation at home is often experienced by other family members as decreasing. . . . The transition from childhood to adolescence marks a loss for the family—the loss of the child. . . . Sometimes parents unable to cope with these transitions experience serious depression. Likewise, adolescents experience feelings of loss as they no longer enjoy the security and self-assuredness of childhood latency.

We are reminded by Williamson (1983) that many parents are simultaneously grieving the loss of a childlike relationship with their own parents. Many employ homeostatic mechanisms in a nonadaptive fashion to maintain previous patterns with both the generation which precedes them and the one which follows them.

Some Typical Family Patterns

Flexible boundaries are needed to allow adolescent swings between dependence and independence. Parents are described by Preto and Travis (1985) as in constant conflict, trying to distinguish "those behavioral choices (on the part of adolescents) which are merely unwise and self-defeating from those that are self-destructive, and even life threatening . . ."

The task of remaining in control while being objective and supportive "may be next to impossible" for parents in the face of open teenage rebellion. Nonetheless, rebellion can serve a positive developmental function if it enhances the processes of redefining rules, roles, and relationships.

The observation that rebellion can be debilitating in families who lack problem-solving and conflict-resolution skills can and should be expanded to include families in which the power hierarchy between the parental and adolescent subsystems is indistinct.

Within such systems, ". . . parents are likely to become overwhelmed and to respond by either attempting to control their adolescents arbitrarily or by giving up control completely." (Preto and Travis 1985). Either of these two patterns becomes more likely if the parents are dealing with their own issues of self-acceptance and self-esteem, or if conflict between the marital dyad is absorbed via triangulation with the adolescent.

The relatively common pattern in which parents attempt to maintain total control over their adolescents can have disastrous effects on the system.

Combrinck-Graham (1983) has suggested the concept of the family life spiral. This concept is useful in understanding the overcontrol pattern.

Life spiral thinking postulates that throughout the life cycle of a three-generational system there is a periodic, normative, nonpathologic, and continuous oscillation between appropriate positions of relative closeness and distance. She refers to those periods of natural and nonpathological enmeshment as "centripetal," and offers the birth of a child as an example. The periods of natural disengagement are considered "centrifugal." The terms "centripetal" and "centrifugal" are used in a completely different way from that found in the Beavers Systems Model (Beavers and Voeller 1983). Combrinck-Graham (1983) is speaking of the periodic swings from closeness to distance and back again which all families experience as the life cycle unfolds. The Beavers system uses "centripetal" and "centrifugal" to characterize a given family's preferred mode of interacting throughout its history, as compared to other families. Combrinck-Graham (1983) suggests that the time at which the first generation is going through adolescence, the second through the forties reevaluation, and the third through retirement is one of normal separation among generations.

If, within this milieu, parents attempt to overcontrol, serious symptomatic behavior may appear. Preto (1988) writes,

> This type of control is often seen in families where . . . centripetal forces operate

> to keep members from leaving the system. For instance, families that have experienced early losses and rejections tend to become overprotective, and parents may try to exert control by reinforcing excessive childlike behavior. The message is given that separation is dangerous . . . Members of families that are so tightly bound attempt to meet each other's needs, but fail to promote growth. As a result, adolescents may become stuck when they feel the urgency to grow, but stay home to meet the parents' needs. Parents experience a similar dilemma when fears of loss interfere with their attempts to help the children grow. The dilemma is often solved by adopting symptomatic behavior.

Another dysfunctional pattern related to separation is found in families who reach resolution via the early expulsion of the adolescent. Preto (1988) describes the ways in which overwhelmed parents may turn over authority to schools, courts, social agencies, etc., and how adolescents may run away or elope in order to effect premature separation. She writes, ". . . parents who were abused or neglected tend to abuse or neglect when they lose control and feel helpless. Especially when parents are emotionally disturbed or substance abusers, adolescents may be forced into premature autonomy."

Preto (1988) is correct when she states that "all change implies the acceptance of loss," and "early loss in a parent's history can make this stage difficult."

So much of what transpires as a family transforms at adolescence involves questions of separation, loss, and grief that it would be wise for the family therapist to become familiar with the literature of this subject. The works of Bowlby (1980) and Mahler et al. (1975) serve as examples.

Minuchin and Fishman (1981) have used the term *holon* for those structures within a system which are simultaneously both wholes and parts of wholes within the system. Individuals are seen by the authors as holons. They write, "The individual holon incorporates the concept of self-in-context. It includes the personal and historical determinants of self. But it goes beyond them to include the current input of the social context."

The works of authors such as Bowlby (1980) are of great value to the systems-oriented therapist if the individual is considered as a holon. The family therapist must also be aware of the bias toward idealizing the autonomous individual. Minuchin and Fishman (1981) state, "This bias has permeated the mental health field, extending even into the field of family therapy. Ronald Laing's concept of family politics demands that the individual be freed from his noxious family shackles . . . Murray Bowen's 'differentiation of self scale' . . . similarly highlights the 'struggle' between the individual and the family. When the individual is seen as being part of any larger whole, somehow she [*sic*] is seen as losing out." A consistent understanding of individual as holon should help minimize the effects of this bias on the family therapist's work.

Some Treatment Approaches

To deal with the conflicting demands of the parental and adolescent holons around the issue of autonomy, Minuchin and Fishman (1981) suggest a technique of "altering affiliation with conflicting subsystems" (p. 172). "The goal of the technique is to allocate in each subsystem a different and complementary expertise, so that instead of competing for hierarchy in the same context, family members explore new ways of relating in a larger frame." The example is given of a fifteen-year-old who feels his parents are too restrictive. The intervention involves supporting the adolescent in the belief that his room is his castle over which he should enjoy complete autonomy, while supporting the parents in their wish to have the boy go to school, be respectful, etc.

To families in which the adolescent and parental holons are enmeshed, the authors suggest the creation of boundaries. For example, the therapist may say, "In this room, I have only one rule. It is a small rule, but apparently very difficult for this family to follow. It is that no person shall talk for another person, or tell another person how this persons feels or thinks. People should tell their own story and their own memory" (p. 149).

Boundaries may also be created by asking the parents to join an adult observing group as adolescents work on a problem, "because children think differently . . . and may have solutions we couldn't even imagine" (p. 149). The therapist may support the parental executive function by asking the parents to give the adolescent a problem to solve, and discussing it with them when a solution has been reached (p. 149). Yet another boundary-making technique involves the spatial relationship within the consultation room. The authors write, "Changing the spatial relationships of family members in the session is a boundary-making technique that has the advantages of being nonverbal, clear, and intense." (p. 150). Variations of any of these techniques could be used with disengaged families as well.

Minuchin (1974) refers to the transitional difficulties of adolescence when he writes, "The parenting process differs depending upon the children's age. When children are very young, nurturing functions predominate. Control and guidance assume more importance later. As the child matures, especially during adolescence, the demands made by parents begin to conflict with the child's demands for age appropriate autonomy." (p. 58). To reflect the changed status of the adolescent, Minuchin suggests the structural move (p. 64):

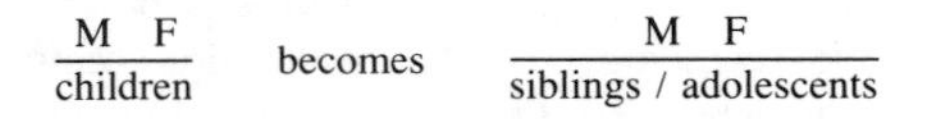

A variation on this move may also be applied with families in which the adolescent is locked in a rigid triad as the result of chronic stress within the parental holon (p. 102):

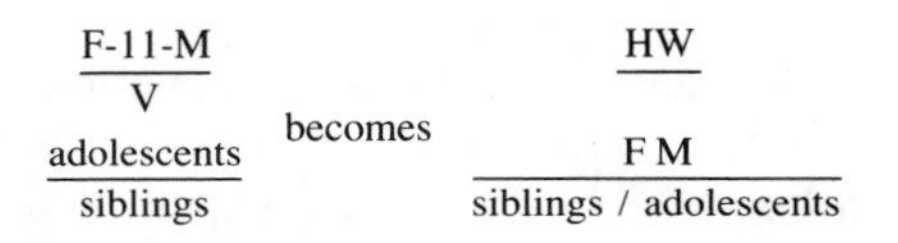

Minuchin also suggests holding individual sessions with adolescents to allow for "exploring issues autonomously and for establishing a relationship with a significant extrafamilial adult that would not be possible within the total family group" (p. 135).

In *Strategic Family Therapy* (1981), Cloe Madanes devotes three chapters to families whose presenting problems concern the behavior of children and adolescents.

Madanes takes the position that the symptomatic child assumes the role of "concerned benefactor or protector" within the family. As the parents focus on the child's problem, they are distracted from their own problems; as the parents try to help the child, they try to rise above their own difficulties.

Madanes contrasts her position to those of Haley, Minuchin, and Bowen. She understands Haley and Minuchin's work as reflecting the belief that "the child is typically thought of as involved in a coalition with one parent against the other parent, or with a grandparent or relative against a parent, or as involved in a conflict between the parents by providing the bond that holds the conflicting parents together. . . . This conflict is said to detour through the child." Bowen's work, as summarized by Madanes, holds that "The child's involvement in a family conflict (is) seen as the replication of family issues in a previous generation."

The differences between her approach and those of other theoretician-clinicians have very important implications in the choice of a therapeutic strategy. Madanes writes, "In this approach, instead of coming into the family ready to look for conflicts, coalitions, and adversaries, the therapist can look at the family in terms of helpfulness and caring."

In chapters four and five of *Strategic Family Therapy*, several therapeutic interventions are defined. Rich clinical examples are offered, illustrative of the techniques and the thinking which underlie Madanes's position. These chapters are highly recommended to any therapist who works with children, adolescents, and their families. The topics described in chapter four include several paradoxical techniques such as a request by the parents that the child have the problem; a request that the child pretend to have the problem; and a request that the child pretend to help the parent. Each of these strategies is designed to attend to the presenting problem and to resolve the hierarchical incongruity which places the child in the position of protecting the parents via symptomatic behavior.

In chapter 5 Madanes describes and illustrates techniques which address situations in which a child's problematic behavior is both a metaphoric expression and an attempted resolution of parental problems. Techniques are discussed which are designed to change the metaphoric action; provide a metaphor for success rather than for failure; and change the metaphorical solution.

In chapter 6 the author suggests a method of allowing a differential diagnosis between adolescent behaviors which serve a protective function within a family and those which reflect powerlessness on the part of the parents. She writes,

> In this author's opinion, when the case involves a first break, a first criminal offense, or a few drug episodes, the therapist should carefully consider whether these behaviors have a protective function in the family: Is the youth expressing metaphorically a parents' problem? Are his acts self-sacrificing? In the more chronic cases, where there have been rehospitalizations or several encounters with law enforcement agencies, the therapist should think mainly in terms of the hierarchical reversal—the power that the youth has over the parents—and focus on understanding the problem from the point of view of how the youth's disturbing acts contribute to maintaining that power.

A family that enters therapy as a result of severe behavioral problems is a family with a long history of incongruity within its power hierarchy. The problems referred to here include "aggressive or self-destructive acts, abuse of drugs or alcohol, bizarre communication, and extreme apathy or depression. With such families the long-standing hierarchical incongruity is maintained by repetitive cyclical interactions. Such a situation calls for a single coherent approach to therapy: the focus of therapy is to restructure the family in a way which ensures that the parents are consistently in a superior power position vis-à-vis the youth. She writes, "[The recommended approach] is intended to be more rigid and less open to variation than the other approaches presented. . . . A certain rigidity of method prevents the therapist from being overwhelmed when there are issues of hospitalization, social control and impending chronicity."

Madanes notes some similarities between families with these more serious problems and those who experience less intense difficulties. For example, in both families the parents' attempt to deal with the problem ensures that they will rise above their own problems. However, in more disturbed families, the power wielded by the adolescent is tyrannical. It threatens the parents and renders them powerless. The meta-communication from the youth takes the form that any attempt at control on the part of the parents will result in the youth doing something very serious. Madanes writes, "The youth might passively threaten that if he is stressed he will go crazy or take drugs or harm himself in some way, or he might physically attack the parents. The parents become unable to attempt to change the young person's behavior because they are afraid that they will cause him harm or that he will harm them."

The incongruity lies in the fact that in one sense the youth is incompetent and dependent upon the parents for his or her survival needs, while in another sense the youth dominates the parents through threats.

In Madanes's view, there exist in such families two power hierarchies, which are incongruous yet function simultaneously. The situation sets up a paradox: how can one be in charge while simultaneously dominated by the others?

With regard to etiology, the author suggests that the child may have originally wielded power in the service of the beneficent functions of protecting or holding the parents together. Over time, the patterns of communication and the roles spawned by the incongruous hierarchies have become chronic, and now function independently of whatever systemic factors occasioned their emergence.

Madanes (1981) writes,

> It is possible . . . to assume that the only (current) function of the disturbing behavior of the youth is the exploitative power derived from it. . . . Whether the youth's behavior originally had a protective function, whether it was meant to prevent a separation between the parents, or whether it was related only to a bid for power is quite irrelevant. The issue is that, to solve the problem, the hierarchy must be restored to one in which the youth does not dominate the parents through helplessness and abuse.

Therapy is predicated on the concept that hierarchies are defined by the pattern of communication sequences. The therapist encourages only those sequences in which the parents communicate as equals with one another in deciding what to demand from the youth. All other patterns are blocked. Madanes (1981) writes,

> Most of the work in the therapy of these families consists in arranging a hierarchy in which the parents are in a superior position to their offspring. The parents must state explicitly what they expect the young person to be doing. . . . The parents should reach agreement on these expectations, which must be phrased as rules for the young person. These rules should be as specific and practical as possible, and consequences should be set if these rules are not followed. Discussion of rules and consequences are the basic work of the therapy.

Parents often contrive to avoid taking a power position. They do so by employing three mechanisms.

"Communicating that the parent is not qualified to participate in the therapy because he cannot occupy an executive position in the hierarchy" is the first of these moves. What follows are some examples of this class of behavior and Madanes's suggested therapeutic responses.

Discussions are also included concerning the therapeutic response to the questions of hospitalization and threats of suicide. The interested reader is referred to chapter 6 of Madanes's impressive work.

In his book *Treating Troubled Adolescents*, Fishman (1988) outlines a therapeutic approach which draws heavily on many issues discussed by other authors. While his concept of the homeostatic "maintainer" is by no means unique, Fishman places great emphasis on its importance.

The maintainers are those homeostatic forces which act in a detrimental way to maintain the status quo. The maintainer keeps the system from changing despite the developmental imperative to grow. He writes, "The family therapist uses the concept of the homeostatic maintainers by attempting to render ineffective the family's stereotyped, stable ways of responding."

After identifying the person or persons who are encouraging the homeostasis, the therapist defines the therapeutic unit as that subsystem which includes the homeostatic maintainer: "Family systems can be like Chinese boxes: individuals are part of a family, which is part of an extended family, which is part of a community, and so forth. The job of the therapist is to identify and focus on the 'box' that may hold the homeostatic maintainer and then treat this unit as the family system."

Fishman's (1988) approach seems as valuable to all forms of family therapy as it is to therapy addressed to adolescent systems. Perhaps his major contributions to therapists engaged in working with families with adolescents is his identification of the most common dysfunctional patterns found in adolescent systems. These include conflict avoidance, complementary and symmetrical schizogenesis, enmeshment, rigidity, and overprotectiveness.

Fishman (1988) lists boundary making, enactment, unbalancing, reframing, and searching for competence as the key techniques to employ when working with adolescents and their families. Fishman warns therapists that it is their responsibility to ensure that the emotional intensity of sessions exceeds the family's threshold. "Below this threshold the family may simply deflect or assimilate information without really getting the message."

Breunlin's (1983) article is highly therapeutically informative, and theoretically very provocative. The author points out that the dominant theoretical position concerning the nature of life cycle transitions is that they result from discontinuous, irreversible second-order change: once a family makes a leap to a new organization, it cannot return to its previous state.

This is the position taken by Hoffman (1988). She proposes a "natural history" for discontinuous change:

> First the patterns that have kept the family system in a steady state relative to its environment begin to work badly. New conditions arise for which these patterns were not designed. Ad hoc solutions are tried, and sometimes work, but usually have to be abandoned. Irritation grows over small but persisting difficulties. The accumulation of dissonance eventually forces the entire system over an edge, into a state of crisis, as the homeostatic tendency brings

Figure 5.1: Therapeutic Responses to Parental Avoidance of Authority

Parents' Behavior	Therapeutic Response
1. Saying that the problem should be solved by some expert, e.g., a psychiatrist, physician, therapist, etc.	1. Therapist relabels the problem to place it in the arena of parental, not expert, authority. Labels the child as misbehaving, confused, childish, rebellious, in need of guidance. Does not use words such as mental illness, schizophrenia, emotional problems, psychological conflicts.
	1a. Relabels inappropriate behavior: Apathy becomes laziness; addicted behavior, choice.
2. Saying that they do not know what expectations they should have of their child's behavior.	2. States and restates the goal of therapy. "I know it's difficult, but he got into trouble because he was confused. So you must be very clear with him. "What I'm driving at are very simple, concrete guidelines. Can he break furniture in your house?"
2a. Using phrases which have no meaning, e.g., "I want him to be good."	2a. "That's a reasonable expectation, but does it mean that he can hit you?"
3. Turns to youth for advice or "Whatever is best for him" or "Whatever he wants from life," etc.	3. Emphasizes that he can be in control of self only when behaving properly. Points out to youth that predictability will make life easier.
4. Youth acts out wildly as parents begin to form a coalition. Attempts to disrupt the parents' conversation.	4. Quiets the youth or asks the parents to do so.
5. Parents give authority to youth and depower themselves by threatening to expel youth.	5. Emphasizes that separation is appropriate only after youth is behaving competently and when parents know and approve of where he will live.
5a. One of the parents threatens separation and divorce if the other will not expel youth.	5a. Returns parents to power by insisting that the expulsion be put off until it is properly planned and until it is used not as a punishment but as a step forward for the youth with the agreement of both parents.

"Parent disqualifies other parent" is the second of this class of behaviors.

Parents' Behavior	Therapeutic Response
1. One parent disqualifies the other as incompetent based on past events.	1. Insists that this is a new situation, that now the therapist is available for help.
	1a. Reframes the disqualification; weakness becomes sensitivity; harshness becomes a desperate attempt to provide clear guidance.

(*Continued on next page*)

Figure 5.1: *(Continued)*

Parents' Behavior	Therapeutic Response
2. Parents state that they cannot work together because of widely different views of what is appropriate.	2. Again emphasizes that this is a new experience.
	2a. Insists that each communicate to the other through the therapist if an argument occurs.
	2b. Reframes the behavior of the disqualifier: a critical person becomes supportive.
	2c. Ignores the disqualification.

"Parent disqualifies therapist" is the third manifestation.

Parents' Behavior	Therapeutic Response
1. Suggests that the therapist is incompetent.	1. Briefly describes qualifications without interpreting parents' suggestion as an attempt to deflect.
2. Cites contradictory expert opinion.	2. States awareness of different positions and that the therapist does not agree with some.
3. Cites previous failures in therapy.	3. Emphasizes the newness of the present situation.
	3a. Suggests that the approach be tried for a limited time, after which a decision can be made.

on ever intensifying corrective sweeps that get out of control. The end point of what cybernetic engineers call a "runaway" is either that the system breaks down, that it creates a new way to monitor the same homeostasis, or that it simultaneously takes a leap to an integration that will deal better with the changed field.

Breunlin (1988) writes,

> The clinical implications of this life cycle model are considerable, because conceptually the therapist is organized to plan the therapy in such a way as to produce a second order change through a discontinuous leap. Not surprisingly, much of the literature concerning therapy based on this model places a heavy emphasis on the use of paradoxical strategies. . . . The net result is an elegant theory on which are based sophisticated interventions that frequently produce dramatic outcomes.

Breunlin (1983) proposes a therapy congruent with a different view of the nature of transitional change, one which understands change as occurring in stages and as vulnerable to forces aimed at undoing the change.

The author presents a four-stage approach to therapy aimed at developmental transitions, based on the work of Haley (1973, 1976, 1981). Although there may be some overlap during the actual course of therapy, Breunlin (1983) sees engaging the family, unbalancing the family, dealing with the consequences of change, and normalizing family functioning as the four stages.

In describing the process of unbalancing the family, Breunlin (1983) echoes a theme from Fishman's (1988) article: therapy is not a gentle, intellectual endeavor; the interventions must be sufficiently powerful to break the developmental impasse; success "requires absolute conviction on the part of both the parents and the therapist."

The author offers several examples of successful clinical interventions so powerful that they may properly be considered ordeals for the families. In one family which included an encorpretic child, "the mother was instructed to have nothing to do with the cleanup procedures. The child continued to soil and tried to reengage the mother by smearing feces on his hands and bringing them to the mother until the mother handed them back, stating to the child in no uncertain terms that they belonged to him and he had to be responsible for the cleanup." If therapy is not unsettling, at least at times, it is not therapy.

Unlike those theorists who view transitional change as discontinuous, Breunlin takes the position that no change takes place without some negative consequences, and these consequences can lead to the undoing of the change. Therefore, successful therapy must address the negative forces which result from the changes achieved through the unbalancing process: ". . . it is not enough to say that the benefit of change will be self-reinforcing or that change itself is permanent because it is irreversible." Breunlin (1983) names regret, anger, fear, and once again, mourning as the negative consequences of change which threaten the success of therapy.

Many other authors have addressed the treatment of families-at-adolescence.

Therapists interested in involving all three generations in therapy can find in the article an outline of how Williamson (1983) conducts his therapy. In addition, Ingersoll-Dayton et al. (1988) describe the intergenerational approaches of Bowen, Boszormenyi-Nagy and Spark, Framo, and Whitaker. Within the specific context of the agencies at which the research was carried out, the authors found that a therapy involving grandparents outside the session was preferable to therapy in which the grandparents were involved in session. Hoverstadt et al. (1985) present and discuss the Family-of-Origin Scale, which may be a useful adjunct for therapists who employ a multigenerational approach.

Karpel and Strauss's (1983) observation that both the adolescent and the parents are aware, at some level, of the losses associated with growth once again raises the issue of mourning as a possible reaction to transformation. They write, "While it often appears as though the struggle is between adolescent and parent, with the adolescent wanting freedom and the parent resisting it, a closer look suggests that this is only part of the picture. Not surprisingly, both parties are considerably more ambivalent. Parents may be torn between their urges to hold onto the child and to see him or her grow up and away, just as the adolescent may be torn between urges to grow out of the family and to remain in it as a child."

Those who work with adolescents know that they can be notoriously "resistant" clients. Karpel and Strauss (1983) provide some very helpful therapeutic strategies for dealing with "functionally mute" teenagers.

Much of the literature on adolescent systems focuses on specific problems. What follows is a small sampler.

Running away and acting out are dealt with from a systemic point of view by

Palenski and Launer (1987) and Frager (1985). Hall (1987) reviews parent-adolescent conflict.

Husain and Vandever (1984) and Patros and Shamoo (1988) have written books dealing with depression and suicide in children and adults. Both contain chapters focusing on family issues. Patros and Shamoo present a detailed school-based program for prevention, intervention, and postvention. Pravander et al., in the *Handbook of Adolescents and Family Therapy* (1985), devote chapters to anorexia nervosa and bulimia, substance abuse, the effects of divorce, adolescent psychosis, suicide, and running away. In addition chapters are included which deal with issues pertaining to the practice of family therapy in various settings. Schaefer et al. (1984) have provided their *Family Therapy Techniques for Problem Behaviors of Children and Teenagers* with an annotated bibliography which discusses conduct disorders, impulsive-aggressive behaviors, fire setting, noncompliance, running away, delinquency, drug abuse, psychosomatic disorders, anorexia nervosa, school phobia, suicide, schizophrenia, elective muteness, incontinence, obsession-compulsion, divorce, handicaps, and crisis intervention. Finally, Fishman (1988) discusses delinquency, running away, violence, incest, suicide, the effects of disability, the single-parent family, and couples therapy. With respect to this last issue, Fishman writes, "The core conflict that sustains most family difficulties can be traced to a profound split between the mother and father." To estimate the magnitude of the concept-expanding effect of the systemic paradigm, the reader is invited to compare this last quotation to those cited in the opening paragraphs of this chapter.

References

Adelson, J. (1980) *Handbook of Adolescent Psychology*. New York: John Wiley.

Beavers, W. R., and M. N. Voeller (1983) "Family models: Comparing and contrasting the Olson circumplex model with the Beavers systems model," *Family Process* 24: 85–97.

Bowlby, J. (1980) *Attachment and Loss*, vol. 3—*Loss* New York: Basic Books.

Breunlin, D. C. (1983) "Therapy in stages: A life cycle view," in H. Liddle, ed., *Clinical Implications of the Family Life Cycle*, in J. Hansen, ed., *The Family Therapy Collections*. Rockville, Md: Aspen Systems.

Carter, B., and M. McGoldrick, eds. (1980) *The Changing Family Life Cycle: A Framework for Family Therapy*. New York: Gardner Press.

——— (1988) *The Changing Family Life Cycle: A Framework for Family Therapy*, 2nd ed. New York: Gardner Press.

Combrinck-Graham, L. (1983) "The family life cycle and families with young children," in Liddle, *Clinical Implications of the Family Life Cycle*, in Hansen, *The Family Therapy Collections*.

Esman, H. (1975). The Psychology of Adolescence: Essential Readings. New York: International Universities.

Fishman, H. C. (1988). *Treating Troubled Adolescents: A Family Therapy Approach*. New York: Basic Books.

Frager, A. R. (1985). "A family systems perspective on acting out," *Social Casework* 66 (3): 167–76.

Haley, J. (1973) *Uncommon Therapy: The Psychiatric Techniques of Milton Erickson*. New York: W. W. Norton.

——— (1976) *Problem Solving Therapy*. New York: Harper Colophon.

——— (1980) *Leaving Home*. New York: McGraw-Hill.

Hall, J. A. (1987) "Parental-adolescent conflict: An empirical review," *Adolescence* 22 (88): 767–89.

Hansen, J., ed. (1983) *The Family Therapy Collections*. Rockville, Md: Aspen Systems.

Hoffman, L. (1981) *Foundations of Family Therapy: A Conceptual Framework for Change*. New York: Basic Books.

——— (1988) "The family life cycle and discontinuous change," Carter and McGoldrick, *The Changing Family Life Cycle,* 2nd ed.

Hoverstadt, A. J., et al. (1985) "A family of origin scale," *Journal of Marital and Family Therapy* 11: 287–97.

Husain, S. A., and T. Vandever (1984) *Suicide in Children and Adolescents*. New York: S. P. Medical and Scientific Books.

Ingersoll-Dayton, B., B. Arnat, and D. Stevens (1988) "Involving grandparents in family therapy," *Social Casework* 69 (5): 280–339.

Karpel, M. A., and E. S. Strauss (1983) *Family Evaluation*. New York: Gardner Press.

Madanes, C. (1981) *Strategic Family Therapy*. San Francisco: Jossey-Bass.

Mahler, M. S., F. Pine, and A. Bergman (1975) *The Psychological Birth of the Human Infant*. New York: Basic Books.

McGoldrick, M. (1988) "Women and the family cycle," in Carter and McGoldrick, *The Changing Family Life Cycle,* 2nd ed.

McGoldrick, M., and F. A. Walsh (1983) "A systemic view of family history and loss," in L. Wolberg and M. Aronson, eds., *Group and Family Therapy—1983*. New York: Brunner/Mazel.

Miller, D. (1974) *Adolescence: Psychology, Psychopathology and Psychotherapy*. New York: Jason Aronson.

Minuchin, S. (1974) *Families and Family Therapy*. Cambridge, Mass.: Harvard University Press.

Minuchin, S., and H. C. Fishman (1981) *Family Therapy Techniques*. Cambridge, Mass.: Harvard University Press.

Montalvo, B. (1988) "Foreword", in H. C. Fishman, *Treating Troubled Adolescents: A Family Therapy Approach*. New York: Basic Books.

Nichols, M. (1984) *Family Therapy: Concepts and Methods*. New York: Gardner Press.

Palenski, J. E., and H. M. Launer (1987) "The 'process' of running away: A redefinition," *Adolescence* 22 (85): 347–62.

Patros, P. G., and T. K. Shamoo (1988) *Depression and Suicide in Children and Adolescents*. Boston: Allyn & Bacon.

Preto, N. (1988) "Transformation of the family system in adolescence," in *The Changing Family Life Cycle*.

Preto, N., and N. Travis (1985) "The adolescent phase of the family life cycle," in M. Mirkin and S. Koman *Handbook of Adolescents and Family Therapy*. Boston: Allyn & Bacon.

Schaefer, C. E., J. M. Breismeister, and M. E. Fitton (1984) *Family Therapy Techniques for Problem Behaviors of Children and Teenagers*. San Francisco: Jossey-Bass.

Settlage, C. F. (1968) *Normal Adolescence*. New York: Charles Scribner's Sons.

Solomon, M. (1973) "A developmental conceptual premise for family therapy," *Family Process* 12: 179–188.

Williamson, D. S. (1983) "Coming of age in the fourth decade" in Liddle, *Clinical Implications of the Family Life Cycle,* in Hansen, *The Family Therapy Collections*.

CHAPTER SIX

FAMILY THERAPY WITH ADOLESCENTS IN A SCHOOL SITUATION

Vita Bollman, M.S.W., *and* Richard Shearman, Ph.D.

The 5-Percent Problem

Sam was an eighteen-year-old "senior" taking ninth grade English for the fifth time. He didn't pass it. Sam dropped out of school yet again.

Every school has its Sams. One administrator says, "Ninety-five percent of our time is spent on 5 percent of the students." There are students who do not seem to improve no matter what the school does. Detentions, resource rooms, principal's hearings, remedial reading, parent conferences, self-contained special education classes, in-school suspension, weekly progress reports all bear fruit only temporarily, if at all. The situation appears hopeless. Staff members become pessimistic. The student may be written off as a "dirtbag" or a "loser."

Placement in a self-contained special education class is, by law and in fact, utilized when other less restrictive measures have failed. In some cases, especially in elementary school, it is effective. However, in other cases it is just one more unsuccessful "solution," and the feeling of pessimism persists.

In principle, the objective of special education is to return the student to the mainstream. This occurs in a significant number of cases. But for students who reach secondary school and remain in—or are then placed in—special education, there is often a feeling of futility, anger, and bitterness. Their resistant and often blatantly hostile behavior does nothing to increase their chances for success and makes it very hard for the special education teacher to teach and for other students to learn. Many of these students behave in contradictory ways, on one hand claiming that if they were just given a chance they could easily succeed in the mainstream, while on the other, behaving both in the special education classroom and in the rest of the school in ways that clearly signal their dysfunction. Because they so often require more time and patience than average students and because many of them, by their actions, clearly do not fit in, they are allowed by tacit and mutual agreement of both student and school to withdraw into the self-contained classroom. For the student who is ostensibly unhappy there, the classroom is at least familiar, and the rest of the school has one less troubling drain on its resources. Reducing the number of outside interactions with students simplifies things immensely for the classroom teacher, but at the same time the role of special education as a bridge to the outside, mainstream world is thwarted.

Learning disability is the predominant classification, but emotional problems are also rife in the special education classroom. Some students are identified and classified as emotionally disturbed, but it is the rare secondary level special education student who does not manifest nonacademic interferences with learning. Years of frustration in school intensify the student's feeling that he is "stuck" in special education, and this can arouse resistance or despair. (Regardless of the official label, special education classes are often referred to by both regular and special education students as "retard" classes, and the minibus that transports special class students is called the "tart cart.")

Not only do special education students feel banished, they are also abandoned by staff members outside of special ed who feel that these students are now being taken care of by specialists and are no longer a concern of the larger school. This can cause special education teachers to feel almost as isolated as their students.

The two of us, psychologist Shearman (R.W.S.) and special education teacher Bollman (V.B.), started at Berner High School in the same year. Each of us had considerable prior experience working with young people. As a classroom teacher of learning disabled and emotionally disturbed adolescents, V.B. had experienced many years of frustration and an ever-increasing awareness of the difficulties of working with students without their families' involvement and cooperation. It became apparent very early that the chances of effecting genuine change were heightened when at least one family member was successfully engaged. Hostile, school-resistant youngsters often had hostile, school-resistant parents who undermined, consciously or not, any efforts to win the student's attention and cooperation. This realization led to V.B.'s spending an increased amount of time trying to involve families. After school hours, evenings, and weekends were often filled with telephone conversations with parents, who were not then at work and could talk more comfortably. The considerable time this took proved worthwhile, because engaged parents, once they understood and supported the efforts on their child's behalf, helped to reduce the youngster's reluctance and negativism in the classroom.

As a psychologist working in a school for the first time, R.W.S. had a strong need to continue developing effective intervention procedures, and to continue working with families and with colleagues regardless of their professional affiliations. Our complementary needs led us to form a working relationship which has continued for eleven years. Our first efforts focused on the student alone, and were usually precipitated by some classroom event—e.g., verbal or physical abuse directed toward a classmate or teacher. We would meet with the student, carefully making these contacts low-key, direct, and laced with humor. While pulling no punches, we reminded the student that our very presence at the meeting testified to our concern and caring. When student contact alone did not work, we contacted the parents by telephone and eventually invited them to meet with us and the student. From this evolved the model we present here, which we call Focused Family Counseling.

Focused Family Counseling (FFC) applies to the range of school-based problems not primarily caused by lack of ability. These included attendance difficulties, disciplinary situations, and failure to complete schoolwork and homework. FFC is applicable in regular and special education settings from elementary school through high school. The present description is set in a secondary school.

On the Shoulders of Giants

Lasers cut through steel by focusing enormous power on a tiny spot. Focused Family Counseling operates analogously. The failure of the school's corrective measures indicates a need for more powerful intervention. The *power* comes from the concern and effort of people with a strong interest in the student's welfare (parents, school staff, outside agencies, and the student). The *focus* is achieved by gathering these concerned people in a short series of meetings devoted to limited, though ambitious, ends.

This model is not new. It draws on several major currents in contemporary counseling and psychotherapy and integrates them into a practical approach which has been effective in our school. The model is constantly evolving; each new case introduces challenges, successes, and failures which affect our approach to the next case.

FFC is eclectic. It uses behavioral, cognitive, dynamic, family, and short-term therapies. Carl Rogers (1951) stressed respect for the client as the authority on his own life. Ivan Boszormenyi-Nagy articulated multidirectional partiality—i.e., taking sides with everyone at one time or another (Boszormenyi-Nagy and Krasner 1986). Milton Erickson and Jay Haley stressed family hierarchies, a developmental view of family life, home assignments, constructive use of therapist power, and openness to unorthodox techniques (Haley 1973, 1977; Zeig 1982). The Mental Research Institute in Palo Alto articulated the concept that people's solutions become the problems they present to therapists (Fisch, Weakland, and Segal 1982). Steve deShazer (1985) and Joel Bergmann (1985) are among the many family therapists who propose and demonstrate brief treatment methods. A method of brief psychodynamic psychotherapy has also been developed by Davanloo (1980) and bases its powerful intervention techniques on analytic conceptualizations. Behaviorists such as Goldfried and Davison (1976) present behavior altering concepts and techniques using small steps, behavior monitoring, and contingency management. The behaviorist believes in doableness. Other sources include Minuchin and Perls (Minuchin and Fishman 1981; Perls, Hefferline, and Goodman 1951). But these concepts and ideas are not the sole possession of the people credited, nor are their contributions limited to these citations. Our operating concepts and techniques include these and many more, whose origins are now obscured, which have become integrated into our style. To all the named and unnamed giants upon whose shoulders we stand, we give credit.

FFC is an integrative approach drawing from these sources worked into a reasonably consistent model. Among the integrationists we particularly wish to acknowledge the Wachtels and Boszormenyi-Nagy (Wachtel and Wachtel 1986; Boszormenyi-Nagy and Krasner 1986). Our approach is also evolving. Each case offers challenges and lessons that nourish our planning and action in future cases.

Although they are not sources drawn upon us in formulating FFC, two recent presentations in school psychology journals include similar concepts. Conoley argues for effective partnerships between schools and families, and provides an extensive bibliography to support her procedures. Hughes reviews a British book, *The Family and the School: A Joint Systems Approach to Problems with Children*, edited by Dowling and Osborne, whose approach is much like ours and whose method is at one point referred to as "focused family consultation" (Conoley 1982).

Philosophical Foundations

Our philosophical foundations lie in three areas. We have a model for normal functioning of humans and their families, a model for growth and change, and a model for intervention.

Our model of normal human functioning is actually our own cognitive map of reality. People need to act and react to things as they "really are" instead of indulging in wishful thinking, avoidance, unrelenting attack, or other strategies that maintain or exacerbate problems. A model of reality can involve extensive philosophical explication. Here we will simply say that we believe some major elements of healthy functioning include moderation, maintenance of basic functions (e.g., eating, having shelter), addressing and satisfactorily resolving issues raised in the life stages of the individual and the family, learning effective problem-solving strategies, developing and maintaining satisfying interpersonal relationships, learning how to work and use one's resources effectively, and learning to function within and to respect hierarchies.

Growth and Change

Problems are opportunity's squeaking wheels, nature's smoke alarms, warning us of what might happen if we don't act. In the FFC approach, problems are reframed as opportunities and are welcomed as providing a chance for staff to succeed where others have failed.

Individuals, families, and schools are relatively homeostatic, but small changes in root areas (e.g., beginning to see a youngster as insufficiently developed to study nightly, instead of as willfully refusing or disinterested) can generate larger changes in time.

Hopes and aspirations are two-edged swords. They inspire striving, but if they are unrealistically high, they can doom to discouragement. "Perfect is the enemy of good."

People act in accordance with their world view, their subjective reality. They move within the borders of their cognitive maps. If their views or maps are altered, they may seek different routes to their goals ("I'll go around these mountains which weren't on my original map;" "Instead of copying test answers from Charlie, I'll study myself") or change destinations ("I'd rather go fishing on the Delaware River than go to Disney World"; "I want a high school diploma more than I want to cut twelfth grade English twice a week.") Changes in cognitions and perception often lead to behavioral change.

As individuals grow and mature, their cognitive (and affective) maps become more extensive (cover a larger field) and more detailed and accurate within the field they cover. Therapy exposes people to such broadening experiences.

People, like flowers, do not thrive in hostile environments. Many people, out of their own suspicion and defensiveness, perceive or elicit hostility or indifference from others. One primary concern of therapy is to evoke an environment that allows openness to growth.

Intervention Model

There are four essential elements of our intervention model: relationship, problem-focused intervention, system/cognitive map revision, and sharing of responsibility. Only a few of the myriad specific intervention techniques adopted from the many theorists who have influenced us are actually used in any particular case. We will first discuss the intervention model and later the specific interventions.

We are presenting the way in which we were able to integrate and adapt available ideas to forge a reasonably effective tool for use in a secondary school, and we are presenting the conceptual framework which we now and in retrospect use as our own cognitive map for effective intervention.

Relationship

Without relationship, nothing. *Relationship* here means the bond connecting school personnel, student, and family. Its specifics include a reasonable degree of liking, respect, and shared belief that improvement in the situation is worth trying for. The families involved in FFC are those in which the student and/or family have been unresponsive to the usual school interventions. Many of these are difficult families—families who relate poorly to outsiders, who are resistant to change, who are markedly dysfunctional, etc. They resemble the difficult families that Joel Bergman describes in *Fishing for Barracuda*, and we, like Bergman, try to "capture the family" (Bergman 1985). Sometimes we also have to capture staff members whose commitment to the student or to the possibility of change is marginal. The success of our next three stages depends on our ability to elicit trust, liking, and hope, as indicated by therapy research studies such as Strupp's. He concluded, "Therapy tended to be successful if by the third session the patient felt accepted, understood and liked by his therapist" (Strupp, as cited in Squires 1986).

Problem-Focused Intervention

The elicitation of hope has many positive consequences, including increased effort, movement toward positive instead of negative expectations, improved physiological functioning, and other benefits frequently described today in the popular press (e.g., *Psychology Today, American Health*) and in the professional literature. When students and their families experience an elimination of habitual tardiness, improved grades, or telephone calls from school reporting good behavior instead of another disruptive outburst, they begin to believe that all is not hopeless. We want to instill that hope in staff members as well, to encourage them to put forth effort for the targeted student.

Solving a vexing problem with the student achieves several ends. It elicits hope, enhances willingness (of student, family, and school) to try more demanding tasks, establishes the credibility of the school staff as effective, strengthens the working relationship between school and home, opens students and parents to influence by the school, and makes them less likely to evade responsibility by blaming the school. Consequently, as we establish the working relationship with the family, we also move in on the identification and formulation of a suitable immediate problem.

An appropriate problem is relevant, solvable, and can be behaviorally stated.

The most relevant problem is apt to be the one that occasioned the FFC meeting—e.g., repeated truancy, failure to complete the schoolwork, or obnoxious behavior. However, if exploring the problem reveals no solution within reasonable reach (for example, if the parents appear minimally capable of following through on a controlled wake-up routine), the problem should be redefined or another problem selected, one that does promise success. Finally, the problem should be stated behaviorally so that it is clear when and if it is solved.

During the exploration with the family to select the problem for immediate intervention, all family members are asked to give their views, negative opinions are respectfully noted, reluctant participants are asked if they can cooperate on the selected problem, and a consensus is established. This step, of course, is part of the relationship building, and here, as throughout, specific intervenor statements, questions, or interventions are directed toward multiple objectives. In addition, the four major foci are not pursued sequentially, but are interwoven. Broadly speaking, relationship comes first, specific problem intervention second, system/cognitive map alteration third, and shared responsibility with the family permeates all.

System/Cognitive Map Alteration

As we establish both the therapeutic relationship and the problem focus, we also examine the individual's and the family's views of the world, to identify any dysfunctional beliefs or strategies. These, too, are objects of intervention, because change here may result in significant modification of the individual's and the family's functioning by modifying the faulty premises which lead to maladaptive behavior. Some examples of dysfunctional strategies are secretiveness, manipulativeness, dictatorial parenting, excessive deference to children's desires, and use of threats to influence behavior. These actions are generally taken in the interest of "good" as perceived by the actor, and are solutions to perceived problems. However, as proposed by the Mental Research Institute, these solutions often become a significant part of the problem, as when harsh parental discipline provokes increasingly violent rebellion by a teenager, or when perfectionism creates discouragement because adequate achievement is impossible (Weakland, Fisch, and Segal 1982). To combat the maladaptive functioning of the family, we teach or elicit active, appropriate coping. We move toward our ideal of reality-based functioning and away from maladaptive extremes, such as being too active or too passive.

Sharing Responsibility with Student and Family

We believe that our success comes not only from the above three goals, but from another goal that pervades all we do. We see ourselves in partnership with the family. Our role alternates between directiveness and consultation, gradually moving toward a preponderance of the second, if possible. As we work, we require from each family member as much as she/he is able to give. We see our sessions as joint efforts of family, student, and school—joint efforts by necessity, because each separate entity has thus far been unable to resolve the student's problems. Our strategy is to win the family's cooperation and trust, to assess their present functioning (strengths as well as faulty patterns), to provide sympathetic assistance (functioning as allies with great respect for both the student and family as people who are living their lives in the best way they know how), and to gently but persistently require them to stretch and to do as much as they can to resolve their difficulties. Our ultimate objective is to transfer control to the student and family. We convey the expectation that student and family (or at least *one* individual in the family) are willing to actively work to relieve the situation. Assessment and encouragement of motivation to change (not merely to be passive recipients of relief) is an essential part of our procedure.

Case Selection and Organization

There are three criteria for case selection. First, ordinary methods have failed with the student. Second, school personnel have hopes for the student, care about him or her, and see a possibility for positive change. Third, at least one individual in the family (besides the student) cares and will invest time and effort. These criteria are stretched when the student is continually obnoxious and disruptive; relief for the teacher may require taking on a less than ideal case.

To arrange sessions, a concerned staff member floats the idea with other staff. When there is concurrence that involving the family may pay off, the specifics are delineated. Parties with an investment in the student are identified and invited to come. These include staff, family members (from one to several), others in the student's life (such as grandmothers or concerned neighbors), and outside helpers such as the probation department, local clinics, or private therapists. An initial meeting is held to establish mutual interest in helping the student, to delineate the apparent problem, to solicit each party's view of the problem and of its possible solutions, to set attainable goals, to begin action to reach those goals, and to establish the times and the approximate number of subsequent meetings. It is generally agreed to meet three to six times, and then to evaluate progress and determine a future course.

Deborah: A Disguised Case History

Deborah was a tenth-grade school-avoiding youngster of above-average intelligence. Her continued absences and consequent poor academic performance had resulted in her placement as an emotionally disturbed student in a self-contained special education class. She had repeatedly come to the school's attention because of her frequent absences. Over the years there had been many generally unproductive contacts with parents, child, and therapists. Deborah's behavior and work habits in the special education classroom suggested that she really did not dislike school as much as her absences indicated.

Although Deborah's attendance was problematic, what made her noteworthy was that she suffered from enuresis. The stench emanating from her was obnoxious, overpowering, and ubiquitous. Repeated attempts to broach the matter delicately were met with angry resistance or sullen unresponsiveness. Deborah had the matter well in hand: if a teacher chose to bring up the subject of Deborah's hygiene, Deborah would stay home from school the next day. Teacher and student were locked in an inexorable two-step, each knowing with dead certainty what the other's next move would be. The student would have two or three good days in school; the teacher, sensing the development of some degree of confidence and trust, would bring up "the subject"; the student, recoiling in disappointment and anger, would take the next two days off.

Contacts between the parents and the school nurse brought repeated promises from the mother that a visit to a urologist would be scheduled. Deborah did not want to see a doctor, however, and Deborah's mother could not tell her what to do. Contact with the junior high school nurse revealed that a similar scenario had been played out earlier—Deborah had travelled this same road before. Something, however, had to be done at this point, because the classroom teacher was temperamentally incapable of turning a numb nose to Deborah's smell for an indefinite period of time. The teacher was also becoming uncomfortably aware of her ability to choreograph Deborah's absence from school simply by broaching "the subject," and was beginning to look forward to those absences because they provided relief from the noxious odors.

Call in the Family

The matter came to a dramatic head one day when the odor was especially overpowering and the teacher brought up the subject in a more forthright and less delicate manner. She told Deborah that her odor was indeed her own business, but that—contrary to Deborah's repeated assertions—its effect on the teacher's environs caused it to become the school's business as well. Therefore, the teacher was sending her out of the classroom and to the school nurse. This statement brought an unexpectedly violent response, which included throwing books, kicking and overturning desks and chairs, threats against the teacher, and a highly colorful string of obscenities. The display resulted in Deborah's being sent to the attendance office (A.O.) and suspended from class for the remainder of the day. The A.O. initially wanted to keep Deborah in the suspension room, but her unpleasant odor caused them to decide, out of consideration for the other students and for the staff, to send her home. A series of meetings with a psychologist, attendance officers, and other teachers made it unhappily clear that, while Deborah was generally well-liked as a person and seemed genuinely capable of acquiring a high school diploma, because of her vile odor no one was happy to have her around. Matters appeared deadlocked, but because her potential as a student had been recognized, the school decided to view the problem as an opportunity and to use the uncharacteristic outburst as leverage for engaging the parents. (*Exacerbation of problem provides impetus for FFC meeting and makes continued parental inaction less possible.*)

The school moved rapidly, and in less than forty-eight hours had devised a strategy. The administration determined how much pressure could be brought to bear on the parents if the odor continued. Administrators indicated that, if no action was taken, they could contact Child Protective Services with a referral for possible parental neglect. This option was to be a last resort. The school district's head nurse was consulted, and decided that the district could pay for a urological examination should the parents claim financial difficulties. (*Assessment and planning among staff before parents contacted.*) Because of the violence of Deborah's outburst, staff convinced her parents that despite her cavalier attitude toward her odor, she was really deeply disturbed by it and sensitive to its effects on others. (*Parents led to see Deborah more accurately. Deborah's defense of denial invalidated.*) Deborah's parents were instructed to keep her home until the meeting, two days after the outburst. (*Deborah's anxiety and her receptivity to the meeting heightened by preventing a routine return to school. Action taken promptly while the issue is hot.*)

By the time the parents came in, the psychologist, an A.O. staff member, the teacher, a school nurse, and the vice-principal were at the meeting. The agreed strategy was to express the school's concern about Deborah's enuresis and its effect on her mood and attitude toward school, to give the parents some information about enuresis, and to reassure them that, although the school would not tolerate either the violent outbursts or the odor, the staff was at the meeting for the express purpose of accepting Deborah and supporting her and her parents in every possible way. (*Meeting is carefully planned and set up and staff resources are not skimped. Impact of meeting on parents and Deborah increased by having five school-district staff present.*) Both parents appeared extremely anxious and tense at the beginning of the meeting, so the school's position was presented clearly and in a low-key and empathic manner. The parents relaxed noticeably as the meeting progressed, and a generally congenial and productive atmosphere prevailed. (*Working relationship established and receptivity elicited.*) Staff effectively managed to reframe the problem in more universal, benign, and hopeful terms. (*Changing the family's cognitive map, decreasing problem aversiveness, and enabling the family to approach possible solutions constructively.*) The parents were asked to share their concerns about Deborah and their perceptions of the effect her enuresis had on them, the rest of the family, and the school. They were gently probed for their responses to the nurse's earlier referrals. (*Information gathering adds the parents' data to the picture and actively involves them in the problem-solving process.*) Staff shared some of their perceptions of Deborah, as well as medical information about enuresis. (*Staff functions as partners and then as experts.*) The meeting, in fact, became so good-humored and relaxed that staff members and Deborah's father were able to share some of their own personal and family experiences regarding bed-wetting. (*Strategic self-disclosure by staff establishes a feeling of mutuality which, along with the humor elicited, increases the family's receptivity.*) In this more relaxed atmosphere, the discussion naturally turned to helping Deborah. The parents were now willing to take her to a urologist even if she objected, and referrals were made. Financial need was a consideration, so the district's willingness to pay the fee was presented (*Parents, and even Deborah, are less threatened, more receptive, and see the problem in a less blameful light, which enables them to consider and take constructive action.*)

Deborah was taken for the urological examination, medications were prescribed, and the family followed through with the medication regimen. Deborah became odor free, her parents no longer had to wrestle with smelly laundry and concealed urine-soaked sheets, and the teacher inhabited a more normal classroom. (*Parents and Deborah are no longer denying, angry, and resistant. They are able to act in their own best interests.*) The control of the enuresis, however, was not the sole outcome of the school's intervention. As a result of the positive feelings generated by the meeting, Deborah's parents became extremely supportive of the school and communicated more openly and frequently with staff. In addition, Deborah's attendance and academic progress showed significant improvement. She was less embarrassed to be at school and felt more like a normal student. Her attachment to the school and the teacher were increased by this positive outcome. The parents' positive and more trusting attitude toward the school was modeled for Deborah and also explicitly communicated to her. The school's and the parents' authority had been established (since she had been required to come to the meeting and to have the urological examination despite her attempts to refuse) and it became easier to require her presence in school and her completion of schoolwork. (*Much more than the original, limited goal of the counseling meeting is achieved, and the stage is set for an accelerating amelioration of Deborah's overall situation.*)

(Deborah's case is atypical in that the problem was so focused that a single session was sufficient for resolution, but the procedures illustrated are typical of our work.)

Goals

The case of Deborah illustrates the goals we pursue. Amelioration of a specific problem is sought. The student attends school, is attentive rather than disruptive during class, completes his or her homework, no longer smells of urine, etc. The broader goals are to move the family's attitudes in a more positive direction, to align their cognitive maps more closely to reality, and to elicit increasingly responsible and competent action. The long-term outcome when these broader goals are reached is a cooperative ongoing relationship with the parents and a collaborative enterprise involving student, parents, and school in which further difficulties are effectively addressed. From these follow improved grades, deportment, attendance, and benefit from the educational services provided.

Equally important in achieving these ends is the goal of changing the school's perception of the student and the parents so that they are seen as sincere, struggling, but basically decent people for whom there is hope and in whom it is worth investing time and effort. More broadly, we seek a change in staff so that more behaviors are recognized as modifiable, and so that families' and students' strengths and positive desires are noticed as readily as their negative behaviors and attitudes. System changes in the school as well as in the family are sought. (Conoley 1982).

Our goals follow our model of intervention. The first goal is to establish a working relationship or a strong therapeutic alliance among the student, the family, and all others present at the meeting. The second goal is modification of the presenting problem, or some other current, troubling behavior. The third goal is to bring the student's and the family's cognitive maps and strategies for coping into more productive alignment with reality. Finally, we aim to engage the student and the family in a cooperative relationship with the school, in which they help themselves as much as they are able.

We also have strategic subgoals, whose consequences move us toward the major goals.

Working Relationship

1. We convey our genuine concern and empathy for the student and his or her family. This is done by active listening, multidirected partiality (Boszormenyi-Nagy and Krasner 1986), calculated self-disclosure, and inconveniencing ourselves for them (e.g., by coming in early for 7 A.M. appoint-

ments when needed). This concern elicits commitment and a reciprocal investment in the counseling, along with increased hope, trust, and openness.

2. We pursue behavior and attitude changes using the methods described below. As change occurs, the therapeutic alliance strengthens, and student and parents become more willing to follow subsequent recommendations and more apt to persist in them. Additionally, there is less blaming of the school and more receptivity to action taken or recommended.
3. A time limit is set for the number of sessions. This conveys urgency and helps mobilize the participants.

Problem Resolution

We use a wide variety of techniques to achieve problem resolution. Our subgoals can be subsumed under the problem-solving model.

1. Identify a solvable problem (one which is distressing, behaviorally definable, and for which short-term intervention is likely to be successful).
2. Determine what measures the student and family have previously taken to solve the problem. Make a judgment about the probable causes of prior failure (e.g., the solution exacerbated the problem, or the solution was not effectively applied).
3. Devise a potential treatment. (Of course, each treatment method will have its own goals and subgoals.)
4. Propose the treatment plan and obtain family and student acceptance of the method as worth trying and as consonant with their values and abilities.
5. Work out the nuts and bolts of the plan with the student and family. It is essential that this be done carefully and in detail, since these families, by definition, are ones for whom ordinary methods have failed. They are often very skilled at unconsciously thwarting limits and requirements and also at seeing complete failure if success is less than 100 percent.
6. Implement the intervention plan.
7. Follow up on the results, and modify the plan as needed.
8. Evaluate the final outcome, obtaining the student's and the family's honest assessments. If they differ substantially from our appraisal, we discuss our differences and examine the data and the criteria which we carefully devised *with them* in step 5. Arrive at a consensus about the outcome.
9. Decide what to do next. Choices include terminating sessions as successful, selecting another problem to work on, and terminating the sessions as ineffectual.

System/Cognitive Map Change

To achieve changes in cognitive maps, life approach strategies, and family systems, our subgoals include the following:

1. Identifying maladaptive behavior patterns.
2. Intervening during the sessions or with homework assignments (Bergman 1985; Shelton and Levy 1981), so that the old patterns are challenged and new patterns are presented.

For example, we may want to teach the family how to use the problem-solving model. As homework, an intrusive mother and a passive father may be assigned a week's role reversal in which the father checks up on the student while the mother busies herself with an out-of-house project. We may present such concepts as the need to respect privacy, the need for more consultative parenting as the child moves through adolescence, or the need to respect both oneself *and* the other when disagreement occurs. Other intervention goals might be to teach communication skills, to get family members to share responsibility (instead of hogging or dumping it), or to move the perceived locus of control from outside to inside, so that blaming and helplessness can be replaced by competent action.

Intervention Techniques

To achieve our goals and subgoals, we employ techniques drawn from many different schools.

Behavioral techniques include contingency management, modeling (both embedded in the interactions of the family meetings and presented overtly through role playing), rehearsal of new behaviors, and the use of small steps. A useful source for behavioral interventions in the classroom is *Discipline in the Secondary Classroom* (Sprick 1985), which includes detailed intervention plans for forty-two problems, including passive resistance, test anxiety, suicide threats, failing to complete homework, and feeling picked-on by the teacher. Homework assignments are given when appropriate; *Behavioral Assignments and Treatment Compliance* (Shelton and Levy 1981) is a resource describing how to do this.

Considerable use is made of performance monitoring. The student's calling out, homework completion, or lateness to class is carefully recorded. In addition to other consequences, student and the parents receive feedback about the student's performance. Joint feedback is a powerful tool because the student has often manipulated information so that the parents believe the student has, for example, not misbehaved, done so only under provocation, or been assigned no homework. Some students intercept notification of attendance difficulties at the mailbox, and this is revealed during feedback at the FFC meeting.

This performance monitoring (through which the student's cover is blown) is made acceptable to the student by describing it as a way for him to get what he wants—such as hassle-free school days or a high school diploma. The connection between acts of self-discipline (such as impulse curtailment, daily at-home study, or leaving one's friends and getting to class on time) and the student's long-term goals is elicited from the student by the Socratic method. His desire for the long-term goals is whetted, and then performance monitoring is presented as a way to strengthen his ability to conform to his good intentions. A metaphor is used in which a six-year-old's will power is enhanced when his mother can hear the click of the cookie jar lid and his will power is weakened when Mom is known to be hanging up laundry in the backyard.

Use of metaphor and of reframing are only two of the techniques taken from *family therapy, communication therapies, and the work of Milton Erickson*. Family patterns can be traced and made evident to family members by use of the genogram (McGoldrick and Gerson 1985). If straightforward methods are ineffective, symptom encouragement or other paradoxical interventions may be used (Weeks and L'Abate 1982). Simple analogies or extended stories and metaphors may be employed to present ideas (Barker 1985). Communication skills or negotiation skills may be directly taught. (An excellent resource for the latter, written in layman's language, is *Getting to Yes: Negotiating Agreement Without Giving In* (Fisher and Ury 1981). Knowing that attention is very selective and that our clients may be unaware, for instance, of the unpleasantness of their voice tones, we give gentle but clear feedback of our perceptions of their behavior.

We view resistance as a welcome behavior, because it reveals the very actions that prevent satisfactory resolution of the student's and the family's problems. As resistances are revealed (e.g., passivity, blaming, hostility, tantrums), they can be addressed and modified. So instead of seeing resistance as behavior that interferes with our treatment efforts, we see it as an asset. Our welcoming of resistance is unexpected by both student and family, and this welcoming itself (even before interventions to modify the resistance) makes the FFC sessions quite different from the client's prior contacts with the school (Davanloo 1980; Zeig 1982).

Another set of techniques emerges from cognitive therapies. Information is provided through direct instruction or by having family members read recommended books. A problem-solving paradigm may be presented to the family. The Socratic method of guided questioning is sometimes used to draw solutions from the student or other family members. At times entreaty or direct persuasion will be used to urge family members to take beneficial action. However, we apply the minimum pressure possible to obtain action, because we want people to attribute their actions to themselves, not to outside forces.

Techniques not clearly associated with one or another school include self-disclosure, the use of humor, and direct confrontation. Very rarely, one of us will get really angry with the student or the family. This option is acceptable only after much patient work has failed either to produce change, or to convince us that change is impossible. Finally in such cases, we will say, "Give us evidence of change or we quit. We give up." This can be a very useful intervention, if it motivates the clients to get moving and to change. If they refuse or offer only an ineffectual agreement, we can terminate our interventions with a clear conscience. We inform the family that they are either unable or unwilling to change. We do not object to this; we simply recognize it as a—possibly—regrettable but inescapable fact. There are immense therapeutic gains possible at this point: (1) Families or individuals may for the first time confront their "as if" approach to life. They may have been fooling themselves by acting as if they wished to live differently. (2) Recognition of this life position can then lead to new decisions. One decision may be that the person really *does* want to change. Another may be that he or she really is content with life as it is and will no longer waste time pursuing goals that are not as important as maintaining the status quo.

From Here to . . . Eternal Evolution

Our model and techniques are constantly evolving. We learn from both our success and our failures. The implications of this for us and for anyone utilizing this model are that it is never finished, that failures produce as much benefit as successes (if they are analyzed and their conclusions are applied), and that you don't have to be an expert to start.

What *is* needed to start? There are certain minimum requirements. First, faith—faith that the approach is a workable hypothesis and, more important, faith that students, families, and staff are capable of and desire better ways to manage school-related affairs. Second, a general plan of approach to each case—the approach need not, and initially should not, be elaborate. Third, the repertoire of the practitioner must include some intervention techniques relevant to the presenting problem. Fourth, a receptive family—don't start with the toughest case; pick one in which the student and more than one family member are committed to improvement. Fifth, choose a case in which staff members are sympathetic to the student and believe that she/he has some chance of improvement. Sixth, set goals and limit the scope of the intervention. Seventh, practitioners should have empathy for the particular family, and optimism about its chances for success. Eighth, engage in careful planning—remember that doing something for the first or second time takes longer but eventually pays off as the activity becomes second nature. In summary, choose an initial case in which the "hopeless" situation includes many factors to support success.

Addendum

Counseling adolescents is not a task for the fainthearted. Few clients provide the challenge, travail, and sheer exasperation that these troubled young people do. Paradoxically, few groups cry out so persistently for help even while scorning and rejecting it. Those of us who choose this work have often questioned our own sanity, common sense, and value systems for persisting in the face of what are frequently Sisyphian endeavors.

Because special-needs students often come to the attention of the school authorities at a time in their lives when their behaviors have already attracted the attention of social agencies, the police, and even a series of therapists, they and their families may be understandably depressed and demoralized. At this juncture, the school's intervention may represent their last hope.

Because the students we work with have already consumed so many of the school's resources, we may need great diplomacy and tact to reengage the family, the staff, and the outside agencies in new skirmishes and alternative game plans. A high degree of optimism, therefore, is a prerequisite. Without this it would be impossible to generate the energy required to move ahead. It is easy to succumb to ennui with each new case, observing how much this one resembles those others in which all our efforts failed. Controlled amnesia is of immeasurable value: It allows the counseling to proceed with full attention focused on the uniqueness of the individual and of the systems in which she/he participates. It allows us to work giving only token acknowledgement of commonly heard remarks such as "That was tried in the junior high and it didn't work" and "We did that, and it was a failure." Counseling adolescents often requires bulldog tenacity and the willingness to go back to the drawing board again and again.

In terms of systems theory, change in any member of the system can cause a change in the rest of the system. Using the resources of the extended school and family the likelihood that change will occur quickly and will last is increased. Because of the time it takes to work with these students and because they are so often resistant and hostile, school personnel frequently experience fatigue, irritation, and a sense of futility. These feelings must be recognized and controlled if effective interventions are to be implemented. To this end, staff must develop a team spirit to provide them with the support and cohesion they need to pursue their common goals.

The development of team spirit is possible only when members of the team know and trust one another enough to work in a cooperative and collegial manner. It is based on the premise that underneath the most cynical, burned-out, and battle-scarred staff member lies someone who initially got into the profession because of a genuine liking for young people and a desire to help them. When staff come together in a mutually supportive way to solve problems, many of these altruistic and empathetic qualities are called into play. Then it becomes possible not only to problem solve more effectively, but also to generate the support and encouragement that will be necessary when the going gets tough.

In developing a team it helps immeasurably to start out with at least one other staff member who shares your views, attitudes, and goals. Often a very small segment of the staff has a substantial effect on the larger system. If at least two staff members will collaborate in engaging other staff members, rather than in establishing themselves as resident rescuers of the delinquent, they can create an ever-widening circle of influence and support into which the student is drawn. It is important to recognize that for interventions to be effective, staff members must not be jealous of their expertise—they must be willing to share it. They cannot pontificate about the right way—they must be willing to explore varying approaches. When they succeed, the team's members must share the glory, credit one another, and not lay exclusive claim to the solution of a problem. The staff that can produce a nucleus of professionals able to work cooperatively in the best interests of their students and of one another is fortunate indeed.

Staff members who share your worldviews, attitudes, and values protect you against burnout. When the going gets tough—and it will—a colleague who can verify that you are on the right track, or indicate you may be on the wrong track, is invaluable. In addition to all this rational, sensible support, a sympathetic colleague also lets you blow off steam when frustrations mount too high. Bitching may be curmudgeonly behavior, but done in confidence, in the right spirit, and with an understanding colleague, it can send you back to the battlefront with renewed objectivity, measured involvement, and optimism.

References

Barker, P. (1985) *Using Metaphors in Psychotherapy*. New York: Brunner/Mazel

Bergman, J. S. (1985) *Fishing for Barracuda*. New York: W. W. Norton.

Boszormenyi-Nagy, I., and B. R. Krasner (1986) *Between Give and Take: A Clinical Guide to Conceptual Therapy*. New York: Brunner/Mazel.

Davanloo, H., ed. (1980) *Short Term Dynamic Psychotherapy*. Northvale, N.J.: Jason Aronson.

deShazer, S. (1985) *Keys to Solution in Brief Therapy*. New York: W. W. Norton.

Fisch, R., J. H. Weakland, and L. Segal (1982) *The Tactics of Change*. San Francisco: Jossey-Bass.

Fisher, R., and W. Ury (1981) *Getting to Yes: Negotiating Agreement Without Giving In*. Boston: Houghton Mifflin.

Cooney, J. (1982) *School Consultation: A Guide to Practice and Training*. New York: Pergamon Press.

Haley, J. (1973) *Uncommon Therapy: The Psychiatric Techniques of Milton H. Erickson, M.D.* New York: Ballantine Books.

——— (1977) Problem-Solving Therapy. San Francisco: Jossey-Bass.

McGoldrick, M., and R. Gerson (1985) *Genograms in Family Assessment*. New York: W. W. Norton.

Minuchin, S., and H. C. Fishman (1981) *Family Therapy Techniques*. Cambridge, Mass.: Harvard University Press.

Perls, F. S., R. F. Hefferline, and P. Goodman (1951) *Gestalt Therapy*. New York: Julian Press.

Rogers, C. (1951) *Client-Centered Therapy*. Boston: Houghton Mifflin.

Shelton, J. L., and R. L. Levy (1981) *Behavioral Assignments and Treatment Compliance*. Champaign, Ill.: Research Press.

Sprick, R. S. (1985) *Discipline in the Secondary Classroom: A Problem by Problem Survival Guide*. West Nyack, N.Y.: The Center for Applied Research in Education.

Squires, S. (1986) "Should you keep your therapist?" *American Health* (June): 72–77.

Wachtel, E. F., and P. Wachtel (1986) *Family Dynamics in Individual Psychotherapy*. New York: Guilford Press.

Weeks, G. R., and L. L'Abate (1982) *Paradoxical Psychotherapy*. New York: Brunner/Mazel.

Zeig, J. K., ed. (1982) *Ericksonian Approaches to Psychotheraphy*. New York: Brunner/Mazel.

CHAPTER SEVEN

TREATING THE FAMILY WITH AN ADOLESCENT WITH FAMILY ART THERAPY

Shirley Riley, M.A., A.T.R., M.F.C.C.

Conducting therapy with a family that includes an adolescent child is always a challenge. With this family, the therapist anticipates confronting additional resistance to treatment, for a non-compliant attitude is syntonic with the teenage developmental process. The therapist's expectation is reinforced by knowing that all members of a family system are normally resistant to change, fearing that any modification of their familiar patterns may threaten the family unit. However, even greater difficulties are experienced, I believe, when therapists are presented with a troubled family in which both teenager and parents are functioning on an equally adolescent level.

Treatment Dilemmas

Family treatment is built on the premise that certain techniques will start a process toward symptom reduction by interrupting dysfunctional patterned behaviors. However, in an "all-adolescent family," I find more questions than answers about both exact technique and applied family theory.

One treatment approach to parent/child dysfunction is to establish hierarchical boundaries, shore up the parent's adult strengths, attend to the child subsystem, and perform other structural maneuvers (Minuchin et al. 1981). With the family in which an adult has not reached adult psychological development, we do not find these agents of change particularly effective. I believe it would be useful to examine how the family art therapist can construct a treatment plan to meet the needs of the developmentally delayed family.

Developmental Concerns

To better understand the difficulties involved in treating what I will call the *adolescent family*, it is first necessary to briefly reexamine the basic process of adolescent development.

When puberty thrusts the child toward his/her next step in physical growth, a simultaneous intrapsychic realignment occurs. This change is called adolescence. In this process youth must give up attachments to parental figures and their protective positions. Youths must turn their attention to the unexpected, uncomfortable changes they are experiencing both physically and in their perceptions of themselves (Mirkin and Koman 1985).

Detachment from the primary adults of childhood and single-minded focus on self is recognized as the "narcissistic stance" of adolescence (Blos 1962). Particularly in the pre-adolescent and early adolescent child, approximately eleven to fourteen years old, the pervasive feeling of emptiness and the constant introspective attention to self limit the available empathy or interest they can share with another person. Moving from a strictly narcissistic involvement to the capacity to care for another is one essential task accomplished during the adolescent development (Carter and McGoldrick 1980).

Unfortunately, many persons falter on the way to achieving empathic caring and remain in an earlier emotional stage. It is nearly impossible for the youth to be giving, since the capacity to demonstrate caring feelings for another person has not yet been achieved (Malmquist 1978). How will a psychologically delayed adult, as a parent, be able to protect and nurture a child when that parent still views the world narcissistically? Younger children of such adolescent-adults fare more or less well during childhood if they maintain rigid defenses and if environmental demands are not excessive. Youngsters cannot clearly express their unmet needs. However, as a child moves into adolescence, where rebellion and resistance to parental authority are the name of the game, the real struggle begins. We now have a situation in which both parent and child attempt to gain attention for themselves, giving little or no empathic understanding to the other. Both child and adult experience emptiness and distress, which are often handled through impulsive actions that distract from the pain. This unfortunate developmental parallel in parent and adolescent child requires a specific series of therapeutic interventions to encourage maturation in the adult while simultaneously keeping the adolescent child developing as normally as possible. This is easier said than done.

This family system recalls the environmental and systemic background of the borderline adolescent which Masterson (1985) delineated so eloquently. The grave consequences of an adolescent's failure to achieve separation and autonomy is described by him:

> The passage of time presents these unfortunates with inevitable life tasks and thereby faces them with truly a Hobson's choice: to avoid the challenge of growth, marriage, and parenthood with the consequent loneliness and suffering that this entails or to take on the challenge though emotionally ill-equipped. Should they opt for the latter they receive the additional dividend of becoming an appalled and helpless eyewitness to the repetition of their own unresolved problems in their children.

These borderline families are often headed by an aggressively active mother who resists the child's desire for individuation to answer her own needs for fusion, and a passive, distant father who encourages this symbiosis. Since 1972 Masterson (1985) and others have relieved the mother of full responsibility for the pathology, and modified this dynamic.

Another very common malfunctioning family system can interfere with child development: the alcoholic or violently abusive system, in which the visible pathology is most often demonstrated by the father. The dependent role in this pattern is taken by the mother.

Many patients recall their own childhoods as ones in which fathers were either violent or alcoholic or both—a home life in which they were unprotected by Mother and triangulated into the parental relationship. These abused children, now parents, often engaged in heavy drug or alcohol abuse during their own adolescence, adding to their developmental failures. In all of these, it is the adolescent youngster who is delegated by the family to attract attention and gain therapeutic treatment by engaging in various acting-out behaviors (Stierlin 1979). Once in therapy, I have observed that parent and child expect the therapist to provide quick answers and prompt symptom removal. Contrary to treatment expectations, resistance is not encountered when the family first accepts professional help but is demonstrated later, when the parents feel reluctant to relive painful depressive periods of their pasts.

In considering an approach to treatment, the configuration in these adolescent families that I find most fascinating is their mixture of strengths and weaknesses. As in normal adolescent development, there is in this delayed adolescence an overriding component of narcissism, but there are also idealism, creativity, intellectualization, and other qualities that may be encouraged in seeking more adult solutions to problems. In addition, these families often fall into a gray area of diagnosis. Although they suffer from borderline or abusive parental backgrounds, they received just enough caring from some related source to give them a notion of "how it might have been better" (Winnicott 1976).

Environmental Factors

These adolescent families are frequently headed by a single parent. Traditionally, these clients have separated from mates whose behavior reproduced stress patterns they had experienced in their families of origin. However, contrary to the notion that these patterns are fated to be reproduced again and again, in many instances the mother or father is *cognizant* of this repetition and determined *not* to repeat the same mistake. Although awareness of past patterns may be used protectively, it may also lead to an additional difficulty for their children. The adult, rather than risk failure, often withdraws from peer-friendships and looks to his or her adolescent child for companionship. This closeness enhances the diffusion of boundaries between parent and child and promotes symbiosis.

The single-parent factor compounds the challenge of conducting treatment. The therapist cannot piece together the strengths of two parents to create a composite executive position to which the adolescent child can either rebel or turn for protection. Too often we see that the teenager moves into the role left unfilled by the missing parent, and is thus deprived of healthy rebellion. The drive to separate continues, but since it is directed against the self (in the substitute parent role), it turns into self-destructive acting-out behavior.

An additional dilemma in treating adolescents in family therapy arises from the realities of the community mental health setting in which they seek help. Constructions of time and frequency of treatment are serious considerations. Obviously, it is not always possible to conduct ideally effective therapy for developmentally damaged persons in a one-hour, once-a-week, short-term contract. So we must cautiously offer therapy that can be helpful within these restrictions, and must not attempt to remove defenses or weaken coping mechanisms that serve positive functions. A systemic/strategic theoretical approach is designed to focus on strengths, reframe behavior, and achieve symptom relief within a time-limited frame. Therefore, I feel art therapy is the most successful therapy to utilize with the families described above (Riley 1985).

I will attempt to show, by case illustrations, some art therapy techniques to which adolescent families have seemed to respond, and which have resulted in a positive outcome of treatment.

Assessment

The presenting picture of the confused, frustrated parent and the defiant, rebellious adolescent is painfully common. The description of the problem that brought them into the clinic does not provide sufficient clues to the underlying cause of the behavior. However if, during the joining phase of family art therapy, the therapist observes an unusually prolonged competitive struggle between adult and child, the hypothesis of mutual adolescence should be considered. To explore this possibility further, the art therapist instructs the family to engage in a mutual art task to provide an arena for enactment of the suspected behavior.

Often, the behavior seen by the therapist during a dual drawing demonstrates the diffusion of authority. The parent and teenager vie for attention. Both may draw or refuse to draw, both may grab for the same color pen, or the parent may defer to the directions given by the child rather than to those given by the therapist. These actions, together with the messages conveyed in the art product, suggest that there is little adult functioning in this family.

After continued observation, an assessment is made of how family patterns repeat themselves. If it is established that in this family both parent and child are developmentally in adolescence, some strategic moves are necessary.

Setting Goals and Treatment

The first goal is to create within the parent an image of competency. This will enable him/her to face the normal trials of raising an adolescent. To accomplish this goal the therapy focuses on the parent and apparently neglects the child and his/her symptoms. If necessary, the counselor invents strengths in the adult's character and, paradoxically, the adolescent experiences relief. A shifting of the system will not be easy, since both parent and child are accustomed to supporting each other in egalitarian positions in the hierarchy. However, the parent who gains satisfaction and approval from others by acting more in charge will learn to continue this change, and thereby to gain narcissistic rewards in an appropriate manner.

Unfortunately there is often such paucity of ego strength in these individuals that the therapist must use a variety of techniques to achieve the treatment goals. Cloe Mandanes (1981) speaks of how she helps a client to playact, or *pretend* to behave in a proscribed manner. In this case a parent is coached on how to pretend to be an efficient and effective adult. Following this experiment in effectiveness, the client tests whether the child perceives the difference between the pretense and the reality. The aim is to start a feedback loop in which the parent pretends to provide structure for the family and a welcome release from stress results. Positive reinforcement of better family function helps the behavior to be retained and integrated as part of the real self. Adolescent parents feel less threatened if they are told that *they have to pretend to be grown up only for the short period of their child's adolescence.*

In the early stages of treatment, the therapist openly attends to the parent, while still supporting the teenager. The alliance is productive for several reasons: (1) When the therapist aligns with mother and/or father, the parentified or symptomatic child feels less needed and more free to be a teenager. (2) As the youth experiences the freedom to be an adolescent his or her need for acting-out behavior is reduced. (3) The child actively participates in art therapy, but the main attention is deflected from her or him, thus diminishing age-appropriate resistance. (4) It is more difficult to assist a developmentally delayed adult through the growth process than it is to aid a child who is doing a similar task on time. Therefore, as the art therapist helps the parent mature, the teenager can achieve a more appropriate relationship with the parent.

To further the attainment of individuation, the therapist suggests art therapy productions which allow the client to observe past patterns of his or her family of origin, and also to observe if these patterns function in the present. Seeing a parallel between past and present maladaptive relationships provides essential information that leads to the desired change. The therapist, when reviewing old behaviors, uses positive connotation to create a new reality and transform present perceptions. By seeing his/her problems represented in the art therapy, the client can develop and utilize his/her ego observer. The skill of monitoring one's own behavior is one of the major tasks of adolescence, an important step toward realizing the goal of maturation for both parent and child.

Brief Case Examples*

Shamar, a Caucasian thirteen-year-old, entered treatment with her mother and younger brother, although she did not feel she had any problems. She was getting satisfactory grades, ran the family efficiently, directed her mother's relationships, and competently parented her younger brother. In contrast to Shamar's grandiose self-perceptions, the mother, Joanne, was filled with anxieties. She tearfully admitted being unable to set rules, to oppose her daughter, or to enjoy her boyfriend, of whom Shamar did not approve. The parents had been divorced for eight years, but the father was very active in the family and intruded at will. Mother complained, "He bosses me just as my daughter does." In spite of the teenager's protestations that she was untroubled, her behavior belied her words. She prefaced every statement to her mother with phrases such as "Now don't be hurt" and "Don't cry, Mother, but . . ." Then she was able to list all her frustrations. Her problems reflected her need for structure in the home, her ambivalence about maintaining her overcontrolling role, and her desire for relief from adult duties. As the therapy progressed the mother bootlegged many individual sessions on one pretext or another, in order to deal with her own issues. She dwelt on her abusive and critical relationship with her father, whom she still feared. She said she wanted better relationships with men

* Case material presented has been modified to preserve confidentiality. Names, circumstances, and dynamics are representative, but are generalized to protect privacy.

and an escape from her ex-husband's rule, and she had other complaints that were obviously unfinished business from her own adolescence. Joanne was so fixated on her own needs that she had little time or desire left over for her children.

The treatment was particularly difficult for the therapist since the daughter's suggestions were very sensible, and the mother's contributions were much less workable. However, it would be destructive to allow this complementary relationship to continue: no matter how well the girl performed adult duties, she was neglecting her own development.

Family art therapy was very useful in achieving separation and in counteracting their enmeshment. Both mother and daughter were artistic and were skillful in using the media. Each could see the other's product and could absorb both overt and covert messages. Most important, the art was often nonverbal, so it avoided negative blaming and provided a new problem-solving device. Joanne gained Shamar's respect when she began to teach art and hold a full-time job. The girl was more cooperative when she realized that her mother had a therapist (a grown-up) to lean on, rather than herself. There was a lively period of treatment during which the mother, in her own quest for autonomy, was extremely distracted. This made the daughter insecure, and she sought attention by getting lower grades. This device succeeded in involving the mother, but in an authoritarian role—a positive surprise in this relationship.

As therapy progressed, it became apparent that Shamar's mother was not going to quickly achieve the desirable adult status; therefore therapist honored the daughter's contributions to the family. Shamar remains a junior partner in the family, and plays the role openly, with structure and limitations set in the sessions between her and Joanne. The six-year-old brother has been given clear rules about who is the real mother and how much authority his sister may exercise. The chance that this threesome will ever become the ideal family we have constructed as our paradigm is extremely slim. However, the mother can now ask openly for individual sessions and articulate the problems she wants to address. The daughter joins the sessions every third week, and then the focus changes to family problems. This is the beginning of a realignment of roles allowing both mother and teenager to begin the work of individuation.

Art Therapy Expressions: Case I

A brief sampling of the art work done by the mother and daughter discussed above dramatizes the difference in their personalities. The first two figures were drawn in response to the question: *What are the family's problems?* In figure 7.1, Joanne drew a pair of clouds obscuring the sun and producing rain. She related that to their conflicts at home. In figure 7.2, Shamar drew a picture of going shopping, explaining that she never got enough clothes from her mother and that, if she did, they wouldn't fight. The contrast between the empty, minimal drawing of the mother and the concrete, pragmatic statement of the daughter revealed their positions in the relationship. Plates 1, 2, and 3 are drawings done by Shamar on two different occasions when we were discussing the struggle over who would get the privacy of the one bedroom. Shamar first drew herself in pastels, a rather flattering rendering. In the subsequent session, after some rules had been imposed, she gazed intently at her mother while

Plate 1: Shamar's self-portrait

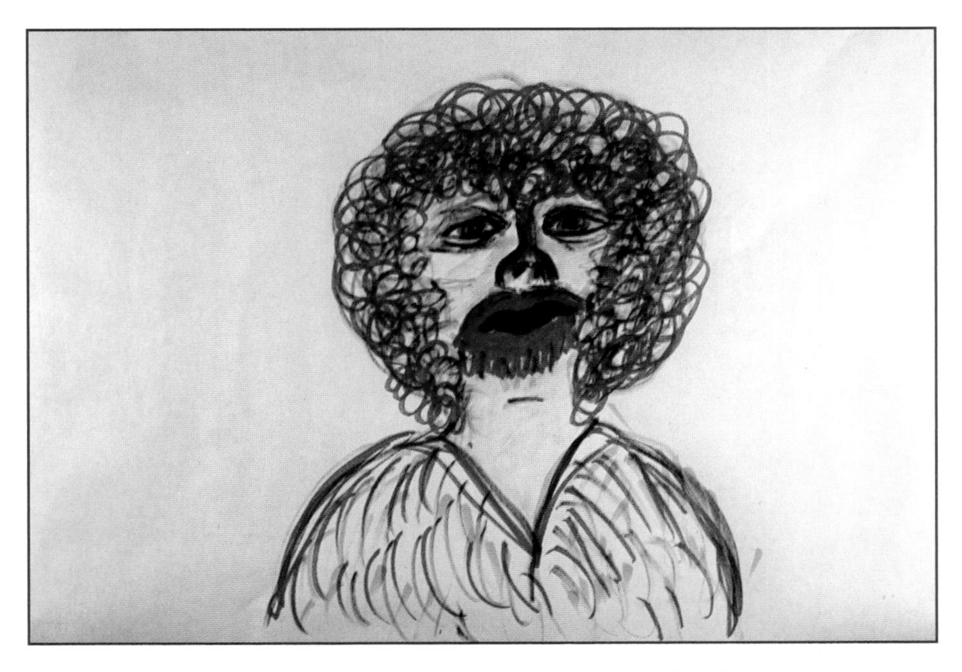

Plate 2: Shamar's drawing of her mother. Was the beard an "accident?"

Plate 3: Shamar's drawing of her mother. Is the woman "happy?"

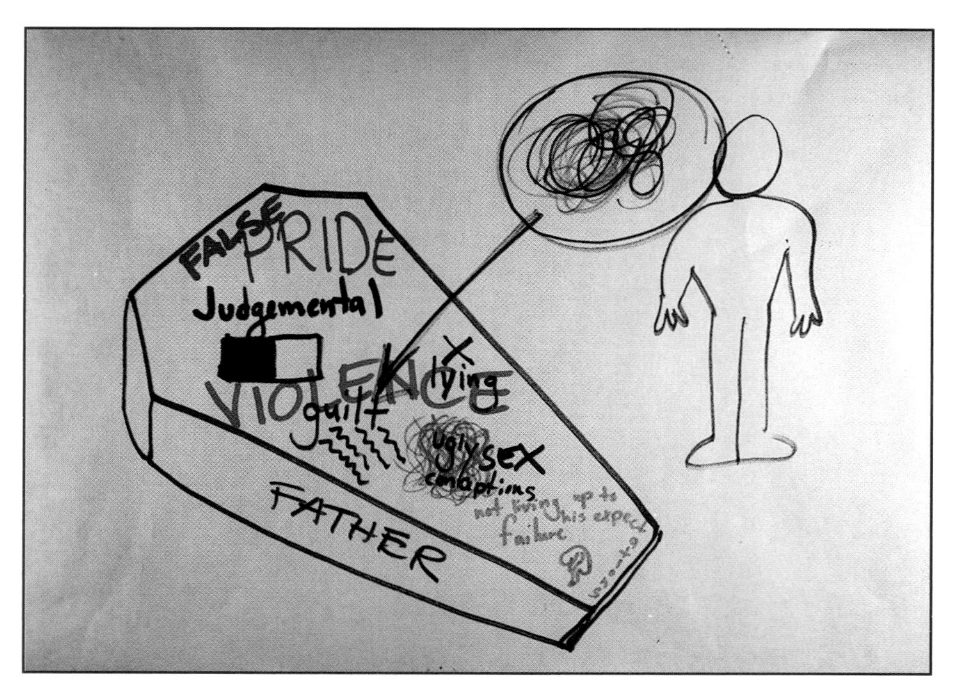

Plate 4: Joanne's "burial" of feelings about her father and her ex-husband

Plate 5: Joanne's perception of the "fuzzy parent" and the "adult parent"

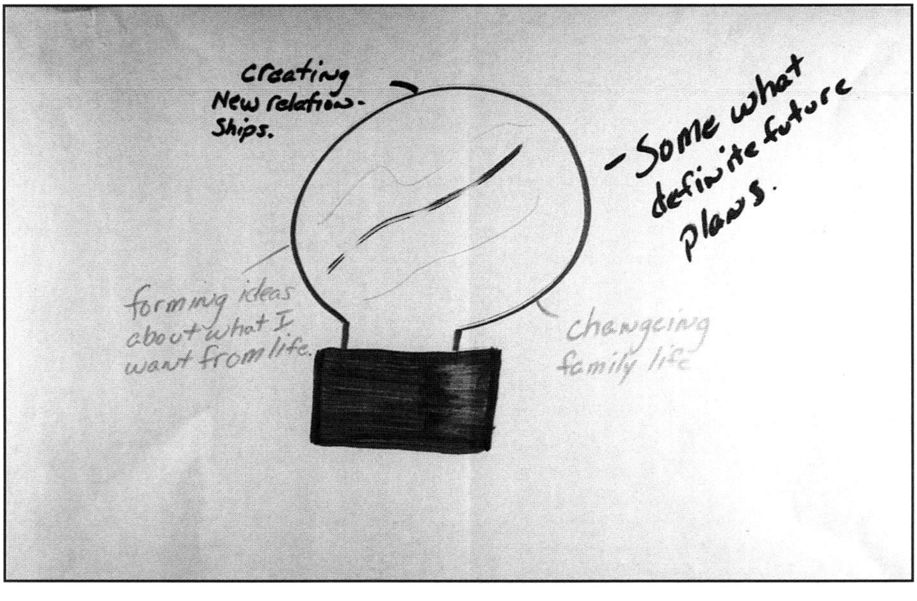

Plate 6: Light bulb symbolizes Joanne's new ideas.

Plate 7: Christi and Jerry's cooperative drawing

Plate 8: Jerry's view of his room, before and after therapy

Figure 7.1: Joanne's view of family conflict

Figure 7.2: Shamar's view of a shopping trip

drawing these two "portraits." She excused the red beard as an accident and thought the other woman was happy. Joanne, a delicate and fragile woman with long, fine, straight hair, did not resemble these renditions. However, the quality of anger and the aggressive affect were extremely confrontative and were shared by both daughter and mother.

Plate 4 shows Joanne's way of dealing with her feelings about her father, feelings which she felt were identical to her emotions toward her ex-husband. She felt burdened by their characteristics of false pride and guilt, their conceptions of ugly sex, her inability to live up to their expectations and, most of all, their violence. She boxed these up and buried them. She felt that the guilt experienced in her present life was derived from past criticism. Some weeks later she drew a very insightful rendition (Plate 5) of the difference between a "fuzzy parent" (on the left of the page) and an "adult parent" (on the right). I quote her explanation: "The broken pink line means no boundaries, the blue cloud is a dream world that holds back the warmth from the heart, the growth is without roots, and the blue waves show turbulence of emotions. The right drawing has a firm base, calm emotions, growth reaching out, and the dreams do not stand in the way of warmth. The most important feature is the firm but open boundaries." Her final drawing, plate 6, indicates that the process of individuation and maturation is beginning. The words around a light bulb are, "forming new ideas about what I want from life, creating new relationships, some definite future plans, and a changing family life."

One important aspect of the art in this treatment is the information it supplied, which assisted the art therapist in her ongoing assignment of the client's growth and development.

Art Therapy Expressions: Case II

In the second session, a hypothesis for treatment was formed by the art therapist based on drawings done by a Latino father and his twelve-year-old son. For two years these two had lived together, gone on the father's dates together, and moved together from one unstable living situation to another. The father and son had the same name and borrowed each other's clothing. The boy's mother had retained custody of his younger sister, but had turned her husband out of the house because of his immaturity and irresponsibility. Bob, Jr. had decided to go with his dad.

The presenting complaint centered on the son's poor school performance. However, it was clear that Father did not respect the school's concern, but felt persecuted and humiliated when called in to speak to the teachers. His distress was aimed at the school, not at the boy. He recalled that he was never successful at school and that his father was never around to defend him. Figure 7.3 and figure 7.4 were completed after the clients were asked to *show how you could help with the problem*. The father drew a single horse whom he jokingly said was going to escape from the corral; the son suggested that they should try to be more "thoughtful, honest, kind, helpful, understanding, and happy."

These two drawings show which person was more aware of the problem and which was going to run away as soon as possible. Treatment focused on helping a man who never grew up mature so that he could appropriately support his son. The boy was encouraged to break away from the symbiosis with his father and to gain his own identity. There was progress until the father, as was his pattern, moved them away. It was encouraging that some

Figure 7.3: The lone horse looks for a way to escape (father)

Figure 7.4: A list of attitudes that might relieve stress (son)

Figure 7.5: Christi's before-and-after appraisals

Before
1) I was ready to give up trying to be a mother and friend to ___
2) I was also tired of myself
3) I was losing control and hitting ___
4)

Now
1) I very happy with my attitude toward
2) I have a lot of patience c̄
3) I can deal with most things that bother me.
4) I am no longer hitting him.
5) I can also him the love I have for him (physical) and spiritually.

change had been made: he followed through with a referral suggestion and continued treatment elsewhere.

Art Therapy Expressions: Case III

This case was court-referred: a black mother and her thirteen-year-old son. The boy had been taken from his home because of child neglect. The mother, Christi, claimed that Jerry was intractably oppositional and never did anything she asked. His divorced father, in jail for drug dealing, was completely out of contact. The boy wanted to stay at home and said he wanted to learn to control his temper. It became apparent that Mother was primarily interested in her excellent job and that she wanted Jerry to run the house for her, to clean and cook. My perception of this case was that the mother and son acted out in similar ways with physical violence, a behavior that often masks adolescent depression. Each had his/her own form of temper tantrums, and both ran away from their problems, and both handled stress in an adolescent manner.

To test their ability to work together, I suggested a dual drawing. This colorful, solid drawing, plate 7, gave them great satisfaction and a pleasurable experience. The empty interior of the house was not interpreted at this time, but the tree leaning tenderly on the house and the stop sign were discussed at length. A positive connotation was used to refer to all images in this significant drawing. The mother-and-son dyad rallied strongly after this experience. Work was done with Mother on her parenting skills; then a few individual sessions focused on her extremely immature fantasies about being rescued by a "wonderful" man. The termination drawings are shown here. Figure 7.5 is Mother's *be-*

fore-and-after therapy appraisal list. *Before*, she was "ready to give up trying, tired of herself, and losing control and hitting." Now she feels "happy with her attitude, has a lot of patience, can deal with most things, is no longer hitting, and can show him her love." These improvements were reinforced by the happiness of finding a very solid, successful man to marry, a man whose son happened to be her boy's best friend.

In plate 8, the teenager pictured the mess his room was in *before he came to therapy* and himself crying as Mother berated him. Now *after therapy* he and his mother go horseback riding together. He claimed that these drawings indicated that they had moved from sorrow to pleasure. The minimal use of space and the cramped imagery, suggest a very careful and controlled—perhaps skeptical—perception of the permanence of this change.

Summary

The three cases reviewed above had a broad common base. Although the families were divergent in ethnic backgrounds, their extended families shared similar histories. In each case—as with countless other families seen in our outpatient clinic—the parent's childhood was extremely deprived. Role models, nurturance, and self-acceptance were sadly lacking. These parents passed through the pubescent years without completing adolescent developmental tasks. In particular, they were unable to identify appropriate persons of the opposite sex with whom to engage in a long-term relationship. Because of their own identity confusions, they became parents with no notion of what parenting entailed, and they did not learn these skills during their children's early years, because they were focused on their own unmet adolescent needs. When their children entered adolescence, they forced their parents to struggle with issues of narcissism, identity, and autonomy, both within themselves and in their teenaged progeny. Families attempting to survive these tumultuous times are helped by a family art therapist who sets realistic goals and adheres to a specialized treatment plan.

The combination of systemic theory and art therapy has proved helpful in treating these adolescent families. (1) The parent is the main focus of treatment, in the early phase of therapy; however, the art work keeps the youth involved and allows him/her to make a statement in every session. (2) Attention is directed to the parent and deflected from the teenager. This technique is syntonic with the teenage developmental stance, so the youth is willing to come to the sessions. (3) As the parent is led toward achieving, or pretending to achieve, adult skills, the child is relieved of inappropriate roles in the family. She or he then turns toward making his or her own adolescence more successful. (4) The treatment of these families takes into consideration the need for compromise in defining clear hierarchical boundaries. The teenager will often continue to take part in adult duties and decisions, but these activities will be overt, not covert, and will therefore be open to negotiation and readjustment.

The essential tool for the family art therapist is a broad knowledge of adolescent development and the acuity to recognize delayed patterns when they manifest in an adult. This assessment is made through observation of the dynamic between parent and adolescent, and through recognition of their perceptions as displayed in their art therapy expressions.

References

Ackerman, N. J. (1980) "The family with adolescents" in E. A. Carter and M. McGoldrick, eds., *The Family Life Cycle: A Framework for Family Therapy*. New York: Gardner Press.

Blos, P. (1962). *On Adolescence: A Psychoanalytic Interpretation*. New York: Macmillan.

Carter, E. A., and M. McGoldrick (1980) "The Family Life Cycle and Family Therapy: An Overview," in Carter and McGoldrick, *The Family Life Cycle*.

———, eds. (1980) *The Family Cycle: A Framework for Family Therapy*. New York: Gardner Press.

Erikson, E. H. (1968) *Identity: Youth and Crisis*. New York: W. W. Norton.

Haley, J. (1980) *Leaving Home*. New York: McGraw-Hill.

Landgarten, H. (1987) *Family Art Psychotheraphy*. New York: Brunner/Mazel.

Madanes, C. (1981) *Strategic Family Therapy*. San Francisco: Jossey-Bass.

Malmquist, C. (1978) *Handbook of Adolescence*. New York: Jason Aronson.

Masterson, J. (1985) *Treatment of the Borderline Adolescent*. New York: Brunner/Mazel.

McGoldrick, M. (1982) "Ethnicity and Family Therapy: An Overview," in M. McGoldrick, J. K. Pearce, and J. Giordano, eds., *Ethnicity and Family Therapy*. New York: Guilford Press.

Minuchin, S. (1974) *Families in Family Therapy*. Cambridge, Mass.: Harvard University Press.

Minuchin, S., and H. Fishman (1981) *Family Therapy Techniques*. Cambridge, Mass.: Harvard University Press.

Mirkin, M., and S. Koman (1985) *Adolescents and Family Therapy*. New York: Gardner Press.

Riley, S. (1985) "Draw Me a Paradox," *Journal of the American Art Therapy Association* 2 (3).

Stierlin, H. (1979) *Separating Parents and Adolescents: A Perspective on Running Away, Schizophrenia and Waywardness*. New York: Quadrangle.

Watzlawick, P., J. H. Weakland, and R. Fisch (1974) *Change: Principles of Problem Formulation and Problem Resolution*. New York: W. W. Norton.

Winnicott, D. (1976) *The Child, the Family, and the Outside World*. Harmondsworth, England: Penguin Books.

CHAPTER EIGHT

FAMILY THERAPY AND ADOLESCENT SEXUALITY

Estelle Weinstein, Ph.D., *and* Efrem Rosen, Ph.D.

Introduction

The period between childhood and adulthood commonly known as adolescence is marked by rapid physical maturation and increased demand for separation and individuation from the family. Yet despite the major psychological adaptations characteristic of adolescence, the majority of young people negotiate this transition with few lasting signs of turmoil or stress (Carrera 1983). For some adolescents, however, the physical and emotional changes, including the need for mature decisions about lifestyle and sexuality, are filled with anxiety. The ability to achieve mature, sexually intimate relationships is a developmental marker expected by the end of adolescence. For some young people, this process carries considerable potential for conflict and crises, and sometimes leads them to seek counseling.

An understanding of the adolescent's perception of the experiences that determine sexual intimacy and their function in interpersonal relationships is crucial to an understanding of adolescent sexual behavior. These experiences are a process in whose earliest stages, the specific sexual behaviors participated in determine the degree of sexual intimacy in the relationship. Thus, if a young person is participating in sexual intercourse with someone, he or she is considered to be "intimate" with that person. The sexual activities themselves, rather than the couple's feelings for each other as expressed through sexual behaviors, are what some young people see as the basis of a sexually intimate relationship. Love is expressed by being sexual.

Sexual activities may also elicit acknowledgement, by the peer group or social system, that the relationship is serious and that the participants have achieved some mature status. In the early stages of adolescent development, sexual activities often meet one person's needs while the other person is being coerced or pressured into them. Guilt, fear of pregnancy, and fear of parental disapproval frequently accompany sexual activities. There is limited communication between partners, love and passion are often confused, and the peer group standard is maintained by peer pressure.

In later development, the adolescent

begins to perceive sexual activities in relationships as expressions of closeness, sensuality, respect, responsibility, and mutual concern. In such an intimate relationship each partner can reveal personal thoughts and feelings and can accept those revealed by the other in an atmosphere of caring and trust. Neither partner in a mature sexually intimate relationship is coerced or exploited by the partner's desire for sexual activities, and both can experience a fusion of love and sex. Thus, while young adolescents are physiologically capable of engaging in sexual or erotic activities, they generally lack the knowledge, judgment, and development needed for mature sexual intimacy. (For a more detailed discussion of developmental models see Erikson 1968; Gagnon and Simon 1983; Kohlberg 1964; Piaget 1970.)

Many factors can affect the course and speed with which one achieves mature sexual intimacy. In this chapter we will elaborate on the way sexual intimacy develops, introduce the reader to some problems associated with the connection of sex with love, describe associated adolescent sexual behavior problems (e.g., unintended pregnancy and sexually transmitted diseases), identify some psychological implications associated with prevention of sexual problems and some family issues that may inhibit the achievement of mature sexual intimacy (e.g., incest, sexual abuse), and discuss strategies for counseling.

Maturing Sexual Intimacy—A Transitional/Relational Model

The process of developing mature sexual intimacy can be visualized as consisting of two stages: A transitional stage and a relational stage. The transitional stage is characterized by a search for an understanding of the sexual self. Sexual activities are expressions of inquisitiveness, experimentation, self-driven needs, societal expectations, peer and family influences, early personal values, and the search for individuation. Regardless of whether early sexual behaviors are masturbatory or involve another person, they answer "Who am I" questions: How will my body perform? How will I look disrobed? Will my experience or inexperience with sexual activities show? These "Who Am I" questions are answered by self-expectations in the sexual interaction.

The physical changes of puberty stimulate comparisons of the physical self with peers, from a need to answer "Am I normal?" questions. This self-examination contributes to the development of self-concept and self-esteem. If emerging adolescents view themselves as in sync with their peer groups, their self-esteem is nourished. If they view themselves as noticeably different, their self-esteem suffers.

As transition continues, those with whom the adolescent sexually interacts becomes important. This interaction may include interest in discussions and/or disclosures about sex and sexual exploration. Regardless of whether the initial experiences are with opposite sex partners or with same sex partners, they not only answer "Who am I?" questions but also "Who are you?" questions: What are your needs and how can they be met? How will your body function? How will you interpret this sexual experience?

The next developmental component of mature sexual intimacy is the relational stage. This stage includes couple considerations in the sexually intimate experience: Who are we? How do these sexual experiences contribute to our relationship? How do they define our commitment to each other? How are we meeting each other's needs?

The adolescent who emerges from the transitional stage of sexual development into relational sexual intimacy may be interested in participating in sexual activities (including sexual intercourse) in mature and responsible ways. During this stage the sexual activity in the relationship becomes an expression of the relationship's meaningfulness and not a yardstick by which the relationship itself is measured. The partners will not use sex to satisfy some unmet social or personal need. The sexual intimacy supports each partner's sense of self-respect and self-esteem. The sexual activities are neither exploitive nor coercive, and they occur in an atmosphere in which each person feels free to accept or refuse.

The sexual activities themselves produce not fear or revulsion but rather pleasure. They are planned activities without guilt, responsibly participated in to prevent unwanted pregnancy and to avoid sexually transmitted disease. Individuals who achieve relational sexual intimacy accept their sexuality and can be fairly comfortable with their chosen behaviors and partners. Sexual activities complement their individual lives and their relationships.

Physiological Changes in Puberty

Adolescence, although a definite stage in a person's life cycle, does not have clearly defined limits. Most authors, however, agree that its onset is closely correlated with the biological changes called puberty (Chilman 1983). A complex set of biological and physiological responses, which manifest themselves in rapid growth and development, result from a sudden onset of hormone flow from the hypothalamus and pituitary glands. Adolescent boys may not begin this rapid growth until well into their teens, and may not complete it until the beginning of their twenties. (For a complete discussion of the physiological changes in puberty, see Katchadourian 1977). In boys the result is a growth spurt especially noticeable in height, development of pubic hair, and increase in the size of the genitalia. This is accompanied by a deepening of the voice, skin problems such as acne, and a first ejaculation, often achieved during initial masturbation activities or nocturnal emissions (wet dreams). Nocturnal emissions may occur once or several times during the night. Unprepared for this experience, many young men wake frightened after having "wet the bed," thinking that they lost urinary control. Family discussions about the normalness of these experiences are best introduced before the initial episode and can prevent terrible embarrassment for the adolescent male after this experience.

The fear that they are not as big as, as capable as, or as knowledgeable and experienced as their peers puts a great deal of pressure on early adolescent males. Many resist sleeping at friends' houses, going camping, or participating in athletics because they do not want to be seen undressed. Pressure is placed on them by parents to perform as men. These parents may be searching for evidence of how normal their adolescent really is.

In girls, the onset of puberty occurs some two years earlier than in boys. This reinforces the physical and emotional separation between boys and girls of the same age. A sudden surge of hormones triggers pubic hair growth and the development of breasts. Menarche (the first menstruation) occurs shortly before the end of this growth spurt, but does not indicate reproductive maturity. At first, cycles can be sporadic and generally occur without ovulation. Ovulation and regularization of the menstrual cycle are usually achieved by the end of the first year following menarche.

Because of the many myths and misconceptions about menstruation (e.g., the amount of bleeding that occurs, the degree of discomfort one can expect, moodiness, the safety of physical or sexual activity, bathing, internal protective devices, etc.) and the language used to describe it (i.e., "the curse"), many young women are unsure of what is normal for them. Confusing beliefs may result. Some young women experience various physical or psychological symptoms associated with hormonal shifts during the pre-menstrual or menstrual state. They may pattern their behaviors and even their symptoms after the experiences of other women in their families, especially their mothers. Some common emotions reported by women, especially after they have reached their adult years, are anxiety, anger, depression, sadness, irritability, or general hostility, which can affect their interpersonal relationships. Women who experience these pre-menstrual symptoms (PMS), report that during "that time" there is heightened arguing within the family, usually about problems that have existed throughout the month but that seem to surface just before menstruation. There may also be an increased sensitivity—they cry at the "drop of a hat" (Atwood, Weinstein, and Rosen 1991). For some adolescent women, menstruation is associated with severe physical and psychological symptoms which require medical and psychological diagnosis and intervention.

Along with new physical sensations, early to middle adolescents begin to experience sexual urges which they may satisfy through masturbation. Masturbatory activities can be observed in early infancy, but early puberty experiences of sexual excitement, coupled with sexual fantasies during masturbation, may be a significant developmental activity leading toward mature sexual intimacy. The masturbatory activities of young adolescents are explorations of their sexual selves and can give them a sense of control over their own bodies and sexual needs. Yet for some young adolescents, guilt about masturbation, particularly about the fantasies that accompany it, may be a source of anxiety that inhibits self-worth and intimacy development.

Pressures similar to those experienced by adolescent boys (e.g., to be as physically mature as their peers) are experienced by adolescent girls, but for girls there is less pressure in early adolescence to be sexually knowledgeable or experienced. Feelings about such matters as breast development or the first menstrual period can have lasting effects on a girl's self-image and self-esteem. If "all of their friends" are wearing a bra or menstruating, girls who are not may feel embarrassed and different. Shyness, irritability, and other acting-out behaviors may result as an expression of their displeasure with themselves.

Adolescence is also the time when young women receive messages about investigating their sexuality (if they receive any information at all). Messages like "good girls don't," "masturbation is wrong for girls," "all that men want is sex," and "women don't need sex as much as men" are common messages. Even in more sexually liberal families, a double standard of information is often applied—"women want sex only with commitment." At the same time, the adolescent is receiving other messages—to be pretty, be popular, get invited to the right parties, have the right friends—from both the family and social system.

The wide variation in development among peers can arouse much anxiety, especially if an individual's growth pattern is significantly different from others in the peer group. Group acceptance may well depend on the similarity of growth pattern of individuals in the group. A positive self-image may depend on the quality of feedback from the group and on reinforcement by the family.

Psychological Factors

In addition to physical development, adolescence is a stage of rapid personality development and psychological maturation. Its central and foremost task is the formation of a personal identity (Erikson 1968; Havighurst 1972). In establishing this identity, the adolescent confronts self-image, career choice, sexuality, autonomy, and social conformity. There is a gradual shift from dependence, narcissism, and egocentricity to autonomy, self-control, and awareness of socially acceptable activities.

Havighurst (1972) has identified seven life tasks that adolescents can expect to master during their transition into adulthood. All these tasks are directly associated with the level of development of sexual intimacy.

Accepting One's Body

Within the context of the earlier discussion of the physical changes and their psychological implications, the task of accepting one's body becomes a matter of incorporating these changes into a body image closer to what one has, rather than to what others say one should have.

Choosing Sex Roles

One's sense of masculinity or femininity develops as a result of strong environmental influences. In an atmosphere of changing cultural notions of masculinity and femininity, some boys and girls are encouraged to be traditional and others to be unconventional in their choices of careers, sexual behaviors, family responsibilities, friendship styles, etc. For example, young women are traditionally encouraged to develop intimate, open relationships with same-sex friends, sharing their secrets and feelings. Young men are traditionally encouraged to be strong, independent and private about their feelings. Yet there is increasing opportunity and encouragement in certain employment systems and family systems for these traditional behaviors to cross. Men, for example, may be encouraged to nurture small children and women may be encouraged to pursue high-powered careers. Thus, sex-role stereotypic values and behaviors are not always taught or reinforced. For many young people these changes have "increased their freedom and expanded their opportunities for self-exploration and fulfillment" (Roberts 1980, p. 7). Others face guilt and confusion about the future. The task of choosing sex roles becomes one of establishing a sense of comfort with whatever social roles an individual becomes identified with (Weinstein and Rosen, 1988).

Establishing Peer Relationships

Early adolescent social systems involve peer group selection. As adolescence continues, the groups become same- and opposite-sex groups, with internal sub-groups or couple relationships developing. Regardless of sexual orientation (homosexual or heterosexual), many different peer relationships are possible and are usually established around social conventions and common interests and activities. Given the individual cultural context, the task of establishing peer relationships involves experimentation in and the development of appropriate socio-sexual skills for effective interaction.

Resolving Dependence on Parents

The social or peer system increasingly influences interests, goals, ideas, and values. Gradually, adult rules of behavior are substituted for peer-influenced or individual motivations. Adolescents swing between complete dependence to independence as they establish their own rules of conduct. It is difficult to establish social or sexual independence while depending on the family for financial and other needs. Sexual conduct can become a source of conflict when communication is inconsistent and individual values are not clear. The task becomes to determine which behaviors are characteristic of self and which are simply ways acting out independence.

Choosing a Career

With increased technology and diminished sexual discrimination, the range of available career choices, especially for women, has both increased and become more difficult. The effects of gender stereotypes are still felt. Young men still feel pressured to be the breadwinners and young women still feel pressured to fit careers to potential childbearing and childrearing responsibilities. The need to be aggressive and competitive in certain areas may confuse women who seek to establish a feminine identity. For men, the need to be artistic or nurturing in some careers can seem incompatible with the establishment of a masculine identity. The task becomes to determine the extent to which *expected* responsibilities are really *chosen* responsibilities and the degree to which gender is narrowing or expanding the choices.

Planning a Family

The task of planning a family structure for adulthood has become difficult to master because of the wide variety of family systems in which adolescents are growing up. The American dream of two parents, two children, a dog, and a station wagon is still alive and well, but few adolescents have experienced it.

Achieving Socially Responsible Behavior

The development of a moral structure occurs in sequential steps (Kohlberg 1964; Piaget 1970). The task of achieving socially responsible behavior requires that moral conflicts be resolved and a value system and personal ideology be established that complement one's life and health. Within this framework, sexual behavior reasoning is influenced first by family, then by social groups, and finally, when it is achieved, is autonomously organized in a self-established ethical system.

Parental Influences on Adolescent Sexual Behavior

Although family influences on adolescent sexual development are fraught with confusion, most adolescents do reach mature relational sexual intimacy. The child reaching adulthood frequently achieves an adult-to-adult relationship with his or her parents and embraces may of their values and attitudes. In many cases, the conflicts children experience during the transitional stage become resolved as they and their parents mature.

During transition these adolescents may see their parents' values and attitudes (especially those related to sexuality) as old-fashioned, inhibiting their freedom and marking them as different from and unacceptable to their peers. The rules or moral codes of the family or religious group may offer a sense of security on the one hand, while on the other, the peer group exerts pressure to emulate its behaviors and attitudes. This conflict can generate frustration, anger, disagreement, poor communication, and sexual acting out.

Conflicts between individuals in the family can also inhibit the development of sexual maturity in the adolescent and interfere with the adolescent's other interpersonal relationships. Sometimes parents become fearful, protective, and restrictive when they observe budding physical development and sexual interest. They may be projecting their own negative early sexual experiences onto their children, or guarding against what they interpret as their failures with older siblings. In this case parents may set strong, non-negotiable curfews and establish strict rules and regulations about such matters as opposite sex guests or when and where adolescents may entertain their friends. If the underlying purpose of these restrictions is to help the adolescent delay sexual activity, that goal is rarely achieved. These restrictions are interpreted by the adolescent as a lack of trust. The adolescent may respond by stretching the rules or by overtly disobeying them. Issues of power and control are acted out as parents become more demanding and assert more control. Adolescents may become more defiant in an attempt to achieve more autonomy. Antisocial and other rebellious behaviors displayed through sexual acting-out or sexual risk-taking sometimes serve to engage a disengaged family.

The marital sexual relationship or the single parent's sexual experiences may also influence parental responses to adolescent sexual maturity. Adults with sexual problems or communication difficulties are likely to be ineffective in communicating with their children. Also, a couple's sexual problems can be exacerbated by the need to deal with an adolescent's sexuality. The couple may try to focus on the adolescent's sexual issues, to avoid their own problems. Family counseling in this situation would concern itself with uncovering the couple's sexual issues and helping them communicate overtly with each other about these issues, instead of deflecting them onto their adolescent.

The changes during puberty produce a sexually and physically mature and youthful body. This can be threatening to parents, especially if it seems a symbol of their own aging. Societal preoccupation with youth coupled with a child's youthful attractiveness can cause lowered self-acceptance, jealousy of the child, and increased youth-seeking by many parents.

The demonstration of a new independence by maturing adolescents may deprive some parents of their accustomed parental roles and force them to redefine themselves. If they are not ready to do so, or if they have few interests and achievements outside of parenthood, they may resist and become over-protective, causing fearfulness, low self-confidence, and decreased individuation or, conversely, resistance and hostility in the adolescent. If the parents' relationship relies heavily on issues surrounding child-rearing, the marital relationship may be threatened by the child's beginning independence. Sometimes adolescents recognize, on some level, that their dependence is important to the marital relationship, and they may resist independent development and show increased dependency, thereby refocusing the couple's problems onto themselves. In such cases the family system can work to decrease the adolescent's socialization experiences, self-sufficiency capabilities, and general achievement of independence.

Sometimes parents try to live out their own unresolved adolescent issues through their children. An adolescent may feel pressured into social situations for which he or she is not ready by parents who are shy and socially reserved themselves. As a result young adolescent males may be pressured into early sexual experiences as a way of fulfilling their fathers' failed adolescent expectations. Women who did not experience the lauded sexual freedom that today's women are supposed to be enjoying, may place unwarranted pressures for early sexual activity on their daughters. For example, mothers may take their daughters to family planning clinics to select a birth control method long before the daughter considers becoming sexually active.

During adolescence, physical contact between parents and children may go through radical changes. Sometimes parents feel guilty when they associate physical changes in their adolescent with arousing sensations in themselves—for example, a sudden awareness of the sexual development of a daughter's breasts by her father, during a casual hug, may produce guilt if he associates them with erotic sensations or fantasies; the seductive or flirtatious behavior of a son toward his mother may seem sexually stimulating to her. These common feelings, unless accompanied by inappropriate sexual behaviors, are normal. Yet many parents become uneasy being close to their developing adolescents and may separate themselves without explanation. They may stop hugging or caressing. In turn, their children may misinterpret this distancing as rejection or displeasure.

In this society in which rules of teenage sexuality are unclear, some families simply have not made clear their own values about acceptable adolescent sexual behavior. Parents run the gamut from wanting their children to be popular and accepted by their friends (which in adolescent terms may imply being sexually active) to wanting them to be sexually celibate. They may not disapprove of sexually intimate behaviors for adolescents under certain circumstances (e.g., "love relationships"), but they may be unsure about how to teach their adolescents to recognize these.

Parents are often fearful of giving information about sex because it may be interpreted as giving the child permission for sexual "promiscuity". Most parents want their children to display responsible sexual behavior, but know how to describe this only in terms of contraceptive use: "If you are responsible, you will use contraception!" So adolescents come to believe that responsibility means protecting themselves against pregnancy. Those parents who are certain about their sexual values are sometimes inflexible and cannot deviate from their position. Many adolescents, therefore, reach the stage of sexual experimentation with much confusion and little concrete information.

An adolescent's sexual maturity and behavior can upset the family's homeostasis. What matters is how the family responds to the budding sexuality of the adolescent and what part the adolescent's sexual behaviors play in the family's dynamics. Counseling can include exploring the parents' belief systems so that they can effectively transmit this information. It could include teaching communication skills and discussing unresolved sexual issues in the marital relationship. The family may find in the sexual issues of the adolescent a legitimate outlet for the expression of other stress or anger. Resolution, then, requires identifying and dealing with the covert stressors that are being acted out.

Sexually Abusive Families

The sexual maturity of adolescents may be severely hampered if children experience sexual abuse. Most reported cases of sexual abuse of children concern sexual activity between members of the same family or persons well known to the family. It is sometimes difficult to determine what constitutes sexual abuse or incest because the behaviors and relationships are not clearly defined by a universally accepted criteria. Behaviors at one end of a continuum of activities involving intercourse, mutual masturbation, oral sex, child pornography, etc., between an adult and a child are clearly inappropriate. What is not so clear are fondling or stroking behaviors, mouth-to-mouth kissing, nudity, and other behaviors interpreted by some families as expressions of affection and by others as seductive, coercive, and abusive. When the sexual roles (and rules) within a family are confused and a child is called upon to meet the sexual needs of an adult (be it natural parent or pseudo-father, mother, grandparent, a much older sibling, or any extended adult family member), the family needs help.

The child who reaches adolescence in such a family may have a variety of problems inhibiting his or her ability to experience satisfying sexually intimate relationships. Adolescents who survive incest often feel responsible for their own abuse. They are fearful that the sexually abusing adult will be jailed or that the family will break up if they tell. They mistrust other adults, especially the inactive parent. They feel unprotected and lacking nurturing, producing extremely low self-esteem. They may tolerate sexual intimacy until they become aware that a younger sibling is becoming a victim, or until they can run away or commit suicide.

Often their only skills for relating to adults or getting adult attention are sexual, so they act especially seductive and sexually knowledgeable. Because the sexual secret is so important for maintaining the family balance, the adolescent and other children in the family will go to great lengths to contain it. They will mistrust others and be unable to form meaningful friendships. Sometimes they will behave perfectly so as to be invisible, and at other times they want so much to be noticed that they will commit anti-social behaviors—e.g., taking drugs, resorting to prostitution, etc. Sometimes they suppress their incestuous experiences so deeply that they have no conscious recall until adulthood, when they realize that they have been unable to develop satisfactory, mature relationships and are experiencing various psychological symptoms that bring them to counseling.

Many underlying factors contribute to the development of a sexually abusing family system. Some factors are associated with the adults' families of origin and some are socio-cultural in nature (e.g., the attitude that children are their parents' possessions). The father rejected by his wife who abuses his daughter or who turns to alcoholism demonstrates the codependency that surrounds sexual abuse.

There are several alternative treatments for sexually abusing families. However, it is not clear from the research which is most effective (James and Nasjleti 1983; Porter 1984). One increasingly acceptable treatment—if the children can be assured complete protection from further abuse—is family therapy with an intact family. An understanding of each family member's contribution to the maintenance of the abuse and the abusing parent's acknowledgement and acceptance of responsibility for the abuse is of great significance in changing the family's behaviors.

When a sexually abusing family is publicly identified and outside intervention is established, a change occurs in the family system. "The abuse becomes multiprofessional as well as a family problem, and the reactions in the professional system directly influence family relationships and the social and emotional interactions between different individuals within the family" (Porter 1984, p. 27). We have only recently become aware of the extent of sexual abuse in our society and of ways to diagnose and treat abusing families. (For a more complete discussion of intrafamily sexual intimacy see Weinstein and Rosen 1988; Vander Mey and Neff 1982.)

Sexual Problems Associated with Adolescence

A variety of problems may arise during sexual development. Among the ones highlighted in this chapter are those associated with masturbation, sexual orientation, premarital sexual activities leading to an unintended adolescent pregnancy, and sexually transmitted diseases.

Masturbation

Most people masturbate—stimulate their genitals for pleasure—because it is sexually satisfying and a natural part of sexual exploration. Participating in self-pleasuring sexual activities provides young people with information about the sexual self (Who am I?).

The research literature is replete with myths and misconceptions about the physical and psychological harm masturbation can do. Some religions consider masturbation sinful. While most adults and middle-adolescents recognize myths and misconceptions and accept or reject religious parameters based on their personal affiliations, masturbation still carries negative connotations. People who participate are thought to do so because of unsatisfied sexual relationships. Because of its negative connotations, extreme secrecy about masturbation practices prevails, participation is generally denied, and pleasure sometimes becomes associated with guilt. Yet most people do masturbate at some time during their sexual lives. Some people incorporate masturbation into the regularly practiced sexual behaviors, alone and with their partners.

First experiences with masturbation occur between thirteen and twenty-five years of age. The Kinsey et al. studies (1948, 1953) revealed that many people experience their first orgasm during masturbation. There are noticeable gender differences in participation. Males begin earlier than females, and by age twenty, 92 percent of men and 33 percent of women have masturbated to orgasm. Males seem to masturbate more frequently during adolescence, while females participate more frequently during their middle years. However, while male masturbation decreases in frequency with age, female masturbation increases but never approaches the level of male masturbation (Atwood and Gagnon, 1987). In this culture masturbation is more acceptable for men than for women; therefore, men tend to be less secretive about it. Children are often punished or reprimanded if they are found playing with their genitals.

Sexual fantasies that accompany masturbation may be whole stories or simple images and may or may not reveal a wished-for experience. For example, sometimes fantasies involve bondage, rape, orgies, or homosexual images. Young people with no understanding of the separation between fantasy and reality may feel ashamed, guilty, and afraid. Unless there is evidence of accompanying pathology, adolescents need to recognize that these are only fantasies; normal people have them during masturbation, during dreaming, and when they participate in sexual activities with a partner.

Excessive or compulsive masturbatory behavior may be associated with avoidance of social contacts or with symptoms of deeper psychopathology. In these cases, anxiety or fear of sexual intimacy is more likely than the masturbation to be the problem (Kaplan 1979). Psychological assessment may be appropriate when adolescents satisfy sexual urges and social behaviors only through masturbation, excluding other social interactions even when they are available. The issue is: what part does masturbation play in the adolescent's life? (For a more complete discussion of the history of attitudes toward masturbation, see Atwood 1981.)

Homosexual or Heterosexual Orientation

The word *homosexual* refers to sexual activity between people of the same gender, while *heterosexual* refers to sexual activity between people of opposite genders. According to Silberman and Hawkins (1988), these terms are differentiated from the terms *homoerotic* and *heteroerotic*, which indicate preference for intimate emotional and physical relationships with people of the same or of opposite genders.

Adolescence is a time of self-identification, exploration, and sexual experimentation, each contributing to the establishment of one's sexual identity. This includes experiences that influence acceptance of one's sexual object preference, and the formation of intimate emotional and physical relationships with same-sex or opposite-sex partners.

Socialization in this society is designed for opposite-sex relationships that follow specific patterns (Moses and Hawkins 1982). Those adolescents who follow these patterns of development are likely to find role models and positive reenforcement for their sexual behaviors, whereas deviation from this pattern is often met with isolation, family and peer rejection, self-denial, and confusion.

As adolescence begins, there is a strong identification with same-sex peer groups which replace the family as a source of information and values. Activities in these same-sex peer groups may include reciprocal or group masturbation, which is referred to as *homosocial*. (Gagnon and Simon 1973) These homosocial sexual activities occur frequently among teenagers (Hass 1979; Sorensen 1973), and are a normal and integral part of developing a self-concept. Such early sexual experiences are motivated by curiosity and exploration, and should not be considered predictors of future sexual gender preferences.

Having a homosexual experience does not indicate that a person is homoerotic, nor does having a heterosexual experience indicate that a person is heteroerotic (Silberman and Hawkins 1988). Yet most young people who experience homosexual activities early in their development feel guilty, afraid, and ashamed. "They have already heard from peers that homosexuality is abnormal or unnatural, a position widely held in our heterosexual society" (Weinstein and Rosen 1988, p. 44). At the same time, the family is waiting anxiously for confirmation of heteroeroticism in the adolescent. Young people who do not find early acceptance of and opportunities for expressing their sexuality in mating and dating, or who feel inadequate or unsuccessful in their initial attempts at sexual activity, may label themselves homoerotic and avoid all social behavior for fear of confirming this or of being found out by others.

Adolescents who become aware of and accept a preference for homoeroticism frequently report feeling different from their peers, and lacking available resources or role models. They may isolate themselves from friends and not know how to relate to their families. Unless they have been fortunate enough to identify a family member or an adult friend who understands or has had similar feelings, their intra-family dynamics become strained. The constant pressure to bring an opposite-sex date to parties or family gatherings becomes so intense that the homoerotic adolescent may find an opposite sex relationship and pretend to conform, or may leave the family as quickly as possible. Often the family is satisfied with the initial evidence of an opposite-sex attraction and fails to recognize the loneliness, separation, and dissatisfaction that their adolescent is experiencing. The socialization process for homoerotic adolescents is often delayed until young adulthood, when they are more self-accepting and can explore relationships that they feared during adolescence.

Because of the devalued position of homoerotic people in this society, acknowledging same-sex interests often decreases self-esteem and self-confidence. Problems occurring in people's lives are often attributed directly to their homosexual behaviors and desires. Everything that is wrong, including family issues common to all families with adolescents, are seen as relating to or caused by homosexuality. For example, sibling rivalry is often exacerbated because the adolescent sees him- or herself as a disappointment to the family (no matter what other successes the youngster has had) and see a sibling as a more valued person. "The intervention and treatment of homoerotic clients should be able to differentiate those problems that are related to being homoerotic from those that are primarily unrelated to being homoerotic" (Silberman and Hawkins 1988, p. 108).

An awareness of adolescent homoeroticism by the family is likely to upset family homeostasis. Unaware of the "causes" of homosexuality, parents with self-doubts about their parental capabilities or with unhappy marriages may blame themselves or their mates. The other stresses between the marital pair or among other family members may be exacerbated. This can precipitate the expression of long-term underlying hostilities, even among extended family members. For example, grandparents, angry at their children for other interpersonal problems or displeased with their marital choices, may blame them or the in-law spouses for a grandchild's "deviance." Counseling in such a case would include differentiating problems associated with the homoeroticism from problems associated with other family issues.

"Coming out" and the experiences and feelings associated with it are especially difficult during adolescence, because many aspects of identity are being tested and clarified. Also, adolescents are generally financially dependent on adults, often parents who control critical portions of their life. Additionally, parental acceptance and approval are important to most young people, even though that importance may decrease in intensity over time.

Some questions that adolescents considering "coming out" to their parents or guardians might contemplate are:

1. Do my parents want to know? How are they asking? Are they avoiding any possibility of homoerotic orientation?
2. Do I need to tell both parents? Should I tell them separately or together?
3. Am I aware that their responses may become more accepting or less accepting over time?
4. Am I aware that honesty might not always be the best policy, that living a partial lie needs to be explored against the possibility of total rejection?
5. What is the worst possible reaction, and what steps can I take to handle myself in that situation?
6. What are the best ways to tell them?
7. How can I assess what their reactions might be?"

(Silberman and Hawkins 1988, p. 109)

Intervention includes a review of belief systems, decisions about the importance of maintaining specific interpersonal relationships, refocusing of problems, and reestablishment or strengthening family alliances.

Premarital Sexual Intercourse and Unintended Adolescent Pregnancy

Much existing literature about premarital sexual activity deals with heterosexual behavior, since most homoerotic adolescents do not "come out" or engage in much homosexual activity until early adulthood. Heteroerotic adolescents may establish their sexual identity and seek to confirm notions about themselves through premarital sexual activity. Premarital sex no longer means that marriage will follow. Sexual patterns vary with social background, geographical region, age, etc. Cultural, religious, community, family, and social group values also influence the onset and extent of sexual activity (Kinsey et al. 1948, 1953).

Early adolescent sexual experiences generally center around school activities such as dances or sporting events. Although flirting is common, young people come to and leave these events with same-sex friends or in groups more often than they pair off. For 50 percent of all teenagers, sexual activity begins with "light petting" and kissing that progresses to ejaculation, orgasm, and sexual intercourse. These sexual experiences can be filled with awkwardness and anxiety, as the participants worry about what their partners think about them, whether they are liked, and what their sexual expectations are. For most, the first intercourse occurs during their sixteenth year, and it is no longer unusual to see sexually active thirteen- and fourteen-year olds (Zelnick and Kantner 1980).

These early sexual experiences often reflect gender double standards (males initiate, females permit), but later adolescents, especially at college age, seem to begin more reciprocal participation (Sarrel and Sarrel 1979). As suggested earlier in this chapter, gender differences probably arise from gender-specific messages about sex, overtly or covertly reinforced by parents in their own behavior patterns. Recent data indicate that if there has been no great increase in the number of teenagers participating in intercourse, young people are more willing to acknowledge it.

Adolescent pregnancy most frequently occurs during the transitional sexual intimacy stage, when adolescents are most vulnerable. Sexually active teenagers who participate in sex to seek attention from or act out against parents or society, and those who use sex as proof that they are loved, are involved in self-defeating behaviors that often lead to sexual risk-taking. Families who deny their teenagers' sexual activity and resist educating them, and those who reinforce male sexual prowess and female sexual ignorance, set the stage for unintended adolescent pregnancy. Young women who cannot "say no" because they fear rejection but believe that a girl is still "good" if she just gets carried away in the heat of the moment" are likely candidates for unintended pregnancy. These young women tend to exhibit low self-esteem and to be less assertive, especially about contraceptive use.

Some families see sexual activity involving intercourse as inappropriate and completely unacceptable for teenagers. These families will generally not provide effective sexuality education, and may therefore place their adolescents at risk. Other families may also view sexual intercourse as inappropriate for adolescents but be uncertain whether their influence is powerful enough to dissuade their teens. These families will encourage abstinence *and* provide appropriate information for protection against pregnancy.

While it is obvious that many sexually active young people are ignorant about contraception and that their knowledge is mixed with myths and misconceptions, highly knowledgeable teenagers also become pregnant. This paradox raises questions about what factors inhibit a person's ability to assimilate and use birth control information when it is effectively provided (Rosen and Weinstein 1988). Some of these young people become pregnant as a statement of independence; some see pregnancy as a means of escape from a destructive family situation (neglect, abuse, rejection); still others assert their masculinity or femininity when more effective ways to serve these purposes are unavailable. For example, youths of low socio-economic status (especially blacks and Hispanics) often find little opportunity for education or for employment that will lead to financial success. Affirmation of their fragile masculinity or femininity can be made through fatherhood or motherhood.

Pregnancy and motherhood are a powerful means of achieving attention from friends and family members. Adolescents hungry for attention observe that pregnant peers become centers of conversation in the peer group. Pregnancy seems a viable escape from their loneliness or outsider feelings. But the peer group that rallies around the pregnant teenager drifts away shortly after the birth of the child. Other teens go back to their activities, while the teen-aged mother's burden of responsibilities keeps her out of the mainstream. In an increasing number of cases, as these teen parents become more isolated from their social groups and less able to resume developmentally appropriate activities, they decide some twelve to fifteen months later to give up their babies for adoption.

Unintended adolescent pregnancy is a crisis that upsets family homeostasis. Although most families engage around the pregnancy problem, conflict can emerge between the parents, who blame each other for ineffective child-rearing, or between the child and one or both parents:

How did you let this happen? How could you do this to us?

Decisions about pregnancy often compromise the family's belief system. Abortion may seem an effective solution, but it may be in direct conflict with the family's religious beliefs. Adoption may seem an effective solution, but giving away a family member may violate family policy and history.

Each family member's responsibility to the pregnant adolescent, and her choices regarding her pregnancy, may create other family problems. If an adolescent keeps the child and remains in the family setting, what family roles will have to change? How will the adolescent's mother feel about the adolescent and/or other family members if she becomes the primary caretaker? If she refuses that responsibility, how will she feel about herself "as a mother"? On the other hand, will this new responsibility give the adolescent's parents a return to familiar activities that can sustain them for another few years? Many parents about to experience the problems of the empty nest, which might require them to reengage each other in ways long since discontinued, may be "saved" for a short time by the responsibilities they assume during their teen's pregnancy and parenthood.

What burdens will the new baby place on the family's financial structure or on the parental plans for retirement, decreased home responsibilities, etc.? What role will the adolescent play in the family setting—adult or child? How will pregnancy and child-rearing responsibilities affect the developmental accomplishments that usually occur during adolescence? How will the teen-aged father and his family be involved? What changes will that bring for the family, individually and/or collectively?

For adolescents who become pregnant and marry because they choose to or are forced to, the statistical probability is that the marriage will end in divorce. These adolescents may have repeated undesired pregnancies, considerably lower financial status, and less education than their peers. If a family applies pressure to marry, what support will they offer the new young family to increase its chances of success? How will their anger and disappointment—especially toward the new family members—be expressed?

If a pregnant adolescent decides, independently but contrary to family pressure, to offer her child for adoption the adolescent may become the focus of family hostility. On the other hand, if she is forced to give her baby up for adoption she may experience a short period of relief, and confront anxiety, guilt, and grief later—perhaps when she is planning a pregnancy.

The short-range counseling issues for families with pregnant teens include helping the pregnant adolescent decide the outcome of the pregnancy in concert with her own needs and those of the family. Sometimes her decision is heavily influenced by the prospective teen father and his family, by peers, and by the social group. Counseling must also determine those issues that will influence the long-term consequences of pregnancy on the adolescent, her mate, her family, and her other interpersonal relationships.

The prevention of adolescent pregnancy rests primarily with the adolescent and his/her family. Often the conflict between the desire to control an adolescent's sexual activities and the inability to do so causes power struggles that block effective communication between parents and children. Expressing concerns and disapproval about early sexual involvement are appropriate in an atmosphere that sustains communication even if the adolescent chooses to participate in sexual activity anyway. Effective communication about sex, birth control, and available community resources are our defense against unintended adolescent pregnancy.

Sexually Transmitted Diseases

Another important consequence of adolescent sexual activity is the rising incidence of sexually transmitted diseases—STDs (Weinstein and Rosen 1988). With an increased incidence of early sexual activity, a greater number of partners, and a greater variety of sexual behaviors, more young people contact STDs. Until AIDS, the primary STDs were herpes, chlamydia, nonspecific urethritis, crabs, and the more commonly known syphilis and gonorrhea. These STDs are of concern to families and to medical professionals, but adolescents either do not take them very seriously—in the common "it can't happen to me" manner—or do not consider them important enough to influence sexual behavior. Because of the myth that only "dirty" people got STDs and that cures were accessible and easy, adolescents denied or ignored their own susceptibility. Though parents were embarrassed if their children became infected, STDs did not substantially influence the way families treated or communicated about sexual activity. Then AIDS appeared on the scene.

Now families are aware of AIDS, but confused. They are afraid that by providing appropriate information about protective behavior, especially condom use, they are promoting or accepting adolescent sexual activity.

We are now in the midst of a health crisis so frightening that it will eventually supersede family belief systems to determine what adolescents will be told about sexual behavior and prevention. At this point society is still denying the possibility of devastation to the non-drug-abusing heterosexual population by blaming the disease on deviant or anti-social people (gay men, prostitutes, and IV drug abusers), or those few who could not help themselves (hemophiliacs, pre-1985 blood transfusion recipients, and babies born infected).

Some families with strong religious affiliations, and some religious organizations themselves, contribute to limiting the education of adolescents to prevent the AIDS epidemic from spreading. In their fears that explicit information will lead to increased sexual experimentation, they restrict discussion about condoms and about high-risk behaviors such as anal intercourse. Since neither immunization nor cure is currently available, education remains our only means of intervention.

Prevention can occur only through the elimination of high-risk sexual behaviors. Since the HIV virus that causes AIDS is fairly well understood and does not spread through casual contact, the *correct* use of a latex condom with nonoxynol-9 spermicide placed in the tip before any sexual intercourse (vaginal or anal), or the use of a condom or dental dam before any oral-genital contact, will provide the most effective protection other than sexual abstinence. Condoms and dams are not, it is true, 100 percent effective 100 percent of the time. Nevertheless, they are the only available protections, apart from avoidance of sexual intercourse. Additional "safer sex" behaviors involve staying in a long term monogamous relationship, or petting or non-intercourse sexual practices which provide sexual satisfaction. These safer sex practices significantly reduce the risk of infection.

The notion of high-risk groups has also subverted our ability to educate. Families, believing that their children are not at risk if they are not gay or drug abusers, are contributing to the problem. Also, some families assume their children are always obedient, and deny the possibility that they may be sexually active, so they teach only abstinence.

Since many married people who experience extra-marital sexual activities and many sexually active single parents are unable to require safer sex behaviors on their own behalf, they are likewise incapable of communicating about these behaviors to their adolescents. Often, scare tactics are used in the hope that teens will be afraid to participate and will abstain. Scare tactics have not generally been successful in preventing other adolescent crises (pregnancy, substance abuse, drunk driving), and are unlikely to be effective against AIDS. The adolescents' belief system—that they are invulnerable and that illness and death cannot happen to them—maintains their high-risk behavior.

The belief system of adolescent men often maintains that "good girls", even if they are not virgins, don't sleep around and must therefore be "clean." "Good girls" believe that men will not respect them if they plan for sex and carry condoms. When "the pill" is used for contraception, a young man may fear that discussion of condoms will be insulting to the young woman. Unsophisticated young people have difficulty acknowledging these underlying behavioral assumptions and belief systems and therefore will often not employ safer sex practices.

Misinformation about the incubation period or the transmission patterns for HIV infection also contributes to the incidence of unsafe sexual practices. Many adolescents believe that if they have known each other for a few months and neither of them has any symptoms they cannot be infected, or that, if they have engaged in sexual activity together a few times, it is too late to protect themselves now.

It has become obvious that some young people do not have the information necessary for self-protection, that some deny the risk, and that some, for social and psychological reasons, have a difficult time using protections. An important part of family counseling includes assessing self-esteem levels and self-image issues, knowledge, values, attitudes, and belief systems that influence the sexual practices of adolescents and their families.

Conclusion

Frequently families who come to therapy about adolescent sexual issues present problems that they believe reside in the adolescent. The adolescent's behaviors, they claim, affect the psychodynamics of the family. "If it weren't for him/her, everything would be fine." The circular effect of the adolescent's behavior on a parent whose reaction in turns affects another sibling or parent or causes the adolescent to intensify his or her behavior, which in turn leads the adolescent to affect the parent, are concepts the family must begin to understand in order to take responsibility for contributing to an escalating crisis. Uncovering family resistances—such as unwillingness to discuss sexual activity, pregnancy, or STD prevention with adolescents for fear that they will see the discussion as permission to become sexually active—can lead to change and family growth.

The adolescent transitional/relational model described earlier in this chapter suggests that while an adolescent is negotiating the transitional stage of sexual intimacy, effective family and peer support will decrease the risky behavior that results in serious consequences. With strong family influence, an adolescent will more readily achieve the relational stage of sexual intimacy, with its possibilities for mature and positive sexual experiences, strong relationships, and love.

Finally, adolescent sexual maturity can be explained by the conceptualizations of *sexual unfolding* offered by Sarrel and Sarrel (1979):

1. An evolving sense of the body—toward a body image that is gender specific and fairly free of distortion (particularly about the genitals).
2. The ability to overcome or modulate guilt, shame, fear, and childhood inhibitions associated with sexual thoughts and behavior.
3. A gradual loosening of the primary emotional ties to parents and siblings.
4. Learning to recognize what is erotically pleasing and displeasing and being able to communicate this to a partner.
5. Resolution of conflict and confusion about sexual orientation.
6. A sexual life free of sexual dysfunction or compulsion.
7. A growing awareness of being a sexual person and of the place and value of sex in one's life, including options such as celibacy.
8. Becoming responsible about oneself, one's partner and society (e.g., using contraception and not using sex as a means of exploitation of another).
9. A gradually increasing ability to experience eroticism as one aspect of intimacy with another person—not that all eroticism occurs then, in an intimate relationship, but that this fusion of sex and love is possible (pp. 91–94).

In families in which effective parenting is observed, a positive sense of self and sexual identity is also present. With these characteristics, adolescents are more likely to achieve "the cognitive and emotional development necessary for contraceptive planning and nonexploitation of others" (Group for the Advancement of Psychiatry 1986, p. 56).

References

Atwood, J. D. (1981) "The role of masturbation in socio-sexual development." Unpublished dissertation: Stony Brook, N.Y.

Atwood, J. D., and J. Gagnon (1987) "Masturbation in college youth," *Journal of Sex Education and Therapy* 13 (2): 35–42.

Atwood, J. D., E. Weinstein, and E. Rosen (1990) "Pre-menstrual mood change: implications for family counseling," *New York Journal of Mental Health* 10 (3): 161–68.

Carrera, M. A. (1983) "Some reflections on adolescent sexuality," *SIECUS Report* 11 (4): 1–2.

Chilman, C. S. (1983) "The development of adolescent sexuality," *Journal of Research and Development in Education* 16 (2): 16–26.

Erikson, E. H. (1968) *Identity: Youth and Crisis*. New York: W. W. Norton.

Gagnon, J. H., and W. Simon (1983) *Sexual Conduct: The Social Resources of Human Sexuality*. Chicago: Aldine-Atherton.

Group for the Advancement of Psychiatry (1986) *Crisis of Adolescence—Teenage Pregnancy: Impact on Adolescent Development*. New York: Brunner/Mazel.

Hass, A. (1979) *Teenage Sexuality*. New York: Macmillan.

Havighurst, R. J. (1972) *Developmental Tasks and Education,* 3rd ed. New York: David McKay.

James, B., and M. Nasjleti (1983) *Treating Sexually Abused Children and Their Families.* Palo Alto, Calif.: Consulting Psychologists Press.

Kohlberg, L. (1964) "Development of moral character and moral ideology," in L. Hoffman and M. Hoffman, eds., *Research,* vol. 1, *Review of Child Development Research.* New York: Russell Sage Foundation, 383–431.

Moses, A. H., and R. O. Hawkins (1982) *Counseling Lesbian Women and Gay Men: A Life Issues Approach.* Columbus, Ohio: Charles E. Merrill.

Piaget, J. (1970) "Piaget's Theory," in P. H. Mussen, ed., *Carmichael's Manual of Child Psychology,* vol. 1, 3rd ed. New York: John Wiley.

Porter, R., ed. (1984) *Child Sexual Abuse within the Family.* London: Tavistock Publications.

Roberts, E., ed. (1980) *Childhood Sexual Learning: The Unwritten Curriculum.* Cambridge, Mass.: Ballinger.

Sarrel, L. J., and P. M. Sarrel (1979) *Sexual Unfolding: Sexual Development and Sex Therapies in Later Adolescence.* Boston: Little, Brown.

Silberman, B. O., and R. O. Hawkins (1988) "Lesbian women and gay men: Issues for counseling," in E. Weinstein and E. Rosen, eds., *Sexuality Counseling: Issues and Implications.* Pacific Grove, Calif.: Brooks/Cole.

Sorenson, R. C. (1973) *Adolescent Sexuality in Contemporary America.* New York: World.

Vander Mey, B. J., and R. L. Neff (1982) "Adult-child incest: A review of research and treatment," *Adolescence* 17 (68): 720–30.

Weinstein, E., and E. Rosen, eds. (1988) *Sexuality Counseling: Issues and Implications* Pacific Grove, Calif.: Brooks/Cole.

Zelnick, M., and J. Kantner (1980) "Sexual activity, contraceptive use, and pregnancy among metropolitan teenagers," *Family Planning Perspectives* 12 (5): 230–38.

SECTION THREE

Families in Transition

This section, comprised of five chapters, addresses what happens to families and their members when the family structure no longer fits the intact, normative, nuclear model of the two-parent household. The chapters focus on divorce and its aftermath, single-parent families, and remarriage, with special attention stressed to divorce mediation, custody, and visitation issues. As in section 2, these five chapters adhere to the systemic framework, while emphasizing changes in the life-cycle transitions of the family and its members, including cognitive-behavioral intervention approaches. Practical issues that face the family and its members during such changes in the family structure are stressed in this comprehensive section. Adjustment problems related to family transitions and aspects of diagnosis, assessment, and treatment are also discussed in this section.

Chapter 9, George Meyer's "Family Therapy with Divorcing and Remarried Families," discusses the transitional stage of divorce, the concomitant changes in the family structure, and in spousal and parent-child relationships. It specifically describes the task-demands that confront divorcing spouses. Divorce is a three-stage process—Preseparation, Separation, and Postseparation—each with its own associated emotions and challenges; Meyer illustrates the emotional changes. He then discusses the impact of failing to move through the stages appropriately, and the emotional problems that may result. Therapeutic strategies for managing areas of potential conflict are discussed. Diagnostic prescriptions and strategies are discussed from a systemic framework, focusing on structural and strategic approaches. Specific attention is given to discouraging either spouse from abdicating parental responsibilities, and to helping ex-spouses maintain appropriate parenting functions. The chapter ends with a discussion of recoupling and marriage, along with therapeutic strategies for managing problems of this stage.

Chapter 10, "Family Therapy with Problems of Custody and Visitation," also by George Meyer, is offered as an aid to both beginning therapists, and experienced clinicians working with divorced and/or divorcing families with children which face problems of custody and visitation. Guidelines for ways to structure and manage the therapeutic process with this type of family are presented.

Chapter 11, by Leonard Marlow, "The Family Therapist and Divorce Mediation," focuses on the nature of the post-divorce relationships of ex-spouses and children, the entire family's adjustment to the new family structure, and the children's ability to create and maintain future interpersonal relationships. Marlow describes the divorce experience, its psychological impact on each spouse, and the additional problems that emerge when divorce is negotiated from the usual adversarial positions. Ex-spouses may use their children as extensions of their own self-esteem or as possessions, instead of dealing directly with the psychological impact of the legal proceedings on themselves and their children. Marlow's thesis is that couples involved in such disputes have achieved a physical separation but not an emotional one.

He offers a detailed description of divorce mediation and its benefits compared to adversarial divorce. The divorcing process, rather than the legal divorce itself, is emphasized. In this way the needs of each spouse, the children, the marital history, and the levels of self-esteem and motivation are addressed. Divorce is presented not as a goal, but as a task: that of ending the marital relationship while maintaining the co-parenting relationship, and thus allowing each spouse to maintain a positive self-concept.

Joan D. Atwood's chapter 12, "A Systemic-Behavioral Approach to Counseling the Single-Parent Family," begins with a discussion of the basic functions of a family and continues with a description of the three types of overload (responsibility, task, and emotional) that single-parent families experience. It ends with a thorough discussion of the use and purpose, in terms of diagnosis and assessment, of working within a systemic framework while using cognitive-behavioral interventions for goal identification and attainment and for behavioral reinforcement. The author gives the reader a diagnosis descriptive procedure for assessing single-parent families, noting their variability. One aspect of the therapist's role is that of educator, whose function is to help the family restructure and clarify its boundaries and roles, develop appropriate child-rearing practices, and acquire age-appropriate behaviors. Therapy in this sense serves the purpose of enhancing family members' psychological growth and maturation. Therapeutic strategies for managing typical single-parent-family problems are described, and a case history is presented.

Chapter 13, "Family Therapy Issues with Those Who Are Sexually Single Again," also by Joan D. Atwood, discusses the social, psychological, and sexual issues faced by individuals who are single due to divorce, separation, or widowhood, along with the socio-historical reasons for the increase in the number of divorces. The problems of psychological adjustment to divorce include positive and negative images associated with being a divorced/separated single; social and psychological adjustments are necessary in negotiating the identity transition from married to single again. Divorcing is a highly stressful and emotionally conflicted process, with four psychological transitional stages: denial (accepting the separation), conflict (realizing the loss, and accepting what the marriage represented and the role the individual played in its successes and failures), ambivalence (identifying and trying on new identities), and acceptance (renewed ability to sustain emotional relationships with others). Being single again poses new concerns about how and with whom to obtain sexual satisfaction. Four common sexual outlets for singles, along with the difficulties associated with each are discussed in depth: sex with the ex-spouse, masturbation, short-term partners, and a long-term, pre-existing affair.

This chapter, rich in research documentation, describes the incidence and frequency of sexual intercourse, the number of partners, who initiates, and the quality of sex. The author then discusses the impact of reengaging in sex as a single mother or father, and the more generic issues facing parents who begin to date and engage in sexual relationships: financial and physical energy restrictions, and the impact of dating on their lifestyles and on their children. Comparisons and differences between the divorcing process and widowhood are examined, as well as a consideration of widowhood from a social, psychological, and sexual point of view. A new model for sexual therapy is proposed, with a presentation of the psychological and sexual situations that may present at each of the four transitional stages. Therapeutic guidelines are then explored.

CHAPTER NINE

FAMILY THERAPY WITH DIVORCING AND REMARRIED FAMILIES

George Meyer, Ed.D.

This chapter is designed as an aid and guide for beginning therapists. It covers: (1) the structure and process of therapy with divorced and divorcing families with children, including such topics as historical intake and data collection concerning custody and visitation arrangements, and patterns of ex-spousal relationships; (2) the stages of emotional divorce, including two models of emotional divestment and reinvestment; (3) management by objectives, divorce mediation, and ethical and legal considerations for the therapist; (4) a legal section reviewing the history of custody determination and the problems of psychological evaluations.

The Structure and Process for Divorced Families with Children

More than ever before, therapists are confronted with clients who enter their offices with postmarital relationships as either the major or a secondary issue. These concerns challenge the experienced therapist and overwhelm the novice, arousing in both concern over their adequacy to manage these therapeutic demands.

This form of therapy may, for example:

1. Involve changes in role from a marital therapist to child or individual therapist, divorce mediator, forensic evaluator, or expert witness.
2. Exceed the therapist's knowledge of:
   a. the background and history of the divorce,
   b. litigation and legal agreements, or
   c. legal and ethical issues that arise in postmarital therapy (e.g., the therapist was the couple's marital therapist, and now is a therapist to only one of the ex-spouses. After the divorce, is this therapist ethically and professionally capable of providing testimony regarding custody or visitation matters?).
3. Raise questions of whether such therapy can be appropriately conducted with one ex-spouse without the involvement of other significant parties, and whether the therapist can maintain a therapeutic neutral role while dealing with issues that significantly affect the lives of others who

may or may not be involved in the therapy. How effective can the therapy be, if the therapist is permitted to deal with only one member of the former family unit?

Getting One's Orientation

Entrance into postmarital therapy occurs in one of two ways: either the spouses have failed to resolve marital issues, and have decided to pursue separation and divorce, or they arrive at the therapist's doorstep (a) as an announcement of one client's intent to divorce the other, (b) as a result of being involved in court proceedings, or (c) due to postmarital adjustment concerns.

Except for couples who have been in therapy and have decided to obtain a divorce, therapists often meet new clients and must rapidly assess the situation, the role they can play, and the role the clients expect them to play. Once arrived at a basic understanding on these points, the therapist must make a number of decisions.

The therapist must first decide whether she/he can work within the identified area of concern. If the therapist does not feel comfortable with this, she/he must tell the clients and possibly make a referral to a competent colleague.

If the therapist assumes the case, she/he needs to define his/her role and gain the client's agreement about the therapeutic structure and its limitations. A client's unwillingness to work within that structure may indicate referral to a colleague who can work within a therapeutic structure closer to the desires and capacity of the client(s). For example, as a therapist, you may prefer to manage a visitation dispute with a systems approach, which requires the ex-spouses to be present together for a number of sessions. This suggestion may prove abhorrent to your client, who wishes only to learn how to deal effectively with the situation and to protect his/her interests. The client may be better suited to a reality therapy approach, which is not within your repertoire or expertise.

Structuring the Therapy

This is a critical facet of therapy. A therapist must immediately probe and press for the possible involvement of significant others in therapy sessions before a thorough history is taken. This is true regardless of what approach the therapist ultimately uses. The structure of sessions determines:

(1) who is in control of the therapy (e.g., members attending the sessions or those not attending);
(2) whether seeking therapy is a ploy to:
  (a) gain allies or seduce the therapist;
  (b) increase the legal stakes, in hopes of getting the ex-spouse to back down;
(3) how rigid or flexible the client(s) are;
(4) what they don't want you to know; and
(5) what impact any movement would have—and on whom.

Historical Intake and Data Collection Concerning Custody and Visitation Arrangements

A thorough history, involving assessment techniques such as genogramming, tracking, and circular questioning, helps the therapist gather multiple viewpoints on what purpose the problem serves, what meaning various members attach to the problem and its possible outcomes, who is contributing to the problem, what roles each person assumes in the problem, how the problem began, what part it plays in the lives of these people, and what solutions they seek, especially regarding the role they wish the therapist to play.

When confronted with any postmarital concerns, the therapist needs information about the final divorce arrangements and any subsequent formal or informal changes. The following questions can serve as an inquiry checklist for the beginning therapist.

1. **Custody Questions:**
   Who wanted custody and why?
   Who appears to have the best interests of the children in mind?
   Who is capable of caring for the children?
   Who is considered the more psychologically fit parent?
   Which parent appears best fit to be responsible for the children in terms of emotionality, etc.?
   How civil are the parents to each other?
   Was joint custody an option? Why and how will it work?
   If there is more than one child, were they separated or kept together?
   Who does the child want to be with and why?
   What if the children want to live with the parent who does not have custody?
   Were the children consulted in the custody decisions? If so, how?
   Did the children have to be uprooted from familiar surroundings?
   Are the parents dating, and how will this affect the children?
   Who has legal custody of the children?
2. **Parenting Differences:**
   What about differences in lifestyles, values, and disciplining?
   Is one parent the "good guy"—buys gifts, etc.—and the other parent the "bad guy"—disciplines, etc.?
3. **How the Ex-Spouses Relate to Each Other:**
   What happens if each parent disapproves of the way the other parent treats the children?
   Do the parents have a civil relationship, or do they argue in front of the children?
   Do the parents see each other when the children are picked up and dropped off for visitations?
4. **Visitation Arrangements:**
   What are the visitation arrangements and rights of each parent?
   What are the visitation arrangements if the children have separated?
   What are the visitation arrangements for accommodating children of different developmental ages?
   What are the parents' working schedules and how does the visitation schedule accommodate these factors?
   Are both parents satisfied with this arrangement, or is it too often/not often enough?
   Is the visitation arrangement convenient for all parties involved?
   Are these visitation arrangements/privileges adhered to by both parents?
   Are there provisions for renegotiating the visitation arrangements?
   What provisions are made for national and school holidays, Father's/Mother's Day, birthdays, vacations, etc., in the visitation agreement?
   How does the visitation arrangement affect the noncustodial parent's family?
   Are there any provisions for altering

the visitation arrangements for unanticipated future changes such as job/residence relocation, or remarriage of either parent?

Are there provisions governing the children's travel outside the United States?

5. **Child Support:**

What are the child support arrangements?

How are the payments made?

How are medical, school, and clothing expenses arranged?

6. **Broken Agreements:**

What options are available to the custodial parent if the other parent neglects to live up to the visitation/child support agreements?

What happens if the noncustodial parent says she/he is going to visit the children and then does not?

What if the parent does not bring the children back when she/he is supposed to?

What happens if one parent wants to send the children out of the country to private school and camp, etc., and the other does not?

If a parent doesn't pay child support, can his/her salary be garnished and can she/he go to prison?

What are a client's legal options if the noncustodial parent kidnaps the child(ren)?

7. **The Children's Reaction to These Agreements:**

How do the children feel about the visitation arrangement?

How do the children feel about visiting Mom/Dad?

Do they enjoy their visits, or do they feel compelled to go?

How is the visitation time spent?

Does anything out of the ordinary occur before, during or after a visit (changes in behavior, depression, moodiness, etc.)?

Do these arrangements interfere with the child(ren)'s daily routine or interests? If so, how is this resolved?

What does the client do if one parent moves out of state so that it is difficult for that parent to visit his/her children?

What about visitation with grandparents and other relatives?

8. **The Integration of New Spousal Relationships:**

How are new husbands and wives (stepparents) integrated into the stepfamily?

How are conflicts with the stepfamily resolved?

What happens if the children do not get along with them?

What happens if the ex-spouse does not like the way the new spouse treats the children?

How are differences in childrearing or rules for step- and biological children resolved by new spouses, custodial, and noncustodial parents?

Patterns of Ex-Spousal Relationship

The therapist needs to determine whether the client's ex-spousal relationship is:

1. cooperative—cooperative
2. cooperative—uncooperative
3. uncooperative—uncooperative
4. oppositional—oppositional

This information will help determine the therapeutic structure and approach the client(s) require. For example, except in the first type of relationship, the possibility arises of endless conflict between the ex-spouses, which often makes the children pawns in a battle to determine which ex-spouse has the greatest ability to control and/or injure the other. This tactic often forces the children to take sides, whether they were actively recruited into this battle or not.

With cooperative—uncooperative ex-spouses, the endless conflict is caused and maintained by one ex-spouse, often the abandoned one, who consecutively breaks and seeks to make agreements. The abandoned spouse may not have wanted divorce, did not initiate the divorce, but was forced to move out or leave.

The uncooperative—uncooperative ex-spousal conflicts often arise from what might be described as a "rubber-band effect," in which both parties have extended themselves and spent considerable energy to save their marriage, but have failed. Now that it is apparent that their efforts were not good enough, each goes out of his/her way to make life miserable for the other as punishment. With these ex-spouses, direct contact and communication are avoided, since both are fearful of igniting an escalating, all-too-familiar fight. They are subject to sporadic hostile encounters, followed by periods of hibernation. During these recuperative periods, they work on each other indirectly through the children. Unfortunately, the children suffer from these indirect attacks, even if they themselves are not victims.

Oppositional—oppositional conflicts often result from two ex-spouses who have grown to hate or despise one another. This relationship arises either from an acute or prolonged history of injury or hurt, such as spousal/child/sexual abuse, extramarital affairs, desertion, or loss of financial solvency through gambling or addiction. Sometimes these relationships contain a love-hate component, in which sudden hostile outbursts are followed by "honeymoon" periods. These ex-spouses fight frequently and directly, as if they have found fighting the only way to relate effectively to each other.

In these scenarios, conflictual relationships signify that emotional divorce has not yet occurred (Kalter 1977). In the interim, the children experience increasing stress and uncertainty, with no place to hide (Hauser 1985; Isaacs et al. 1986). The child's developmental level of mental ability will determine the effect of a missing parent or a change in his/her living arrangements on him/her. Unilateral moves made by an ex-spouse, affecting the children or their visitation and communicated to the other ex-spouse through the children, ignite reactive responses in the children. Sometimes these moves cause a child to choose sides, in hopes of putting an end to his/her feeling of being kicked around, and in an effort to resolve his/her own and his/her parents' conflicts. It is a child's defense mechanism.

For example, in the oppositional-oppositional ex-spousal conflict, extreme fluctuations in parental moods create tension and instability. The oscillation between fighting and withdrawing creates uncertainty in children. Out of frustration and the need for structure, children may seek to paint one parent as the "good guy" and the other as the "bad guy." If they fail or refrain from choosing sides, they are likely to become symptomatic (Lowery and Settle 1985; Pfeffer 1981; Kalter 1977; Johnston, Campbell, and Mayes 1985; Wallerstein and Kelly 1977; Benedek and Benedek 1979; Ellison 1983; Chess et al. 1983; Block, Block, and Morrison 1981). A child's symptom, if severe enough, may cause a temporary cease-fire and cooperation between the parents in order to help the child. In more chronic conflictual ex-spousal relationships, one or both adults may be emotionally disturbed and the children may have symptomatic disorders. In addition, such ex-spouses often pull in their own parents to help them gain leverage (Isaacs et al. 1986; Wallerstein and Kelly 1977).

Conflictual ex-spousal relationships usually require a structural, if not a strategic-structural, approach. Highly conflictual ex-spousal relationships appear to function better within a behavioral contract approach which has definable and enforceable consequences and options. This type of imposed relationship often helps maintain their conflicts within tolerable limits. The threat of the court's arbitrarily making decisions or resolving problems is often a strong reminder that each ex-spouse has at least some ability to control the situation. This contract is usually effective with ex-spouses who would prematurely withdraw from, or not cooperate in, attempts to resolve their relationship difficulties, or who are reluctant to assume parenting responsibilities.

These clients have entered therapy either at the beginning of a divorce or in its aftermath. In contrast, there are those who have failed to salvage their marriage in therapy or who have entered therapy in hopes of achieving an amicable divorce, while attempting to maintain a positive regard for him/herself and the other. With them, the therapist already largely understands the issues and most of the answers to basic questions.

In addition, this therapist has the advantage of:

1. Working with two highly motivated and cooperative spouses
2. A greater understanding of what causes them, individually and collectively, to fail or succeed on joint issues
3. Observing how they function independently and together
4. Knowing what they are capable of doing, individually and together, in terms of extending themselves, reconciling differences, and retaliating
5. Predicting what significance present and future options will have for each spouse
6. Knowing each one's ability to cope and to carry out homework assignments

The Stages of Emotional Divorce

Every psychological divorce requires dismantling an emotional relationship between the ex-spouses, so that emotionally free and independent persons may reemerge.

Each ex-spouse must learn that it is in his/her best interest to bury hostility with the dead marriage, and to begin living his/her new life. Mature ex-spouses bury the past, plan their futures, and get on with life. As G. H. Raggio (Raggio, Halverson, and Kydd 1987) emphasized, "life is too short to be wasted in a running battle to get the better of the person you once loved and who is the parent of your children. Shalom!" (p. 14). Not to act in one's own best interests causes a person to remain stuck in the divorce process and to become a victim of the other ex-spouse's antagonism. Legal ploys—motions, dispositions, interrogatories—cause expenses to skyrocket, and the ex-spouses, and their children, to suffer major emotional and psychological trauma. Also, these maneuvers only postpone the necessary resolution of a failed relationship. If ex-spouses cannot act responsibly in regard to financial and custody decisions, then professional help is required, through either a divorce mediator or a marriage and family therapist.

Prior to and during the divorce process, ex-spouses find it very difficult to disengage from an emotionally enmeshed battle. Each is flooded with feelings of vulnerability, loss, low self-esteem, shattered dreams, guilt, anger, misuse or betrayal, etc., all of which require addressing. These feelings are too often disguised as concern over the children, property, or finances. Sex role differences may be observed in ex-spouses' reactions to divorce, although they often suffer from the same divorce-induced emotional problems. For example, females fear that they will not survive economically, while males fear the loss of assets, home, and contact with children. But neither these feelings nor the sexual differences in their psychological reactions to divorce is a license to begin trading blows. Once conflict escalates into legal battles, it is extremely difficult to stop the destructive process. A court battle is a disastrous way to end a marriage or settle parenting issues.

Two models demonstrate the process of psychological divorce and emotional recovery: Fisher's Rebuilding (1981) model and Meyer's Self-Expiation and Re-Individuation (1987) model.

Fisher's Rebuilding Model

Dr. Bruce Fisher's rebuilding model offers criteria by which to determine passage and readiness to enter different stages. His model also recognizes that individuals differ in their abilities to grow emotionally, to recover from, or pass through these stages. He views divorce as an opportunity to reconsider one's basic values structure, and challenges each ex-spouse to decide whether she/he is capable of learning and growing from the experience. His model consists of three stages: Denial, Letting Go, and Renewal.

Stage 1: Denial

This stage deals with the aftermath of failure, feelings of rejection, loneliness, and loss, their expressions, and the required grief work. It marks the onset of separation and accompanying feelings of isolation and devastation. Introspective questioning—"What went wrong?" "Why did this happen?"—permeates an ex-spouse's thinking.

An ex-spouse's ability to manage this phase both depends on and reflects how well she or he managed the first six stages of Erikson's psychosocial development (Trust versus Mistrust, Autonomy versus Shame, Initiative versus Guilt, Industry versus Inferiority, Identity versus Role Confusion, Intimacy versus Isolation). Those who develop favorably can expect to adjust to divorce more easily than those who have had difficulty with any of these developmental steps. Extending his concept of spousal development ability, Fisher has labelled the spouses in a divorce as either *dumpers* or *dumpees*. Dumpers will probably have an easier time adjusting than dumpees, since they are already geared to leaving the relationship.

Part of either spouse's initial natural reaction to divorce is feeling devastated. This feeling usually prompts a desire to be alone. Feelings of abandonment, or the need to retreat after delivering a death blow to the other, prompt a reassessment of one's worth. Whether one is a dumper or dumpee determines in part one's evaluations. For example, dumpers tend to accept attacks by the ex-spouse as punishment for wrong-doing. They are more willing to relinquish things and to work on their own relationships. Dumpees, on the other hand, tend to believe they have done something wrong, and something that they could figure out and correct, enabling them to restore the relationship. They tend to accept anything the other is willing to give them as a means of maintaining, or as a sign of the other's willingness to reestablish, their relationship. They are willing to work on the relationship, rather than on themselves.

In either case the children pick up and internalize these attitudes and behaviors from both parents, as part of their own personal make-up, and adapt these tactics as their own coping styles. When the concept of dumpee is extended to children, most feel guilty for causing the divorce by doing something displeasing to one or both of their parents. They react by taking out their feelings of fear, rejection, and frustration on the parent who brought about the divorce or abandoned them.

Once grief feelings are acknowledged, they need to be constructively managed. Fisher (1981) describes this management as a growth process achieved by living and working through such emotions, mastering them, and learning to use them to benefit oneself and others. Initially, feelings of hurt, devastation, abandonment, etc., give rise to anger, which helps each ex-spouse establish the necessary emotional distance from the other. This distance permits an ex-spouse to function independently and to regain a sense of self. Ultimately, constructive use and management of this anger, with professional help if necessary, yields the serenity to forgive oneself and the other. Instead of asking him/herself "What went wrong?", Fisher believes that an ex-spouse would be better off if she/he would honestly take stock of him/herself. Ex-spouses having difficulty with this stage can be identified by their ability to honestly and satisfactorily answer the following questions:

- Were you and your partner friends?
- Did you confide in one another?
- Did you share friendships?
- Did you go out together socially?
- Did you make major decisions jointly?
- What interests did you share? Attitudes toward life? Politics? Religion? Children? Hobbies?
- When you got angry with each other, did you deal with it directly, hide it, or try to hurt each other? (pp. 26–27).

Fisher also indicates that easily-arrived-at answers to these questions are usually incorrect and dishonest.

Following the initial shock of divorce, according to Fisher, the ex-spouse must learn to grow through loneliness to aloneness. This process begins with the desire to be alone, allowing the person to become more comfortable with doing things by him/herself and for him/herself alone. This process resembles Kubler-Ross's (1969) five stages of coping with death, which requires the ex-spouse to realize, acknowledge, and accept the death of a relationship, in order to free her/himself to be able for meaningful emotional involvement with life, family, children, and significant others. The refusal to acknowledge and express these associated feelings causes a person to become emotionally stuck in an non-existent relationship, and hence emotionally unavailable to others.

During this vulnerable and volatile time, necessary adjustment and growth can be short-circuited if either party immediately seeks another relationship to replace the failed one. Rebounds offer only temporary relief. Their long-term effects only delay coping with the reality of the divorce. Likewise, a counterattack on the divorcing ex-spouse is a delusional ploy to place blame. It is based on magical thinking: If one ex-spouse can make the other feel responsible for the failure, maybe the other ex-spouse will feel guilty enough to correct his/her alleged wrongdoing, and to restore the former relationship.

Fisher's (1981) checklist helps determine whether an ex-spouse is ready for the next stage:

1. I am able to accept that my love relationship is ending.
2. I am comfortable telling my friends and relatives that my love relationship is ending.
3. I have begun to understand some reasons why my love relationship did not work out, and this has helped me overcome my feelings of denial.
4. I believe that even though divorce is painful, it can be a positive and creative experience.
5. I am ready to invest emotionally in my own personal growth, in order to become the person I would most like to be.
6. I want to learn to be fulfilled as a single person before committing myself to another love relationship.
7. I will continue to invest in my own personal growth, even if my former love partner and I decide to get back together. (p. 27)

Stage 2: Letting Go

The second stage consists of several sequential phases. First, each ex-spouse must redirect his/her own emotionality, spending it not on attempts to maintain a relationship but on efforts to maintain him/herself. Second, and equally important, each ex-spouse must redefine him/herself in terms of individual values and attributes rather than as a member of a partnership that has ceased to exist. Each ex-spouse should reemphasize his/her good points, abilities, personality traits, etc., and end the self-blaming cycle. During this process, an ex-spouse may feel as if she/he has regressed to a former stage of development—to being a single person in search of social relationships. This regression may prompt other partially- or fully-resolved feelings of loss to reemerge, perhaps some unresolved premarital developmental problems of family or parent-child separation, or any of Erikson's (1963) developmental tasks of Identity versus Role Confusion and Intimacy versus Isolation; these issues will now require additional grief work. In essence this stage, according to Fisher (1981), requires the ex-spouse to learn or relearn to love him/herself, in order to be able to love and be loved by others, a capacity basic to all productive, vital, growth-oriented relationships. This process is developed by investing oneself in new social relationships, with emphasis on creating "safe" friendships, not love affairs, through which one may define oneself, take risks, experiment, and learn. In this way, self-definition can result from factual, self-evaluated observations, rather than from others' expectations.

Failure to appropriately manage this stage signals self-esteem problems or less than desirable self-definition. This condition may have existed before the marriage, may even have contributed to its demise, and may prevent any other meaningful relationship from being established and maintained. Becoming stuck in this letting-go stage is directly related to one's refusal to redefine the self. Stuck persons tend to dwell on the positive or negative aspects of their ex-spouses, of their lives, and of themselves. According to Fisher (1981), this emotional immobility is expressed in one of two ways. The ex-spouse will become completely other-directed, attempting to please and win others' approval, etc., as a means of defining him/herself; or she/he will actively deny his/her emotional involvement, attempting to act as if she/he does not care about the other spouse or about him/herself.

In addition Fisher indicates that children may become caught up in their parents' reactive ways of coping with each other and with themselves. This only prolongs the children's adjustment to the divorce. Children may not only tend to mimic the custodial ex-spouse's way of dealing with others, but may also adopt this reactive way of presenting themselves. This will limit the child's capacity to emotionally engage others and to develop socially.

How does each ex-spouse know when this stage has been processed? Fisher simply states that one will know it when one gets there.

Stage 3: Renewal

The third stage is concerned with reaffirmation of self, emotional independence, and the capacity to relate again. It is based upon trust in oneself to be responsible for the self and to relate emotionally to others; to act independently in decision-making and to be in charge of one's emotions; to be able to risk, afford disappointments, regroup, and apply oneself anew repeatedly, etc. Trust in oneself permits trust in others, not the other way around.

At this time ex-spouses may reenter the world of sexual relationships, but within comfortable limits, since old fears and moral strictures must be reexamined, reworked, and applied in terms of the regained self. Ex-spouses can now relate to others as adults and associate with others who treat them similarly. Singleness has become comfortable; each ex-spouse can now choose whether she/he wishes to stay single or to remarry, and choose his/her degree of involvement with significant others. She/he has gained freedom from the history of involvement and expectations that formerly controlled him/her. She/he is free to determine his/her lifestyle and emotional investments.

If this stage is not achieved, limited independence and emotional involvement in relationships, if not a skewed type of emotional involvement, can result. Similarly, the children will feel either freer or more restricted in their emotions and interpersonal relationships, because of their identification with either their custodial parent or their fantasized non-custodial parent.

Meyer's Expiation and Reindividuation Model

This model emphasizes an adaptive process that involves accepting and learning to cope with the demise of a primary relationship (i.e., a break in the parent-child relationship or a divorce). It requires the realization and acceptance that to some extent a parent has died, and so a part of the self has also died. The model has three stages: Mourning the Loss, Extrapolation, and Reapplication.

Stage 1: Mourning the Loss

Mourning requires that any and all feelings be acknowledged and accepted, including feelings of hurt, anger, and ambivalence. Feelings are to be experienced and expressed, not denied or repressed.

In addition this stage requires a review of the ex-spouse's life as it was with the child or parent and as it now is, apart and separated. The ex-spouse can then come to terms with his/her changes and losses. This review permits grieving but not wallowing, rejection, repression, or denial of what has transpired. It encourages us to say to ourselves, "Life is unfair, but it is all we've got. Let's get on with it," instead of, "This should not have happened to me. I am not going to permit it. I'm going to fight it."

It encourages retaining the relationship's positive moments without obsessing over its negative aspects, or "turning shit into gold." The process asks the ex-spouse to channel the pain and anger—into sports, creative writing, helping others, etc.—in other words, to expand, to involve him/herself in the world and life, rather than withdraw from them. It is a process of incorporation rather than of dissociation.

Stage 2: Extrapolation

The extrapolation process requires an ex-spouse to separate him/herself from the relationship, in order to regain objectivity, freedom of movement, direction, and purpose. Bowen (1978) describes this process as one of individuation. This is accomplished by teaching or helping the ex-spouse, the child, or others to differentiate themselves—in terms of their actions, feelings, and thoughts—from others. For example, "If your ex-spouse is emotionally distraught, does that mean that you have to become emotionally distraught, too? How is his/her problem your problem?"

Separating him/herself permits the self and others to reestablish and reorder values, expectations, and self-beliefs. As a consequence, she/he is able to reapproach and reconnect more appropriately to new and old relationships. For example, in M. Williams' (1958) children's book *The Velveteen Rabbit,* the rabbit who wished to become real had first to separate himself from a loving relationship. After doing this, the rabbit gained self-definition by differentiating between others and himself by contrasting his behavior with others', as illustrated in Cooley's (1902) "Looking Glass Self." Although the ex-spouse is apart from the relationship, she/he learns that she/he still exists and can still be loved and desired. Through this process, she/he becomes free to engage, disengage, and reengage relationships, in which she/he can give and take, accept and reject, be accepted and be rejected. In this way primary relationships become flexible, workable, and satisfying. Survival, combined with a newly acquired sense of self and of renewed hope, permits old relationships to be readjusted and new ones to emerge.

Stage 3: Reapplication

This is the process of reapplying oneself, of getting on with life. At this point a child or ex-spouse can recommit him/herself to others by dealing with his/her own positive and negative feelings toward the ex-spouse or absent parent and toward significant others, without feeling compelled to bond with them through obligation, reciprocity, retaliation, or guilt. Achieving this stage, an ex-spouse also understands that a cooperative and satisfying relationship of choice is possible.

This metamorphic process is akin to Winnicott's (1965) transitional state, when the child moves from symbiosis to self-autonomy. The child, weaned from a rich diet of "mother's milk," needs to experience the loss of the parent. As a result, the child feels as though a part of her/himself that reflected the introject parent has died or been wounded. However, the child emerges more developed personally and more intact socially than before the rift. He or she is more capable of moving "into" and "out of," while experiencing a greater sense of self. This capacity is fostered by acknowledging his/her own and his/her parent's survival through the stormy transition, without either one being destroyed, and with both still loving and being loved.

Difficulty working through any of this process usually reflects the presence of secondary gains or the consequences of negative reinforcement—better known as avoidance learning—in divorce therapy. For example, a child who, in regard to the divorce, experiences stress, may be benefitting from parental attention that reinforces the symptomatic behavior. The reinforcement of such behavior elevates the child into the executive subsystem and can lead to a parentalized child.

Secondary gains can be neutralized by associating the secondary gain situation with unpleasant percepts, reframing the client's actions (i.e., lavishing excessive attention on the child) as behavior that lowers self-esteem or attempts to please the ex-spouse. This type of intervention is similar to the reframing used by Haley or Milton Erickson. For example, the therapist may tell the client, "They've really got you where they want you. You are playing right into their hands" (Haley 1976) or, "I see. You believe that if you act that way, your ex-spouse will feel sorry for you or feel guilty and relent or alter his/her behavior toward you." (Erickson's "spitting in their soup").

Avoidance learning exists when dysfunctional behavior operates on a non-verbal level or when such behavior has been positively reinforced. In this case, the therapist needs to help the individual raise unconscious behaviors, beliefs, feelings, etc., to the conscious and verbal level. Action-oriented therapy and play therapy for children can help achieve this goal. When dysfunctional behavior is conscious, however, reassociating the behavior with negative reinforcement will do the job.

Management by Objectives

Once these historical data, issues, and questions have been identified, addressed, and answered and the client-therapist relationship has been satisfactorily negotiated, the client and therapist are ready to proceed.

Management-by-objectives is an excellent method to use in conjunction with any theoretical orientation to manage therapeutic sessions. The therapist's dogmatic adherence to such a methodological management of the sessions will:

1. Objectify a very subjective relationship
2. Keep ex-spousal agendas visible
3. Help ex-spouses be honest with each other and with themselves
4. Keep negotiations and options open
5. Help maintain a relatively stable, versus a volatile, emotional state and relationship

The client, in turn, is helped to:

1. Stay goal-oriented
2. Become less easily emotionally aroused

This methodological procedure surrounds the therapy, with the question, "How does this help you get what you want from this limited relationship?" Management-by-objectives also requires the client to establish a ranked-order listing of what she/he most and least desires as the outcome of spousal negotiations.

Divorce Mediation

Divorce mediation is applicable to managing both divorcing and post-divorce matters. The management-by-objective approach works well in any therapeutic setting involving emotionally enmeshed or conflictual spouses/ex-spouses. However, divorce mediation produces superior results with highly enmeshed or conflictual spouses/ex-spouses because it permits the therapist to (1) take a much more hard-nosed position, (2) be more dogmatic in approach, and (3) constantly challenge either ex-spouse's attempts to sabotage or manipulate the other. The therapist, assuming a take-it-or-leave-it stance, is better able to keep the spouses/ex-spouses on a constructive course because the clients know that their only alternative is arbitrary court decisions about what is best for their children and for the ex-spouses. In divorce mediation, disputes about property, finances, custody, and support have a better chance to be cooperatively worked out than they have through power tactics or clever manipulations. Divorce mediation is mandatory in many states, but not at present in New York. Divorce mediation operates on two assumptions:

First, the ex-spouse(s) has/have failed to (a) achieve an emotional divorce and (b) re-individuate. Either condition may be fueled by feelings of anger, hurt, resentment, abandonment, depression, guilt, loss of face, etc., which must be put to rest.

Second, divorce attorneys and courts encourage spouses/ex-spouses to feel insecure, threatened, depressed, and/or hostile. They indirectly help clients to maintain emotional dependency upon a former spouse.

Divorce mediation works only when:

1. The spouses or ex-spouses would rather solve problems than fight.
2. The therapist keeps the spouses/ex-spouses focused on workable objectives while dissipating their emotional enmeshment.
3. The clients fear the capricious decision-making power of a court, escalating attorney fees, and loss of control over their situation.

Divorce mediation has disadvantages too.

1. It is often voluntary so either party can terminate the process at any time and begin or resume court litigation.
2. It may heighten one party's sense of vulnerability to the extent that she/he feels uncomfortable to continue negotiating openly and honestly.
3. It may cause the issue of control to become too large for either spouse/ex-spouse to handle. Feeling threatened, one ex-spouse withdraws from mediation to pursue a course which provides to maintain his/her control or to save his/her "face".
4. It may be unable to reconcile ex-spouse's spousal/ex-spousal value systems. Negotiation becomes impossible in such cases because one client's issues of loyalty and/or self-worth are at stake.
5. It works only fifty percent of the time, since many spouses/ex-spouses cannot sufficiently cooperate with each other.
6. It may inadvertently heighten conflict, because it invites self-expression.

Ethical and Legal Considerations for the Therapist to Ponder

This section consists of self-directed questions about the therapist's role, position, and legal involvement in post-marital therapy.

Q: What are the legal implications and what is your responsibility as a therapist, if in either the custodial or non-custodial parent's home, there is the presence of:
a. physical, sexual, or emotional abuse?
b. drug or alcohol abuse?

A: In most states, you are legally required to report physical and sexual abuse or be prosecuted yourself. Failing to do so may cause licensed or certified therapists to lose their ability to practice their trade.

Other legal responsibilities are less clearly defined. Given a therapist's understanding of a situation, however, various professional associations' ethical committees require the therapist to operate in a manner that will support healthy development, and not subject any one client to harmful effects.

Q: What is your responsibility as a therapist if you find your client is an unfit parent, psychologically or otherwise?

A: This is often a difficult question, especially if custody has been determined by joint agreement or by the court. Changing it may prove more disruptive to all and have unforeseen consequences. Except in cases in which the law requires action, most therapists want to support their clients, and to help clients learn effective parenting skills.

Q: As a therapist, what are your values concerning custody and visitation? To what extent do your biases influence your testimony or evaluation? Do you indicate that your findings are influenced by these biases?

A: Here, a therapist must be aware of his/her value structure, countertransference, etc. She/he must maintain the best interests of all parties concerned, especially with regard to any children involved.

Q: Given certain research findings (Wallerstein and Kelly 1977; etc.), would you recommend that:
a. same-sex children be in the custody of the same-sex parent?
b. the father be sole custodian of the children?
c. young children (including pre-teens) always be awarded to the mother?
d. teenagers decide, if possible, with whom they prefer to live?
e. children remain with their primary caretaker?
f. siblings always remain together?

A: The therapist must be very careful to maintain as much objectivity as possible, putting aside his/her own values to meet the needs of the client family. If this is not possible, the therapist should state his/her values or biases and let clients decide whether they can continue to work with him/her.

Q: What is the therapist's role when she/he is involved in a custody battle as an evaluator or when she/he is asked to testify on a client's behalf?

A: The present and growing legal sentiments are against "hired guns"—expert witnesses hired by one ex-spouse or his/her lawyer to attest to his/her suitability for custody—and in favor of awarding such evaluation to non-partisan evaluators with no previous allegiances or affiliations with a client. Unless requested by the court or by both ex-spouses' attorneys to conduct such an evaluation, the best a therapist can offer is a better understanding of the parties she/he has worked with, knowledge that will be limited and biased by the absence of significant others' input and feedback.

References

See page 177 for references used in chapters 9 and 10.

CHAPTER TEN

FAMILY THERAPY WITH PROBLEMS OF CUSTODY AND VISITATION

George Meyer, Ed.D.

Legal Issues

Perspective

Child custody determination has undergone several changes over time.

1. Initially custody was seen as a purely legal issue of property and inheritance, which was determined by the existence of a surviving male heir.

   Beginning in 451 B.C., a father had ultimate authority and right over his children, even to the extent of disposing of them in any way he wished—including selling or killing them. Marriage itself was a social arrangement which the husband had the right to dissolve as he pleased. Until 1500 custody was always awarded to the father because his children were his property and he needed to maintain his lineage. (Goldstein et al. 1973)
2. Custody determination became a psychosocial issue with the introduction of the *tender years doctrine,* which emphasized the special importance of the mother-child relationship during early childhood.

   In what is described as non-common-law cases, the father continued to receive custody unless he was proven unfit. In the 1800's and early 1900's, the courts reversed their viewpoint and embraced the tender years doctrine, awarding women custody of the children in recognition of the woman as wife and mother. In 1839 under the common-law rule, custody of children under seven was awarded to the mother. In 1880 mothers were awarded custody of all children under sixteen, but only in the United States.
3. By 1970 emphasis on due process supported more uniform matrimonial and divorce rulings, embracing the "child's best interest" concept. Most courts continued to award custody to mothers. However, as fathers became more active parents of young children and women began to enter the work force in large numbers, the psychosocial concept of the *most fit parent* played an increasingly important role. Custody might be contested. Hearings were held to determine custody

on a case-by-case basis (Warshak and Santrock 1981: Santrock and Warshak 1979; Pollock 1985; and Ambert 1982).

4. In the 1980's, courts no longer presumed that gender alone should determine custody. Judges, aided by research and expert testimony, focused on what they considered to be in the best interest of the child. The classic reference was the Salk case, in which both parents were viewed as equally fit, but in view of the father's more enriching lifestyle and financial resources, he was awarded custody.

Since gender is no longer the primary qualification for the custodial parent, more fathers than ever before are being awarded custody. However, a great number of these cases are initiated by fathers several years after the divorce, when the children are entering their pre-teens or adolescence. The large number of fathers petitioning the courts for custody long after their divorces raises questions—"Why at this time?" and "What are their motives?".

Another problem is that the "child's best interest" doctrine causes ex-spouses to try to disqualify each other as suitable parents on the grounds of sexual promiscuity, sex/child abuse, substance abuse, etc. Such efforts tend to (1) heat up the adversarial situation; (2) traumatize the child(ren), who are seduced or coerced into taking sides and even into testifying in court on behalf of one parent against the other; and (3) financially drain both ex-spouses, often causing one (usually the woman) to withdraw from the action out of unwillingness to subject the children to such proceedings, or for financial reasons.

Today the theoretical "child's best interest still prevails, despite the lack of any clear legal definition of the inadequacy of research supporting this concept. As an alternative to designating either parent as the superior caretaker, courts, lawyers, and ex-spouses have embraced joint custody as the solution of choice. Joint custody offers both parents a way to keep their children.

However, legal joint custody has never been explicitly and consistently defined—indeed, it has often been left deliberately ambiguous. The ambiguity of such a custodial statement allows new interpretations to be read into it and grievances to be raised over it. A conflictual ex-spouse can attempt to *save face* by threatening court action, thus forcing the other ex-spouse into a "compromise." This gives ex-spouses a basis for continued emotional enmeshment and manipulation of each other. Even when every conceivable area of a joint custody agreement has been spelled out in great detail, joint custody works well only with highly amicable and cooperative ex-spouses. Even then the effects of physical joint custody on children, who must change residences periodically, remain largely undetermined.

Problems with Psychological Evaluation

A major problem clouding child custody and visitation evaluation is that such litigation often becomes a weapon in the hands of the dissatisfied ex-spouse and his/her attorney (Wallerstein 1983; Wallerstein 1985a; Johnston et al. 1985b; Thies 1977; Perkins and Kahan 1979). Consider the following example of the inadequacies and abuse of an evaluation as reported by Isaacs et al., (1986):

> Every clinician and every divorce lawyer is familiar with the situation in which the

> parent who looks best "psychologically" and with whom the child obviously wants to stay is in fact overtly or covertly blocking the child's relationship with the other parent. Also commonplace is the situation, in which it becomes clear over time that a child's insistence on living with a particular parent is based on the belief that he or she must save that parent from falling apart.

Also familiar are cases in which "once the decision is made, the losing parent is likely to sabotage the court's decision or to appeal it, thus leaving the child in limbo for some time" (p. 222).

A more inherent problem with psychological evaluations ordered by the court or an attorney to determine either custody or visitation is that often only the most minimal evaluation is performed: a spousal interview, a history of each parent, a mental status examination, and an assessment of each parent's thoughts about child-rearing. In addition, research findings of dubious interpretative value are often introduced. These represent retrospective research that offers information only to the extent that the researcher asked the right questions. Furthermore, these evaluations often are found to contain inconclusive, contradictory findings or to suffer from inadequate research design, which leads the other ex-spouse's attorney to debate the merits of the evaluations. This research, upon which most mental health professionals base their interpretative findings is retrospective in that present conditions are viewed as an outgrowth of identifiable past events. Despite this, courts often utilize such research as a basis for their decisions, horrifying researchers with the liberties taken by judges, attorneys, and evaluators.

A more disturbing part of the psychological evaluation process is that courts and evaluators assume no responsibility for the outcome of their decisions. They do not follow up on cases to see whether their decisions improved the quality of life for the children of divorce and their parents, and whether therefore, they should continue using such bases for decisions. The follow-up procedure requires periodic review of custodial and visitation arrangements in order to determine whether the divorced family members have met most of the criteria for adequate adjustment:

1. Have the children and the adults settled down into more "normal," healthy patterns of behavior?
2. Have the adults begun and continued good parenting skills?
3. Do the parents respectfully and effectively communicate with each other about important issues concerning the children?
4. Does the structured visitation allow the children comfortable and quality access to both parents?
5. Do the in-laws promote family harmony by respecting boundaries, rather than forming intrusive and warring alliances?

Given the questionable use of research findings, and the shortcomings of such findings in terms of applications and interpretations, many evaluators believe that a new kind of custody evaluation is needed (Lowery and Settle 1985; Kelly 1981; Wallerstein 1985a, b; Ollendick and Otto 1984; Cliongempeel and Repucci 1982; Benedek and Benedek 1979; Huntington 1985; and Hauser 1985). Most custody and visitation decisions are made from a snapshot assessment, examining the family and its members at a single point in time. Isaacs et al. (1986) strongly recommend the inclusion in custody and visitation decisions of ex-spousal dynamics to move beyond the inadequate question of who is the better parent, and explore the potential for change and ongoing development in the entire family situation. Custody and visitation decisions still, directly and indirectly, appear to be awarded on the merits of each ex-spouse's attorney in the eyes of the judge, rather than through examination of the conditions which will afford the children with the best upbringing. Aspects to be examined include:

1. the powerful effect of the couple's ongoing fight;
2. the kind of participation other members of the social network have in the ongoing fight;
3. the degree of commitment each parent has to cooperating with the other parent, to setting boundaries in their respective networks, and to promoting the other parent's relationship with the children;
4. the willingness of each parent to deal directly with the other about the children and to share crucial parenting information;
5. the willingness of both parents to curtail the reciprocal destructiveness that often accompanies divorce and litigation.

Many of their recommendations are concerned with the *balance of power* between the participants, as emphasized in their last point. This focuses on shifts in the balance of power that may either help conflicts surface and be resolved, or keep them submerged and damage the parental relationship. This balance of power concept also includes the limits of the ex-spouse's flexibility in response to ongoing changes in developmental life-cycle stages (e.g., pre-teens becoming teenagers, ex-spouses remarrying). A two-part, family-based evaluation is clearly recommended. The first part of the evaluation examines each member of the divorced family individually, collectively, and in every conceivable combination, using both objective and subjective measures. This evaluative process seeks to determine the family's and each member's flexibility through measured requests for change in critical areas. It assesses the ways in which ex-spouses typically succeed or fail to deal with divorce and accompanying changes and to profit from recommendations made by the court or evaluators. Which parent is more adaptable to change? Who is more willing to explore alternative solutions to child-related problems? Who is willing and able to live by negotiated agreements? The evaluation also assesses parent-child, sibling-sibling, and parent-parent interactional patterns for possible problems of triangulation, the parentified or spousal child, the symptomatic child, alliances and loyalty issues, fixation at the oedipal stage, regression, cut-offs, etc., any of which may prove detrimental to either the children's or the parents' adjustment and development.

The second part of the evaluation, more costly and difficult to achieve, examines a parent's consistency over time. Such a process would require courts to make initial and interim determinations to be followed by reevaluation after two years. As Wallerstein (1985a, b) has indicated, varying degrees of stress, change, and adjustment occur during the pre-, peri-, and postseparation periods. At present, most of these evaluations are performed during the highly unstable pre- and periseparation periods, resulting in skewed, temporary findings of chronicity or abnormality. What is proposed is that a single evaluator have several meetings with the entire family during the pre-, peri-, and post-separation periods. This approach would allow the evaluator and the court to observe the parents' behavior with the children and each other, as well as how the children position themselves around the parents. Do they go quickly to one parent? Are preferences displayed? Is there a pecking order among them? Who adheres more willingly to the court's or evaluator's recommendations? How do the children thrive under the present arrangement? Which parent demonstrates greater flexibility, willingness, adaptability, and consistency in dealing with the children, with each other, and with these issues over a two-year period?

In addition, the children's school performance should be reviewed, to determine whether:

1. The children had school problems before the divorce/separation, whether the problems have changed, and how severe these problems have been.
2. The children had any initial reactions to the separation.
3. The school has been given instructions about contact with (inclusion or exclusion of) the noncustodial parent.
4. Household circumstances have undergone significant changes, such as a move, financial changes, changes in stepparent and stepsiblings, or parent returning to work.
5. Academic performance has changed, and in what way.
6. Children express their feelings more or less freely since the divorce or separation.
7. Relationships with the same or opposite sex peers have altered.
8. Relationship with the mother has altered, and in what way.
9. Relationship with the father has altered, and in what way.
10. Relationships with teachers have altered, and in what way.
11. Overall adjustment has altered, and in what way.
12. What the school is prepared to do to help the children with these problems.

Testing the Limits

Testing the limits is a method of evaluating antagonistic ex-spouses. By using hypothetical situations, the ex-spouses are pushed to their respective breaking points in order to demonstrate the effect of such situations on the parents, their child(ren), their interactive patterns, and the single-parent family unit as a whole. Testing the limits provides both the evaluator and the court with a greater understanding of ex-spousal dynamics, parent-child relationships, etc., upon which to make custody and visitation decisions at any point in divorce proceedings.

References [chapters 9 and 10]

Ambert, A. (1982) "Differences in children's behavior toward custodial mothers and custodial fathers," *Journal of Marriage and the Family* (February): 73–86.

Benedek, E., and R. Benedek (1979) "Joint custody: Solution or illusion?" *American Journal of Psychiatry* 130 (12): 1540–44.

Blau, T. H. (1984) *The Psychologist as Expert Witness*. New York: John Wiley.

Block, J., J. Block, and A. Morrison (1981) "Parental agreement-disagreement on child-rearing orientations and gender-related personality correlates in children," *Child Development* 52, 965–74.

Bowen, M. (1978) *Family Therapy in Clinical Practice*. New York: Jason Aronson.

Chess, S., et al. (1983) "Early parental attitudes, divorce and separation, and young adult outcome: Findings of a longitudinal study," *American Academy of Child Psychiatry* 22 (1): 47–51.

Cliongempeel, W. G., and N. D. Reppucci (1982) "Joint custody after divorce: Major issues and goals for research," *Psychological Bulletin* 91 (1): 102–127.

Cooley, C. H. (1902) "Looking-glass self," in E. H. Cooley, *Human Nature and the Social Order*. New York: Scribner's 120–32.

Ellison, E. S. (1983) "Issues concerning parental harmony and children's psychosocial adjustment," *American Journal of Orthopsychiatry* 53 (1): 73–80.

Erikson, E. H. (1963) *Childhood and Society*. New York: W. W. Norton.

Fisher, B. (1981). *Rebuilding*. New York: Impact Press.

Goldstein, J., A. Freud, and A. J. Solnit (1973) *Beyond the Best Interests of the Child*. New York: The Free Press.

——— (1979) *Before the Best Interests of the Child*. New York: The Free Press.

——— (1986) *In the Best Interests of the Child: Professional Boundaries*. New York: The Free Press.

Grisso, T. (1986). *Evaluating Competencies: Forensic Assessments and Instruments*. New York: John Wiley.

Hauser, B. (1965) "Custody in dispute: Legal and psychological profiles of contesting families," *Journal of American Academy of Child Psychiatry* 24 (5): 575–82.

Huntington, D. (1985) "Theory and method: The use of psychological tests in research on divorce," *Journal of American Academy of Child Psychiatry* 24 (5), 583–89.

Isaacs, M. B., B. Montalvo and D. Abelsohn (1986) *The Difficult Divorce: Therapy for Children and Families*. New York: Basic Books.

Johnston, J., L. Campbell, and S. Mayes (1985a) "Latency children in post-separation and divorce disputes," *Journal of the American Academy of Child Psychiatry* 24 (5): 563–74.

Johnston, J., L. Campbell, and M. Tall, (1985b) "Impasses to the resolution of custody and visitation disputes," *American Journal of Orthopsychiatry* 55 (1): 112–29.

Kalter, N. (1977) "Children of divorce in an outpatient psychiatric population," *American Journal of Orthopsychiatry* 47 (1): 40–51.

Kelly, J. (1981) "The visiting relationship after divorce: Research findings and clinical implications," In I. Stuart and L. Abt, eds., *Children of Separation and Divorce: Management and Treatment*. New York: Basic Books.

Kubler-Ross, E. (1969) *On Death and Dying*. New York: Macmillan.

Lowery, C., and S. Settle (1985) "Effects of divorce on children: Differential impact of custody and visitation patterns," *Family Relations* 34 (October): 455–63.

Meyer, G. J. (1987) "Coping with the emotional divorce." Paper presented at the Long Island Association of Marriage and Family Therapists' Seventh Annual Conference, C. W. Post Campus, Long Island University, Greenvale, N. Y.

Ollendick, D., and B. Otto (1984) "MMPI characteristics of parents referred for child custody studies," *The Journal of Psychology* 117: 227–32.

Perkins, T., and J. Kahan (1979) "An empirical comparison of natural-father and stepfather family systems," *Family Process* 18 (2): 175–83.

Pfeffer, C. (1981) "Developmental issues among children of separation and divorce," in I. Stuart and L. Abt, eds., *Children of Separation and Divorce*.

Pollack, S. (1985) "Fathers' rights, women's losses," *Women's Studies International Forum* 8 (4): 593–99.

Raggio, G., L. K. Halverson, and J. W. Kidd (1987) *Divorce in New York*. Lanham, Md.: Rutledge Press, distributed by National Book Network.

Santrock, J., and R. Warshak (1979) "Father custody and social development in boys and girls," *Journal of Social Issues* 35 (4): 112–25.

Stuart, I., and L. Abt (1981) *Children of Separation and Divorce: Management and Treatment*. New York: Basic Books.

Thies, J. (1977) "Beyond divorce: The impact of remarriage on children," *Journal of Clinical Child Psychology* 11 (Summer): 59–61.

Wallerstein, J. (1983) "Children of divorce: The psychological tasks of the child," *American Journal of Orthopsychiatry* 53 (2): 230–43.

——— (1985) "Children of divorce: Preliminary report of a ten-year follow-up of older children and adolescents," *Journal of the American Academy of Child Psychiatry* 24 (5): 545–53.

Wallerstein, J., and J. Kelly (1977) "Divorce counseling: A community service for families in the midst of divorce," *American Journal of Orthopsychiatry* 47 (1): 4–22.

Warshak, R., and J. Santrock (1981) "The impact of divorce in father-custody homes: The child's perspective," *New Directions for Child Development* 9 (March): 29–46.

Williams, M. (1958) *The Velveteen Rabbit*. New York: Doubleday.

Winnicott, D. W. (1965) *The Maturational Process and the Facilitating Environment*. New York: International Universities Press.

Wolley, D. (1979) *The Custody Handbook*. New York: Summit Books.

CHAPTER ELEVEN

THE FAMILY THERAPIST AND DIVORCE MEDIATION

Leonard Marlow, Esq.

A very dramatic rise in the incidence of divorce in the United States began in the early 1960s. While the rate of divorce had been increasing for more than one hundred years, that increase had been slow and relatively steady. Now, in the space of only a decade, it doubled: There had been approximately 413,000 divorces in the United States in 1962—2.2 divorces per thousand persons; by 1973 that rate had increased to 4.4 per thousand persons, for a total of approximately 915,000 divorces. The rate continued to climb until it leveled off in the early 1980s, and at present it is approximately 4.9 per thousand persons, a total of almost 1.2 million divorces each year. Since every divorce involves two people, if that number of divorces remains constant some twenty-four million Americans will be divorced every decade.

Nor is this the whole story. In any given year, those 1.2 million divorces affect approximately 1.1 million children under the age of eighteen. Thus, in a ten-year period some eleven million minor children will be directly affected by their parents' divorces. In fact, it is estimated that probably 45 percent of all children born in the 1970s and 1980s will spend some portion of their lives, before their eighteenth birthdays, in a single-parent family. Right now approximately 19 percent of all households are headed by only one parent. Divorce and out-of-wedlock births are the major causes of single-parent households.

Given the tremendous increase in the number of divorces—nearly thirty-three million adults and children are now directly affected in any ten years—it was to be expected that the problem of divorce would attract more and more attention. This was particularly so since marital dissolution, coupled with the changing role of women in the marketplace and in the home, has had enormous and as yet incalculable impact on family life in the second half of the twentieth century. Even more significant for our purposes is the fact that, with the sole exception of the death of someone extremely close, the process of separating and divorcing is probably the most traumatic experience a person can undergo.

As public attention began to focus on

the problem of divorce and its impact on family members, particularly on the children caught in the process, it was only natural that the manner in which couples effectuated their divorces would come under closer scrutiny. It was to be expected that children would be affected by their parents' divorce. Studies such as those conducted by Judith Wallerstein and Joan Kelly (reported in their book *Surviving the Breakup*), however, suggested that it was not the *fact* of a couple's divorce that caused lasting damage to their children, but rather, how the divorce was effectuated and what kind of relationship the parents maintained following their divorce—especially in matters concerning their children. This report led concerned professionals to question the efficacy and appropriateness of the traditional adversarial legal divorce proceedings.

Adversarial Divorce Proceedings

What made those concerned with the problem of divorce question the appropriateness of adversarial divorce proceedings? To answer this it is necessary first to consider the family's emotional climate at the time of a couple's separation and divorce. The decision to divorce, in the vast majority of instances, has been made by only one of the two parties. That party has normally been considering the decision seriously for some time—probably for a year to a year and a half—and has usually been unhappy in the marriage for much longer. Until this point, conflicting considerations have both pulled him away from the marriage and held him to it, and now his decision to divorce means that he has finally resolved those conflicts to a point from which he is able and anxious to move on.

For the other party, however, the situation may be very different. Although there have been signs all over the landscape indicating that her spouse was seriously considering divorce, and although there may have been requests to seek professional help with the problems of the marriage—requests which were either ignored or not seriously pursued—the other party is, nevertheless very much taken by surprise. She may even be in a state of shock and unwilling to accept the reality of the situation. Even if she has passed the stage of shock and denial, it may still be too early for him to participate actively in the process of divorce. As a result the parties come to their divorce unequally prepared and, therefore, not emotionally in step.

In addition one or both parties are usually struggling with very difficult feelings. People do not get married to get divorced. Their divorce represents a great disappointment. That disappointment may be greater for the party who has had the decision thrust upon her, but contrary to popular belief, the one who has initiated the divorce is usually disappointed too. To make matters worse, it is very hard for either party to see her own role in the unfolding drama. On the contrary, both parties tend to see themselves as blameless, and as not deserving what is happening to them. As a result, both spouses feel that they are where they are because of what the other spouse has done or failed to do. If a man is very hurt about the divorce, he sees himself as his spouse's victim. The offended party all too often feels that the spouse must pay for this great injustice.

Yet a third factor complicates the picture. The terrible disappointment which the marriage now represents in the couples' lives has inevitably given rise to conduct by one of them, or to actions and reactions by both of them, which, though usually only symptoms of the underlying malaise, are nevertheless viewed as its cause. This conduct can range from silence and indifference to verbal and even physical abuse. It often leads one of the parties to seek solace and support in an emotional relationship outside the marriage. In any event, before long, hurt usually gives way to anger and sometimes to a sense of betrayal. None of this is helped by the fact that, as very often happens, one party is overwhelmed by feelings of fear and by a sense of profound loss in the face of the impending divorce.

This is the usual emotional state at the time of a decision to divorce, and under these conditions the parties must now deal with each other. What the couple should do now is sit down and make arrangements for themselves and for their children, and address the many practical problems arising from the decision to divorce. Unfortunately, they are rarely able to do this. The very complex feelings with which one or both of them are struggling make communication difficult and painful, sometimes impossible. Then, too, one party—usually the one who has had the decision forced upon him—is simply not able to put aside the wrongs of the past and address the issues of divorce in a reasonable manner. For that party there is nothing reasonable about the breakup of the marriage—it is simply a tragedy. Nor is this spouse willing to engage in a process whose businesslike approach denies this tragic aspect. He does not want sense and sensibility; he wants revenge and retribution.

Unable to address the issues on their own, the spouses look to others for help. Principally because they view divorce as a process that will guarantee them certain legal rights, and because each feels threatened, they have traditionally turned to lawyers. Unfortunately, these lawyers do not solve their problems for them—as they had hoped—and may even make the problems worse.

Why? To begin with, the legal structure views the spouses as parties with conflicting interests. Lawyers do not operate from the premise that their clients have a common problem to be solved in a constructive atmosphere. Rather, they assume their clients are adversaries, and—in the way of self-fulfilling prophecy—the assumption makes adversaries of them. The name of the game quickly becomes "Look out for Number One," with the object being to get as much as you can and to give as little as you must. The rules of the game permit anything that the law allows. And as each party quickly learns, the law allows a great deal.

Something else about those proceedings tends to obscure the real issues. By talking in terms of legal rights and obligations, the lawyers lead the spouses to believe the issue is to determine and secure certain rights and to impose certain obligations rather than to resolve the difficult conflicts raised by the decision to divorce. Further, by reinforcing the idea that the goal of the divorce proceeding is to secure justice, lawyers may reinforce the mistaken belief of at least one spouse that the object is to make the other spouse pay for all her crimes—real and imagined—and not to help them both settle the divorce and get on with their lives.

Perhaps the worst aspect of such proceedings is their tendency to exacerbate rather than minister to the very difficult feelings with which one or both parties are struggling. Almost by definition, the process is long and costly; the divorcing parties must tread water with their lives while divorce proceedings slowly wend their way to a conclusion. Nor, despite all the trumpeting about rights and justice, does either party ever feel that the conclusion was fair. On the contrary, the divorcing parties are left with equivalent levels of disappointment. The resolution is not achieved by any triumph of right over wrong, but instead by a slow war of attrition. In the end the agreement is accepted by the parties only because the spouses want it to be over with. The parties' agreement does not bring emotional closure to the process. Instead, in-fighting usually continues, with money and children as the principal weapons. The law has handed each spouse a document symbolizing a legal divorce; the law does not, however, help them conclude an emotional one.

Those who usually suffer most from this nightmare are the children, caught in the parental cross-fire. Wanting only the assurance that they will be taken care of, they quickly find their security very much in question. While they desperately need the care and concern of two parents, each of whom they love without any feeling of disloyalty to the other, they find their loyalties divided. Sometimes this means hearing each parent vindicate his own positions by slandering the other's. All too often it means becoming a pawn in the parents' struggle. In either event, the children lose what is perhaps most important to them—the bond of unity that held their family and their world together.

Divorce Mediation

It is hard to imagine a process as ill-designed as this legal system. As one commentator observed, if you set out to create a procedure to help separating and divorcing couples address their problems, and if at each turn you purposely did the opposite of what made sense, you would be left with our adversarial system. Professionals sought a better way and found mediation.

Mediation had been employed by civilized societies throughout history. It had a long history in China, was greatly influenced by Confucian teachings, and was employed in the United States by many immigrant cultural groups. More recently, it was widely employed in the resolution of labor disputes. Labor and management both knew that, when all was said and done, they had to go back into the factory and work together. The situation of separating and divorcing couples was very much the same, particularly if they had children. To be sure, they might not want to do any more business than they had to with each other. But they did want to be able to manage the business at hand.

Mediation is an informal procedure whereby parties to a dispute use a third person as an intervenor to help them resolve issues that stand between them. Unlike a judge or an arbitrator, a mediator has no binding power on the parties to the conflict. A mediator does not hear each party out and then make a determination. Instead, she attempts to help them hear each other and recognize what each considers important, so as to effectuate an agreement that both can live with.

Implicit in mediation are certain assumptions markedly at variance with those underlying adversarial legal proceedings. First, the appropriate result does not conform to some external, objective yardstick. The result conforms to far more subjective criteria specified by the parties themselves. Even though legal rules vary considerably from place to place, we expect a court to give us what is within our rights, so disputes resolved through the application of legal rules are disputes about legal rights and obligations. An agreement that conforms to these rules is considered appropriate—even if the parties cannot live with the adjudicated agreement.

This is not to suggest that legal rules are unimportant in mediation, only that they are important in a very different sense. From the standpoint of the mediator, legal rules do not necessarily embody wisdom. Nor does their application guarantee that justice is done. Although these rules attempt to define society's attitude about the obligations of people to each other and to their children following a divorce, they express this imprecisely. Furthermore, they are arbitrary rules, having little to do with the realities of individual lives. In the final analysis, they are applied not because they guarantee justice but because the parties cannot find better ones. Finding better rules—rules relevant to the considerations that motivate each spouse—is the mediator's primary concern.

Second, implicit in mediation is the belief that resolving the dispute is an end in itself. In traditional adversarial legal proceedings, the emphasis upon justice, equity, and legal rights tends to obscure this. In fact, adversarial lawyers become so preoccupied with getting what they feel their client deserves that all too often they fail to concern themselves with resolving disputes. The real issues are not abstract principles, like liberty and justice. The issue, first and foremost, is the crisis that each family member is experiencing.

Third, people try to control what happens in their lives. That is what they did during their marriage, and that is what they still have a right to do, and should be helped to do, at the time of their divorce. Mediation rejects the idea that lawyers, judges, mental health professionals, or even mediators are better qualified than the spouses themselves to decide what should happen in the divorcing couple's lives. From the standpoint of mediation, the problem is that the parties have lost the ability to address and resolve issues in their lives as they did before, without the intervention of third parties. They need a process that will restore that ability. But traditional adversarial legal proceedings leave the parties feeling powerless, which adds to their state of crisis.

Last, the process employed must help the couple bring some emotional closure to the relationship. It is not enough simply to hand a couple a piece of paper and tell them they are legally divorced. It is important to help them effectuate an emotional divorce for both practical and personal reasons. In most instances it will be necessary for the parties to work together in the future, which they will not do successfully if they are still burdened with disappointment, hurt, and anger. Even if they need not do business with one another in the future, they must get on with their lives—they must stop looking back and start looking forward. To do that, however, they must find a way to bring closure to those very painful feelings.

Divorce Mediation and Mental Health Professionals

In the past, when contesting parties sought alternative means to resolve their disputes—arbitration in commercial matters or mediation in labor disputes—lawyers still occupied center stage. The parties were still advised and represented by lawyers, who in most (though not all) instances acted as arbitratrors and mediators. When it came to mediating disputes between separating and divorcing couples, then, why were so many mental health professionals at the forefront of the movement, acting as mediators?

First, they were available. Thus, while the instinctive reaction of each spouse once they had decided to divorce may have been to turn to lawyers, couples were increasingly seeking mental health professionals before they got to that point. In the past most mental health professionals viewed their job as helping the parties address their marriage issues and felt that their obligation ended once a couple decided to divorce, but they began increasingly to question the wisdom of that assumption. For more and more mental health professionals had become family therapists. This caused them to reevaluate their role, because a divorce might dissolve a marriage but it does not—when there are children—dissolve a family.

Second, mental health professionals felt comfortable helping separating and divorcing couples, and they also considered themselves far more qualified to assist than were lawyers or judges. Mental health professionals knew that the best interests of children would be better served if important issues could be resolved by the spouses themselves. This was much more likely to happen in the therapist's offices than in the offices of the attorneys or in the judge's chambers.

Third, mental health professionals attempted to repair the damage done by lawyers in the adversarial legal system. If mental health professionals were going to confront the problem anyway, why shouldn't they get in there before more damage was done, damage they might be able to prevent?

Fourth, although mental health professionals had no monopoly on the skills and understanding necessary for mediation, by both training and experience they had these to a very high degree. Whether as marriage or divorce counselors, they worked toward the resolution of conflicts between the parties. And more than any other professional group, they were qualified to do this successfully.

Finally, and perhaps most important, mental health professionals shared most of the assumptions implicit in mediation, particularly in mediation of disputes between separating and divorcing couples. When a mental health professional worked with couples in marriage counseling, his guide was reality, not a set of abstract principles. Thus, rather than concentrating on what the ideal marriage was like, he worked with what he had. His goal was to effectuate sufficient change to make this marriage acceptable to both parties.

As she had accepted a limited role as a marriage counselor, so she was able to accept a limited role as a divorce counselor. She did not expect to solve all the problems that a divorcing couple had been unable to solve in their marriage. What she could do was help them get beyond those problems. She hoped to counsel effectively, and in a manner that would not add to the couple's emotional injuries. For mental health professionals, mediation provided the necessary vehicle.

What about the more technical aspects of the problems with which the parties were faced? There are equitable distribution laws and tax laws, of which mental health professionals could not speak with any authority. There are evaluations of homes, businesses, and pensions, and questions about medical insurance, life insurance, and college education expenses—all issues with which mental health professionals are not generally conversant. Finally, the understanding concluded by the parties must be reduced to a formal agreement drawn up by an attorney.

On the face of it, these limitations might seem to disqualify mental health professionals from divorce mediation. They persisted, however, for two reasons: First, they firmly believed that, contrary to lawyers' understanding, a couple's divorce was not essentially a legal problem, but a personal problem with legal implications. Second, mental health professionals believed no one was more competent than the couple themselves to determine what would happen in the lives of a divorcing couple.

Was the couple capable of deciding all these things on their own, without assistance? Of course not. They would hire an architect to help them design a home, and they would retain an attorney to help them design a will or a contract. But these experts were there to help the couple make a decision, not to make it for them. Therefore, mental health professionals realized that decisions involving expertise in other fields did not disqualify them—they simply had to incorporate the expertise of others into mediation practice.

Mental health professionals were aided in two other respects. First, since the results of mediation would be embodied in a legal document, lawyers were going to be involved. In that case, there was no reason not to call upon these lawyers to answer legal questions, to assist in arranging for valuation of pensions, businesses, or other assets, and to provide whatever other expert help they could. It became the practice of many mediators to have each party consult with separate lawyers, for their unique expertise, during the course of mediation. This matter of separate lawyers stemmed from the legal profession's traditional belief that one attorney should not represent parties with conflicting interests.

The practice of mediation was not without its problems. Lawyers and nonlawyers alike who entered the field of divorce mediation unthinkingly accepted the mythology that each party needed independent legal counsel to protect his or her interests. Mediators quickly learned, however, that this counsel all too often reintroduced the counterproductive adversarial attitudes they had tried so hard to eliminate. In time mental health professionals began to find attorneys sympathetic to mediation. This was particularly important in drafting of the final agreement, when the mediator all too often lost control of the process. In the hands of separate, adversarial attorneys, the agreement the mediator had so carefully helped the parties conclude often fell apart.

Many mental health professionals felt they knew only half the story, so to speak, and they found many attorneys who wished to become involved in mediation because they felt similarly disadvantaged. That is, while they knew the law and a great deal of technical information, they lacked many skills critical to successful mediation. The logical conclusion was to join forces, so the field of mediation has increasingly been populated with mental health professionals and lawyers working in tandem, each providing, at different stages of mediation, the expertise that the other lacks. Moreover, even if one attorney was precluded from representing both parties in an adversarial setting, a single attorney was not necessarily prevented from assisting the mental health professional in concluding a mediated settlement.

Numerous training programs began to

spring up around the country to provide would-be mediators with necessary technical and legal information, and to teach them the skills needed to mediate successfully. These training programs were not intended to make mental health professionals experts in the law or to make attorneys experts in conflict resolution, but to make mediators more familiar with areas outside their normal professional competence, and to make them thereby more comfortable in their work.

State and national organizations were founded by practicing mediators. These organizations afforded mediators the opportunity to meet and learn from one another by providing workshops and seminars on an ongoing basis, as opportunities for mediators to advance their training and education.

Divorce Mediation and Therapy

While many assumptions and skills brought by mental health professionals to divorce mediation assisted couples with their separation and divorce agreements, these professionals quickly realized that there were significant differences between their traditional roles as marriage counselors and their new roles as divorce counselors. It was important to keep these differences in mind.

There was no unanimity of opinion here, but most mental health professionals—at least when they were consulted by both parties together—were initially committed to preserving the marriage. They believed their role was to try to improve the relationship between the spouses.

In divorce mediation, the orientation is in the opposite direction. To be sure, if both parties, even at this late stage and in spite of serious misgivings, are willing to address the problems in their marriage with a view to maintaining it, the mediator's task is the equivalent of marriage counseling. But this is rarely the case. In most instances, the decision to divorce is made by one party. The problem, therefore, is that one spouse looks to the mediator to persuade the other to reconsider the divorce decision, while the other spouse looks to the mediator to get her through this process as quickly as possible.

The mediator cannot please both—in fact, in a real sense he must choose between them. The choice may be hard, but it is nevertheless clear. As the mediator understands and accepts the desire of one party to maintain the relationship, he must also respect the other's decision to end it. More important, the party who has chosen divorce did not come to the mediator to justify himself, and the mediator has no right to require that. Contrary to conventional mythology, he did not choose divorce casually; rather, he struggled with it for months or even years. Again contrary to conventional mythology, the decision was probably very painful. The mediator has an obligation to respect it.

Another very practical consideration binds the mediator to respect a decision to divorce: there is very little likelihood that he could dissuade the party who is pressing for a divorce, and get her to join in attempting to maintain the marriage. Most couples who have come to this point have already attempted to address their marriage problems through therapy. This may or may not have been a joint effort or a lengthy one; nevertheless, this therapy reflected what the parties were willing and able to do. Even if the mediator could convince them to try therapy again, it would presuppose that she could succeed where others had failed.

As religions may require leaps of

faith, so divorces are not based on logic alone. The instigator of divorce needed to go an extra, and more difficult distance. Perhaps he used a bridge relationship with a third party as a support system during this difficult time. Perhaps he simply forced himself to stop questioning, to stop looking backward, and to take a bold step into the future. That was not easy and he did not necessarily take the step without serious misgivings. He, therefore, does not want to retrace his steps and will not thank the mediator for forcing him to. On the contrary, he will view a proposal of marriage counseling as a bias or predisposition on the mediator's part which may disqualify the mediator and even the mediation process for him. (If he does find a bridge relationship and it is an ongoing one, there is an even more formidable obstacle to reconciliation.)

What benefits would come from marriage counseling? In all likelihood, none. The mental health professional, acting as a mediator, must always respect the decision of the party who has chosen divorce, even if she personally disagrees with it. In respecting that decision, a mental health professional might initially feel that she has violated the precepts of her primary profession. That is not the case. On the contrary, she has relied on one of its most important understandings: that she must always start where the client is. Therapists do not start with idealized goals. Rather, grounded in reality, they do what is possible.

Mediation is far more task-oriented and goal-directed than therapy. All couples come to mediators for the same purpose: to help them settle the issues resulting from their decision to separate and divorce. To be sure, there may be many other subgoals which they and the mediator would like to achieve. The mediator would certainly like to help them adjust to their divorce. He would like to help them maintain (or develop) a relationship that will enable them to handle whatever business remains after their divorce. And, of course, he would like to assure a continuing bond between each of them and their children. As important as each of these may be, all are ancillary to the primary purpose. Thus, if the mediator cannot help the couple conclude an agreement regardless of what other benefits he has bestowed upon them, the mediation is not a success. Conversely, if the couple concludes an agreement, the mediation is successful even if the mediator has not secured any of these other benefits.

Perhaps the most important distinction between mediation and therapy concerns the reaction of the mental health professional to the feelings expressed by the parties. In therapy, these feelings are everything. As a by-product of the two individuals' internal conflicts and of the conflicts between them as a couple, these feelings represent the key to the couple's problems. The therapist believes that he will not be of any value to the couple unless he addresses and reduces their level of emotional conflict. Thus, it is an inconsistency in terms to suggest that a mental health professional's efforts to resolve the conflict between the parties have succeeded, even though he has left them with the same level of feelings that they had before.

Just the opposite is usually the case in divorce mediation. Rather than being the key to their problems, the feelings which so overwhelm the parties are usually the impediment to resolution. The problem for the mediator is that the spouses feel too much and understand too little. In fact, these feelings have so encrusted the couple's practical problems that both are blinded to these problems themselves. The mediation will be successful only if both parties realize that they can agree only if they find a way to control their feelings.

Both husband and wife are overwhelmed by these feelings. Their sense of having been wronged, and their need to believe that there is some sense (justice) in all this, compel them to express feelings. The party to whom these feelings are directed does not share the other's view, and replies with an expression of his/her own feelings. Rarely will this benefit anyone. On the contrary, expressing their feelings may well jeopardize the possibility of the couple's ever concluding an agreement. One of the mediator's jobs is to subtly underscore this.

A mental health professional engaged with a couple in therapy might view the surface calm, knowing that it masks feelings which she and the couple will have to uncover, but in mediation the same mental health professional must learn not to disturb that surface calm. It represents the conscious and unconscious decisions of the parties to get through the divorce. Their conclusion, therefore, is that they must somehow rein in their feelings, if only for the moment; that decision is reality-based, and the mediator must respect it.

What will become of those terrible feelings? After all, being on one's best behavior is not changing one's behavior, and reining in feelings does not mean that they have been adequately dealt with. If they are not, won't they come back to haunt the parties and their children in the future? In that case wouldn't it be more appropriate for the mental health professional, acting as a mediator, to address them?

The answer is no. The couple has come to the mediator for the very limited purpose of addressing certain practical problems with which they are faced. It might make sense also to address these emotional problems. The mediator may not be able to help the couple effectuate the desirable emotional closure unless he does. Nevertheless, the couple has still not come to him for that purpose.

That should be sufficient reason, but there is an even more important one. The mental health professional acts as a mediator because she is committed to the idea that she will help the couple if she can bring them to an agreement. In that respect, although mediation is not therapy, she believes that a successful mediation will be therapeutic. Why? Because, speaking metaphorically, the mediator believes in a natural healing process—a natural tendency of human beings toward health and adaptation. The mediator, then, does not believe that it is necessary for her to heal their wounds. All that is necessary is for her to establish conditions which will permit that natural healing process to proceed unobstructed.

For that to happen, however—for the couple to begin looking forward, rather than continue looking backward—there must first be a resolution of the issues they now face. The mediator believes this resolution is his primary obligation, and he cannot allow anything to interfere with it. Although he would like to address, and hopefully resolve, some difficult feelings with which one or both of the parties are struggling, he cannot permit such an excursion to interfere with his primary obligation.

What about those feelings after the couple has reached an agreement? Here again the mediator falls back on her belief that the agreement itself will set in motion conditions that will enable the couple to come to terms with these feelings, either on their own or with professional help. In this sense the mediator believes that the process itself, although it is not therapy, is therapeutic.

When, if ever, should a mediator attempt to address these feelings? Only when one party is having such difficulty dealing with them that they interfere with the mediation. Obviously, as part of his work with the couple, a mediator will be supportive and will express his understanding of how difficult and painful this experience is. However, he does this not to address feelings directly, but to help both parties deal with them on their own. If they can keep those feelings from substantially interfering with the mediation's progress, he will ignore them. On the other hand, if those feelings are so overwhelming that they interfere with the work at hand, the mediator has no choice but to address them. Even so, however, he will address them only in a limited way. His goal is not to resolve the conflict those feelings express. (That will be the job of others once the mediation is concluded, if the party in question seeks help.) The mediator's goal is simply to help the troubled party gain sufficient control over his feelings so that the mediation can proceed.

Conclusion

Divorce mediation presents both a new opportunity and a new challenge to mental health professionals. It is a new opportunity in that it permits mental health professionals to help separating and divorcing couples. It is a new opportunity, also, in that it permits those professionals to more meaningfully address one of the most significant factors affecting family life in the second half of the twentieth century.

That opportunity is also a challenge. Mental health professionals must broaden their skills and expand their traditional horizons. More important, they must be willing to reexamine certain assumptions and refine them in answering the question, "How can I best help the parties and their children through this crisis?"

Suggested Readings

Erickson, S., and M. Erickson (1988) *Family Mediation Case Book*. New York: Brunner/Mazel.

Fisher, R., and W. Ury (1981) *Getting to Yes: Negotiating Agreements without Giving In*. Boston: Houghton Mifflin.

Folberg, J., and A. Taylor (1984) *Mediation: A Comprehensive Guide to Resolving Conflicts without Litigation*. San Francisco: Jossey-Bass.

Gold, L. (1985) "Reflections on the transition from therapist to mediator," in J. A. Lemmon, ed., *Mediation Quarterly*, vol. 9—*Legal and Family Perspectives in Divorce Mediation*. San Francisco: Jossey-Bass, 112–26.

Kelly, J. (1983) "Mediation and psychotherapy: Distinguishing the difference," in Lemmon, *Mediation Quarterly*, vol. 1—*Dimensions and Practice of Divorce Mediation*, 73–79.

Marlow, L., and R. Sauber (1989) *The Handbook of Divorce Mediation*. New York: Plenum Press.

Milne, A. (1983) "Divorce mediation: The state of the art," in Lemmon, *Dimensions and Practice of Divorce Mediation*.

Saposnek, D. T. (1983) *Mediating Child Custody Disputes: A Systematic Guide for Family Therapists, Court Counselors, Attorneys and Judges*, vol. 2. San Francisco: Jossey-Bass, 104–126.

Chapter Twelve

A SYSTEMIC-BEHAVIORAL APPROACH TO COUNSELING THE SINGLE-PARENT FAMILY

Joan D. Atwood, Ph.D., C.S.W.

Abstract

Since 1970 the number of single-parent households has doubled. Of these households, 70 percent are the result of divorce. Fourteen percent are the result of death of a parent, 6 percent are temporary because one parent is away, and 10 percent have never included a married couple (Weiss 1979). In 1985 there were 1.2 million divorces (Diegmuller 1986). By the end of this century, single-parent and remarried families will outnumber the traditional nuclear family in this country. Because of the problems inherent in this type of family system, the single-parent family frequently comes for counseling. The purpose of this paper is to present systemic/behavioral counseling techniques which the author has found very successful. A brief description of systemic/behavioral theory relevant to single-parent family counseling is presented. A single-parent case history, through which behavioral/systemic counseling techniques with the single-parent family are illustrated, is then discussed.

Most parents, whether in a two-parent or a single-parent situation, are not aware of the functions of a family. According to Parsons and Bales (1955), the functions of the family are to socialize the children; to provide models for relationships with others; to establish cultural norms; to provide religious and ethical values and emotional support; to politically indoctrinate the children; to provide financial care; to give guidance; and to educate the young. When these tasks are accomplished, a functional family provides the children with a healthy sense of self (Walsh 1982). It teaches them how to relate to other people by providing the nurturing, support, and security necessary for each member of the family to develop to his or her fullest potential. The dysfunctional family is not carrying out these tasks satisfactorily, and so is stuck in its development (Walsh, 1982).

These are not easy tasks even when there are two adults in parenting roles. The situation becomes even more difficult in a single-parent family household, with only one person responsible for providing the young with an adequate foundation for psychological development. In addition, there are many variations among single-parent families. The distinction between the types of single-parent families is important because they differ considerably with respect to their access to economic and social resources. Widows have much higher incomes and experience less social disapproval than do other groups, whereas never-married mothers have the fewest resources and are most likely to become dependent on government welfare assistance, leading to the feminization of poverty (Kohan et al. 1979). In 1983 one of two children in female-headed households was poor (Congressional Budget Office 1985).

General Concerns of Single-Parent Families

Even though there is no one type of single-parent family system (Mendes 1979), certain generalities can be made about the problems inherent in this system. For example, Weiss (1979) has identified three levels of possible overload for the single parent. First, responsibility overload: The single parent has to make all decisions regarding family life and the children's behavior. From financial details to daily domestic duties, there is no one else to give direction. The parent can feel overwhelmed by these demands. Although children may begin to take on responsibilities, they are unable to make some of the bigger decisions regarding their lives. It is in this area of increased responsibility that the single parent may feel the greatest effects of lacking a system of interaction in which many decisions are shared. Instead of feeling free to make decisions without interference, the single parent may suffer from tension, pressure, and confusion (Ahrons and Rodgers 1987).

The second area pinpointed by Weiss (1979) is task overload: Too much to do. The parent has to earn money, prepare meals, clean house, discipline the children, make doctor and dental appointments, pay rent, insurance, and other bills, and so on—all alone. Most single parents have little time for friends or social life, which often leads to social isolation.

Weiss's (1979) third level of adjustment is emotional overload: The single parent must be available to his or her children emotionally, even when exhausted or drained of all reserves. While some single parents have family, friends, or an ex-spouse to consult, many have no one to turn to for needed attention, or to discuss the children's growth and personality development. Many have no other person to step in when the parent is feeling so stretched that she or he may be irrational or thoughtless with regard to the children. Emotionally overburdened parents may lash out, physically as well as verbally, against a child, not because the child has done anything wrong but simply because he or she is there (Isaacs and Montalvo 1986).

The loss of the other parent is also significant in other ways. The parent may no longer have an ally to help him or her in disciplinary efforts. The single parent, with new responsibilities, can suffer in ways that are passed on to the children, and that are detrimental to the functioning of the whole family. A depressed, hostile, and aggressive person may see his or her children acting out some distress and may be unable to stop them. The major point is that the single parent is the focus, especially for younger children, around which all task performance occurs, and through which all anxiety and stress must be processed (Beal 1980).

Other pressures on the parent in the primary home are conflicts between parents regarding child-rearing practices and expenditure of time and money on the children. The absent parent may sabotage the other parent's efforts by trying to align the children with him or her against the primary parent. In all situations the absent parent must be included in consideration of the system (Beal 1980). Grandparents and other relatives may take sides with one parent, confusing the children with divided loyalties. Or they may align with the children against the custodial parent, creating a cross-generational coalition that leaves the family system ripe for dysfunction. Thus, whether through necessity or choice, single-parent families share certain basic problems: coping single-handedly with day-to-day decisions, the supervision and discipline of children, and compensating for the absence of the other parent.

General Systems Theory

General Systems Theory is the major underlying theory of most forms of family therapy. Systemic family therapy applies general systems theory to family constellations. The systemic approach to family counseling looks at the symptoms or problems presented in a counseling situation in terms of the whole family. Systems theorists assume that behavior is a communication about relationships (Haley 1977). Behavior can be understood only within the context in which it occurs, and is defined by (as well as defines) and influenced by (as well as influences) all other behavior in that context or system.

The basic assumption of the family systems counselor, then, is that all parts are interrelated. Change in any one part of the system can cause change in another part. Each part of the system has a unique function, and the parts work together to achieve common family goals (Hoffman 1981). Families also have boundaries that separate them from the environment. The family boundary is structured by the values, norms, and attitudes derived from the family's cultural heritage (Minuchin 1974). Boundaries are the rules and regulations which govern interactions among family members, and between the family and the surrounding society. These rules and regulations define how specific family functions are to be carried out (Minuchin and Fishman 1981). For a detailed examination of general systems theory, see von Bertalanffy (1968); for a description of its application to family therapy, see Bateson (1979); Bowen (1978); Haley (1977); Hoffman (1981); Madanes (1981); and Minuchin and Fishman (1981).

For example, if a mother in an intact family comes to counseling distressed because her teenaged son has run away for the fourth time in three months, a family systems counselor might insist on seeing all members of the family, to find out how running away (the presenting problem) is functional for the ongoing maintenance of the family system. It is possible that at certain times tension between the marital pair mounts so high that divorce is imminent. The son (identified patient, or I.P.), sensing this on some level, runs away. For the moment, attention shifts away from the marital pair onto the runaway. In this manner, running away maintains the balance (homeostasis) of the system; divorce is put off while the parents shift their focus onto their runaway child.

Systems counselors believe that to counsel only the identified patient is to miss the point. Persons exist in environments, and to look at the problem from an individual frame of reference is to take the person out of context, to see the person as existing in a vacuum. Thus, an important question frequently asked by a systems counselor is, "What function does the symptom serve within the family system?" (Minuchin and Fishman 1981).

According to systems theory (von Bertalanffy 1968), family systems have the property of self-regulation. Any input to the family (i.e., change of any one member) is acted upon and modified by the system itself through the mechanism of feedback. Family stability or equilibrium is generally maintained through negative feedback mechanisms, while change (learning, growth, or crisis) is maintained and increased through positive feedback (Walsh 1982).

A typical intact nuclear family system might look like this: There are a mother and a father, representing an executive authority bloc from which all authority flows. The mother-father bond is stronger than all other bonds. Chronologically the bond between the mother and the father, who have greater wisdom and judgment, come first and endures longer (Nichols 1984), thereby establishing the authority hierarchy. The natural division occurs along generational lines. In any given family system, there are four subsystems: the children (the sibling subsystem); the husband-wife interactions (the marital subsystem); the parental subsystem (parent-child interactions); and nuclear family interactions with external systems and individuals (extra-familial subsystem) (Nichols 1984).

In a healthy, functioning system, the boundaries are clarified. There are relationships between the mother-father subsystem, the mother-children subsystem, and the father-children subsystem. In the single-parent family system, the husband-wife subsystem no longer exists; however, the mother-father subsystem may (Ahrons 1980). In single-parent family systems in which women are most often the custodial parents, the father may be an important part of the children's lives, available to the mother as a resource person for caretaking and decision-making concerning the children (Wallerstein 1980).

The single-parent family system has one parent absent from the household or has a single parent ghost (i.e., the influence on a family of a dead husband kept alive by the wife) in the case of death or birth out-of-wedlock. A parent-ghost could also exist for either the children or the parent in a single-parent home with no contact with the absent parent. In any case, the gap in this type of family system is typically filled by one of the children. This child, called the "parental child," is usually the oldest (Ahrons 1980).

The presence of a parental child can create a cross-generational coalition; it almost always leads to the formation of a pseudo-adult, overwhelmed and burdened by adult responsibilities (Weiss 1979). As mental health professionals, it is important for us to recognize the presence of parental children and to encourage the return of the child to the sibling subsystem, reinforcing the sibling coalition.

The systemic approach enables us to conceptualize what is happening in the family and what motivating force originally produced and currently maintains the symptoms. Through this framework we can answer the question, "What is the function of the symptom in this family?"

In addition we can assess the hierarchy within the system, examine the boundaries of the family members, explore the nature of the subsystems, and look for coalitions.

Cognitive-Behavioral Principles

In addition to assessing the family on a systemic level of analysis, cognitive-behavioral psychological principles may help provide the therapist additional information about the system, and aid in utilizing behavioral therapeutic interventions to induce systemic change. Cognitive-behavioral approaches have been shown to be effective in treating marital distress (e.g., Jacobsen and Margolin 1979; Weiss 1980). Until recently, little attention was paid to the potential success of applying it to family therapy. The behavioral approach contributes specific, step-by-step intervention strategies, through which the underlying goals of the family are achieved using positive and negative reinforcers and punishers (Jacobsen and Margolin 1979). Since a basic assumption of cognitive-behavioral therapy is that emotional disturbance is caused by the persistence of irrational or untrue beliefs, these interventions may help produce perceptual shifts in thinking, feeling, or acting (Jacobsen and Margolin 1979). Thus, the family is assessed at a systemic level and specific cognitive-behaviorial therapeutic interventions are used. The level of analysis is systemic; the interventive strategies are behavioral.

As an example, here is a case history depicting a "typical" single-parent family system, a systemic analysis of the family structure, and a description of the behavioral goals utilized to bring about change in the structure.

Single-Parent Case History

Nancy M, a 39-year-old assistant bank manager, was referred for counseling by her family physician. She had been divorced for about three years and was having a hard time coping with her two sons, Steven (eight) and Craig (five). Prior to counseling, she had been in group counseling for a drinking problem.

In counseling, although Nancy stated that her marriage was not good before the divorce, she often expressed both "negative and positive feelings in abrupt alternation" about Roger, her ex-husband. The main reason Nancy gave for her divorce was Roger's infidelity: he had had an affair with his secretary. At the beginning of counseling the relationship between Nancy and her former husband was antagonistic, often culminating in very unpleasant arguments about financial arrangements, visiting arrangements, or any other topic. Because of the constant arguing, the two children began to suffer, each in his own way. Steven started to do poorly in school. He did not listen to his mother, frequently called her names, told her he hated her, and had temper tantrums. Craig, the younger child, also had temper tantrums, but his tantrums resulted in his hiding in his closet for many hours.

Most of the time Nancy aligned herself with Craig. He was behaviorally a better child, achieving more in school and having more friends at home. The other son, Steven, looked like his father. This resemblance affected Nancy's interactions with Steven and was the basis for their somewhat distant relationship. Steven was a loner and, although there was no learning disability involved, schoolwork was difficult for him. Complicating the matter even further, Nancy and her ex-husband often argued about whose fault Steven's low school grades were, and Steven frequently heard these arguments.

Nancy came from an upper-middle class family background, and all her basic needs were taken care of while she was growing up. At the time of the divorce, Nancy had not psychologically separated from her mother, who fostered attachment and dependency. She invited Nancy and the boys to live with her. She told Nancy that she would take care of her, which at times was quite appealing to Nancy, even though their relationship was generally conflict-ridden. As Weiss (1975) points out, "For the separated woman the parental invitation is not without attractions. Going back home can offer a brief moratorium from responsibility, a breathing space during which the woman can pull herself together without feeling guilty for neglecting her children. But . . . the cost would be reduced autonomy" (p. 141). For Nancy, this move would be psychologically costly. In certain European cultures with an accepted extrafamilial subsystem, the psychological cost of moving back home would be much less.

Nancy, who originally had little job training, was unprepared psychologically and technically for the work force, and began working at a low-paying clerical position. When she was growing up, and during her entire marriage, she had very few extrafamilial responsibilities. After her divorce it became necessary for her to work to help support the children financially. This was the first time in Nancy's life that she was totally responsible for her own and her children's needs. She appeared fragile, overwhelmed by the slightest thing. When she first came for counseling, she was unsure of her mother role, sometimes using the rationale that "It's okay not to cook dinner for the children, because I'm exhausted. I've had a hard day, and I need to relax. It won't kill them to eat bread and butter for one night." This, unfortunately, stretched into more than a few nights and was in the counselor's opinion, becoming problematic for the children.

The basic family pattern was chaotic. All fended for themselves. Things would go along smoothly for a while, but then a crisis would occur and problems would arise. Nancy seemed to suffer from each and every one of the specific problems presented by Bloom, White, and Asher (1979): ". . . difficulties with children, the need to work, sexual problems, problems with reestablishing social relationships, financial difficulties, and the feelings associated with failure and shame" (p. 193). The communication issues involved Nancy either pleading with the boys to behave or giving in to their whims to prevent them from annoying her. There was very little positive reinforcement given to the boys. Nancy tried to keep their behavior under control through punishment. Their positive behavior went unnoticed; their negative behavior was punished—sometimes. Most of the attention they received from Nancy was negative. This quickly led to an increase in their bad behavior, for that was the way to receive attention from their mother. Transactions occurred mainly surrounding functional issues, such as, "Did you do your homework?" or "Put your toys away!"

For the most part Nancy tolerated the children's misbehavior, becoming upset but disciplining them inconsistently. When their behavior became very disruptive, she would call Roger and argue with him about his lack of responsibility for the children.

It was hypothesized that Nancy's inability to consistently reward and punish the children was a symptom functioning to insure Roger's participation in their lives. The children contributed their misbehavior to ensure that Nancy would become upset enough to call Roger. Roger would then come to the rescue, but make only feeble attempts to resolve the problems with the children, usually managing to blame Nancy. This ensured that the children would continue to misbehave and that Roger would be called again in the near future.

This is an example of how dynamics, viewed through a behavioral lens, act to mold the family system in a damaging way. This also illustrates the sequence of events that leads to family symptoms and their functions. It is called *tracking the symptom*. Once we know the pattern of the family communication around the symptoms, we can find alternate healthier ways to "language" about the symptom.

In a typical dysfunctional single-parent family system such as Nancy's, the husband-wife bond is usually dissolved; there is generally conflict and hostility between the two parents and the siblings. Sometimes one child enters the executive subsystem as the parental child, creating a cross-generational coalition, replacing the absent father and taking on adult responsibilities.

Counseling Techniques

This case history presents one type of single-parent household—a white, middle-class, single-parent family system with young children. It is not typical of other types of single-parent family systems, so the principles stated in this paper are not generalizable to other single-parent family systems. Even among white, middle-class, single-parent family systems there are many variations (Hodges 1986), but there are also similarities and therefore certain principles that mental health professionals can use to deal with such families.

The focus in this type of counseling is always on the family. The goals are to change the family structure and the behavioral sequence that has led to the symptoms, and to teach effective coping skills necessary to fulfill the functions of the family (see Minuchin and Fishman 1981). These goals are achieved through planned behavioral counseling techniques, based on a systemic analysis of the family's hierarchy, boundaries, and subsystems. In this case the goal was changed from fulfilling the mother's dependency needs by drawing her ex-husband back into family life even at the expense of the success and self-esteem of one of the sons to helping the mother develop enough independence to fulfill her own needs.

Some specific cognitive-behavioral interventions were used in this family in order to create systemic change. While these interventions are discussed in relation to Nancy's family's case history, there are certain structural similarities among single-parent systems (Minuchin and Fishman 1981). These counseling techniques are therefore generalizable.

1. Reinforce the Parental Role

Since most parents are unaware of the functions of the family, it is useful for the mental health counselor to educate them. In single-parent families, a child may take on one of two roles to maintain the post-divorced family's equilibrium (Ahrons 1980). A child may become a parental child, relinquishing childhood play and taking on many adult responsibilities. A child may also take a spousal role, becoming an emotional confidante for the single parent. Both these situations indicate cross-generational problems in the custodial parent-child subsystem, and are indications for counseling (Ahrons 1980).

Another problem in the custodial-parent subsystem may occur if the parent lacks the coping skills necessary to care for the children. In Nancy's case, it was important to reinforce her caretaking role (Berman and Turk 1981). This became a long-term goal of the therapy. Nancy, initially, was still dependent on her own mother, and had not been dependent on her husband. She could not become independent without first learning basic caretaking skills. This was accomplished by using short-term behavioral goals (Jacobsen and Margolin 1981). For example, the therapist worked with her on setting up a schedule to utilize her time more efficiently. This was reinforcing for her because she could spend more time with the children and felt less guilty about her mothering capabilities.

She was helped to set up a behavior modification chart for the boys. Topics on the chart included brushing teeth, making beds, putting toys away, clearing the dinner table, doing homework, studying, and getting good grades. Each topic was fully explained to the boys. For example, after school from 3 to 4 P.M., the boys were to do their homework and study. If they did this, they would get a gold star for the day. For every six gold stars (they did not have to study on Sundays) they received a prize. The prizes were reasonable—e.g., a trip to Friendly's for ice cream. The purpose of the chart was to create structure, to restore some order to the children's lives.

Not only did the chart create structure for the boys, it also taught them to be independent and to take care of some of their own needs, which their mother had been unable to model for them. This had the secondary result of freeing some of Nancy's time. It was no longer necessary for her to come home from work tired and begin yelling at the boys to do their homework. Her interactions with them became more positive, and she began to enjoy spending time with them.

2. Help the Parent Become a Nurturing Supportive Figure in the Children's Lives

Divorce creates systemic disequilibrium. Although this is often a period of increased strain on family members, it can also be a time of growth and development (Beal 1980; Isaacs and Montalvo 1986). When a system is in flux, it is most conducive to change. Much can be accomplished during this crisis when roles are ambiguous, boundaries are permeable, and rules are temporarily suspended (McPhee 1985).

Nancy needed to establish a nurturing, supportive relationship with the boys. Once again short-term behavioral goals were utilized to accomplish this. The counselor attempted to help the client maximize the time she spent with the boys so that it was beneficial to all and was not wasted in argument. It was suggested that Nancy make a list of places she was interested in visiting. She was very interested in gardening, so it was suggested that she plan day trips once a week during which she would take the boys with her to places—gardens or nurseries—that she was interested in seeing. As a result, she would not resent "not having any time to do the things I want to do," and the boys would have the chance to spend enjoyable times with their mother.

In counseling Nancy learned how to make small amounts of time very valuable for both mother and children. For example, if it was necessary for Nancy to drive the children to their various after-school activities, it could be a fun time for all. She learned to create very special moments for the children in the car. It was a time when they had her attention. She realized that she did not need to spend large blocks of time with the boys to have meaningful time with them. This helped to alleviate some of her guilt about her mothering abilities.

Another behavioral goal was to help her to cook efficiently for the boys. Nancy loved to cook but felt overwhelmed by it on nights when she came home from work. She decided that it would be more enjoyable for her to cook several meals at once. It was suggested that she do the cooking on Sunday mornings, when the boys were usually with their father. Then she could focus completely on the cooking, without interruptions.

Soon Nancy began to cook all the meals for the coming week, package them and freeze them. During the week, she would take them out one at a time and heat them in the microwave oven. Again, because she was cooking decent meals for the children, all family members benefitted. Nancy felt positive about her capabilities as a cook and the boys were finally eating nutritious meals. Because Nancy did not have to shop and cook during the week, she also had more time for herself and the boys.

3. Help the Client with Separation/Individuation Issues

The issue of separation/individuation from the family of origin can be important in therapy with single parents. There must be clear boundaries around the single-parent family system—the single-parent family system must not be confused with the extended family system (Isaacs and Montalvo 1986). Nancy was responsible for a great many matters, and the overwhelming feelings she was experiencing were perfectly normal. In counseling she realized that these matters could be broken down into smaller parts for easier management. In so doing, she learned not to depend on her mother for help with everyday activities and chores.

Nancy's mother presented a problem, inasmuch as she wanted Nancy to move back home with her. Nancy's father had died about five years before Nancy's divorce, and her mother was lonely. This is a trap into which single parents often fall. On the one hand Nancy felt it would be easier to move in with her mother. Nancy's mother was financially well off, and Nancy would not have to worry about paying her mortgage. Single-parent families are often economically disadvantaged, so the single-parent's family of origin may represent rescue from financial ruin. Moving back to her family of origin also meant that food shopping, cleaning, chores, and babysitting would be taken care of by her mother.

In most cases, though, the psychological price is too high. Nancy's mother was very controlling, demanding to know Nancy's whereabouts at all times. According to her, there was one right way to do things; no other way was acceptable. Nancy was much more relaxed than her mother wanted her to be, and because of this, moving in with her mother would set her up for constant failure.

The other problem with moving in with her mother was that of authority. When Nancy's mother visited she became the person-in-charge, and Nancy's authority with her children was undermined. This created a triangle which produced conflicting feelings in the children. It was no longer clear whom they were supposed to obey since mother and daughter had different ways of doing things. The potential for all sorts of alliances was created, with Nancy never quite sure whether she was the child or the mother. This was probably a pattern repeated in her relationship with her ex-husband. Even though the offer to move in with her mother initially seemed quite appealing, it would have been a psychological disaster for Nancy. In future counseling sessions Nancy learned to assert herself with her mother, and to remain in authority when her mother came to visit. During one session, Nancy said that she finally felt "grown up."

Nancy's case shows that in single-parent family systems, there are times when the power gets confusing. It is important for mental health counselors to ask, "Where is the power base? Are the children mothering the mother? What is the role of the mother's mother? The mother's father? Other family members?"

4. Help Dispel Feelings of Abandonment

Nancy's own feelings of abandonment were crucial and were discussed throughout the sessions. This problem is also discussed by Weiss (1979). "The disruption of attachment is a major source of emotional disturbance following a separation" (p. 205). When Nancy felt overwhelmed or abandoned, she wrote her feelings in a journal, which she then brought to counseling sessions to discuss. A connection was pointed out between unrealistic expectations and unnecessary painful feelings.

Nancy's children also experienced fears of abandonment, as exemplified by their not wanting to stay with a sitter. They would often ask their mother, "Are you sure you're coming back? Tell me exactly what time you'll be home." In counseling Nancy learned how to supportively help her children get over these feelings. She often reassured them of her love. She also involved them in planning future activities in which they would all participate. The children's opportunities to project themselves into these future situations assured that their mother would be there with them.

5. Help the Mother Involve the Children in Her Goals

At the beginning of counseling, Nancy and her children were alienated from each other. It seemed as though they simply lived in the same residence, with very little positive communication and/or affection flowing between them. During the adjustment period after separation or divorce, this is typical. One way to increase the positive aspects of the parent-child relationship is to help the mother involve her children in her goals. This was accomplished for Nancy when the boys joined her every other Sunday and helped her to prepare the meals for the next week. They were given choices about their meals and were encouraged to cooperate in the food preparation. Soon after this process was begun, preparing the meals became a fun-filled family activity. Through behavioral activities such as these, the roles of the family members became defined, the responsibilities of each member became known, and the family system began to function more effectively (Ahrons 1980).

6. Help the Mother Develop a Support Structure and Social Interests

It is important for mental health counselors to help clients make contact with and attach to another system. A single-parent system can be quite successful if there are other strong systems to which the client can look for support (Morawetz and

Walker 1984). These outside systems may be women or men friends, a group of single parents which meets on a regular basis, a sports activity, or even a return to school. This network can introduce people and material resources to help the single parent reach out and form new relationships (Warren and Amara 1985). Initially, Nancy was so overwhelmed with basic survival that she had little time for anything else. Her entire world consisted of working, cleaning, cooking, and shouting at the boys to behave. Her life was devoid of fun and relaxation. She felt she had little to look forward to and was in a state of depression. What she missed most was someone with whom to discuss her day. Her life was filled with professional conversations with people at work or conversations with her children about things important to them. There was no one with whom she could have an adult conversation—no one with whom she could share an intimate relationship. In short, there were no reinforcers in her life, and according to one cognitive behavioral psychologist (Beck 1970), depression is defined as a lack of reinforcement in one's environment.

During counseling Nancy was encouraged to seek out other single parents in her neighborhood, and begin to develop friends. In this way she was able to share her career dreams, her daily trials and tribulations, and the fun moments that began to occur more frequently. In other words she began to develop a support structure of women, a network of comrades to make her life more pleasant. Her children were now free to play with their friends and to engage in the extracurricular activities young boys enjoy—the sibling subsystem was reinforced. They no longer had to feel guilty about leaving their depressed and distraught mother.

7. Help the Client Work Out a Reasonable Relationship with His/Her Ex-Partner

Wallerstein and Kelley (1980) found that a supportive and cooperative divorced coparenting relationship is essential for continued growth and development of the children in single-parent homes. Many problems arise, however, in the coparental subsystem. Some of the more common ones concern raising children, as in one of the parents using the children as a go-between, competition with the other parent, one parent spoiling the children, and lack of support and caring by the other parent (Morawetz and Walker 1984). Along with these problems, in single-parent family systems there is often unresolved anger and hostility between the two parents. Too often the children become involved in this anger and hostility (Isaacs, Montalvo, and Abelson 1986). Typically a child feels that he or she cannot express anger to the noncustodial parent because that parent might completely disappear. This forces the child to express anger and complaints to the parent with whom he or she is living. This in turn may cause the parent to resent the child (Wallerstein 1980). In counseling sessions with single parents, it is important to discuss these issues, helping the client work through feelings of resentment and anger to understand the necessity of not conveying that anger and resentment to the children (Jacobsen 1974).

In some cases clients react differently to the ex-spouse. These individuals deny the impact of their divorce and report no strong feelings associated with the loss of their marriage or partner. It is as if the marriage or divorce never happened. This has been likened to Bowen's (1978) concept of emotional cut-off. Here the individual cuts off the ex-spouse either by physical distancing, brief and infrequent contact with him or her, or total withdrawal and avoidance. Bowen's solution to emotional cut-offs is to have the client recontact the family member involved. Sometimes divorced spouses need to reestablish contact in order to truly divorce. This, however, can be a very complicated process.

Working through her relationship with her husband Roger was another goal in counseling with Nancy. This was discussed in session, and she attempted to speak with her ex-husband about taking some extra responsibility for the boys and possibly coming to joint therapy sessions. Involving the absent parent is important when working with single-parent families, for seeing the primary parent alone—in this case, the mother—reinforces that the problem is hers alone. Thus, another goal of the therapy is to increase the involvement of the non-custodial parent. Roger did seem to want to be involved with the boys. The counselor suggested that one way to increase his involvement with them was to drive them to and watch them during their sport activities. In this way Nancy need not leave the bank to drive the boys to their games, which would alleviate some of her anxiety and pressure. At the same time, the boys' father would become more involved, which would ultimately have positive consequences for the whole family.

8. Help the Clients Mourn Unresolved Losses

Help clients deal with issues of unresolved mourning. Often when depression is the presenting problem, issues of relationship loss underlie the sadness. Clients in these situations must mourn the loss of the relationship (Walsh 1982). In divorce these losses are experienced by all members of the family system. Fulmer (1983) believes that the single-parent family is especially vulnerable to problems of unresolved loss. Hoffman (1981) describes the children's misbehavior as "collusive mischief" to offset the mother's depression. Seeing her depression, they become anxious, begin to misbehave, and by their disobedience "impel (her) to take an active position" (p. 84). This was typified in Nancy's family. Whenever Steven sensed his mother's depression, he acted out by not doing his homework or by fighting with his brother. This behavior mobilized Nancy to action, taking the focus away from her depressed state.

In counseling Nancy expressed her sadness about the loss of the relationship, the loss of her dreams and expectations for her marriage, and the loss of Roger. In family sessions the boys also expressed their sorrow at no longer having an intact family and at not seeing their father as often as they did before their parents separated.

9. Help the Client Recognize That His/Her Single-Parent Family System Is Very Different from the Intact Family Model

As Hodges (1986) points out, "One of the most important tasks for counseling with single-parent families, regardless of their lifestyle, is to help liberate families that are tyrannized by the two-parent family model. They need to see that it is impossible for one parent to be both father and mother" (p. 195). In this society, people are socialized to believe that the two-parent family is the norm. Between 1970 and 1978 there was a 46 percent increase in female-headed family systems. What matters, though, for the single parent is that the intact system is considered ideal. This may make the single-parent family member feel inferior—a product of a less-than-ideal arrangement. During counseling it is important for the individual to evaluate his or her definitions of what a single-parent family system should be like, emotionally and realistically, to challenge unrealistic "shoulds." Help clients evaluate the cost of doing everything. Help them see that by sharing family tasks, they can reduce the inevitable anger felt by an overburdened parent.

It is true that if Nancy's and Roger's family were still intact, some of the existing problems would be alleviated if two people shared the responsibilities for the children, finances, and household chores. The interparental conflict would be much less. There also would be another person to share emotions, someone for Nancy to talk with about the frustrations of her day. If this were an intact-parent family, the focus of the therapy would be on helping Nancy share with her husband her feelings of being overwhelmed and to work out task-sharing between the two adults. While it is true that some problems would be solved simply because another adult person would share responsibilities, it is crucial to realize that some of the same issues would exist even if this were an intact-parent family—for example, the lack of separation from Nancy's family of origin, her lack of coping skills, and Roger's detachment and aloofness.

Aside from these issues, this society presents an intact-parent family norm. This norm defines what a family should be. Unfortunately, the single-parent family system cannot live up to this norm and is therefore considered a failure (Beal 1980). In counseling it is important to talk these issues through with clients and help them resolve their uncertainty, ambiguity, and loss of self-esteem. For a consideration of other therapeutic issues in the single-parent family system, see Morawetz and Walker (1984).

During therapy, the structure of Nancy's single-parent family system changed. The boundaries between the generations became more clear. The father grew more involved, less alienated from the family situation. The children lived in a more "normal" environment, with a strong sibling subsystem. There was more structure, more rules and regulations. The executive boundary was reinforced. Nancy now behaves in a more "mother-like" way. She is less overwhelmed and more bonded to her children, causing them to feel more secure which helps her feel more fulfilled, more needed, less isolated and guilty. As a result the children have fewer temper tantrums, and the anxiety level in the house lessens. Nancy even has time to go to an occasional movie with her friends.

Some long-range goals for Nancy were to help her establish a support network, administer career-oriented tests, help her with career planning (something in which she was very interested), and help her reenter the dating situation (something which she also mentioned as desirable). Emotionally Nancy still sometimes relied on alcohol for relaxation, so more help was needed in this area. She also needs to continue to work through her anger at Roger for abandoning her. There is much more work left to do with this single-parent family, but positive changes have started to occur.

While a single-parent family is difficult to run, it can be run very well even in the most difficult cases. For example, it may be easier to make executive decisions when there is one executive. Cashion (1982) found that children from female-headed families have "good emotional adjustment . . . self esteem . . . intellectual development . . . and no higher rates of juvenile delinquency" than do other children of comparable socioeconomic status.

Summary

There are many areas to investigate when working with a single-parent family system. The emphasis on assessing the family as a whole is an obvious one. Also necessary is the role of the counselor as an educator, helping the family to restructure and clarify boundaries and roles. The model for intervention was based on facilitating "good enough" arrangements between divorced parents and their children (Isaacs, Montalvo, and Abelson 1986). The basis of this approach is to include children's open access to the non-custodial parent and assurance that two parents are raising them. Part of the family counselor's role is to teach the family good child-rearing practices and help them to learn age-appropriate behaviors. The basic theme of single-parent family counseling is to stimulate psychological growth, always a developmental process, and to encourage the future psychological maturation of all family members.

References

Ahrons, C. (1980) "Redefining the divorced family: A conceptual framework," *Social Work* (November): 74–96.

Ahrons, C., and R. Rodger (1987) *Divorced Families: A Multidisciplinary Developmental View*. New York: W. W. Norton.

Bateson, G. (1979) *Mind and Nature: A Necessary Unity*. New York: Dutton.

Beal, E. (1980) "Separation, divorce, and single-parent families," in E. Carter and M. McGoldrick, eds., *The Family Life Cycle: A Framework for Family Therapy*. New York: Gardner Press.

Beck, A. (1970) "Cognitive therapy: Nature and relation to behavior therapy," *Behavior Therapy* 1: 184–200.

Berman, W., and D. Turk (1981) "Adaptation to divorce. Problems and coping strategies," *Journal of Marriage and the Family* 43: 179–89.

Bertalanffy, L. von (1968) *General Systems Theory: Foundations, Development, Applications*. New York: George Braziller.

——— (1974). "General systems theory and psychiatry," in S. Arieti, ed., *American Handbook of Psychiatry,* 2nd ed. New York: Basic Books.

Bloom, B., S. White, and S. Asher (1979) "Marital disruption as a stressful life event," in G. Levinger and O. Moles, eds., *Divorce and Separation: Context, Causes, and Consequences*. New York. Basic Books.

Bowen, M. (1978) *Family Therapy in Clinical Practice*. New York: Jason Aronson.

Cashion, B. G. (1982) "Female-headed families: Effects on children and clinical implications," *Journal of Marital and Family Therapy* 8: 77–85.

Dell, P. F., and A. S. Applebaum (1977) "Trigenerational enmeshment: Unresolved ties of single parents to family of origin," *American Journal of Orthopsychiatry* 47: 52–59.

Fulmer, R. H. (1983) "A structural approach to unresolved mourning in single parent family systems," *Journal of Marital and Family Therapy* 9 (3): 259–69.

Gardner, R. (1982). *Psychotherapy with Children of Divorce*. New York: Jason Aronson.

Glasser, P., and E. Navarre (1965) "Structural problems of the one parent-family," *Journal of Social Issues* 21: 98–109.

Hackney, G., and S. Ribordy (1981) "An empirical investigation of emotional reaction to divorce," *Journal of Clinical Psychology* 36: 105–110.

Haley, J. (1977) *Problem Solving Therapy*. San Francisco: Jossey-Bass.

Hodges, W. (1986) *Interventions for Children of Divorce*. New York: John Wiley.

Hoffman, L. (1981) *Foundations of Family Therapy*. New York: Basic Books.

Holman, A. (1983) *Family Assessment: Tools for Understanding and Intervention*. Beverly Hills, Calif.: Sage Publications.

Isaacs, M. B., B. Montalvo, and D. Abelson (1986) *The Difficult Divorce: Therapy for Children and Families*. New York: Basic Books.

Jacobsen, D. (1978) "The impact of marital separation/divorce on children: Parent child separation and child adjustment," *Journal of Divorce* 9 (1): 47–64.

Jacobsen, D., and G. Margolin (1979) *Marital Therapy: Strategies Based on Social Learning and Behavioral Exchange Principles*. New York: Brunner/Mazel.

Kitson, G. C., and P. Mason (1982). "Family social support in crisis. The special case of divorce," *American Journal of Orthopsychiatry* 52 (1): 161–65.

Kohen, J., C. Brown, and R. Feldsberg (1979) "Divorced mothers: The costs and benefits of female control," in G. Levinger and O. Moles, *Divorce and Separation: Context, Causes and Consequences,* 228–45.

Levinger, G., and O. Moles (1979) *Divorce and Separation: Context, Causes, and Consequences*. New York: Basic Books.

Madanes, C. (1981). *Strategic Family Therapy*. San Francisco: Jossey-Bass.

McCollum, E. (1985) "Recontacting former spouses: A further step in the divorce process," *Journal of Marital and Family Therapy* 11 (4): 417–20.

McPhee, J. (1985) "Ambiguity and change in the post-divorce family. Toward a model of divorce adjustment," *Journal of Divorce* 8 (2): 56–73.

Minuchin, S. (1974) *Families and Family Therapy*. Cambridge, Mass.: Harvard University Press.

Minuchin, S., and H. C. Fishman (1981) *Family Therapy Techniques*. Cambridge, Mass.: Harvard University Press.

Morawetz, A., and G. Walker, (1984) *Brief Therapy with Single Parent Families*. New York: Brunner/Mazel.

Nichols, M. (1984) *Family Therapy: Concepts and Methods*. New York: Gardner Press.

Scanzoni, J. (1979) "A historical perspective on marital dissolution," in Levinger and Moles, *Divorce and Separation*.

Tessman, L. (1978) *Children of Parting Parents*. New York: Jason Aronson.

U.S. Bureau of the Census (1978) *Household and Families by Type* (March): 1.

Wallerstein, J., and J. Kelly (1980) *Surviving the Breakup: How Children and Parents Cope with Divorce*. New York: Basic Books.

——— (1976) "The effects of parental divorce: Experiences of the child in later latency," *American Journal of Orthopsychiatry* 4: 256–69.

Walsh, F. (1982) *Normal Family Processes*. New York: Guilford Press.

Warren, N., and I. Amara (1985) "Educational groups for single parents: The parenting after divorce programs," *Journal of Divorce* 8 (2): 104–119.

Weiss, R. (1975) *Marital Separation*. New York: Basic Books.

——— (1979) "Growing up a little faster: The experience of growing up in single-parent household," *Journal of Social Issues* 35: 97–111.

——— (1980) "Strategic behavioral marital therapy: Toward a model of assessment and intervention," in J. Vincent, ed., *Advances in Family Intervention. Assessment and Theory*. New York: Brunner/Mazel.

Chapter Thirteen

FAMILY THERAPY ISSUES WITH THOSE WHO ARE SEXUALLY SINGLE AGAIN

Joan D. Atwood Ph.D., C.S.W.

American society has traditionally sanctioned monogamous marriage as the institution within which heterosexual activity legitimately takes place. The script for heterosexual behavior has always been clearly specified. Historically, individuals were expected to abstain from premarital sexual activity and to marry at approximately a certain age. From that point on they were supposed to conduct all their heterosexual activity within that marital relationship. There has never been total adherence to this sexual script in American society. Extramarital sexual activity has always occurred, and alternatives to traditional monogamous marriage have been practiced by at least some people since the 1800s. "Free love" and sexual freedom movements as well as communal marriages were widely known in the nineteenth century (Murstein 1974).

Currently, major alternative heterosexual relationships can be seen as falling into two categories: (1) alternatives to traditional marriage and (2) alternative sexual relationships within marriage. The first category includes both "singlehood" and cohabitation. The second category includes multilateral marriage, open marriage, and "swinging." We are concerned here with a specific instance of the first category: singlehood.

Definition: Who Is Single?

Single persons are found in every age group. The term *single* was traditionally applied only to those who had reached the age at which most people married without having done so themselves. Currently, however, there are many types of single person. Some individuals have never married but are cohabitating and sexually active. Others have never married, are cohabiting, but are not sexually active. Some single people have been married but are now separated, widowed, or divorced. Divorced individuals who do not remarry have typically been called "divorced," not "single." This distinction is somewhat misleading and may be of little use in that it suggests two different types of person. More important than prior marital status is the person's age, the existence of children, past sexual and relationship experience, attitudes toward marriage, and future life and relationship goals. Thus, within the category "single" are two major versions of this status: never having married and having divorced. (A third subgroup—widows and widowers—spouse, is relatively small, although it is the major subgroup among people past middle age.)

Since people in these categories must confront life in a totally new role, both situations create special problems. Individuals involved in these readjustments encounter important personal and social issues as they try to find a new place for themselves as social and sexual beings. This chapter primarily explores one segment of the single population—those who are separated or divorced. The focus is on the specific problems, adjustments, and social and sexual issues faced by this growing population, along with the techniques employed by counselors who work with these individuals.

U.S. Divorce Rates

The divorce rate (number of divorces per 1000 marriages) began to increase in the United States early in this century. It seemed to peak after World War II and drop back a bit, but it has been rising again in recent years (Ditzion 1978), with an increase of 34 percent in the 1960s and about 80 percent during the 1970s. Most of the increase during the 1970s was among younger couples. In 1975 there were 460 divorces per 1000 marriages. Current estimates are that there are approximately 500 divorces per 1000 marriages, or approximately 1 divorce for every 2 marriages. Each year there are approximately 2.2 million marriages and 1.1 million divorces in the United States, so that more than 1 million people enter single status in this way each year. The divorce rate is higher for nonwhites than for whites and generally higher among lower-class whites than among middle- and upper-class whites (Glick and Norton 1971). The average age at divorce from first marriage in the United States today is 27 for females and 29 for males. Divorce appears to have become so common that 60% of Americans who get married today report that they do not expect the marriage to last the rest of their lives (Yankelovich 1981).

In addition to the divorced, many people are between marriage and divorce. Individuals separated from their spouses constitute a very large population. In March 1985 the U.S. census reported that 1.5 million men and 2.4 million women were separated (U.S. Department of Commerce 1985). It should be noted, however, that these are probably underestimates, inasmuch as an unknown number of people report that an absent spouse is "visiting relatives." It is basically impossible, then, to measure separation through agreement to separate or through desertion, since there are basically no reporting techniques to cover couples who do not go through the formalities of legal separation.

These statistics mean that American society has the highest divorce and separation rates of any industrial country. Thus, from both available divorce statistics and estimates of separations, it is clear that a large segment of the population is confronted with readjusting to postmarital life.

Explanations of Increased Divorce

A growing number of marriages are ending in divorce, but there are many ways to interpret such figures. Rising divorce rates are a common topic in the popular media and are often interpreted as signs of societal rejection of the institution of marriage. This explanation, however, is questionable. First of all, available divorce statistics are not necessarily an entirely reliable indicator of the current state of marriage. It may be true that fewer people value the commitment of marriage, but it is also possible that expectations of marriage are higher than they were historically and that people are more easily disappointed. In the days of arranged marriages many people tolerated and adjusted to unhappy or unsatisfying situations. Now, fewer people are kept from divorce by religious prohibitions, legal barriers, or social disapproval and sanctions. Therefore couples dissatisfied with their marriages are more likely to terminate the union. Divorce is probably also more common now because women have more economic opportunities to support themselves and their children and to receive financial aid from governmental agencies. (About one family in seven now has a woman as the head of the household.) Finally, changes in gender roles and gender-role expectations may have led to increased dissatisfaction with the institution of marriage in general.

It is important to keep in mind that the number of divorces may reflect dissatisfaction with a particular marriage more than with the institution of marriage. Most people who divorce eventually do remarry, indicating that their dissatisfaction was with the choice of partner rather than with the institution of marriage. There is no single summary of the positive and negative features of divorced life compared with married life. How postmarital individuals feel about marriage versus singlehood is perhaps best revealed by an interesting statistic: five out of six divorced males and three out of four divorced females eventually remarry.

Several other factors could bear on the way divorce statistics are interpreted. Only half of the states have developed uniform standards for divorce record keeping (Glick and Norton 1971). This probably means that the records reflect variable data-collection procedures. There have been many recent changes in divorce laws. Thus, the current rise in divorce rates could also reflect the increased ease of obtaining a marital dissolution rather than a rise in dissatisfaction with marriage itself. In many states obtaining a legal divorce has become a relatively simple legal process in recent years. Furthermore, a significant portion of the divorce rate represents individuals who have had more than one divorce. This means that more first marriages remain intact than is obvious at first glance. Using most measures, though, the research does appear to indicate that the proportion of marriages ending in divorce has almost doubled since the 1950s. Thus there is a large and still-growing population of divorced men and women confronted with the emotional task of adjusting to a new social, psychological, and sexual role.

Socially Single Again

There are many social stereotypes of the divorced or separated person. Traditionally, the divorced male or female was seen as a social loser, sitting alone in his or her apartment with four or five cats and newspapers piled to the ceiling. This stereotype invokes the image of the sad, depressed, or psychologically devastated victim of divorce, struggling through the trauma of this life change and experiencing severe problems in his or her interpersonal and sexual relationships. Today this image of the single person has changed. Beside the lonely loser image is another picture of the contemporary divorced single—a young, swinging, upwardly mobile career person without a worry in the world for whom sexual fantasies have become reality. This person, released from the bonds and burdens of marriage, supposedly lives amid constant parties and entertainment, plentiful sex, and general abandonment in sexual and other areas of life. Of course, neither stereotype is accurate, but both probably contain elements of truth applicable to many people's adjustment to divorce or separation. Becoming single again for most people falls between these extremes.

Individuals report both desirable and undesirable aspects of singlehood. On one hand, for some it offers an independence they rarely obtained in their marital relationship. Singlehood also offers time alone. It provides the opportunity to examine the individual needs and desires that concern many young people today. For individuals who value privacy and time alone, singlehood may be defined as a positive lifestyle. People can come to know what kind of persons they are in the absence of day-to-day living with a partner who may be the primary focus of their self-definition. Singlehood offers variety in terms of both interpersonal and sexual relationships. Some people believe that only singles can truly experience human diversity in interpersonal sexual relationships, an opportunity that many people find rewarding in terms of the uniqueness of each new partner and each relationship.

On the other hand, many people report disadvantages to being single. Some define singlehood as being lonely rather than as being alone. Perhaps more important for the average single person, there are many times when the price of independence and time alone is the absence of intimacy and sharing. Individuals report that little things become problematic. Such necessary tasks as running errands during the day, doing laundry, washing the car, and the like must be accomplished alone.

Many social adjustments must be made when becoming single again. People who have established friendships and social relationships as couples rather than as individuals may feel awkward being alone or with others who are in couples. At the same time, couples may not be comfortable including a single person in their activities. Often, then, a sense of security or belonging that accompanies being part of a couple is replaced with sudden autonomy. Divorcing individuals often need to establish new social contacts, including new groups of single people. Many cities have organizations to help single people meet and form new friendships. For many individuals, however, giving up old relationships and seeking out new friendships can be frightening.

Divorced men and women undergo a radical change in social role, from "wife" or "husband" (part of a couple) to unattached person for whom society has established no role or expectations. For this reason recently divorced people often feel anxious and rootless. They may watch helplessly as friends who saw them as half a couple drift away. These social definitions, expectations, and assumptions about marriage and divorce, which delineate the appropriate contexts for sociosexual behavior, create the setting within which individuals experience their psychological reaction to the divorcing process.

Psychologically Single Again

Although the chain of events leading to marriage is varied, people generally marry with the hope and expectation that the marriage will last. Divorce often represents loss of this hope as well as other losses: of one's spouse, sometimes of one's children, possibly of a lifestyle, often of the security of familiarity, and, perhaps most important, of part of one's identity. Changing status from being married to being single presents varied difficulties in emotional adjustments. It usually takes two to three years to form a strong attachment to a spouse. For counselors to assume that couples married thirty years necessarily suffer more than couples married seven years is to accept a myth. In each case the individuals involved suffer the same syndrome, separation shock. Individuals going through the divorcing process typically and predictably pass through a series of psychological stages. It is crucial for counselors to be aware of these stages in order to aid their clients in this sociopsychological process. For purposes of clarity, the four stages are labeled *denial, conflict, ambivalence,* and *acceptance*.

Denial

Stage 1 of the emotional divorcing process, denial, is manifested mainly in separation shock. During separation shock the individual experiences relief, numbness, or panic. Relief is often felt when the divorce has been a drawn-out process. The most typical reaction to separation is fear of abandonment. The emotional response to this fear may be apprehensiveness, depression, and anxiety. These feelings are often accompanied by disturbances of sleep or appetite patterns. Those who eat more and sleep less are usually experiencing anxiety. Eating less and sleeping more probably relates to depression. In any case these symptoms indicate separation shock. Often during this time individuals report an inability to concentrate on work or to carry on conversations. They may experience sudden outbursts of tears or anger. Some people report that they often lose control and, for a reason that later seems insignificant, explode in sudden flashes of rage.

Many individuals, though, feel "numb" or report an absence of feelings. Numbness is a way of muting or denying feelings that, if experienced, would be too overwhelming for the individual to handle. In this case the individual temporarily "turns off" his or her psychological system.

During this stage people often vacillate between emotions, feeling first anxious, then angry, then numb. These emotions can be combined with feelings of optimism about their new life. Separation shock can last anywhere from a few days to several months.

Often one partner desires the divorce more than the other, and counselors must be aware of each person's specific emotional reactions to the situation. The person who leaves, for example, is often burdened with enormous guilt and self-blame, whereas the other partner potentially feels more anger, condemnation, hurt, and self-pity. The person who requests the divorce may fear being labeled a deserter, whereas the person who is left may feel embarrassed and fear being labeled a loser. It is important to recognize that *both* individuals suffer. The process of divorce has effects far beyond the dissolution of an unworkable marriage. Even when the marriage ends because one partner has fallen in love with someone else, there can be profound pain for the partner who asks for divorce. In sum, Stage 1 emotionality involves coming to grips with the fact that the marriage is ending. The emotional task at this stage is to accept the reality of the separation.

Conflict

Once the reality of separation is accepted, people who are divorcing enter Stage 2, conflict. Shortly after separation shock they may begin to experience a multitude of emotions, one right after the other. One minute they may feel perfectly comfortable with their new lifestyle, and a minute later may find themselves in tears, reminiscing about their former spouses. Shortly thereafter, remembering a negative event or an argument, they may feel enraged. Feelings of disorganization may arise. One day there may be a sense that the entire world is upside down; the next day they may feel perfectly comfortable with their newfound freedom. Volatile, explosive emotions may unexpectedly surface at this time. Individuals typically feel as if they may fall apart. Feelings of guilt and anger grow strong. People feel enraged at their spouse and then, a few hours later, ashamed and guilty about their angry feelings. They experience periods of anger at themselves and their spouses for having failed at their marriage or at having been left alone in their current situation. Along with these feelings they may also ponder whether they should have stayed with their spouse; they may feel that they made a mistake. At times, there may be feelings of regret. These feelings usually come in waves, and may catch people off guard. This stage is typified by conflicting and unpredictable emotions.

Also during this second stage people may do what is called scanning (Krantzler 1975). They reminisce about what went wrong with the marriage, who was to blame, and what their own role was in the failure. They also relive the best times in the marriage and mourn the loss of its more intimate aspects. Scanning may, in many ways, be an attempt to preserve attachment bonds; it may also provide insight to individuals into their own constructive and destructive relationship pattern. In this sense it can be a valuable learning experience. The review process goes on for months and is a major contributing factor to the mood swings that divorcing people experience. Each memory and each new awareness causes them to feel different emotions. This process, although emotionally uncomfortable, enables individuals to release pent-up feelings, which might otherwise cause them distress at later points in their lives.

During this stage of emotional upheaval, a sense of loss and loneliness frequently develops. Loneliness in this phase manifests itself in many ways. Some individuals sit in front of the television set for hours. Gradually, they withdraw from social contacts. Others experience a more active loneliness. Instead of sitting at home, they frequent old restaurants, pass their spouse's home, or go from one singles bar to another, desperately looking for solace from their loneliness. During this time also, negative feelings and emotions experienced as a child—such as separation anxiety, low self-esteem, or feelings of worthlessness—may resurface, causing them much distress. During the strong emotional swings typical of this stage people may experience periods of euphoria. Hunt and Hunt (1977) found that a small percentage of individuals in their sample felt a sense of relief, increased personal freedom, and newly gained competence, and also reinvested in themselves emotional energy that had previously been directed toward the marriage. These euphoric feelings appear suddenly and for no apparent reason, causing people to feel "on top of the world." These happy feelings may last for days or weeks. The danger during this phase is that people may think the worst is over, then suddenly plunge into the depths of depression. Unfortunately, it is usually during this time of rapidly changing emotions that people are required to deal with lawyers and make major decisions. In sum, for most people Stage 2 is an emotional seesaw, characterized mainly by psychological conflict. The emotional task of individuals at this stage is to achieve a realistic definition of their marriage, their role in its maintenance, and their responsibility for its failure.

Ambivalence

Stage 3, ambivalence, involves changes in the divorcing person's identity. In many ways this is the most psychologically stressful of the divorcing process. Being married is a primary source of self-identity. The two partners develop identities that include who they are and where and how they fit into the world. They create social identities consonant with the social definition of marriage. When their relationship ends, they may feel confused and fearful, as though they no longer have a script telling them how to behave. They may "try on" different identities, attempting to find one that is comfortable for them. At this time the divorcing person faces a major change in self-perception. Instead of being a husband and father, a man may find himself a bachelor living in a small apartment and seeing his children every other weekend. Instead of being a wife and mother, a woman may find herself labeled a "divorcée," a term that may imply promiscuity to the uninformed. Some people go through a second adolescence, becoming very concerned about how they look and how they sound. They may buy new clothes or a new car. Many of the struggles they experienced as teenagers may reappear, and they may find themselves trying to decide how to handle sexual advances or when to kiss a date good night. Sexual experimentation may occur as people explore their new sexuality outside the marital situation. The emotional task for the person at this stage is to make the psychological transition from being "married" to being "single" again.

Acceptance

Finally (usually not until several months or a year have elapsed), the person enters Stage 4. In this stage individuals typically feel a sense of relief and an acceptance of their situation (Krantzler 1975). They start to experience new strength and confidence. For the most part, they feel quite content with their lifestyles and no longer dwell on the past. They have a new awareness and knowledge of their own needs. If after months of separation an acceptance of the past is not developing, the person may seek professional help. Hunt and Hunt (1977) and Weiss (1975) write that the most painful aspects of mourning over divorce peak within the first several months and tend to level off by the end of the first year. They believe that the complete emotional resolution of a divorce usually takes two to four years. Although many of the feelings triggered by divorce are painful, discussing them in therapy allows them ultimately to be resolved, so that the individual will be emotionally able to reestablish an intimate relationship if he or she so desires.

Stress

Under the best of circumstances separation and divorce represent a major life-cycle transition. Even in mutually agreed-on, friendly terminations of a marriage, many significant lifestyle changes occur. The newly single person often faces adjustments in social and sexual relationships, financial arrangements, living arrangements, and parenting roles. Most divorces, however, do not occur under the best circumstances. Typically they are not logical and rational agreements but emotional and irrational conflicts full of bitter contention. During this time people's self-confidence may be shattered because they believe they have failed at marriage. Extensive changes, even if accompanied by relief over ending an undesirable situation, typically cause stress. As stressful events divorce and marital separation rank second and third behind the death of a spouse.

The stress of divorce shows in many ways. Compared with married (or remarried) people, divorced men and women drink more, smoke more marijuana, are lonelier, more despondent, and more likely to feel anxious or guilty (Cargan and Melko 1982). As Muhammad said, "Divorce is the most detestable of all permitted things" (quoted in Epstein 1974, p. 19).

Interview and clinical data indicate that divorced individuals must go through a period of social and psychological adjustment that is very difficult and often quite traumatic. After this period, however, the person's life settles into its own pattern. It is this postadjustment period that we are now interested in: how do divorced and separated individuals adjust sexually to being single again?

Sexually Single Again

Making the transition from marital to postmarital sexual relationships presents many challenges. For men these challenges often involve learning to cook and to fend for themselves in a household. For women the challenge often involves getting a job and learning to function in the work world. Along with these challenges the newly divorced person may experience considerable ambivalence about sexuality in general, as well as fears of intimacy. Feelings of anger, rejection, or fear remaining from the trauma of the divorcing process may inhibit some people's sexual desire, preventing them from reentering intimate relationships. Some individuals, to protect themselves from emotional vulnerability, withdraw completely from potential sexual relationships. Others react by seeking numerous superficial sexual encounters. This section examines the available sexual outlets and the actual reported sexual behavior of those who are sexually single again.

Sexual Outlets

For separated and divorced men and women there appear to be four main outlets for sexual behavior. These outlets are not mutually exclusive, and an individual may choose one or more of them.

Sexual Interaction with the Ex-Spouse

It is not unusual for separated or divorced partners to engage in sexual relations with each other. Clients may be reluctant to discuss or report this behavior in surveys, because in many states it is legally defined as "contamination" and may hinder or invalidate the legal process of divorce. In a clinical setting clients often report having engaged in such relations. Usually this contact occurs while the couple are in the divorcing process, and it typically ceases once one of the individuals begins dating. When it does occur, however, many clients report confusion about what it means. Some feel that it must mean there is "hope" for the marriage. In other words, it may rekindle feelings of caring or attraction for the former spouse. For others it may reinforce feelings of having made the right decision in separation. Thus, having sex with an ex-spouse typically complicates the divorcing process and is frequently a cause of concern for clients in counseling sessions.

Masturbation

Masturbation is another outlet for sexual behavior used by separated and divorced individuals. While masturbation is more commonly reported by men, women also report engaging in this form of sexual activity (Kinsey 1948, 1953). Divorced women also report having erotic dreams that result in orgasm (Kinsey 1953). It is probably true that no other sexual behavior elicits as much guilt as masturbation; yet we know from Kinsey that the vast majority of people do engage in masturbatory activity at some point during their lives. If clients report that they feel guilty about masturbating, it is important for counselors to give them accurate information regarding the widespread use of the activity as a sexual outlet and to explore some of the underlying motivational reasons for their guilt. It is helpful to aid some clients in prioritizing their sexual outlets and options. For some individuals developing autoerotic patterns of sexual expression can help them define themselves as sexually independent.

Short-Term Partners

For many divorced men and women dating several partners is crucial, because they can reaffirm their sense of attractiveness to the opposite sex. In these cases individuals typically engage in short-term, uncommitted sexual encounters and relationships. Ultimately, most individuals report that they would prefer a long-term relationship and that sex with many partners feels shallow. This type of sexuality is more frequently practiced by men than by women. Women tend to prefer sexuality in the context of a relationship with the ultimate goal of establishing a new long-term intimate union. Clients tend to report that they feel guilty when they engage in what they define as meaningless sexual activity. In such cases it is useful for counselors to help clients deal with their feelings, set boundaries around their behavior, and mobilize their willpower. In other words counselors can assist clients in making personal choices about sexual issues and then help them take responsibility for their choices. In light of the AIDS epidemic, it is useful and appropriate for counselors to provide clients with information about the disease and with guidelines for practicing safer sex.

Ongoing Monogamous Partners

Some men and women are involved in a long-term monogamous relationship that began before the divorce. Their sexual needs are typically met within the context of their relationship. In other situations individuals satisfy their sexual needs in a long-term monogamous relationship that began after the divorce. The great majority of men and women report that finding an ongoing relationship is their sexual goal.

Incidence of Sexual Intercourse

With regard to the actual incidence of sexual intercourse among the divorced, Kinsey (1948, 1953) found that divorced men and women were engaging in less sexual activity than were married men and women of comparable ages. However, Hunt (1974) found a very different picture

25 years later. He reported that in his divorced sample 100 percent of the men under age 55 and 90 percent of the women had engaged in sexual intercourse in the year prior to the survey. In a later study involving a national questionnaire given to 984 separated and divorced people and 113 widowed people, Hunt and Hunt (1977) reported that a great majority had become sexually active within a year after their divorce. Only one man in 20 and one woman in 14 reported that they had not engaged in intercourse. In an even later study Zeiss and Zeiss (1979) found that 50 percent of the divorced people they studied had begun having intercourse within a month after their marital separation and 81 percent had done so within a year. From these findings it appears that sexual activity among the divorced is quite a bit higher than previous measures had shown.

Frequency of Sexual Intercourse

Hunt (1974) found that the typical frequency of intercourse for divorced individuals was twice per week. Zeiss and Zeiss (1979) found that their divorced respondents averaged intercourse once every other date. In Cargan's (1981) research 36 percent of the divorced reported that they engaged in intercourse three or more times per week. This level of coital activity is characteristic of a minority.

Even though divorced individuals report the greatest frequency of sexual activity, they still report that they would prefer more frequent sex (Zeiss and Zeiss 1979), indicating some dissatisfaction with their sexual life. This finding cannot be taken to mean that divorced persons are frantically hopping from one bed to another in the search for sexual ecstasy. Despite any initial flurry of postdivorce sexual activity, divorced individuals tended to have sex less often on the average than most married people. Zeiss and Zeiss also found that at any one time the divorced people in their sample were dating only one person and that sexual selectivity was the rule rather than the exception. Many divorced persons, in fact, find sexual and dating exclusivity problematic, because even though the opportunities and attractions may be available, they do not feel comfortable being sexually active with more than one person (Stein 1976).

Number of Partners

There was a definite increase in the number of sexual partners from the time of Kinsey's surveys to the 1970s. In the Kinsey studies (1948, 1953) the typical divorced man reported four partners in a year, while the average woman reported two partners. In a later study divorced men had a median of eight partners in the year prior to the survey, and women reported a median of four partners (Hunt 1974). More recently about a third of divorced individuals reported more than ten sexual partners in a year (Cargan and Melko 1982).

A count of the sexual partners of divorced people may not actively reflect their sexual activity. Many divorced people go through a variety of sexual partners during the first year after their divorce. This stage of sexual experimentation may be motivated by their feeling of having escaped from a sexually restrictive marriage, by a search for intimacy with someone new, by a wish to avoid commitment in another intimate relationship, or by an attempt to ascertain their attractiveness to the opposite sex. Divorced people may also need to prove their sexual desirability with a new partner or partners. The divorced person's new sense of freedom may quickly wane, however, because before long most men are looking for "meaningful relationships" and most women are complaining that casual sex lowers their self-esteem and leads to feelings of depression and even desperation (Hetherington, Cox, and Cox 1976).

Who Initiates Sex?

Approximately two-thirds of divorced men and one-fifth of the women reported that in a new relationship women were sometimes the ones to initiate sex (Hunt and Hunt 1977). Only one in five women reported they had accepted sex the first time it was initiated, whereas four-fifths of men said that women had accepted their advances on the first attempt. It is difficult to ascertain what this disparity between the male and female reports mean. It is possible that because of gender stereotypes regarding male and female sexuality the men in the sample were inflating their sexual desirability and the women were hesitant to express their sexual aggressiveness.

Quality of Sex

The divorced group in Hunt's (1974) study indicated that their sexual life was better in some ways than their marital sexual experiences had been. Divorced men and women both reported greater variety of sexual arousal techniques and sexual positions, and the women reported higher orgasm rates. Women often reported more orgasms in postmarital relationships than in their former marriages, and they also reported higher orgasm rates than wives of the same age (Gebhard 1970). Almost all of the divorced subjects rated their current sex life as "very pleasurable" or mostly pleasurable. In a later study, Cargan and Melko (1982) found that the divorced individuals in their sample reported more dissatisfaction with their sex life than the married, the never-married, or the remarried. The researchers found that married individuals were the most satisfied, followed by divorced people and the never-married. This same pattern was somewhat evident when individuals who were divorced compared their present sexual life with their married sexual life. Marital sex still held a slight edge. Although they rated their current sexual pleasure as higher than they had experienced in marriage, they were probably comparing their present sexual situation with a disintegrating marriage in which they had experienced numerous sexual and related problems. It is also possible that the feelings of inadequacy, communication problems, and financial stress that some had experienced in their disintegrating marriage inhibited their ability to experience satisfying sexual responses and enjoyment in their new relationship. Getting a divorce may resolve some of these issues and thereby allow the person to engage in a fuller sex life. Of course, the opposite can also occur. In these cases the trauma of the divorce can lead to feelings of sexual inadequacy, doubt, and dysfunction (Gebhard 1968).

Thus, the findings are inconclusive. It is probably reasonable to suggest, though, that there is much variation and a great deal of ambiguity on the part of those who are sexually single again.

Hunt and Hunt (1977) maintain that the formerly married are much more open and liberal about sex with new partners than their counterparts were a generation ago. Sneaking around, particularly if children were involved, was once the norm. But in contemporary society at least some divorced individuals appear to be more eager and spontaneous about sexual encounters, and fewer report hiding their activities from their children. It is important to note that because of the recent AIDS epidemic and the resultant fear associated with sexual promiscuity it is likely that many people are altering their sexual patterns, and that if a survey on sexual behavior were obtained now there would be a decrease in the number of sexual partners of divorced persons.

Thus, it appears that immediately following a divorce some men and women engage in a short period of increased sexual experimentation, but in most cases they soon settle down to a more stable sexual style in the context of a longer-term relationship. In some situations this increased sexual activity seems to entail far less emotional attachment and commitment. The interviewees reported confusion about and difficulty with suddenly finding themselves required to date and engage in various courtship behaviors after years of monogamy. They often reported not knowing appropriate behavior in dating situations and feeling insecure with members of the opposite sex. They were unsure of themselves and had value conflicts about their actions. It was not unusual for men to experience occasions of erectile dysfunction as they tried to have intercourse with new partners whom they perceived as being sexually more demanding and aggressive than their former wives. For some men and women these anxieties and insecurities led to postmarital sexual dysfunctions.

After divorce, it appears, most individuals are wary of another involvement. They may feel lonely, rejected, and sexually unsatisfied. A typical reaction is to have casual and friendly sexual relationships with little commitment. These new relationships can serve an important psychological function, for they can heal a wounded ego and thereby encourage people to involve themselves in an intimate relationship again. For some, they even result in more satisfying sexual expression.

Sex and the Single Parent

Many divorced individuals, of course, are single parents, even if they are not primary caretakers. Census experts estimate that about 45 percent of children born in 1978 will live with only one parent for at least a while before they are 18. In 1980, 20 percent of children under the age of 18 were living with only one parent. About 17 percent of all living arrangements for a child under 18 are with the mother only, and about 1.6 percent are with the father only (Glick and Norton 1979).

The Single Mother

Since mothers are more likely to be given custody of the children after separation and divorce, and since widows are more common than widowers, it is not surprising that most children in single-parent homes live with their mothers. Over eight million children in the United States live with their mothers alone, while eight-hundred-thousand live with their fathers alone.

Money is an especially critical problem for single parents. One-parent families in general have considerably lower incomes than two-parent families, and their problems are often economic. Not surprisingly, single working mothers make less than half of what single fathers make, and since child care must often be arranged and paid for, single mothers are constantly burdened with financial worries. It is no wonder that some writers speak of the feminization of poverty. Because of these very real economic pressures, the single mother may find it difficult to attend social events and may be unable to buy new, attractive clothing or to afford a baby-sitter. These factors obviously restrict her dating.

The Single Father

Relatively few one-parent families are headed by a man. When such families do exist, usually the mother has died. In these cases the widower experiences many of the same psychological and emotional problems faced by widowed mothers, such as loneliness, sorrow, bitterness, and a sense of being overwhelmed by the full responsibility of child care. Most motherless families have fewer economic problems than fatherless families. However, if many single mothers are at least initially unprepared for the work role, many single fathers are unprepared for childcare responsibilities and home management tasks such as shopping, cooking, doing laundry, and cleaning house. Some men do these chores themselves, while others rely on relatives or friends for help or hire outside workers. Teenage daughters are sometimes put in the role of the "little mother" or the parental child and given considerable responsibility for the house and the younger siblings. In these cases there is often resentment on the part of the child, who is unable to enjoy childhood activities and often feels overburdened by feelings of responsibility for the emotional well-being of the parent. Other children in the family system may also feel resentment toward the parental child, for they believe that he or she holds a special, favored position in the parent's eyes. The father may rely on the company of this child, and in some cases this may prevent him from seeking appropriate social partners of the opposite sex.

Meeting sexual and intimacy needs while taking care of children without a partner is fraught with problems involving privacy, energy, and time. In an interview study with 38 single parents, Greenberg (1979) reported that most of her sample believed that their sexual activity should not be known to their children. The double standard was evident, since more men than women accepted sex among single parents even if it was apparent to their children. In a study of 127 separated or divorced fathers with full or joint custody of their children, Rosenthal and Keshet (1978a) found that most of their serious dating relationships were with younger, childless women. When the father dated a new woman and stayed overnight, it was more typically at her home than his. The women involved in the sample reported feeling more comfortable and more romantic in their own homes or apartments, where they did not have to worry about their date's children. If a serious relationship developed, the sense of a new couple emerged. Eventually, 75 percent of the single fathers asked their new partners to sleep over (Rosenthal and Keshet 1979b), although they reported that this was initially very difficult. Single fathers also reported that they were generally uncomfortable about having a girlfriend sleep over when the children were present. They reported worrying that their children might feel that sex was ideally totally uncommitted and free. This idea was uncomfortable for them (Rosenthal and Keshet 1979b).

It may be especially important for the single father that his new partner get along with his children. If the relationship leads to marriage, the woman may be expected to assume much responsibility for managing the household and caring for the children. Single mothers, on the other hand, may consider financial security more important in their mate selections. They may consider the possibility that the children's biological father will renege on support payments, thereby making the stepfather more responsible for the child's welfare. In this sense, then, for single mothers the financial security of the future mate is an important variable, while for single fathers the woman's ability to assume responsibility for child care and household maintenance may be more important.

General Considerations

In general, the single parent must confront several issues regarding dating and sexuality. First, there are time considerations. The decision to begin dating may arouse guilt feelings concerning the children. If the single parent works and his or her children are in child care all day, he or she is faced with a choice between going out in the evening and spending time with the children.

Second, a single parent generally looks at the men or women he or she meets not only as potential marital partners but also as potential parents. A new criterion then enters the process by which the single parent evaluates the person. While the individual may be fun to be with, he or she may not be interested in assuming parental responsibilities. This relationship will probably not last. In another situation an individual may be willing to assume parental responsibilities, but the children may be so threatened by his or her presence that they sabotage the new relationship, attempting to maintain the status quo.

Third, there are financial and fatigue considerations, or the costs of dating in time, energy, and money. If the children are small, dating requires finding and paying a baby-sitter. Both men and women need up-to-date clothes in good order. If finances are limited, there may be competition between these needs and the needs of the children. Going out also imposes a cost in fatigue. It means less time to get other things done, less time to sleep and rest, and less time for the children. Single parents who work may feel that they spend too little time with their children as it is. Dating means that the children will be left once again with a baby-sitter. The possibility of dating also creates conflict in the single parent when he or she attempts to decide whether to date in the first place.

Fourth, some individuals, especially those from conservative families in traditional neighborhoods, may worry about their reputations. What will the neighbors think, and what are the repercussions for the children? Single parents may also fear that the former spouse will use their dating to malign them to the children or to argue in court for renegotiation of support or custody. Most single parents who begin to date also worry about their children's reactions. They are likely to be aware that their children now see them as having sexual needs. They may be concerned about their children's reactions to the people they date. The children may actively discourage parents who are already uncertain about dating. And although parents may feel that they relinquish their rights as independent adults by allowing their children to control their personal lives, the children's objections may, in fact, affect their dating behavior.

Fifth, there are personal considerations. Single parents recognize that not only has society changed, but so have they. They are older. They may feel less attractive. They may worry about the condition of their bodies. Women may be concerned about sagging breasts and stretch marks. Men may worry about potbellies, thinning hair, and impotence. And now they come as a package deal: adult with children. They are likely to feel less "marriageable," since many prospective partners are hesitant to take on the added responsibility of parenthood with someone else's children.

Sixth, there are also considerations of a sociosexual nature. Meeting eligible mates can be difficult. When such prospects are met, children may cause immediate problems, either by being negative or by being excessively positive and frightening others off by asking, "Are you going to be my new Daddy?" Furthermore, a single parent must decide whether to permit a date or a lover to spend the night when the children are present. To allow someone who is not the children's mother or father to spend the night is often an important symbolic act for the parent. For one thing, it generally involves the children in the relationship with the person. If there is no commitment to the person, the parent may fear that the children will become emotionally involved with the person. If the relationship ends, the parent will have to deal not only with his or her own feelings about the breakup, but also with the children's feelings. Allowing a date or a lover to sleep over also reveals to the children that the parent is a sexual person. This may make the parent uncomfortable. He or she may feel that the children are passing moral judgment.

Finally, there are "right person" considerations. Single parents, both men and women, can easily despair of finding the right person. Single fathers may have an easier time meeting someone. But they may complain that those they meet are too young or, if older and never married, too involved with their careers or too prudish. Divorced women may feel bitter toward all men, and divorced men toward all women. Widows and widowers may idealize their former husbands, creating an unrealistic fantasy person for the single father to compete with. Single mothers in their thirties or forties express similar complaints. There may be men around, they report, but not the right type. If the men have never been married, it is probably because something is wrong with them and no one else wants them: they are unwilling to settle down, they are still tied to their mothers, or they are homosexual. If the men have been married, they probably still have responsibilities to their former families, wives to whom they must furnish child support and children whom they must see. Many single parents, male or female, come to the conclusion "Why bother?"

As a result of all these difficulties, there is less movement into marriage from the world of single parents than from some of the other unmarried populations. These structural impediments certainly add to the general lack of desire for remarriage of many of these single parents.

Thus, on the one hand emotional, physical, and social needs press the single parent toward finding a new partner. On the other hand very real reasons for hesitancy include the costs of dating and concerns about dignity and self-respect.

Widowhood

Divorce represents what is called a relationship loss. Reactions to such a loss are called mourning processes, and the road back to emotional stability is a healing process. The loss a person feels in divorce is comparable to the loss individuals experience when a loved one dies. In both cases a grieving process occurs, but there are important differences. Divorce is the loss of a relationship; death is the loss of a person. In divorce the former spouse continues to exist and in many cases to interact in legal, financial, and parenting matters. When the grief is caused by a death, social rituals and supports help the remaining spouse adjust emotionally in the mourning process. Unfortunately, there are no recognized grief rituals to help the divorced person. Divorce may be a more difficult adjustment than death of a spouse (Rathers and Nevid 1983). When a spouse dies, legal problems are usually minimal. Divorce may seem to require a ream of documents and endless waiting periods. When someone dies, the family remains intact. In divorce children and others choose sides and assign blame. For the parent who does not have custody of the children, divorce signals changes in the parental as well as the marital role. After a death people receive compassionate leave from work and are expected to be less productive for a while. After divorce people are often criticized. Death is final, but the divorced may nourish "what ifs?" and vacillate in their emotions for many years.

The postmarital adjustment following the death of a spouse is different in some ways from the situation commonly found after divorce. Widowed individuals typically do not have the sense of having failed at a marriage. In addition, the anger and resentment that often help facilitate the emotional separation after a divorce are frequently lacking when a partner dies. The grief may be more intense, and the quality of the emotional attachment to the deceased mate is often quite high. For some people this emotional tie remains so strong that other potential relationships appear dim by comparison.

There are also problems when the widowed individual has adult children living in the area. They may have divided loyalties between the dead parent and any new person the remaining parent is dating. Sometimes adult children feel they must protect themselves from the new relationship. In these cases they tend to deny the existence of the relationship and in patronizing ways laugh at their parent's "childish" behavior. Many adult children also have difficulty viewing their widowed parents as sexual persons.

By far the majority of marriages end with one partner's death. Although a spouse can die during the early or middle adult years, widowhood usually occurs later in life. In most cases, especially in this century, it is the man who dies first. The ratio of widows to widowers in the United States has increased from less than 2:1 in the early 1900s to 5:1 in the 1970s (Hoult, Henz, and Hudson 1978). Widows, particularly if they are older, tend to be less sexually active than divorced women. This is more true for widows than it is for widowers. Older widows are often reluctant to begin new relationships and may be influenced by loyalty to departed husbands and by negative family pressure. The problems of the widowed woman are complicated by the fact that the pool of available men is small relative to the number of women looking for partners.

There have been no direct studies of the postmarital sexual adjustment of widows and widowers. This does not mean that they do not have sexual problems. In fact, their problems may be far more complex than those of younger people. This lack reflects American society's view that older people should be nonsexual and that any sexual interest among the older population is abnormal or immoral. Sexuality researchers appear to have accepted this view, at least as evidenced by their historical ignoring of this group. With increased awareness that sexual interest and activity can continue indefinitely, perhaps there will be greater concern about and interest in the special problems of widowed individuals as they face postmarital sexual adjustment.

A large percentage of the single population is composed of the divorced and widowed of both sexes. Singlehood is often thrust on them by circumstances, not chosen. These people have often been involved in an exclusive relationship for many years. Suddenly they find themselves in the arena of dating and courtship. This transition is particularly difficult because social values have changed so radically since they were a part of the dating scene. The inability to cope with the demands of dating today often leaves older divorced or widowed people in a state of confusion. Some of them retreat into a celibate life.

In many cases the social, psychological, and sexual adjustments and the grieving process described in our discussion of divorce are experienced by widowers and widows.

Implications for Counseling

The decision to separate and divorce is rarely reached quickly or without difficulty and pain, even in unhappy marriages. Counseling during this time may help people reconstitute their sense of stability and focus on their new lives. The general goal of counseling is to help clients optimize personal development as they pursue new lifestyles. It is important for the counselor to examine his or her own assumptions about this particular lifestyle in order to help clients identify their own social roles and attitudes. The counselor's attitude should be that the single lifestyle is legitimate and viable. Counselors need to help clients explore their own personal and interpersonal needs and attitudes, aiding clients to develop and maintain their social identities in realistic ways. In some cases the counseling process may include educating the client about single life. During the stages of divorce adjustment, clients frequently present several common problems that relate to sexuality. Although these problems may not initially appear overtly sexual, the task of the counselor is to tune in to the possible sexual implications, to understand the underlying sexual dynamics, and to be comfortable and competent enough to give clients permission to deal with the problems, confident that they can be solved. However, counselors must be keenly aware of all the emotional processes that individuals experience during the divorcing process. It is impossible to separate sexual issues without considering the other strong emotions that people feel at this time.

The Stage of Denial

During Stage 1 of the divorcing process, as we have seen, clients experience denial. At this time clients may not be interested in sex at all, let alone in sex with a person other than their spouse. Along with denial of their basic emotional state, they may also deny the existence of their sexuality or their fears about it. This is often manifested in a counseling session by a repeated, "I don't have to worry about sex. I'm simply not interested in it. It just isn't important anymore." Most clients still feel married at this point, and to encourage them to date would be detrimental to the healing process. Any sort of denial, repression, fear, or ignorance imperils eventual healthy sexual expression. Clients during this stage usually experience sexual deprivation. Even if the marriage was disintegrating, some individuals, because they still feel married, will continue to engage in sexual intercourse with their former spouses because they feel sexually deprived. Counselors dealing with clients in Stage 1 should help them acknowledge their sexual needs and decide how they could comfortably deal with their sexuality.

The client's reactions to loneliness are also important at this stage. Counselors should help clients explore and deal with feelings of loneliness. Loneliness has many components. First, there is a feeling of emotional insufficiency. People may feel empty and sorrowful. This may be a healthy sign, for it signals that they are without emotional partnership. Another component is anxiety. People may feel as though the world is without comfort for them: they will never meet anyone satisfactory. This mood may be accompanied by a feeling of impending doom. Clients may feel restless and may keep busy with random activities. The single person must, at times, deal with these feelings of loneliness and isolation. A degree of comfort with solitude and with one's self is essential.

Epstein (1974) has suggested that loneliness is a greater problem for divorced men than for divorced women, but that autonomy is a greater problem for women. This is especially true for women with young children still at home. Children may prevent much potential loneliness, because they give structure to everyday life and provide emotional satisfactions. At the same time, however, they impose numerous responsibilities and may further restrict the mother's ability to fully utilize her newfound freedom. Single parents sometimes find solace in their children's presence (some women report that they feel as if they talk to babies all day), but reliance on children for amusement and company is unhealthy if it prevents parents from seeking more appropriate alternatives. Further, it may overburden the child. Some parents blame the children for their loneliness. "If I didn't have the children, I would be able to go out and meet more people."

Loneliness, then, is one of the most painful feelings that accompany divorce. The individual often feels hopeless at the prospect of making new friends as a single person. Clients complain that they do not know where and how to meet people. Loneliness can turn to depression when people have tried the singles bars or experienced the frantic search to pair up that is common in certain self-help divorce adjustment groups. For some individuals loneliness may become a chronic condition—a way of life.

Certain times of day may be more difficult than others. The time after dinner may be particularly lonely for a person who before divorce or the death of a spouse socialized until bedtime. For others the holidays may present a problem. In these cases, the counselor must help clients get in touch with their own motives and needs, explore the extent to which sexual needs are part of their loneliness, understand the extent to which a fantasy of a new ideal partner or of the ex-spouse is dominating their efforts to make new friends, and evaluate options for dealing with the problem in terms of the divorce-adjustment process.

It is important for counselors to help the clients openly face feelings of loneliness and come to understand their own responsibility for those feelings. Denial of these feelings and displacement of anger and blame will only increase the problem. During this time people also feel doubtful of their own capacity to love or to maintain a stable relationship. The counselor should help them understand their loneliness and aid them.

The Stage of Conflict

During Stage 2 of the divorcing process—conflict—clients may feel curious about dating, interested in dating, or even compelled to date. At this point they may in fact enter the social world while remaining unsure of themselves. They may push themselves to date and have sex, only to feel ashamed and depressed afterward. Some individuals at this stage use their sexuality as a weapon to rebel against a sexually restrictive former spouse or a sexually restrictive upbringing. Some individuals use sexuality as self-punishment, much as people allow themselves to be used sexually to prove that they are indeed worthless. In these cases sex is used for manipulation, rebellion, and punishment. Areas for exploration in counseling are self-worth and self-esteem. Sexual needs are legitimate, and in these cases the counselor can help clients understand the basic purposes of sexuality: enjoyment, communication, playfulness, and construction of deeper relationships. At this time it is not unusual for a man to report impotence or a woman to report orgasmic dysfunction or sexual disinterest. At times they may feel quite comfortable dating and engaging in sex, only to find themselves guilty and ashamed later on. Their emotions at this point are too unstable to form any long-lasting impressions of themselves or others.

During this stage it is also important to help clients clarify values about dating, relationships, and sexuality. In this process, they become aware of the beliefs and behaviors that are important to them and that they are comfortable with. This clarification also helps them act consistently on their values and beliefs. Basically, counselors aid clients in sorting through their sexual values and the reasons they hold them. It is also useful for counselors to help clients set up realistic values for themselves so that they do not constantly fail to adjust their behavior to their values. After a sexual value has been clarified with a client, planning can optimize the client's chances of carrying the plan into action.

Anxiety about newly achieved sexual freedom and changes in sexual codes and behavior is another common problem for clients. Some people appear to enjoy the freedom to have many sexual partners without commitment; others find the expectation that they must have sex with every new friend or date oppressive. Somewhere between these two extremes, others explore by trial and error their new sexual self-concept. With clients who feel that sexuality should be free and easy, counselors can help them fit sexuality into their lives. In other words, while sexuality may be very important to some clients, it is not one's whole life. In this sense the counselor helps clients put sexuality into perspective. As clients cope with the dating and the sex games, they often find they have to confront additional feelings of *anger* at having been used sexually, *guilt* over sexually exploiting others, or *depression* when intimacy needs are not met. In addition, both male and female clients often express concerns about the new emphasis on female orgasm and other changes in sexual mores. For these kinds of *sex-related anxieties,* the counselor can help clients recognize specific fears and anxieties; bring to consciousness personal needs, expectations, and values about sexuality; and hasten the reintegration of the sexual self so that they can deal openly and honestly with potential sexual partners and choose whether, when, and on what terms to engage in sex.

Counselors can help clients deal with prioritizing and setting limits and boundaries on their sexuality. This means determining the dividing line between constructive and destructive sexual expression. People in these situations must practice willpower. Once they have established their values and a plan of action, they must mobilize their willpower to incorporate the values into their lifestyles. It is only with this kind of self-knowledge and comfort with one's own needs and values that a person can communicate honestly about sex and take responsibility for his or her own sexuality, thus gaining protection from the hazards of trial and error sexual encounters. After clients have accomplished this and are well on the road to consistency between values and behavior, it is important for them to evaluate and assess their sexual value systems. If they feel comfortable with their actions, they have affirmed their value system; if not, more value clarification work is needed.

The AIDS epidemic is having a draining emotional impact on single people's behavior, forcing many into counseling. Some clients are preoccupied with the fear of getting the deadly virus. Clients report a great deal of distress about dating and sexuality because the virus is spreading into the heterosexual population. These concerns are very real. In such situations the counselor must discourage clients from having multiple partners, encourage them to explore other means of sexual satisfaction, give accurate information about the disease, and in all cases stress safer sex practices. This may involve assertiveness training, because some clients may be reluctant to tell a partner that they will not engage in sexual activity without using a condom lined with nonoxyl-9. Until a cure or vaccine for AIDS is found and the epidemic is over, counselors must address the subject with all sexually active single clients.

Counselors should help clients approach new roles and responsibilities from a positive perspective. People may feel a sense of pride in their newly found competencies. For example, clients can find emotional support in friendships and family relations. It is crucial for single parents to establish a support network outside their dissolved marital system. In this way they can achieve a new level of adult communication with acquaintances whose uncritical acceptance can greatly aid in reducing their feelings of guilt and shame.

The Stage of Ambivalence

In Stage 3 of the divorcing process, ambivalence, people may experiment sexually. They may date and have sex with several individuals in an attempt to learn about their new sexual identity. One client reported having sex three times on one weekend with three different partners. Feeling youthful and free, people may enter a relationship with a much younger person and engage in youthful activities. Some clients seem to be picking up where they left off as socially and sexually involved individuals before they were married. Usually, these relationships are short, and most such clients eventually begin dating someone closer to their own ages, emotionally and biologically. During this time a person may also feel that "my body is not getting any younger. I'd better have sex with this person now." In situations like these people feel as though they are bartering sex for something else. In other words clients may not engage in sex for appropriate reasons; rather, they may act out of curiosity or to affirm their attractiveness to the opposite sex. Counselors should help their clients understand their values regarding sexual motivations. Usually individuals who engage in sexual

Table 13.1 Stages of the Divorcing Process and Appropriate Counseling Techniques

Stages	Issues	Counseling techniques
Stage 1 (*denial*)	Loneliness	Help clients develop outside support networks.
	Sexual deprivation; lack of sexual interest	Aid clients in dealing with emotionality associated with separation shock.
Stage 2: (*conflict*)	Possible sexual acting-out	Help clients clarify values about dating, relationships, and sexuality.
	Emotional instability	Help clients "own" their ambivalent feelings.
Stage 3 (*ambivalence*)	Identity problems (social, psychological, sexual)	Help clients make the identity transition from defining themselves within a "married script" to defining themselves within the context of a "single script."
Stage 4: (*acceptance*)	Maintenance of stability	Help clients internalize their new sociopsychological identity.

encounters based upon these reasons lack self-esteem, commitment, and intimacy, characteristics that most people consider important in sexual and social relationships.

During this stage clients may report specific sexual dysfunctions. At this time counselors should universalize and thereby detoxify these dysfunctions. Loss of sexual desire, erectile dysfunction, premature ejaculation, and orgasmic difficulties may be present alone or in the context of the problems discussed above. Therapeutic assessment of these dysfunctions must encompass the individual's previous sexual functioning, the dynamics of the previous marriage, sexuality within the marriage, the overall impact of the divorce process on the person's sexual self-concept, and the present circumstances in which the sexual dysfunction is manifested. Regarding the extent to which the problem existed in the previous marriage and the possibility that it may have been a factor in the divorce, the counselor may have to accept the client's version of the problem and its causes. The direction that the counseling takes will obviously depend on the overall assessment and on the counselor's level of competence in treating sexual dysfunctions.

The Stage of Acceptance

Only when individuals enter Stage 4 of the divorcing process, the acceptance stage, do they have enough awareness of their own needs and desires to maintain a healthy social and sexual relationship. They have attained a balancing of self and relationship and are now able to enter an intimate relationship. While it is important for counselors working with divorcing individuals to consider their sexual needs, problems, and issues, it is crucially important not to separate the sexual areas of counseling from the psychological or emotional. Human behavior is wonderfully complex, and to ignore any aspect of it is to simplify this complexity. (For a summary of the psychological issues of the divorcing process, see table 13.1.)

Conclusions

The feelings and behavior of individuals who are sexually single again often reflect an ongoing psychological process. A healthy transition from marriage through divorce requires significant identity work, because it involves change in three areas: the social, the psychological, and the sexual. There are also specific sociopsychological problems faced by single parents, especially in dealing with children's responses to divorce.

As people move through the four stages of the divorcing process, distinct sexual issues become relevant. These include loneliness, loss of sexual interest, sexual acting-out, and identity problems. Members of the helping professions can help clients develop new sexual identities by encouraging them to form support networks; by aiding them in coping with the emotions associated with separation shock and in clarifying their values about dating, relationships, and sexuality; and by helping them create single "scripts" with which they feel comfortable.

References

Cargan, L., and M. Melko (1982) *Singles: Myths and Realities*. Beverly Hills, Calif.: Russell Sage Foundation.

Diegmuller, K. (1986) "Divorce exacts its price from parent and child alike," *Insight* 2 (41): 14–17.

Ditzion, S. (1978) *Marriage, Morals and Sex in America*. New York: Norton.

Epstein, J. (1974) *Divorced in America*. Baltimore, Md.: Penguin.

Gebhard, P. H. (1968) "Human Sex Behavior Research," in M. Diamond, ed., *Perspectives in Reproduction and Sexual Behavior*. Bloomington, Ind.: Indiana University Press, 391–410.

——— (1970) "Postmarital Coitus among Widows and Divorcees," in P. Bohannon, ed., *Divorce and After*. Garden City, N.Y.: Doubleday, 81–96.

Glick, P., and A. Norton (1971) "Frequency, Duration and Probability of Marriage and Divorce," *Journal of Marriage and the Family* 33: 307–313.

——— (1979) *Update: Marrying, Divorcing and Living Together in the United States Today*. Washington, D.C.: Population Reference Bureau.

Greenberg, J. B. (1979) "Single Parenting and Intimacy: A Comparison of Mothers and Fathers," *Alternative Lifestyles* 2 (3): 308–331.

Hetherington, M., M. Cox, and R. Cox (1976) "Divorced Fathers," *The Family Coordinator* 25: 417–28.

Hoult, T., L. Henz, and J. Hudson. (1978) *Courtship and Marriage in America*. Boston: Little, Brown.

Hunt, M., and B. Hunt (1977) *The Divorce Experience*. New York: Signet.

Kinsey, A., W. Pomeroy, and C. Martin (1948) *Sexual Behavior in the Human Male*. Philadelphia, Pa.: Saunders.

——— (1953) *Sexual Behavior in the Human Female*. Philadelphia, Pa.: Saunders.

Krantzler, M. (1975) *Creative Divorce*. New York: New American Library.

Murstein, B. I. (1974) *Love, Sex and Marriage through the Ages*. New York: Springer.

Rathers, S. A., and J. S. Nevid (1983) *Adjustment and Growth: The Challenges of Life*. New York: Holt, Rinehart and Winston.

Rosenthal, K., and H. Keshet (1978a) "The Impact of Childcare Responsibilities on the Part-time or Single Father," *Alternative Lifestyles* 1 (4): 465–92.

——— (1978b) "The Not-Quite Stepmother," *Psychology Today* (July): 82–88.

Stein, P. (1976) *Single*. Englewood Cliffs, N.J.: Prentice-Hall.

U.S. Bureau of the Census (1985) *Household and Family Characteristics*, ser. P.20, no. 411 (March). Washington, D.C.: U.S. Government Printing Office.

Weiss, R. (1975) *Marital Separation*. New York: Basic Books.

Yankelovich, D. (1981) *New Rules*. New York: Random House.

Zeiss, R. A., and A. M. Zeiss (1979) *The Role of Sexual Behavior in the Post-Divorce Adjustment Process*. Paper presented at the annual meeting of the Western Psychological Association, San Diego, Calif.

SECTION FOUR

Common Issues In Marital and Family Therapy

This section, comprised of seven chapters, focuses on four problems that frequently appear in marital and family therapy. These chapters specifically focus on "typical" dysfunctional families, sexual issues, bulimia and obesity, and the death of a family member. The final chapter addresses the future directions of family therapy theory, with a specific focus on constructivism. Once again, a systemic viewpoint is taken including aspects of cognitive-behavioral and life cycle approaches. Treatment of each subject area extends beyond reported research to pragmatic therapeutic methods for dealing with such presenting problems. The need for differential diagnosis and procedures is stressed.

Chapter 14, "Family Therapy with a 'Typical' Family System: The Involved Mother and the Peripheral Father," by Joan D. Atwood, demonstrates the greater understanding a therapist can obtain by assessing the family structure and dynamics at a systemic level. The data derived from such an analysis gives a therapist a vantage point from which to maneuver effectively. Structural, strategic, and cognitive-behavioral therapeutic interventions, creating systemic change, are outlined. This approach is demonstrated within a typical family in therapy.

Chapter 15, by Joan D. Atwood and Estelle Weinstein, "Sexual Issues in Marriage Counseling," demonstrates the value of a thorough understanding of sexual therapy issues, disorders, and treatment techniques in marriage and family therapy. There has been an increase in the presentation of sexual problems in marital therapy; however, a sexual problem is often a metaphor for a relationship. The chapter includes a brief historical overview of modern sex therapy and a listing of the major sexual dysfunctions. Specific attention is given to how therapists may incorporate sexual therapy into marital and family therapy, and what function sexual problems may serve from a systemic viewpoint. The authors provide the reader with a diagnostic procedure for identifying organic, psychological, and interpersonal causes of sexual problems. This section is followed by a description of how various structural, cognitive-behavioral, and paradoxical techniques can be used in an integrated way within a systemic framework.

Marvin Glassmann's chapter 16, "Inhibited Sexual Desire: Toward An Integrative Approach," also illustrates the need for marital and family therapists to deal intelligently with sexual issues, particularly stressing sources of inhibited sexuality, namely inhibitions of desire, arousal, and orgasm. After a brief history of the evolution of sex therapy, this chapter focuses on one of the most subtle and often difficult problems to treat: inhibited sex drive. The author discusses the various types and causes of inhibited sexual desire for both its prognostic and prescriptive value. He then illustrates and discusses, through case presentations, the use of various therapeutic approaches, such as cognitive-behavioral, hypnotherapy, and systemic therapy.

Chapter 17, also by Marvin Glassmann, "Family Therapy with Bulimia and Obesity," discusses the possibility that bulimia and obesity are two similar disorders that require a more holistic viewpoint than is typically used. A comparison between the two disorders and their respective causes and treatment modalities suggests that both disorders might be better viewed as symptomatic. The author stresses the need for a differential diagnosis in order to develop an effective treatment plan. A systemic orientation is assumed, while cognitive-behavioral, structural, and hypnotherapy approaches are examined within the bulimic and obesity case presentations.

Chapter 18, "The Book about Daddy Dying: A Preventive Art Therapy Technique," by Maxine Borowsky Junge, demonstrates the usefulness of art therapy within a systemic approach. The chapter begins with a thorough discussion of the many instances in marital and family therapy in which mourning arises. In terms of diagnosis the author stresses the therapist's need to examine clients' developmental life-cycle stage, the nature of the death, whether it involved long- or short-term caring by others, the position of the dead member within the family, the emotional significance of the death, and the openness of the family to change. Art therapy is demonstrated as an effective diagnostic and therapeutic tool. The author believes that failure to mourn the loss completely may result in marital/family dysfunction or the development of individual psychopathology. She particularly emphasizes the use of art therapy, with regard to mourning the death of a family member as a therapeutic ritual ("the book about Daddy dying") that enables family members to come to terms with the death, accept it, and become emotionally capable of moving on.

Chapter 19, "Family Therapy and Bereavement Counseling" by Frank Genovese, presents an integrated approach to the final stage of the life cycle, death and dying. He makes a transition from individual therapeutic approaches to mourning—describing normal and abnormal reactions to grief and loss, stages of mourning, different forms of grief, and therapeutic considerations—to a discussion of mourning in the family system. In so doing he completes the transition from linear to systemic thinking. A discussion of life cycle considerations is presented, along with an exploration of the grief process from a systemic perspective. Unresolved mourning is considered from a therapeutic point of view and therapeutic interventions are presented.

In Chapter 20, with John Mince's "Discovering Meaning with Families," we have come full circle. Dr. Mince begins his chapter where chapters 1 and 2 left off—a paradigmatic shift in family therapy. He explores *constructivism,* the explanation of how we know what we know, and discusses its theoretical underpinnings, demonstrating multidisciplinary contributions to the new language-based family therapy. His historical adventure takes us through philosophy, physics, mathematics, communication, sociology, social psychology, biology, and the new biology. He then focuses on the new biology, discussing its essential concepts such as autopoesis, the closing of the nervous system, perturbations, compensation, mutual perturbation–compensation process, structural coupling, languaging, construction, coconstruction, description, explanation, meaning, reality, and objectivity. These concepts are then evaluated and applied to family therapy. Dr. Mince ends with a discussion of future directions, posing many intriguing questions.

CHAPTER FOURTEEN

FAMILY THERAPY WITH A "TYPICAL" FAMILY SYSTEM: THE INVOLVED MOTHER AND THE PERIPHERAL FATHER

Joan D. Atwood, Ph.D., C.S.W.

Since individuals exist in a family context, it is almost always necessary to involve the entire family in counseling. The family with an involved, overfunctioning mother and a peripheral, underfunctioning father presents a common situation. This paper provides the mental health professional, perhaps experienced but new to family therapy, with a description of counseling such a family system. Included in the paper is a brief description of General Systems Theory as applied to family theory, followed by case material. The family structure is then examined to analyze the family dynamic and the family-of-origin connections. To better aid the mental health practitioner faced with such a family, specific cognitive-behavioral strategies are then presented.

This paper involves a family which, at the beginning of counseling, was on the brink of divorce. Although the children were from a structurally intact, two-parent nuclear family, they appeared to suffer the same fears, sadness, worry, rejection, loneliness, conflicted loyalties, anger, and guilt as do many children in divorced homes (see Wallerstein and Kelly 1980)—evidence that one need not *be* divorced to *feel* divorced.

Theoretical Basis

Before presenting the case material, it is important for the reader new to family therapy to have a basic understanding of systems theory. Family counseling uses specific terms based on general systems theory. Briefly, the systemic approach examines the symptoms or the problems presented in a counseling situation as they are being maintained by the larger context—the family. Basically the family counselor assumes that to examine problems from an individual point of view—to see, for example, an acting-out adolescent as an individual with a mental problem—is to miss the point. People exist in environments; to assume that person and environment (context) are mutually exclusive is a mistake. Thus, for the family counselor the focus is both the interaction within the environment in which the person exists and the individual and his/her place in that environment. The basic assumption of the family counselor is that all parts are interrelated. Change in any one part of the system can cause change in another part. Each part of the system has a unique function, and these parts work together to achieve common family goals. Families also have boundaries. The family boundary is structured by the values, norms, and attitudes derived from the family's cultural heritage. Boundaries are determined by the rules and regulations which govern interactions among family members and between the family and the larger surrounding society and by idiosyncratic family experiences. These rules and regulations define the ways specific family functions get carried out.

Some other basic assumptions of family systems theorists are that it is more productive to focus on the observable family structure and on interpersonal behavioral sequences of the whole three-generational family system in the *present* than to focus on assumptions about nonobservable intrapsychic functioning based on a linear relationship with a nonobservable *past*.

Also, the focus is very much away from blame (for example, on inadequate parenting), and toward regarding all behavior, including individual symptoms, as the family's best efforts at solving life's problems. The goal, then, is basically to define the family's original life problems and to help them find different solutions to these problems.

Further, just as family systems theorists see the person as embedded in the extended family context, with all of its expectations, rules, and roles, so too do they see the family embedded in the societal context with all its definitions, rules, and roles. Therefore family therapists look to at least three generations in the family, as well as to societal influences. Within the family system, therapists focus on meaning systems and on how and who takes part in defining behaviors.

The family portrayed in this chapter is typical of the family structure seen in the practice of family therapy. It is an exaggerated version of the stereotyped male and female social roles that have been with us for so long. The mother and children are very much involved, meaning that for all practical purposes she is in charge of the home and the children. The executive boundary is ambiguous, indicating that the mother often sees herself as being "one of the kids," or sees one of the kids as a parent. The father is outside the family life space, indicating little involvement and possible feelings of alienation. He is in charge of bringing the money home. There is usually strife and discontent between the marital pair. These exaggerated role models do not work very well today. Once the therapist is able to figuratively depict the family structure, the therapeutic strategies with a particular family system become more obvious.

Background of the Family

Dot M. was referred for therapy by her family physician. She had requested the name of a therapist for a daughter with whom she felt she was having a lot of trouble. The initial appointment was set up by Dot alone. When she appeared in the therapist's office, she was visibly upset, reporting that she was at her "wit's end." Her seventeen-year-old daughter, Jan, had run away from home after an intense argument with Dot. Two days later the daughter returned and agreed to go for therapy to see if they could resolve their problems. Dot also stated that she felt she received no emotional support from her husband,

and that she could not handle the family situation any longer.

Jan was the oldest of four children. Next in line was Suzy (15), Roger (14), and Bryan (7). By the end of the second session, which they all attended, it was apparent that the whole family was in trouble and that family therapy was clearly warranted.

Cast of Characters

Jan, the runaway, had been getting into trouble for about a year. She was having difficulty in school, would not participate in family life, and was dating a person named Andrew whom her mother defined as undesirable. Jan was a petite, attractive young woman, nicely dressed and of normal intelligence. She was exceedingly hostile toward her mother, seemed somewhat closer to her father, and hated her sister Suzy, with whom she shared a room. She had a relatively normal relationship with her two brothers. Her relationship with her boyfriend Andrew was generally one of dependency on both their parts.

Andrew, (19) was labeled as undesirable by Dot for these reasons: (1) He was a landscaper and could therefore not "keep" Jan in the lifestyle to which she was accustomed; (2) Jan was totally dependent upon him, thus earning Dot's disapproval; (3) Andrew's father had died a few years earlier and Andrew's mother had moved to California, leaving Andrew with no family at home. Dot felt that because of these circumstances Andrew had latched on to the M. Family, depending upon them for the emotional support he no longer received from his own family.

For the most part Suzy physically resembled Jan, but her coloring was very different. Whereas Jan had dark hair and eyes, Suzy had blonde hair and blue eyes—highly desirable traits, according to Dot, who often mentioned them. Suzy was also different from Jan in other ways. While Jan was very shy and demure, Suzy was outgoing and friendly. Jan basically disliked school, yet Suzy was an honor student, well-adjusted to the school situation. Jan was exceedingly feminine, while Suzy was very active in sports. Dot was proud of Suzy's feistiness and encouraged her to be aggressive—"not wimpy like your sister." Dot appeared to have taken Suzy under her wing, counseling her on what she believed to be the liberated woman. She would tell Suzy not to get involved in a situation like Jan's or to do what she, Dot, had done. She would continually tell her not to depend on men.

Roger was the parental child. As described by Minuchin (1974), "The allocation of parental power to a child is a natural arrangement in large families, in single-parent families, or in families where both parents work. The system can function well. The younger children are cared for and the parental child can develop responsibility, competence, and autonomy beyond his years" (p. 97). Over a period of years, as the father, Ronnie, became more distanced from the family, increasing executive authority was assumed by the oldest son, Roger. Dot expected that Roger would repair broken things around the house, and also take care of the youngest son, Bryan. Roger was the take charge person. If he was baby-sitting and a crisis arose, he would decide whether parents should be called. He was very cooperative, doing everything he was asked and then some. While both Jan and Suzy had many friends, Roger had only one or two; he spent most of his time at home helping his mother, doing his homework, or baby-sitting. Adding to this situation was Roger's guilt over disloyalty to his father. As Gardner (1982) points out, " . . . the child may find himself in a situation where his loyalty was overly tested, where he is required to make decisions and take actions that reveal without question his preferences." Roger, siding with his mother, felt that his father was often to blame and expressed antagonism toward him, which in turn caused him to feel guilty. This situation typifies the meaning for Bowen (1978) of the term *triangulation*—a third person caught in the conflict between two others.

Bryan was described by Dot as a brat. He was very smart and slightly precocious. He was demanding, and was almost always catered to. He would not hesitate to scream at his mother from the family room, where he was watching TV, "Get me some food!" She would respond by getting him food, so that his demand-feeding schedule was continually reinforced.

Ronnie was a 41-year-old male who owned his own business. He and Dot had been married for twenty years. At the point when the family came into counseling Ronnie was a peripheral member of the family structure. He married Dot when he was twenty-one years old and finishing his bachelor's degree in business. After completing the degree, he became absorbed in making a million dollars before he reached forty. He did not accomplish this goal, and although he was very successful, he felt he was a failure. Because of this he was subject to frequent bouts of depression.

While Ronnie verbally expressed his interest in family matters and in keeping the marriage together, he seemed to make little effort to interact with his wife or children. He was frequently unaware of events that took place in the family, and generally would not take the initiative to plan any family activity. His nonverbal communications, then, were in contradiction to his verbal communications.

Ronnie was the product of a single-parent family. His father had died of a heart attack when Ronnie was ten, and he had been raised by his mother. It would seem that in his family life he was perpetuating the pattern of a family with little father influence, which was the only pattern he himself had been exposed to. He had one younger brother, who was married with two children. Ronnie's mother had cancer and frequently needed medical attention. Ronnie's brother Tom lived about two blocks from Anne (their mother) and Ronnie lived about fifty miles away, but Ronnie was defined as more responsible (he himself had been a parental child in his own family of origin) and more financially able, so he was expected to take care of his mother financially and emotionally. Ronnie was willing to do this, but wanted some help from Tom. His connection to his mother seemed stronger than his connection to his wife. His responsibility to his mother thus deprived his wife of the support she needed. To Ronnie it seemed normal that a son should be parentified and respond to his mother's needs. This created the environment conducive for his son Roger to fall into the parental role.

Dot was the family switchboard, in that all messages, requests, and family interactions involved her. Her parents were from the "Old Country," so her family-of-origin was traditional in many ways, including strict stereotypic male/female roles. Her mother was the dominant force in the house, controlling all the men in the family.

For Dot, from the beginning, men were cast in weak, passive roles, a role her brother William fell into easily. Dot was a bitter forty-year-old woman. Her bitterness and hostility often elicited bitterness and hostility from other members of the family. "A spouse's hostility can produce responsive hostility" (Weiss 1975, p. 100). She was tremendously resentful about having spent twenty years of her life "tied down with babies, while he (Ronnie) was off having a good time." She felt that Ronnie was interested only in his business and that he was able to discuss only two subjects: business and sports. She said that she had wanted to go to college when they were first married, but because she got pregnant right away, she was prevented from doing so. Ronnie, however, completed his education, which created great ambivalence for her. She reported that Ronnie was insensitive to her needs—that he was totally involved with himself and couldn't care less about her and the children. She believed that he was never there when she needed him. She often threatened divorce. As Whitaker (1989) points out, "Divorce is a metaphor that evokes a whole gestalt of meaning and feeling. In this early stage of dissolution divorce is in the air as a way to increase the temperature in the marriage" (p. 65). When Dot did not get her way, she often threatened divorce. This heightened tension between the marital pair, and Ronnie often backed down.

Dot used sex as a control mechanism and refused to have sex with Ronnie because she "hated him." She went out of her way to do "vindictive and hateful" (her words) things to him. She was very proud when she annoyed him and never hesitated to tell him so. She said that she wanted a divorce because "now it is my turn." She saw herself as having sacrificed for twenty years, depriving herself of a college education or a career to stay home and take care of her children. She felt about herself very much as did Scanzoni's (1977) owner-property type of woman entrapped in the same kind of marriage (p. 26)—that she was merely a material possession of Ronnie's, like his car, that he could deal with as he wished. She believed that Ronnie did not consider her a valuable resource, and that decisions were made without her opinion or needs being considered.

The Family Dynamic

During the course of the counseling, it became apparent that Jan's acting-out behavior maintained the family structure. Whenever Dot and Ronnie's fighting became so intense as to threaten the family (as evidenced by Dot saying that she wanted a divorce), Jan would act out. By running away from home or creating some crisis, she transferred attention from the marital couple to the identified patient (herself). In this way, Jan helped her parents stay together, and the family system remain intact.

Jan's position demonstrated a triangled alliance between her and her parents. It appeared that she carefully manipulated situations so that her parents remained relatively isolated from each other. Whenever her parents even began to unite, she created a situation whereby they would begin fighting again. On one occasion, she convinced her mother that it was important for the family to go to Vermont on a ski vacation. Dot, excited at the prospect of a "status" vacation, approached Ronnie and demanded that he make the arrangements. Ronnie, overwhelmed by financial burdens, lost his temper at another request/demand from Dot for funds. It seemed that Jan knew from the beginning that this would happen. In this way, dual executive authority remained unattainable, and no parental bloc could arise to control her behavior. Yet she had to be careful not to create too much of a gap between her parents, because then divorce might become a reality.

Dot, angry at herself for her twenty years of dependent, passive behavior, blamed Ronnie for her misfortune in not being able to finish school and start a career. However, Ronnie had initially been very supportive of her returning to school, and there had always been money available for babysitters for the children if she wanted to work. Angry at herself and projecting this anger onto her husband, she punished him by gradually pushing him out of the family unit until he became a peripheral member. This was a role with which he was comfortable, and Dot acted with his complete cooperation. In this way he could maintain his alliance with his mother—his "true" wife—and focus completely on his business. Whenever he attempted to bring Dot into his business world, she told him she was not interested. After awhile he left her out of it. This gave him more energy to focus on his business—which he ultimately wanted—and so the cycle continued. In this manner, the couple cooperated to maintain a certain distance from each other and a level of intimacy with which both were comfortable.

Developmentally the couple were at Solomon's (1983) Stage II. They had long ago stopped working on their marital roles and taken on the parental ones. "One of the traps to be avoided in this stage is relinquishing the marital role in favor of assuming the parental one" (p. 58). This kind of parental role served the M.'s well for twenty years, dismissing any worry about developing intimacy—something they both desperately feared. As was seen earlier, historically neither of them had had good models for intimacy. As Solomon (1983) also points out, ". . . the lack of attention to the continued development of the marital roles will create severe difficulties when the family attempts to move into later stages of development that are focused primarily on the beginning individuation of children and their eventual departure" (p. 58). This, of course, was what was occurring in the M. family. The older children were beginning to separate from their family of origin, causing the parents to focus once again on themselves as the marital pair. They were unprepared for what they saw.

Dot defined herself as a "woman's libber"—very different from the passive, shy Dot of twenty years earlier. By fostering this self-definition onto her children, she almost created the process by which Jan could individuate. In order to become separate from Dot, Jan had to become what Dot no longer was—passive, shy, and demure. Individuation as defined by Karpel (1983) refers to "the process by which a person becomes increasingly differentiated from a past or relational context (p. 38)." In order to individuate, Jan became Dot of twenty years earlier, and in so doing, created the triangle.

As Gardner (1982) points out, "The child of divorce, more than the child living in an intact home, is likely to be deprived of parental love" (p. 270). It is nurturing from both parents that creates self-esteem in a child, yet for the most part Ronnie was alienated from the family system, thereby depriving Jan of necessary support. Jan now, however, reminded Ronnie of his young bride, thereby eliciting positive responses that held him in the family. Jan, however, angered Dot because she reminded Dot of a self she was trying desperately to negate, one that had not brought her happiness. Thus, the triangulation emerged: Hostility between mother and father, tension between mother and daughter, and positive feelings between father and daughter. The parents could now use their involvement with their daughter and the resulting triangulation to act out their own unresolved conflicts.

In the meantime, as a result of the distancing of the father and the resulting overburdening of the family system, Roger became the parental child. He helped to preserve the family system by preventing it from becoming chaotic. He established rules, kept order in the house, and helped everyone with day-to-day living.

Another theme typical of this system was the involvement of the mother with all of her children, in a desperate search for the intimacy she was not receiving from her husband. She followed the children around to make sure they were going where they said they were going. She was very protective of Brian and babied him to a large degree. As Napier (1983) points out, "Infantilization occurs when the parent guides the child through activities that should be done independently . . ." (p. 178). Dot still dressed Bryan and often slept on the floor next to his bed, in case he had a nightmare.

The Family of Origin Connections

Both Dot and Ronnie basically replicated their families of origin in their family of procreation. Dot's mother controlled her own marital relationship, while Dot's father spent little time with the family. Because Ronnie's mother worked to support the family, he was in charge of his brother for most of their growing years. Even so, he reported that each brother went his own separate way—basically, each fended for himself. Thus, no strong family ties developed. Although Ronnie professed to want an involved family life, he also went his own way as an adult.

Family Therapy Strategies

1. Move the symptom from the identified patient to the whole family system, and help family members accept responsibility for their own behavior that maintains the family problem.

Strategic means "planned." It is crucial in family counseling—in any therapy for that matter—for the therapist to plan techniques to use in each session. Once the counselor has determined what the family structure is, as determined by the roles, interactions, rules, and boundaries of the family members, s/he should then plan strategies to help the family help itself to be more functional. S/he attempts to positively connote people's behavior as attempts to solve their problems, but attempts which happen to be ineffective, and s/he suggests, "Let's find some better and more effective behaviors."

Many strategies were used with the M. family. First of all it was important for the entire family to take responsibility for the family problems. Dot needed to take responsibility, too. The other members were more apt to examine their share in the maintenance of the system but Dot liked to portray herself as a saint, all-knowing and terribly self-righteous.

2. If appropriate, implement a behavioral contract to "get things started."

In order to alleviate the overt initial tension within the family system, a behavioral contract was set up with all the members of the M. family. This contract was basically focused on ironing out some concrete problems between Jan and her mother, but it also included negotiation strategies involving the other members.

Some of the initial tension was alleviated, and a working situation in counseling was therefore created. For example, Jan wanted to stay out later than her mother desired. Dot wanted Jan to clean her room. The behavioral contract entailed an if/then statement: If Jan stayed out one hour later, she had to clean her room on Saturday morning. In this manner, both parties won and these two items were no longer family issues.

3. Help the involved, overwhelmed family members become involved with outside systems.

Dot wanted to be drawn outside the system. She wanted to be less involved with the children and more involved with herself and the pursuit of her own interests. It was suggested that she return to school—something which she had professed she always wanted to do. She agreed and registered for her first course. This required a new definition of the role of mother in the family (engaged in rational pursuits).

4. Help the peripheral family members become more involved in the family system.

Ronnie, the husband, needed to be pulled back into the family system. This process was initially accomplished through Jan. Since Ronnie already had a relatively good relationship with his daughter, during the first family session Ronnie was instructed to begin negotiations for the behavioral contract with Jan. This gave him a place of authority and involved him in the system. This also required a new definition of the role of the father in the family (engaged in nurturing, emotional tasks).

5. Help the children form a sibling coalition.

In this family there was no sibling subsystem. Roger was a parental child; Dot was very involved with the children and saw herself as part of any existing sibling subsystem; Suzy was alienated from the rest of the children, as was Jan. In order to accomplish a sibling subsystem (a coalition of children), the children were assigned cooperative tasks. During the counseling sessions they were given home assignments to take turns being in charge of a particular task. They were encouraged in various ways to do things together. At times, the tasks were allocated according to gender—girls and boys. Other times the allocation was according to age—the two oldest and the two youngest. And at other times, they were all assigned a task together—"All the children are to go to the movies together this weekend." They were also encouraged, especially Roger, to focus on their peers as sources of friendship and support. The point of these assignments was to create a sense of boundaries between the children and to get them involved with each other.

6. Help the marital pair focus on the more positive aspects of each other, and further help them to bury the past.

With regard to the couple relationship, much work was needed. Ronnie needed to develop overt assertive strategies. Dot needed to relinquish her aggressive power strategies and substitute assertive techniques. The counselor would deliberately alternate in joining with each of them and reframing their positions in ways which made their behavior more acceptable and understandable to each other. This was crucial, because as Klugman's (1983) article points out, "The structuralist joins the system and then uses his presence to realign coalitions and strengthen or weaken boundaries. Attention is directed at changing the functions of the system" (p. 97). Dot was very eager to hold onto her definition of the situation. Because the counselor sometimes joined Ronnie, enough doubt was cast on her position that she eventually allowed him to win from time to time.

Other times the therapist joined Dot, in order to feel Ronnie's withholding behavior. Dot was very focused on Ronnie's negative aspects. She saw nothing positive whatsoever. Many sessions were spent in which the two reversed roles to gain insight into each other's behavior and into their own and each other's motivations. Minuchin and Fishman (1981) believe that "The therapist, observing the pressures organizing his (her) behavior, may join by choosing to yield to those pressures" (p. 35).

Joining with various members of the M. family helped to unbalance the structure. Minuchin emphasizes aspects of the father that are soft and nurturant (p. 72). This was particularly important in this family network, because Dot saw Ronnie as cold and unemotional, interested only in rational pursuits.

As a result of these techniques, Dot's perception of Ronnie was challenged, for she was presented with alternative possibilities that made sense to her. In the process new, self-reinforcing relationships were set up in the family. As Andolfi (1980) nicely states, "the author was hoping to get into the family to find them, without losing the ability to maneuver" (p. 114).

Both Dot and Ronnie needed to let go of the past and of their entrapment in obsolete gender role stereotypes. It was important for them to focus on the here and now. At times during the therapy sessions, Dot was asked by the counselor to bracket an event and to deal and redeal with it in its many forms and interpretations in the present. She needed to let go of her definition of herself as "victim." Ronnie needed to let go of his resentment toward his wife for, in his perception, alienating him from his children and for her lack of interest in his business activities. Many times he stated that he felt used by Dot—no more than a meal ticket and a provider of material niceties. Both Ronnie and Dot also needed to learn to communicate with each other. Dot used attack statements on Ronnie whenever she could. It was important for her to realize the futility of such behavior. Ronnie needed to learn to express affection and caring, which he found very difficult.

Follow-Up

Jan moved out and is living with Andrew. They are both in school, working toward their associate's degrees. After many sessions, they have established a good rapport with the family. Dot is completing her associate's degree, is very involved in school, and is thinking about continuing her education toward a master's degree in social work. She is less involved with the day-to-day family living and the household chores. Everyone, including Dot, is happy that Dot is in school. She is a straight A student.

Ronnie has become involved in family activities for the first time, and is in the process of establishing relationships with each of his children.

The children are responding well to this arrangement, but are somewhat suspicious of Ronnie's attention. Roger, absolved of much of his parental authority, has become more involved with friends and sports activities.

Ronnie now realizes what Levinger and Moles (1979) so cleverly make clear in their foreword "Peter, Peter, Pumpkin Eater." He has to do more to keep his wife. He is involving himself more with his family and is considering his wife's needs in a more appropriate and thoughtful manner. The marital couple is functioning on a much healthier level. They have learned to negotiate and to see each other's point of view. They are feeling more positive about each other and have resumed having sex on a regular basis. Although their communication techniques have improved greatly, more work in this area is still needed. Both Ronnie and Dot are working on individuating and separating from their families of origin. As Karpel (1983) states, "To enter into a relationship with another or others to become a part of 'We,' is the concept of maturation" (p. 83). Both Ronnie and Dot are now working toward this goal. They are developing the strength of the marital coalition which is the foundation for the structure of the whole family.

References

Ackerman, N. (1966) *Treating the Troubled Family*. New York: Basic Books.

Andolfi, M. (1980) *Family Therapy: An Interactional Approach*. New York: Plenum Press.

Bowen, M. (1978) *Family Therapy in Clinical Practice*. New York: Jason Aronson.

Gardner, R. (1982) *Family Evaluation in Child Custody and Litigation*. Cresskill, N.J.: Creative Therapies.

Hansen, J., and B. Keeney (1983) *Diagnosis and Assessment in Family Therapy*. Rockville, Md.: Aspen Systems.

Karpel, M. (1983) "Individuation: From fusion to dialogue," in *Handbook*. New York: Adelphi University Press.

Kluggman, J. (1983) "Enmeshment and Fusion," in *Handbook*.

Levinger, G., and O. Moles, eds. (1979) *Divorce and Separation*. New York: Basic Books.

Lynch, J. (1977) *The Broken Heart*. New York: Basic Books.

Minuchin, S. (1974) *Families and Family Therapy*. Cambridge, Mass.: Harvard University Press.

Minuchin, S., and J. Fishman (1981) *Family Therapy Techniques*. Cambridge, Mass.: Harvard University Press.

Napier, A. (1983) "The rejection intrusion pattern: A central family dynamic," in *Handbook*.

Papp, P., ed. (1977) *Family Therapy: Full Length Case Studies*. New York: Gardner Press.

Rhodes, S., and J. Wilson (1981) *Surviving Family Life: The Seven Crises of Living Together*. New York: Putnam and Sons.

Satir, V. (1983) *Conjoint Family Therapy*. Palo Alto, Calif.: Science and Behavior Books.

Solomon, M. I. (1983) "A developmental conceptual premise for family therapy," in *Handbook*.

Whitaker, C. (1989) *Midnight Musings of a Family Therapist*. New York: W. W. Norton.

Whitaker, C., and D. Keith (1987) "Counseling the dissolving marriage," *Journal of Marital and Family Therapy* 13 (1): 21–33.

Chapter Fifteen

SEXUAL ISSUES IN MARRIAGE COUNSELING

Joan D. Atwood, Ph.D., C.S.W., *and* Estelle Weinstein, Ph.D.

Abstract

In order to deal with the sexual issues s/he may encounter in his/her practice, the marriage and family therapist needs basic information about techniques used in sex therapy. This paper outlines a method of incorporating the psychotherapeutic techniques used at present in sex therapy into the marriage and family counseling setting when a sexual issue is involved. The paper is separated into a discussion of the problem, a brief overview of the history of modern sex therapy, a classification of sexual dysfunctions, and an overview of the major theoretical approaches to treatment. Next, a diagnosis and assessment guide for marital and sex therapists is presented, including discussions of (a) identification of organic causes, (b) identification of psychological issues, (c) examination of interpersonal issues, and (d) assessment of systemic issues. Some common systemic interventions are then presented.

William Masters describes a situation at his workshops in which three men, with a combined fifteen years in therapy with five different therapists, applied to the Masters and Johnson clinic in St. Louis with impotence as the presenting problem. He explains how, during the preliminary physical examination, organic bases for the dysfunction were tentatively ruled out. During the sex history inventory, the three men were asked if they had ever ejaculated during sexual intercourse. They responded no. Had they ever ejaculated during masturbation? No. Had they ever experienced a wet dream? Again, no. Had they ever ejaculated in their lives? No. Masters then recommended that they be examined by a urologist, who tested them and determined that these men had no ejaculatory ducts. The task of the therapist was to inform the clients that they would never ejaculate.

A young woman was referred for sex therapy for functional dyspareunia. She had been in therapy for this problem for three years. After an organic etiology was ruled out by a physician, a detailed sex history was taken. During the interview, the client was asked if she was at present taking any drugs. She answered no. The therapist asked if she was taking any nonprescription drugs. The client said no at first, then sheepishly admitted that she felt she was addicted to Dristan. Dristan is an antihistamine that dries up the nasal mucous membranes. Indeed, it dries up the mucous membranes everywhere in the body, including the vagina, which happens to *be* a mucous membrane. The client stopped taking Dristan, and her dyspareunia disappeared.

In both cases, no amount or type of psychotherapy would have eliminated these individuals' sexual dysfunctions, because they were not psychologically based.

Marriage and family therapists today encounter more and more clients in treatments for anxieties, conflicts, and problem behaviors in the sexual area. This increase is probably due to the recent social changes which have given people permission to acknowledge and deal with such problems. Unfortunately, though, these therapists have rarely taken more than a three-credit course in human sexuality counseling if they have taken *any* course dealing with sexual problems. Both types of courses generally involve only a short introduction to the field of human sexuality, including research, sexual physiology, a description of sexual dysfunctions, the general treatment strategies, and a broad coverage of other sexual issues such as rape, incest, abortion, etc. Students are then expected to be adequately prepared to treat such problems in a clinical setting. They are not. Some therapists realize that they are not adequately prepared, and the more responsible ones will refer clients to a sex therapist. One of the purposes of this paper is to suggest that it makes no sense to train people to practice marriage and family therapy without giving them adequate training in human sexuality. And it is not fruitful to train people to practice sex therapy without giving them a context in which to apply that training. It is time that the two fields—marriage and family therapy and sex therapy—be brought together. This paper is an attempt to familiarize marriage and family therapists with basic information about human sexuality, and to further familiarize sex therapists with the systemic marital issues which often occur as a context for sexual problems.

Most programs in marriage counseling do not provide adequate training for students in the field of sex therapy, and most training for students in sex therapy does not provide a context in which to place the sex therapy. We have several suggestions for rectifying this situation. We begin with a brief description of the background of the sex therapy field, including a discussion of the general treatment approaches now used. Ways are proposed in which therapists can integrate different therapeutic models to deal more effectively with changing clinical realities. Guidelines for the diagnosis/assessment of sexual issues in marriage counseling are then presented, along with several paradoxical strategies for work with highly resistant couples. The focus of this paper calls for an integration of the fields of marriage counseling and sex therapy (see also Weeks and Hof 1986).

Sager (1976), in reflecting on the evolution of the therapist's role in treating couples with sexual problems, stated that he initially believed in keeping sex therapy and couples therapy separate. He later reversed this view and proposed that the couples therapist ought to be versed in sexual therapy techniques and be ready to shift focus when necessary, rather than refer patients to a "sex therapist." Since many couples use their sexual activity as a metaphor for their relationship, only by integrating sexual and marital treatment can the therapist fully engage the couple. Lief (1982), a pioneer in the area of marital and sex therapies, also believes that it is impossible to do sex therapy without dealing with the couple's relationship. The importance of considering the role of sexual dysfunction in the couple's broader emotional relationship cannot be overemphasized. Yet there are times when both marital partners are unaware of basic physiology. In these situations, information is needed, not a deeper exploration into the couples' relational dynamics.

For some couples the dysfunction plays a functional role in the maintenance of their emotional relationship and lifestyle. A dysfunction may be a means of avoiding intimacy, of expressing hostility, of maintaining control, or of retaliating for other grievances. Sexual symptoms can be a means of sustaining or distancing relationships, a motivation for treatment or for the most determined resistance to it.

When a sexual issue arises, couples tend to request therapy in one of two ways: either directly, by presenting sex as the area of their chief complaints or indirectly, allowing sexual concerns to emerge only after other issues have been discussed. Increasingly, couples request sexual therapy rather than marital therapy. They often appear to be more comfortable with acknowledging sexual problems as isolated issues than with admitting general marital discord. The couple's therapist is therefore presented with a challenge in assessing the nature and etiology of the sexual complaint and integrating it into therapy. Often couples will initially indicate that they do not want long-term therapy, and that they have read about sex therapy and believe it is precisely what they need. However, few sexual issues can be addressed by a sex-therapy approach alone. After a few sessions the majority of clients who present a sexual complaint realize the complexity of their difficulties. For many there is a defensive need to see their problem as sexual, and they therefore resist considering the relationship issues. In these situations it is often effective to accede initially to the request for sex therapy, as a means of establishing an alliance. Couples sometimes have the fantasy that sex therapy does not require much emotional involvement, and that if they follow a prescribed formula the problem will disappear. Often after a few sessions resistance emerges, which may be made manifest by non-completion of the sensate focus exercises assigned as initial sex therapy procedure. Couples will tell the therapist that they were too tired, that they had an argument, that they felt ridiculous, etc. More than likely, failure to complete these exercises occurs because both partners are uncomfortable with the intimacy or effect generated by this degree of closeness. After this experience most couples are more amenable to discussing the broader, more difficult aspects of their marriages, and will engage in more comprehensive couples therapy. These couples who initially defined their problems as "only" sexual are able to see that there are also relationship problems that require attention.

While sex can remain an isolated problem, more often the couple's overall relationship needs to change. Generally, therapeutic intervention is aimed at helping clients express feelings to each other, demonstrate caring and affection, establish a sense of equal involvement in the relationship, problem solve, and reach conflict resolution. Interventions typically involve reconceptualization, communication exercises, role-playing in new or reversed relationship roles, self-monitoring, monitored small expressions of caring, homework practice, showing tapes of client interactions to the clients themselves, and pointing out constructive and destructive communication patterns.

History of Modern Sex Therapy

This section familiarizes the marriage and family student with the background of modern sex therapy. Historically, sexual dysfunctions were seen as manifestations of serious psychopathology with a poor therapeutic prognosis (Leiblum and Pervin 1980; Lederer and Lederer 1979). Originally, anecdotal information from individual clinical case histories was the major source of information. In addition, the clinician attempting to treat sexual disorders did not possess accurate knowledge of human sexuality on which to base that intervention. Sexual behavior had not been systematically studied in the laboratory, so basic data were non-existent. Inquiries into the area of human sexuality whose scientific merit we would now recognize began only seventy to eighty years ago. As a result, the accumulated body of knowledge in this area was relatively sparse and in some cases—for example, masturbation—invisible.

This lack of data resulted in adherence to incomplete and inaccurate therapeutic concepts derived from theoretical speculations and unsubstantiated hypotheses, such as Freud's assertion that vaginal orgasms express normal, healthy, mature female functioning, while a preference for clitoral stimulation reflects unhealthy female functioning. This conception was not corrected until Masters and Johnson (1966) demonstrated that there is a single type of orgasm involving genital vasocongestion perceived either vaginally or clitorally.

Several events hastened the development of sex therapy as a separate entity. Kinsey (1948, 1953) is credited with stimulating the modern sociological study of sex through the documentation of the incidences and rates of sexual conduct and examination of the relationship of certain sociological demographic factors (social class, education, religion, etc.) to several sexual variables. The laboratory research of Masters and Johnson (1966) provided a fairly accurate picture of the basic psychophysiology of human sexual response and reproductive functioning. It was this information about human sexuality that provided the basis for sex therapy. This work confirmed that human beings can be expected to produce biophysiological sexual responses in a typical, predictable pattern or cycle. These responses are more similar than dissimilar in males and females. Understanding of the cycle is particularly valuable in dealing with problems resulting from medical and psychosocial events. The studies by Masters and Johnson and other important researchers (Kaplan, Kolodny) also identified sexual problems or dysfunctions which led to the development of a number of effective treatment approaches.

Classification of Sexual Problems

The sexual problems that a marital therapist encounters fall into several common classifications. *Inhibited sexual desire* exists when one or both partners typically report little desire or interest in sexual activity. This can range from sexual anesthesia—no feeling at all—to avoidance of situations which typically produce sexual feelings. This can also be interpreted as a difference in the partners' sexual scripts or levels of sexual desire, whereby one partner wants sex more or less frequently than the other (Zilbergeld and Ellison 1980). *Inhibited sexual excitement* refers to the difficulties encountered specifically during the phase of sexual excitation. In the male it is usually manifested by problems in achieving or maintaining sufficient erection for sexual activity—in other words, erectile dysfunction, or impotence. In the case of *primary erectile dysfunction* the individual has never experienced erection. With *secondary erectile dysfunction*, the person has achieved satisfactory erections in the past, that is, the person has achieved or can achieve erections under certain circumstances or with particular partners. In the female, inhibited sexual excitement refers to a partial or complete failure to attain and maintain the lubrication response typically associated with high sexual arousal, or a genuine lack of erotic response to sexual stimulation.

In *inhibited female orgasm* a woman is unable to experience climax following adequate sexual excitement or has great difficulty doing so. This, too, can be primary, secondary, or situational. *Inhibited male orgasm*, or retarded ejaculation, is a condition in which the man is unable to experience ejaculation and orgasm following an adequate phase of sexual excitement (this can also be primary, secondary, or situational). *Premature ejaculation* is the inability to voluntarily control ejaculation despite a conscious effort to do so. Primary premature ejaculation is the diagnosis for a male who never had control, while secondary premature ejaculation means that good control was achieved in the past.

Functional dyspareunia troubles women for whom sexual activity, mainly intercourse, results in recurrent and persistent genital pain and discomfort. *Functional vaginismus* is recurrent or persistent vaginal contractions or spasms which prevent the penis from entering the vagina.

For a more detail description of these categories, the reader is referred to the *Diagnostic and Statistical Manual* (1980).

Approaches to Treatment

At present three widely accepted theoretical orientations are used to treat sexual dysfunctions. They are the psychoanalytic, the cognitive-behavioral (including the New Sex Therapies), and the systemic approaches.

Psychoanalytic Approaches

Prior to 1970 psychoanalytic theory and practice dominated the therapeutic approach to sexual problems. Psychoanalytic theory is a slowly evolving collection of ideas for integrating the forces that influence psychological life. It attempts to relate sexual and other symptoms to the patient's past psychological development and current mental state. Psychoanalytic discussions of sexual symptoms include factors such as constitutional predisposition, long-term parent-child relationships, psychosocial development and sociocultural and biological alterations. Even most opponents of the psychoanalytic approach believe its basic tenets: There are important unconscious influences on all mental functioning. No psychological event occurs entirely by chance. There are various schools of psychoanalytic thought, but psychoanalysts recognize the critical importance of the complex internal psychological life.

The typical therapies evolving from psychoanalytic tradition to treat problems are dyadic. Their aim is to achieve a more complete understanding of the person's mental life. The sexual problem is seen as a manifestation of an underlying, usually unconscious, internal conflict. The therapeutic goal is not just to relieve the symptom, but to resolve its infrastructure—the underlying conflict. Insight, understanding, mastery, and psychological growth are highly valued therapeutic goals. Other means of symptom removal are regarded simply as "transference cures" or "suggestion," likely to be followed by symptom substitution. The rate at which psychoanalysis and psychoanalytic psychotherapy proceed is largely controlled by the person's inner life. After the evaluation phase, a married patient with a sexual problem is usually seen alone. Interpersonal problems are viewed as the acting out of the patient's internal conflicts.

Sex Therapy

The outcome data presented in *Human Sexual Response* (Masters and Johnson 1966) and *Human Sexual Inadequacy* (Masters and Johnson 1970) challenged these psychoanalytic attitudes and suggested a radically different therapeutic approach. The rapid acceptance of the new form of therapy by both the lay and the professional public testified to psychoanalytic tradition's inadequacy in dealing with the widespread sexual problems.

Masters and Johnson's initial work suggested many exciting possibilities for dealing with dysfunctions. Both partners are included in the treatment. The concerns of each partner are considered without placing blame for the dysfunction. The symptoms belong to the marital unit, not to the symptom bearer. Masters and Johnson's often quoted statement to dysfunctional couples is, "Sexual dysfunction is a marital unit problem—not a husband's or wife's problem" (Masters and Johnson 1970). The psychological mechanisms of dysfunction may be largely related to current rather than past influences—such as performance anxiety, spectatoring, or anger at the dysfunctional spouse. A new emphasis was placed not on intrapsychic causes but on social forces, including strict Judaeo-Christian religious orthodoxy (e.g., cultural expectations which affect the normal development of female sexual expression). Male and female cotherapy teams were uniquely suited to fostering communication and mutual understanding between spouses. These teams were also more effective in identifying and dealing with the high frequency of serious interpersonal problems. Correction of misinformation and imparting of knowledge were facilitated by cotherapists.

Sensate focus is one of the more common sex therapy techniques used by Masters and Johnson (1970) and Kaplan (1979). It is defined as the use of the dimension of touch to provide sensory experiences in reconstituting natural responsivity to sexual stimuli. The exercises are initially kept at a nonverbal level. In sensate focus the partners touch each other for sexual pleasure, progressing from nongenital to genital touching. Their purpose is to reinstitute sexual responsivity to physical touching. Thus the goal is to create a comfortable, anxiety-free atmosphere for physical contact, with one person providing stimulation that is both pleasing to give and pleasing for the other person to receive.

Feedback, another Masters and Johnson (1970) technique, is a natural part of the sensate focus process. Initiations and refusal of sexual contact are typical issues for individuals with a common dysfunctional pattern. Masters and Johnson (1970) believe that initiations are often surrounded by tension, guilt, anxiety, or dread, and may have become ambiguous, ill-timed, or annoying. In these situations Masters and Johnson recommend that therapeutic time be spent in guiding the couple's discussion of good and poor ways to initiate and refuse a sexual exchange. Clients are asked to develop ways of providing positive as well as negative feedback.

Because many sexual dysfunctions occur when individuals involved are embarrassed to teach each other what pleases them, Masters and Johnson employ the *hand-riding* technique. It involves placing one's hand on the partner's hand and gently and slowly guiding the partner's hand over the body, indicating what is sexually pleasing. Gradually, through the initiation and refusal, feedback, and sensate focus experiences, a basic sexual communication framework is developed.

After ruling out physical causes for premature ejaculation (especially when it is experienced after a period of good control), the *squeeze* or *stop/start* techniques can be administered. The squeeze technique involves the female squeezing the glans of the penis between her thumb and forefinger after the male has communicated to her his feelings of impending ejaculation. When the glans is squeezed in this fashion, ejaculation is postponed and sexual intercourse is prolonged. The stop-start technique directs the female partner to manually stimulate the erect penis until the male communicates impending ejaculation, at which time she immediately stops until he regains control. This is repeated many times over a period of several weeks, until the male partner indicates he has attained some control over his ejaculatory reflex. At that time the manual stimulation is increased to include penile penetration of the vagina, initially in the female-superior position and ultimately including the male-superior position. Each time impending ejaculation is experienced the couple is instructed to stop until control is regained. Premature ejaculation is among the most common and the most successfully treated sexual problems.

Kegeling, named after the physician who discovered these exercises, is designed to strengthen the pubococcygeal muscle in both women and men. Exercises to contract and relax the pubococcygeal muscle are sometimes taught as ways to stop and start the flow of urine during urination. Men can exercise the muscle by raising and lowering the erect penis carrying the weight of a towel. This has the effect of strengthening the muscle, thereby indirectly heightening sexual pleasure.

Masters and Johnson (1970) also believe that an individual's negative cognitions can contribute to sexual dysfunction. According to them, orgasmic dysfunction can result from what women tell themselves about sex or about their partners. In some cases, religious prohibitions lead such women to equate sex with sin. Others fail to become sufficiently aroused because they tell themselves their partner is a social bore, a financial failure, a slob, or a second-rate lover. Premature ejaculation may result from negative self-talk about the need for speedy performance and concern about performing or about being caught. Ejaculatory incompetence is the inability to ejaculate within the vagina. The negative self-talk may involve the fear of impregnating the partner, the thought that the vagina is unclean, the beliefs that sexual activity is immoral, and a negative impression of the sexual partner. Erectile dysfunction in males is the inability to get a sufficiently hard erection to enter the vagina or the inability to maintain an erection after entry long enough to ejaculate. This often results from irrational ideas such as "Sex for pleasure is a sin," "I'm not a good lover, I'm inadequate" or, "What if I should fail in making love?" Treatment involves challenging and changing negative self-talk and false beliefs and attitudes about oneself, sex, and the sexual partner.

Retarded ejaculatory disorders, especially in their mildest forms, are often situational, reflecting the client's guilt about the encounter or anxiety with a particular partner. Other individuals may be unable to achieve ejaculation during intercourse but be able to do so during masturbation. Kaplan (1979) suggests that some impeded ejaculation is manifested after a particular trauma, or as an expression of silent rage, ambivalence toward a partner, fear of abandonment, inhibitions instilled by a strict religious upbringing. Both Kaplan's and Masters and Johnson's treatment plans include a series of progressive exercises, beginning with those with which the couple have achieved some ejaculatory success and progressing toward more complex and threatening ones. The concurrent therapy sessions act to enlighten the clients about their inhibiting fears and cognitions.

Vaginismus is treated by suggesting that both partners observe and investigate the vagina in private. They are told to attempt a one-finger (well-lubricated) insertion. When this is accomplished they are told to move the finger around and then to increase to two fingers. Slowly they are instructed to increase fingers, with the eventual goal of insertion of the penis. Dilators are often used instead of fingers. Since vaginismus is usually a psychologically based disorder, simultaneous psychotherapy is of great importance to successful experimentation and outcome.

Thus, the most comprehensive and persuasive account of direct sexual skills training procedure for the alleviation of sexual distress was provided by Masters and Johnson. Subsequent controlled studies, which compare directive, Masters-and-Johnson-type sex therapy to other approaches, have concurred that a directive behavioral approach is effective in ameliorating sexual difficulties. Even though Masters and Johnson originally advocated the use of a male and female cotherapy team, couples seen individually in an intensive (daily) two-week program have had equal success. A review of the literature evaluating different formats for the delivery of behavioral sex therapy indicates that one therapist is as effective as two, the gender of the therapist does not influence therapeutic outcome, and massed and spaced therapy sessions produced equivalent therapeutic effects. Although Masters and Johnson's later treatment techniques and outcome reports have come under some criticism (Szasz 1980; Zilbergeld and Evans 1980), their physiological data on sexual functioning remain a landmark source on which both medical and nonmedical practitioners have based treatment programs.

With regard to the New Sex Therapies, most sex therapies with couples still consist of Masters and Johnson's basic format: thorough evaluation of psychological and organic factors, use of sensate focus exercises, sex education, improved communications, challenging of negative self-talk, and assistance with apparent personal and interpersonal conflicts. Araoz (1982) has introduced important new concepts such as the processing phase of sexual functioning and negative self-hypnosis. He believes that mental processing pervades the entire human sexual experience, from desire, through arousal and foreplay, to orgasm. These mental processes can interfere with healthy sexual functioning at any stage. Negative self-hypnosis is the result of those nonconscious negative statements that a person indulges in, encourages, and may even work at fostering, while consciously wanting to solve the problem. Araoz demonstrates how hypnosis combined with sex therapy techniques can rapidly and effectively overcome such negative mental processing.

It was the work of Masters and Johnson (1970) that provided the first detailed description of procedures for overcoming sexual dysfunction, stressing the psychological basis of most sexual problems and the role of reeducation in solving them. Helen Singer Kaplan (1979) combined the Masters and Johnson approach on specific problems with a psychoanalytic awareness of deeper conflicts. Kaplan found that fear of intimacy and romanticism may underlie sexual problems such as seeming lack of desire. She claims that unraveling the source of such fears may take months of psychoanalysis before partners develop enough insight into their sexual problems to deal with them constructively. She cautions that when a relationship's deep psychological stresses are not resolved, therapy for overt sexual problems may not help much (1979).

Heiman, LoPiccolo, and LoPiccolo (1981) state that the process of defining a healthy, well-functioning sexual relationship is infused with the sociocultural values of the person doing the labeling. They feel that the specific components of adequate sexual functioning are (1) pleasure from sexual activities, (2) frequency, (3) variety, (4) arousal and orgasms, (5) acknowledgement and acceptance of partner's sexuality. The important general relationship factors are (1) flexibility, (2) openness, (3) active intimacy and involvement, (4) trust and commitment, (5) love, (6) erotic attraction, (7) freedom, autonomy, and responsibility.

Systemic Issues

Sex therapy has not, for the most part, been grounded in or related to systems theory. Sex continues to be treated both theoretically and clinically, as a special area within the family field, and little effort has been made to elaborate the conceptual connections between family theories and theories of sexual behavior. Systems theorists generally see sexuality as only a symptom or a metaphor set forth as a static screen by a couple to avoid dealing with more essential family issues. This viewpoint stresses that sexual dysfunction does not exist in a vacuum, but is often related to problems in the couple's emotional relationship, such as poor communication, hostility, competitiveness or sex role problems. Even in cases in which sexual dysfunction is not related to relationship problems, the emotional relationship can be damaged by the sexual problem in that feelings of guilt, inadequacy, and frustration usually accompany the sexual dysfunction.

Generally, sexual problems have a cyclical position in the couple's interaction. One's demands may result from his or her sexual frustration and feelings of rejection. The other's anxiety may combine sexual conflict, self-doubt about sexuality, and fear of failure to please the partner. Thus, the important features of therapy include interrupting whatever negative cycle has developed, separating yet integrating erections or orgasms from feelings of love, and then reintegrating love with sexuality. Therapy from this viewpoint focuses on the couple's interactions and systems dynamics which maintain problematic sexual patterns.

So the major approaches to sex therapy can be separated into two camps. On one hand, using the Masters and Johnson and the newer sex therapies model, the sexual issue presented IS the problem. On the other hand, using the psychoanalytic more systemically based therapies, sexual dysfunction is a manifestation of some underlying unconscious conflict or a metaphor or symptom of a dysfunctional relationship. These two major divisions represent the division between the fields of sex therapy and marriage therapy. Once again it is time that the two fields come together.

How to Deal with Sexual Issues in Marriage Counseling

This section presents a guide to help marital and sex therapists better incorporate the two therapeutic approaches.

Diagnosis-Assessment Factors

Couples therapists dealing with sexual issues are involved in four areas of assessment which are not adequately described in the literature. They are (a) the identification of organic causes, (b) identification of psychological issues, (c) examination of interpersonal factors, and (d) assessment of systemic issues. Section d is presented as an attempt to relate sex therapy to systems theory.

Identification of Organic Causes

Organic factors can affect sexual functioning. They may be direct causes of problems, the primary causes, or contributing factors. Even in sexually dysfunctional patients who seem organically intact, there are usually some bio-physiological processes implicated in the sexual dysfunction. (For a more detailed description of these factors the reader is referred to Masters, Johnson, and Kolodny 1982). Assessment and diagnosis should include some of these relevant questions:

1. Is there a physical disease or disability (e.g., renal failure, circulatory problems, diabetes)?
2. Does the partner of the person presenting the sexual dysfunction have a disease? The dysfunction may be a response to the partner's postcardiac vulnerability, cancer, prostatectomy, or mastectomy. If illness or injury permanently affects the sexual function of the partner, body image and sexual role behavior may be ignored.
3. Is the client taking any drugs which could affect sexual function (e.g., hypertension medicine, alcohol, methadone)?
4. Has the person had any surgery, such as prostate gland removal or vulvectomy?
5. Is an escalation in the aging process impairing sexual functioning?

Identification of Psychological Issues

Briefly, psychological issues are the complex and unique elements that can shape each individual's sexual attitudes and behavior (e.g., adequate or inadequate sex information and education). The psychological sequences that mediate most dysfunctions are an unwillingness to make love, an inability to relax, and an inability to concentrate on sensation. A major purpose of assessment is to identify the inhibitions which block sexual desire. The most common inhibitions are anxiety, guilt, and reaction to sexual trauma. Once they are identified they must be presented to the couple in a nonblaming, nonjudgmental manner.

Also relevant to an assessment of psychological factors is a sex history interview. The therapist questions the client to learn about his/her:

a. history of sexual behavior, including a psychosexual/developmental overview/exploration of the client's personal childhood history and religious upbringing;
b. current sexual behavior; and
c. attitudinal and cognitive factors, including what the clients think about their sexual dysfunction and whether they have negative attitudes about sex in general.

For a more detailed sex information instrument, see Masters and Johnson, 1970.

Examination of Interpersonal Issues

Interpersonal issues can affect sexual functioning through ineffective sexual communication (e.g., not openly discussing sexual needs). In other words, the couple may have dysfunctional communicational patterns with respect to sexual issues. Some relevant assessment areas are:

1. **Conflict Resolution**—the ease with which differences of opinion are resolved.
2. **Affection**—the degree to which feelings of emotional closeness are expressed by the couple.
3. **Sexuality**—the degree to which sexual needs are communicated and fulfilled by the marriage.
4. **Identity**—the couple's level of self-confidence and self-esteem.
5. **Compatibility**—the degree to which the couple is able to work and play together comfortably, their commitment to their marriage, and the similarity of their attitudes, belief systems, and preferred activities.
6. **Intellectual and Affectual Expressiveness**—the degree to which thoughts, beliefs, attitudes, and feelings are shared within the marriage, as well as each partner's degree of self-disclosure.
7. **Autonomy**—the success with which the couple gains independence from their families of origin and from their offspring.
8. **Relational Structure**—the degree to which the couple has set explicit rules and roles to provide structure and definition.
9. **Sexual Boundary Rigidity**—the degree of the couple's enmeshment or disengagement. Disengagement in a relationship can lead to stimulus and touch deprivation, sexual isolation, and/or body-image anxiety.
10. **Disruptions of Established Power Hierarchies**—Was there a disruption within the couple or their family subsystems around the time when the sexual dysfunction began? For example, a challenge to the husband's decision-making authority could result in inhibited sexual desire or erectile dysfunction.
11. **Life Cycle Crisis**—the capacity of the family structure to transform in response to predictable or unpredictable major life crises.

Assessment of Systemic Issues

Zimmer (1985) believes that clinicians should carefully evaluate a couple's general relationship at the beginning of therapy. Couples in marital distress usually exhibit some sexual dysfunction. These dysfunctions, however, play various important roles in the maintenance of the marital system, such as diverting the couple from other family interactions. They may help the couple maintain emotional distance. They may provide outlets for power plays or hostility. They may sustain role-specific behavior. In these cases treating the sexual dysfunction only in a sex therapeutic modality is likely to fail, in that the sexual dysfunction must be sustained in order to maintain the stability of the marriage. This type of conceptualization enables the therapist to assess and understand the influences within the marriage in the etiology and maintenance of the sexual dysfunction; the relative strength of relationship-enhancing forces that could potentially facilitate and support the process of sex therapy; and the relative strength of relationship-diminishing forces that would potentially inhibit or even undermine the process of sex therapy. Therefore a comprehensive and multidimensional approach to the treatment of sexual dysfunctions must include a thorough evaluation of the marital relationship. Focusing on marital problems helps to facilitate more rapid changes in both marital and sexual functioning.

An examination of systemic issues becomes especially relevant in cases involving resistant couples. Sager (1976) has argued that persons in severe marital distress require different treatment than do those with circumscribed sexual problems, and that severe marital disaffection contraindicates immediate sex therapy (see also Broderick 1979; Kramer 1980). Thus, one aspect to be assessed is the level of marital harmony. This factor must be considered in terms of the couple's responsiveness to sex therapy. The Lock-Wallace Marriage Inventory and the Marital Satisfaction Inventory are psychometric scales which can help the marital and sex therapist distinguish couples with severe marital distress (Mobarak, Tamerin and Tamerin 1986).

Heiman, LoPiccolo, and LoPiccolo (1981) believe that individuals with inhibited sexual desire are treatment-resistant. These individuals often wind up in therapy because their spouses threaten divorce. Better-adjusted couples have a history of resolving conflicts with some success and satisfaction, so they are better equipped to translate the value conflict exposed during the sex therapy into positive change. Better-adjusted partners derive daily gratification from the relationship despite the sexual impasse, and thus are likely to be more cooperative, more motivated, and less resentful.

The working-through aspects of treatment for sexual dysfunction can upset the strained power balance that characterizes certain severely distressed marriages. In perhaps its most culturally salient form, a traditional female partner often enters into an uneasy alliance with a similarly role-bound male, simultaneously reducing her anxiety about dominance and his about submission. While some of these marriages can be quite stable, if such a woman or man becomes dissatisfied, sex therapy may prod her or him to ventilate grievances, try out new confrontation skills, and establish more self-respecting personal boundaries. In the face of these abrupt changes of script, however, her husband may beat a hasty retreat.

Frequently the therapist is faced with a sexually dysfunctional man and his wife. Such couples often delay therapy until several years of frustration have passed. While both may have claimed—verbally—to desire sexual fulfillment, their delay in seeking therapy may be a measure of their nonverbal tendencies in the other direction—i.e., lack of desire. During the course of therapy, the therapist may actually witness the man becoming verbally and nonverbally erect—in his voice tone, his body posture, the tensing of his musculature. At the same time his wife may become increasingly anxious or act in such a way as to stop her husband's erection, although this is precisely what she says she wants.

Few women comprehend the extent to which men's fears, performance anxieties, and self-doubts can affect sexual performance, so women often mistakenly assume that male dysfunction is purposive. A mistaken attribution of voluntariness often contributes to a reaction by the invested partners, creating a vicious circle in which the woman pressures the man for more adequate performance, thereby raising his anxiety level and contributing to the dysfunctional pattern.

One partner may feel threatened by the other's improvement. A woman may worry that her own deficiencies will be more clearly revealed by his improved functioning, or that his demands on her may increase to an extent that she cannot handle. She might fear that he will now become involved with other women, and no longer be as dependent on his relationship with her. Sexual dysfunction does not occur in a vacuum; it must be viewed within the context of the total marital system (Hof 1986).

With highly resistant couples or in situations with a high degree of marital stress, the therapist can ask several relevant assessment questions.

1. What is the central theme around which the problem is organized? The central theme is the highly charged emotional issue around which the conflict arises. Who has the control or power in the relationship? Have there been any recent shifts in the balance of power? How is power distributed, and what is the level of satisfaction with this distribution? How are decisions made and roles negotiated or renegotiated?

   Does the sexual dysfunction serve to maintain emotional distance? This is the typical situation of the distancer/pursuer: The husband complains that he continually approaches his wife for sex, and she continually rejects his advances. In such cases therapists often suspect that if the situation were reversed—if the wife approached her husband for sex—he would find some excuse to avoid her. Both these individuals are comfortable with a certain amount of emotional distance and will maintain this distance at all costs. What is the extent of each partner's commitment to the other and to the relationship? How are intimacy and affectional issues handled? Are the partners satisfied with their intimacy/affectional level?
2. What is the cycle of interaction? To answer this, the therapist uses *tracking*. For example, the therapist asks the wife, "What do you do when he does that?" Then the therapist asks the husband, "And when she does that, what do you do?" In this manner, the therapist explores the cycle of interaction that maintains the dysfunctional behavior.

   Thus, the therapist creates a hypothesis about the function of the symptom in the relationship by inferring the payoffs for the wife who constantly avoids sexual interactions with her husband and for the husband who ignores his wife. Does this symptom create distance between the spouses, or does it elicit closeness? Many individuals cannot tolerate the closeness that sex entails (Schover and LoPiccolo 1982). If these individuals are involved with partners who want a great deal of contact, they will often withdraw even more. According to Zilbergeld and Ellison (1980), "Sex often provides a way of maintaining optimal distance for one or both partners in a relationship. When maintaining distance through sex leads to desire discrepancies or arousal problems, the issue of distance is what requires consideration, because the problems are merely a reflection of it" (p. 65). But if low sexual desire is unacceptable in the relationship, the therapist must help the clients find other ways to establish their optimal levels of distance.

During this phase of the assessment, the therapist attempts to determine what functions the dysfunctional behaviors serve. A dysfunction can serve purposes very useful to the structure of the relationship and to the psychological needs of the individuals. Interactions between the couple regulate the relationship. An argument between a wife and her husband may keep him at home rather than out with his friends. The therapist identifies how interactions lead to marriage-maintaining functions or to interpersonal payoffs for each person.

3. The next question is crucial. The client is asked, "What would be the consequences of changing the problem behavior? For example, how would your relationship be different if the problem disappeared?" A 56-year-old man was in therapy for erectile dysfunction. A urologist ruled out physical bases for the problem. Although the man was unhappily married for over thirty years, he did not want a divorce because he feared being alone and did not want to deal with the financial pressures that he believed a divorce would create. For the past five years he had been involved in a very happy relationship with another woman, who also did not want a divorce because she did not want to risk her financial security. When asked how his relationships would differ if he did not have this problem, he replied that the whole applecart would topple because then he would feel closer to, more intimate with, his mistress and would probably want to escalate their relationship, which he was afraid to do. As Watzlawick et al. (1967) point out, sometimes the solution to the problem *is* the problem.

Interventions

The paradoxical element in sex therapy is worth considering. Most approaches emphasize spontaneity, yet paradoxically, they totally direct the clients' sexual activity. The paradoxical command to "Be spontaneous" is therefore consistent in sex therapies. In addition, some non-demand exercises are paradoxical in nature. The male may be instructed to lose his erection with his wife several times, freeing him eventually to defy the therapist and keep the erection. The couple is often prohibited from having intercourse at the beginning of treatment, allowing them to experience sexual desire without having to perform. Are clients responding to the paradoxical nature of the sex therapy directives? More research is needed. In any case, several interventions are useful when dealing with resistant couples who have a sexual problem.

Relationship Focus

Immediately at the onset of therapy, the therapist takes the focus off the individual and places it on the interactions that maintain the sexual dysfunction. The therapist does not want the couple to continue seeing the problem as the fault of the person with the sexual dysfunction. This is accomplished by asking questions and making comments about the role each partner plays in the problem. The therapist asks about the process the couple uses to deal with their problem instead of asking about the problem itself. For example, the therapist might say, "So, when you attempt to initiate sex with your wife, she becomes upset because she is tired. What do you do when you are disappointed?" Then, to move the focus of therapy toward mobilizing the resources of the couple, the therapist would ask, "When you initiate sex with your wife and she responds positively, what do you do?"

The couple is more likely to be motivated to change if the emphasis is placed not on the individual with the problem, but on the relationship that maintains the dysfunctional behavior. Thus the therapist must move the couple from a singular-cause way of thinking to thinking about how interactions, not specific behaviors or feelings or thoughts, create problems. The couple can see themselves as a set of relationships rather than as bad or sick individuals. The therapist paints a picture of the connectedness of their behavior and examines their interdependent properties through comments that link the two—e.g., "So when your wife follows you around the house asking you questions, do you feel angry and leave?" The goal is for the couple to leave the session understanding that they are not to blame anyone. Each contributes to the problem and they are therefore both victims. Consequently, they begin to see that change is in their best interests.

Reframing

It is crucial to change each person's conception of the problem. When a woman has been labeled by her husband as undersexed and unloving, she becomes defensive. The therapist must relabel her. For example, she may become an unselfish woman, who does not want to be demanding of her husband. She may be a hard worker who is too busy taking care of her family to enjoy herself. She may simply be a woman sincerely interested in developing other aspects of her marital relationship. In subsequent sessions the therapist can help the woman find better ways to be unselfish. In other cases, when the wife is called a nymphomaniac by her husband, the therapist may describe her as a woman interested in enriching all dimensions of their relationship, or as a woman who enjoys pleasing her husband. The therapist may redefine excessive control as concern and depressive withdrawal as sensitivity to the relational problems at hand.

People interpret their own and others' behavior in a way that makes for continuing difficulties. If the therapist can positively relabel the meaning of the behavior, it can have a powerful effect on attitudes, behaviors, and relationships within the family. Any behavior can be considered an asset or a liability. The therapist should point out the positive aspects of the behavior. These new labels create more positive feelings about constructive change. For example, the therapist instills hope that the husband can find better ways to show his concern than by being hostile.

Prescribing the Refusal

The inability of a spouse or couple to do the exercises is often one of the most troublesome situations for a marital therapist. It is difficult to avoid becoming impatient or attempting to steer the couple toward a particular decision. This inability can be approached systemically by prescribing that it be continued. To do this the therapist must describe the inability in systemic terms rather than as an intrapsychic event. Then it is possible to develop a positive rationale for the desirability of the status quo. This rationale should be couched in positive terms, but ideally it should be unpalatable to one or both partners. For example, in situations that show considerable underlying hostility, one partner can be credited with attempting to protect the spouse or to make the spouse look good.

For most therapists the ideal outcome of such an intervention is to have the couple move in one direction or the other and actually make a decision. The third possibility is that the couple may make an explicit decision to stay on the fence. At this point the therapist should not show enthusiasm for their reaching a choice, but should continue to promote indecision. If the couple opts for fence-sitting, this should be validated as a wise decision. To maintain such a therapeutic stance, it is necessary for the therapist to develop a real appreciation of what keeps the couple stuck, instead of criticizing them. So whether the couple does or does not do the exercises, the therapist can switch to marital counseling. The therapist must be prepared to suspend therapy if only he or she is becoming the person with the greatest investment in change. If termination is recommended, it should be presented as a validation of their wise choice not to do the exercises.

Implications for Education and Training

Unfortunately, while marital therapists feel that clinical sex training is not a discrete area and should be integrated into core courses, what actually happens is that it remains in the province of the specialist with postgraduate training. There are few opportunities for even experienced family therapists to obtain training that would be considered comprehensive during their undergraduate education. Rather, family therapists take isolated workshops and courses that allow them to feel confident enough to move into sex treatment.

Heiman et al. (1976) believe that in order to do sex counseling, the individual should (1) be trained in general assessment-diagnosis and psychotherapy; (2) have a theoretical knowledge of human sexuality and sexual disorders; (3) have exposure to and use of more than one theoretical system; (4) have experience working with couples; and (5) be supervised. Kaplan (1977) points out that the clinician should (1) be sensitive to the special vulnerabilities of clients with sex problems; (2) be relatively conflict-free about his or her own sexuality; (3) view sexuality as a positive, life-enhancing force; and (4) be mature and unbiased in regard to gender role differences in love and sex. What these theorists suggest is that the marriage and family therapist who deals with sexual issues should not only have academic training in general psychotherapy, marriage and family therapy, and sex therapy, but should also possess psychological maturity.

Summary

The need for the integration of the fields of marriage and family therapy and sex therapy seem apparent. Sexual dysfunctions rarely exist in a vacuum, and must be diagnosed, assessed, and integrated into the treatment of dysfunctional couples and families. The training of marriage and family clinicians in sex counseling and sex therapy and the skills for integrating these with a systemic approach is essential to comprehensive and effective therapy.

References

Abramowitz, S., and H. Sewell (1980) "Marital adjustment and sex therapy outcome," *Journal of Sex Research* 16 (4): 325–37.

Ard, B. N. (1977) "Sex in lasting marriages: A longitudinal study," *Journal of Sex Research* 13: 274–85.

Aroaz, D. (1982) *Hypnosis and Sex Therapy*. New York: Brunner/Mazel.

Berman, E., and L. Hof (1986) "The sexual genogram," *Journal of Marriage and the Family* 12 (1): 39–47.

Broderick, C. (1979) *Couples—How to Confront Problems and Maintain Loving Relationships*. New York: Simon and Schuster.

Diagnostic and Statistical Manual, 3rd ed. (1980) Washington, D.C.: American Psychiatric Association.

Erikson, E. (1978) *Childhood and Society,* 3rd ed. New York: W. W. Norton.

Glick, I. D. 1986 "Treating the new American couple," *Journal of Sex and Marital Therapy* 12: 297–306.

Gottman, J. (1976) *A Couple's Guide to Communication*. Champaign, Ill.: Research Press.

Hartman, L. M. (1980) "The interface between sexual dysfunction and marital conflict," *American Journal of Psychiatry* 137 (5): 576–79.

Heibert, W. J. (1984) "Talking with couples about sexual problems," in W. Hiebert and R. Stahmann, eds., *Counseling in Marital and Sexual Problems*. Lexington, Mass.: Lexington Books.

Heiman, J., L. LoPiccolo, and J. LoPiccolo, (1976) *Becoming Orgasmic: A Sexual Growth Program for Women*. Englewood Cliffs, N.J.: Prentice-Hall, 6–7, 10.

Hof, L. (1986) "Evaluating the marital relationship of clients with sexual complaints," in L. Hof and G. Weeks, eds., *Integrating Sex and Marital Therapy*. New York: Brunner/Mazel.

Kaplan, H. (1977) *The New Sex Therapy*. New York: Brunner/Mazel.

——— (1979) *Disorders of Sexual Desire*. New York: Simon and Schuster.

Kinsey, A., W. Pomeroy, and C. Martin (1948) *Sexual Behavior in the Human Male*. Philadelphia, Pa.: Saunders.

——— (1953) *Sexual Behavior in the Human Female*. Philadelphia, Pa.: Saunders.

Lederer, W. J., and D. D. Jackson (1968) *The Mirages of Marriage*. New York: W. W. Norton.

Leiblum, S., and L. Pervin (1980) "Introduction: The development of sex therapy from a sociocultural perspective," in S. Leiblum and L. Pervin, eds., *Principles and Practice of Sex Therapy*. New York: Guilford Press.

Leif, H. (1977) "Inhibited Sexual Desire," *Medical Aspects of Human Sexuality* 11: 94–95.

Libman, E., C. Fichten, and W. Brender (1984) "The role of therapeutic format in the treatment of secondary orgasmic dysfunction: A Review." Montreal, Que.: Sir Mortimer B. Davis Jewish General Hospital.

Libman, E., J. Takefman and W. Brender (1983) "A comparison of sexually dysfunctional, maritally disturbed and well-adjusted couples," *Personality and Individual Differences* 1: 219–27.

LoPiccolo, L. (1980) "Low Sexual Desire," in S. R. Leiblum and L. A. Pervin, eds., *Principles and Practice of Sex Therapy*. New York: Guilford Press.

——— (1977) "From psychotherapy to sex therapy," *Society* 14 (5): 60–68.

Masters, W. H., and V. E. Johnson (1966)

Human Sexual Response. Boston: Little, Brown.

——— (1970) *Human Sexual Inadequacy*. Boston: Little, Brown.

Masters, W. H., V. E. Johnson, and R. Kolodny (1982) *Human Sexuality* Boston: Little, Brown.

Mobarak, A., J. Tamerin, and N. G. Tamerin (1986) "Sex therapy: an adjunct in the treatment of marital discord," *Journal of Sex and Marital Therapy* 12 (3): 229–38.

Patton, D., and E. Waring (1985) "Sex and Marital Intimacy," *Journal of Sex and Marital Therapy,* 11 (3): 186–98.

Perlman, S., and P. Abramson (1983) "Sexual satisfaction among married and cohabitating individuals," *Journal of Consulting Clinical Psychology* 8 (2): 104–109.

Pomeroy, W. B. (1982) *Taking a Sex History*. New York: Macmillan.

Sager, C. J. (1976) "The role of sex therapy in marital therapy," *American Journal of Psychiatry* 133: 555–58.

Schover, L., and J. LoPiccolo (1982) "Treatment effectiveness for dysfunctions of sexual desire," *Journal of Sex and Marital Therapy* 8: 179–97.

Sedere, L., and N. Sedere (1979) "A family sex therapy gone awry," *Family Process* 18: 315–21.

Sullivan, H. S. (1962) *Schizophrenia as a Human Response*. New York: W. W. Norton.

Szasz, T. (1980) *Sex by Prescription*. Garden City, N.Y.: Anchor Press.

Todd, T. C. (1981) "Paradoxical prescriptions: Applications of consistent paradox using a strategic team," *Journal of Strategic and Systemic Therapy* 1: 28–44.

Treat, S. P. (1987) "Enhancing a couple's sexual relationship," in L. Hof and G. Weeks, eds., *Principles and Practice of Sex Therapy*. New York: Guilford Press.

Waring, E., et al. (1981) *Psychiatry* 44 (May): 169–75.

Watzlawick, P., J. H. Beavin, and D. D. Jackson (1967) *Pragmatics of Human Communication*. New York: W. W. Norton.

Willi, J. (1982) *Couples in Collusion*. New York: Jason Aronson.

——— (1984) *Dynamics of Couple Therapy*. New York: Jason Aronson.

Zilbergeld, B., and C. R. Ellison (1980) "Desire discrepancies and arousal problems in sex therapy," in Leiblum and Pervin, *Principles and Practices of Sex Therapy,* 65–101.

Zilbergeld, B., and M. Evans (1980) "The inadequacy of Masters and Johnson," *Psychology Today* (August): 29–43.

Zimmer, D. (1987) "Does marital therapy enhance the effectiveness of treatment for sexual dysfunction?" *Journal of Sex and Marital Therapy* 12 (3): 193–207.

CHAPTER SIXTEEN

INHIBITED SEXUAL DESIRE: TOWARD AN INTEGRATIVE APPROACH

Marvin Glassmann, Ed.D.

Abstract

Current research and practice indicate that sexual desire is only one phase in the three-phase response of desire, excitement, and orgasm. The manifestation of inhibited sexual response can be a function of a difficulty within a limited context, or may be a symptom of intrapsychic and/or interpersonal dysfunction in a dyad. Treatment methods are explored: e.g., behaviorally oriented sex therapy and psychodynamic psychotherapy, systemic marital therapy, and hypnotherapy. Case studies are presented to illustrate the efficacy of some of these approaches. The need for an adequate diagnostic evaluation is pointed out, as well as the need to be aware of the purpose the symptom serves for both the individual and the couple.

Introduction

Sexual desire essentially refers to that phase of the sexual functioning process in which the individual experiences a need not unlike the hunger for food. There is, of course, a dissimilarity between the two hungers. To deny the nutritive one, as in anorexia, results ultimately in death; this, of course, is not true of the sexual one. There may be physiological and/or physical correlates to this inhibition of sexual release, such as feelings of tension or irritability. According to the *Diagnostic and Statistical Manual III-Revised* (American Psychiatric Association 1987) the diagnosis of *inhibited sexual desire* is indicated when there are "persistently or recurrently deficient or absent sexual fantasies and desire for sexual activity." This lack of desire, though rather widespread, has apparently resisted therapeutic attempts to ameliorate it. It appears to be the sexual dysfunction most intractable to intervention (Kaplan 1979).

Historical Review

Although various approaches to this problem have been tried, the traditional psychological approaches are behaviorally oriented (Marks 1980)—e.g., short-term sex therapy (Masters and Johnson 1970) and marital therapy (Margolin 1985). The latter's major focus would be on the nonsexual aspects of the couple—i.e., on relationship dynamics—while the former focuses more closely on the so-called presenting complaint.

This paper will attempt to determine the efficacy of dealing with one aspect of the problem (sexual or relationship) and the effect of that approach on the total relationship.

From a historical perspective, the concept of sexual dysfunctioning grew out of Freudian thinking (Freud 1938), identified as a unitary phenomenon caused by repression of libidinal impulses. This blockage and accompanying anxiety were the result of unresolved oedipal conflicts, unacceptable longings for the mother or father. These theorists believed that inhibited sexual functioning was more common among females because of their constitutionally lower sex drive. Treatment was generally long-term and attempted to deal with the etiology of the problem.

Much later, James Semans perceived inhibited sexual desire as a particular aspect of sexual disorder (Kaplan 1979).

It was, however, Masters and Johnson (1970) who fundamentally revolutionized the approach to treating sexual dysfunction. They view sexual dysfunctioning as a result of traumatic events, inadequate learning, and/or social experiences which lead to anxiety and fear. This anxiety and fear act as blocking agents to influence the natural biological experience of sexual functioning. Masters and Johnson treat sexual dysfunction with a cognitive-behavioral approach, focused on the symptom in and of itself. Through direct counseling they attempt to remove both the evaluation of sexual performance and spectatoring of the sex act by the partners. Both of these practices are effective in reducing and even eliminating the spontaneity of the sexual act. As Masters and Johnson point out, the participant cannot will arousal or orgasm, and in fact, attempting to do so actually reduces the likelihood that these will occur. Homework is prescribed for the couple (e.g., sensate focus, the squeeze technique, etc.) which is aimed at reducing performance anxiety and increasing sexual communication, thereby changing attitudes. Usually the couple is seen for two weeks by a therapeutic team (a male and a female). Under specific circumstances a partner may be seen privately by the like-sex therapist in order to ensure and maintain a high degree of motivation. The dysfunction is ascribed to the marital unit and not to the identified patient (I.P.). For this reason, the couple is generally seen together by the male and female therapy team.

Masters and Johnson (1966) viewed the sexual experience in four segments: excitement, plateau, orgasm, and resolution. Essentially, however, the concept is biphasic, since excitement and orgasm are the only aspects that relate to physiological reality.

The 80 percent success rate of Masters and Johnson's reported treatment electrified the sex therapy field when it was first announced. Currently, however, serious questions have been raised as to the actual success of their methods. Zilbergeld and Kilman (1984) believe that Masters and Johnson's results cannot be taken at face value because of the criteria they used for success and failure, and because of a significant difficulty in replicating their research findings. In fairness to Masters and Johnson, specific variables are present now which were not available in 1970. The population they dealt with was more naive, not as well educated sexually as today's population which is exposed to current self-help books and explicit media presentations. Therapists now counsel a treatment population which may not need simple educational techniques, and whose problems are less amenable to direct treatment than those of Masters and Johnson's patients of 1966 and 1970 (when they did their original research). The positive manner in which the treatment population viewed Masters and Johnson may also have contributed to the positive results.

Current Theory—Helen Kaplan

If Masters and Johnson revolutionized the treatment of sexual disorders, Kaplan (1974, pp. 187–188) institutionalized it by combining it with the more traditional psychodynamic base. She (Kaplan 1979) believes that the human sexual response is triphasic, as compared with Masters and Johnson's four phase model which did not deal with the desire phase of the human sexual response. They did not consider desire a mental and physiological phenomenon separate from excitement. According to Kaplan the three phases—desire, excitement, and orgasm—are discrete and mutually exclusive, and dysfunction in one will give rise to a discrete difficulty. If, for example, the orgasm phase is disrupted, it is very likely that premature or retarded ejaculation (in males) and orgasmic inhibition (in females) will result. Blockage of the excitement phase can lead to impotence in males and to limited excitement and lubrication in females. Kaplan (1979, p. 6) goes on to say that "desire phase inhibition occurs in both males and females and is evidenced by low libido in both genders." Although it is possible to have a disruption in all three phases, resulting in an asexual experience, what usually happens is that one of the phases is blocked while the others continue. An individual may feel desire but have difficulty with arousal or erection, or may suffer from inhibited desire but be capable of arousal—lubrication and orgasm.

The sexual dysfunctional desire phase can be subclassified into several types: Primary, secondary, global, and situational. Within the primary context, the individual has never experienced sexual desire. Secondary inhibited sexual desire means that the individual experienced desire at one time in his/her life but does so no longer. Global inhibition indicates that the lack of desire is complete, while the situational inhibition suggests a lack of desire in specific situations—e.g., with the spouse, but not with a lover. This classification is helpful for both diagnostic and prognostic purposes. The more circumscribed and less chronic the condition, the more amenable it is to intervention.

Patients often feel more comfortable presenting their problems as arousal or orgasm blockages, because admitting to desire inhibition implies a deeper problem or a lack of love for the partner, which may be more threatening to the patients. It is important for the clinician to determine if the patient is experiencing desire inhibition because the other two phases are significantly more amenable to short-term, behaviorally oriented sex therapy.

Low sexual desire is not always pathological, not always a result of dangerous circumstances, repulsive feelings for an unattractive partner, or a wish to restrain oneself until one finds the right partner. (Of course, one can always believe that not finding the "right person" fully explains not experiencing desire.) Endocrinological factors, physical illness, depression, drugs, and stress are among the many organic factors which can contribute to ISD.

Some patients, Kaplan (1979, p. 83) finds, are able to switch on their "emergency circuits" of fear or anger in order to turn off their sexual desire, a form of what Araoz (1982, pp. 74–76) describes as negative self-hypnosis. They focus on negative thoughts or past events to control or negate their desire by stimulating the parasympathetic nervous system. The individual may not be aware that he/she is evoking negative images, but may instead see himself/herself as a victim.

Intense anxiety is a significant causal factor in inhibiting sexual desire. Dynamically, this may relate to an increasingly uncomfortable feeling about intimacy, romantic success, or commitment. The high value placed upon the partner, along with sexual desire, may become too intense for the individual and create a need to "shut down." These difficulties are *mid-level*: They are neither so superficial as to be alleviated by minimal intervention, nor so intense that they cannot be resolved with psychodynamic sex therapy. However, unresolved conflicts, intense anger, and marked marital and/or individual disturbance with very deep roots are not amenable to the new sex therapy; traditional psychotherapy is needed in these instances.

Kaplan's (1979) approach is essentially a combination of short-term dynamic insight therapy and cognitive-behavioral sexual therapy, with the latter used to probe the resistance of the couple. As each level is confronted, using sensate focus in graduated stages, resistance is encountered; this resistance is analyzed, or diluted, allowing a movement to the next step. She uses this approach because of the refractory nature of ISD when it is dealt with by traditional psychotherapy or short-term behavioral-cognitive sex therapy. The latter may be effective in dealing with the antecedent causes, while the former is better suited to the more intractable and hidden causes of ISD.

During the course of the sessions, secondary gains are explored, i.e., what is it that the individual achieves through his/her inability to achieve sexual satisfaction? Often it is a fear of sexual and romantic success and a related fear of pleasure and intimacy.

Alternate Findings

Using a somewhat similar model, psychoanalytic psychotherapy with sex therapy, Levay and Kagle (1983) report that despite long and intensive treatment they were unable to extricate ten couples from their entrapment. Some limited progress was achieved with sex therapy, but then the couple cycled into a regression. The depth and intensity of the women's aggressive hostility and the men's passivity distinguished these couples from others. Papp (1983) takes issue with Levay's conclusion and, rather than blaming an individual member of the dyad, felt that dealing with the couple systemically might change both the focus and the results. She felt that the couples needed to maintain their distance and positions.

Fish et al. (1984) support the view that ISD may be a distance regulator in which sex is seen as a route to intimacy. However, inhibited desire may be manifested when an individual feels a lack or loss of control over his/her body. ISD may define who is in control of the relationship, particularly if one member *feels* she or he is losing or has lost that control. "Structural family therapy views the symptom as both system-maintained and system-maintaining."

Case Study

This writer was involved with a case of ISD which may help to illustrate this need for control and distance. The wife experienced no desire, was unable to achieve orgasm, initiated sexual contact only once and often rejected the husband's advances. The one instance of initiation occurred when she believed her husband was having an extramarital affair. Earlier in their marriage, she was reportedly more sexual and able to achieve orgasm. At present, during intercourse she felt on the verge of experiencing orgasm but doubted that it would happen, and of course it did not. She was a fairly controlled individual, speaking even more softly when she was angry. She never masturbated, remembering her mother's prohibitions against it. When she attempted masturbation on three separate occasions, she experienced no pleasure, only disgust. She related feelings of dissatisfaction with herself regarding her appearance, productivity, and general competence. Objectively, she was only minimally overweight and had recently graduated from college with honors. She felt more adequate and in better control of her life when she was working or going to school. During those times she felt more sexual. Despite this, she engaged in only token attempts to get a job and continued to set unrealistic goals. This is possibly due to her concern about the adequacy of her performance.

During one session hypnosis was attempted, in order to determine if previously satisfying sexual feelings could be bridged with current experiences. She admitted to feeling body sensations in her arms and reported feeling fairly relaxed. During the following session, she expressed anger at the therapist for "trying to hypnotize her" because it had never worked in the past. When she realized what was happening, she decided hypnosis was not going to work. She made the connection between the hypnosis experience and what she experiences when she is on the verge of orgasm. In response to a question about what the lack of sexual desire did for her, she stated that it prevented her from feeling vulnerable and open to harm or injury. Her husband was very dominant, outgoing, sexually demanding, and open about his feelings and thoughts. Sex for him provided intimacy and reassurance, and reduced anxiety. He was less selective about what he found sexually stimulating.

It became increasingly clear that the symptomatic lack of sexual desire could not be dealt with using a behavioral model, such as sex therapy. Previous attempts at sensate focus with this couple had had very limited success. The wife needed to develop a more functional way to protect herself and a more adequate sense of herself. Having greater control over her own life made it less necessary to control her impulses. Feeling more separate and individuated precluded her need to avoid the sense of fusion which can occur during sex. Her husband needed to learn how to deal with his anxiety in other ways so that he need not pressure her for sex. For him, sex was the primary technique for reducing anxiety. He needed intimate contact to ease his sense of isolation, and sexual performance to negate his feelings of powerlessness. He overcame his fear of intellectual impotence by enrolling in college studies, which he is successfully completing. He became more competent in other areas as well, so that his sense of power emanated from his sense of himself. He is now gradually giving up some of his need to control and is sharing responsibility for certain aspects of their lives; he now "allows" her to initiate sex at times, to drive the family car, to learn about their financial situation, and to have more input into managing their finances. They have both developed more power, yet there is less need to use that power to control each other.

Additional Findings Continued

Fish et al. (1984, p. 8), point out that a family needs to be distant enough to differentiate and together enough to feel a sense of belonging. They believe that structural family therapy and sex therapy are very similar, in that both focus on changing the presenting problem, assign behavioral tasks, and reach therapeutic goals in a limited period of time. Essentially they state that the treatment of ISD can be effectively accomplished using structural marital therapy. The therapist can unbalance the structure that supports the ISD by creating intensity that will change repetitive sequences.

Zilbergeld and Ellison (1980) emphasize the importance of distinguishing between arousal (the feeling of excitement) and desire (the feeling that one wants sex). The latter is closely tied to the relationship and to the differences in sexual desire between partners. They state that when there is a discrepancy, when one partner wants sex more frequently than the other, there are usually problems in the relationship. They do not suggest that the low desire is a symptom or that low desire causes a difficult marital relationship, but rather that it is a function of circularity, one variable reinforcing the other. They conclude that sex therapy should not be instituted unless there is a strong commitment to the relationship.

Case Study

Involvement in a relationship outside the marriage can affect therapeutic progress. In this situation the partner already has pleasure and satisfaction without needing to engage in the work and pain of treatment. This is an important issue, one which can be amply illustrated by one of this writer's treatment failures.

The thirty-year-old husband suffered from premature ejaculation, while the wife experienced no sexual desire or arousal. There had been no sexual experience for either of them before their marriage when both were twenty. He was Catholic, neither of them had been brought up in a very warm familial setting, and neither had ever masturbated. He also had a fetish: in order to feel excited he had to wear a suit or have his wife wear a tie. He blamed his wife for his lack of excitement. The wife, though attractive, was doll-like in appearance and flat in affect. Attempts were made to delay ejaculations through squeeze and sensate focus techniques. Initially success was marginal because of the wife's limited involvement, though the husband was very motivated. Eventually, he gave up his fetish by using the squeeze technique both on his own and with his wife during intercourse. His involvement with the fetish was diminished by having him focus on his own body, specifically on his penis, and become more aware of the pleasure he was able to gain from it. He came to realize that the feeling came from his own body and not from an inanimate object such as a tie or a coat. The fetish had served as an intervening focus permitting him to experience sexual desire because he felt it was unacceptable to him to take responsibility for his own sexual desire and to direct it toward his wife. It was important not to see her as desirable. Through reframing and refocusing, he was able to get in touch with his sense of arousal. Women became less taboo for him. Later in a private session, his wife admitted that she had been sexually involved with a neighbor and had achieved sexual satisfaction with him. She also reported her rage at her husband for blaming her for their sexual problem and for forcing her to engage in ritualistic behavior. She planned to leave him, but was waiting for an opportune time. It was now obvious that no amount of sex or marital therapy could help, because there were hidden agendas creating resistance to modifying the system. Perhaps divorce counseling would have been more appropriate. It was also clear now that her ISD was not global, but situational.

Additional Theoretical Models

Chapman (1982) reinforces the view that it is important to determine whether the couple is presenting the sexual dysfunction as the main problem or as a difficulty concurrent with personal and/or relationship problems. An indication of the latter may be the couple's inability to complete their homework assignments. "Absence of significant individual pathology, presence of basic communication skills, excessive amount of relationship-relevant material withheld, mutually compatible life and relationship goals" are all necessary in order for sex therapy to progress.

Regas and Sprenkle (1984) further reinforce the view that although ISD is a symptom of marital dysfunction, the latter must be dealt with before the former can be effectively approached. They use a "Functional Family Therapy" model, a brief systems-behavioral approach, to clarify their position.

Heiman (1986), as a proponent of systems theory, sees the sexual problem as a symptom or metaphor put forth by the couple as a smokescreen to avoid dealing with more essential relationship issues. For example, managing anger may be the first step with a desire-phase disorder. She states that therapy should include the couple's acceptance and understanding of the problem's purpose for both individuals and for the relationship. Couples must learn to manage anxiety through relaxation, hypnosis, sensate focus exercises, in vivo exposure, and relationship adjustment, and to increase effective communication skills in the therapy sessions.

A Complementary Technique: Hypnosis

A somewhat different approach to ISD is presented by Araoz (1980) and Araoz and Kalinsky (1987) utilizing hypnosis, or hypnotherapy. Araoz deals with sexual dysfunctions on a couples-only basis, unless the affected individual is not involved in a stable relationship. His treatment model presupposes a good relationship, stable and committed, based upon trust of and respect for each other. He first determines that the presenting problem has a psychogenic base, with physical and/or medical problems ruled out. Heiman (1986) and Zilbergeld and Kilmann (1984) both indicate positive results with hypnosis, particularly with reducing anxiety. Araoz sees hypnosis as more than just a tool to reduce anxiety. He believes it is also a means to get at the roots of the problem, to make a differential diagnosis, and to reawaken desire.

According to Araoz (1982), the new hypnosis, as originally conceptualized by Erickson, is rather different from the more traditional model. Hypnosis is essentially a skill which most individuals can and do engage in every day. It involves utilizing the right (emotional, not rational) part of the brain to tap into the unconscious process. The hypnotist is not the manipulator or doer, but only the teacher or guide who helps the individual increase his/her skill in this area. Continued daily practice leads to greater and greater skill.

A clear example of how all individuals use this technique on a daily basis is evident in the examination of negative self-hypnosis (NSH). NSH is essentially negative statements made to oneself on a repetitive and daily basis. The continual repetition of the thought reinforces the belief, attitude, behavior, etc., making it a self-fulfilling prophecy. If an individual concerned about his sexual performance focuses on the likelihood that he will not be able to achieve orgasm or maintain an erection and continually repeats this worry in his mind, the probability is high that he will malfunction sexually. This is known as the "hidden symptom" and consists of the self-defeating affirmations of mental imagery in which patients engage, based upon the differential symptoms they experience" (Araoz 1987, p. 102).

Case Study

A case in point is that of J, a middle-aged man who, having been separated from his wife for several years, found he had little or no sexual desire. This apparent lack of interest stemmed from previous unsuccessful attempts to have sexual relations. He experienced phobic responses not unlike those he experienced in another situation—traveling on public transportation. In both travel and sex, he anticipated panic-like reactions and feelings of shame, originating from the exposure of his inadequacy. He was helped to see that belief in his success (positive self-hypnosis) could lead to actual success. He focused on his own pleasure, not on his performance, with therapist-placed limitations on the extent of sexual involvement with his current companion. His acceptance of the idea that he did not have to engage in sex if he did not want to, and that any sexual behavior he did engage in was experimental, relieved the pressure he felt. He became less concerned about success and failure, and looked forward to having a good time. He was able to experience more intense sexual pleasure than he had when he was married.

The first step in sex hypnotherapy is to uncover this hidden symptom and to help the couple become aware of other, more positive parts of their sexual relationship. They must have a balanced picture, but the couple may be so problem-oriented that they block out the enjoyable, pleasurable part of their intimacy—i.e., sensual experiences in the non-sexual parts of their bodies. Getting the couple to focus "hypnotically" on sensations by relaxing, closing their eyes, and mentally "seeing" this touching can be a diagnostic tool. If the couple cannot focus, there may be significant relationship or individual difficulties, such as anger, communication, or intimacy problems. If they do focus on the positive aspects, self-hypnosis is engaged with a resolution of the problem.

In dealing specifically with ISD, Araoz (1980) uses hypnotherapy to attain three goals: Revivification (patient relives part of his life when sexual functioning was exciting, or tries to imagine possible sexual situations and scenes), uncovering (learns when and why a change occurred in his/her sexual desire), and mental rehearsal (imagines a life of greater sexual interest and enjoyment). When this last goal is reached, traditional sex therapy can be instituted. Posthypnotic suggestions are given, so that good feelings experienced under hypnosis return in the bedroom. The patient is always given a choice about whether he wishes to act upon his feelings. Araoz (1980) believes hypnotic imagery can reawaken natural impulses responsible for sexual interest, desires, and stimulation.

Discussion and Conclusions

As theoretical orientations proliferate, there is a greater and greater need to emphasize their differences rather than their similarities. The theoretical constructs and the language used for them are often very specific and unique, setting each theory apart from all the competing ones. Although a theoretical conceptualization is necessary to help the clinician organize and formulate his/her treatment plan, it is striking that so-called different approaches are at times not very different. For example, Regas and Sprenkle (1984) speak of *relabeling* in their functional family therapy approach. This does not appear markedly different from the more commonly known concept of *reframing*. To further support the idea that, once strict theoretical lines and approaches are broached, distinctions become blurred, is Levay's (1983) response to Papp's (1983) attack. He states, in part (1983, p. 17), ". . . no one therapy has all the answers, but . . . the various approaches together can go a long way toward solving even the most difficult cases. . . ."

It has become abundantly clear that ISD is a complex phenomenon not easily dealt with in therapy. Sexual interaction, particularly for a couple committed to each other, has been described as a microcosm or reflection of their total relationship. It is also an important and separate part of the relationship. It is sensitive and responsive to the quality of other aspects of the dyad's interaction, and also contributes to its feelings and tone. It may reflect power, intimacy, and dependence. Essentially, then, the couple's sexual difficulty may be a cause, symptom, or a reflection of the marital problem. It can also be an isolated phenomenon in an otherwise satisfactory relationship.

If sexual dysfunction is a microcosm of the couple's difficulties, dealing with either sphere—sexual or relationship—can ameliorate the problem in the other sphere. If the sexual difficulties are part of the system's difficulties, disrupting the homeostatic balance in the sexual sphere can lead to a change in the total interaction. Diagnosis is particularly important in each and every case. It is important to determine whether there is, in fact, a desire phase disorder, but it is also important to determine the extent to which the symptom maintains a particular relationship and the individuals within it. In making a differential diagnosis, the picture is often clouded. For example, an individual may experience frustration at not being able to achieve orgasm or erection and so, rather than confront this discomfort, may avoid it by ceasing to feel sexual desire.

In treating this population, it is important to be aware that ISD may be either a symptom or a learned behavior. Removing the "cause" of the symptom—e.g., anger or the need for distance—does not necessarily remove the manifestation of the symptom. Nor may reeducation, after the root cause is dealt with, lead to an emergence of sexual desire. Intervening steps, such as learning to relax or to deal with stress in a more functional manner, may be necessary.

Adequate diagnosis may determine the outcome of treatment for ISD. The utilization of a competent medical consultant is essential, to rule out significant medical, physical, and physiological causes, contributing or primary to the difficulty. Closely tied to this medical area are the equally important variables of depth and extent of individual pathology. Marital and/or sex therapy do not necessarily deal with such conditions as severe depression or borderline character disorders.

The importance of determining the commitment of the dyad, and of each individual, to the relationship cannot be overemphasized. Assessment of this commitment can be accomplished by seeing each individual alone during the early stages of evaluation. Learning about hidden agendas and/or involvement in outside relationships will determine the treatment strategy and the possible fruitfulness of treatment.

An important, but at times overlooked, diagnostic clue to the treatment of ISD is the ability or inability to complete homework assignments. Reasons or justifications for not doing them offer significant material for recognizing the resistances.

A further complication in the diagnostic picture, and therefore in the treatment plan, concerns the definition of ISD for each couple. How does a therapist determine that ISD is based upon the discrepancy of desire between the individuals in the dyad? The presence or absence of ISD is clear at the extremes. One partner desires sex twenty times a week, while the other wishes it only seven times. This is obviously a discrepancy, but does not seem to indicate ISD. Conversely, if one partner desires sex once every few months while the other wants it two or three times a week, there is little problem making a diagnosis of ISD. It is in the middle ranges that determination is more difficult.

There is also a bias on the part of clinicians toward increasing frequency of desire in one partner rather than decreasing it in the other. In the first example the totally rational practitioner would be hard-pressed to make such a decision—to try to increase the frequency of the less active partner's desire.

Far from having all the answers, this writer finds himself faced with more and more questions. This paper did not solve the dilemma of the efficiency of one treatment modality over the other in dealing with ISD. However, the reader is now acquainted with the complexities of a specific sexual difficulty, and is exposed to the different theoretical approaches and modalities that can be used in treating it.

References

American Psychiatric Association (1987) *Diagnostic and Statistical Manual for Mental Disorders* rev. ed. Washington, D.C.: APA, 293.

Araoz, D. L. (1980) "Clinical hypnosis in treating sexual abulia," *The American Journal of Family Therapy* 8 (1): 48–57.

——— (1982) *Hypnosis and Sex Therapy*. New York: Brunner/Mazel, 74–76.

Araoz, D. L., and E. Kalinsky (1987) "Sex hypnotherapy with couples", in G. R. Weeks and L. Hos, eds., *Integrating Sex and Marital Therapy*. New York: Brunner/Mazel.

Chapman, R. (1982) "Criteria of diagnosing when to do sex therapy in the primary relationship," *Psychotherapy: Theory, Research and Practice* 19: 359–67.

Fish, L. S., R. C. Fish, and D. H. Sprenkle (1984) "Treating inhibited sexual desire: A marital therapy approach," *The American Journal of Family Therapy* 12: 3–12.

Freud, S. (1938) "Three contributions to the theory of sex," in A. A. Bull, ed., *The Basic Writing of Sigmund Freud*. New York: Modern Library.

Heiman, J. R. (1986) "Treating sexually distressed marital relationships," in N. S.

Jacobson and A. S. Gurman, eds., *Clinical Handbook of Marital Therapy*. New York: Guilford Press, 361–84.

Kaplan, H. S. (1974). *The New Sex Therapy: Active Treatment of Sexual Dysfunctions*. New York: Brunner/Mazel.

——— (1979) *Disorders of Sexual Desire and Other New Concepts and Techniques in Sex Therapy*. New York: Brunner/Mazel.

Levay, A. N. (1983) "Response to Papp's comment," *Journal of Marital and Family Therapy* 9: 15–17.

Levay, A. N., and A. Kagle (1983) "Interminable sex therapy: A report on ten cases of therapeutic gridlock," *Journal of Marital and Family Therapy* 9: 1–9.

LoPiccolo, L. (1980) "Low sexual desire," in S. Leiblum and L. A. Pervin, eds., *Principles and Practice of Sex Therapy*. New York: Guilford Press, 29–64.

Margolin, G. (1985) "Building marital trust and treating sexual problems," in A. S. Gurman, ed., *Casebook of Marital Therapy*. New York: Guilford Press.

Marks, I. M. (1980) "Review of behavioral psychotherapy, II: Sexual disorders," *American Journal of Psychiatry*, 138: 750–56.

Masters, W. H., and V. E. Johnson (1966) *Human Sexual Response*. Boston: Little, Brown.

——— (1970). *Human Sexual Inadequacy*. Boston: Little, Brown.

Papp, P. (1983) "Comment on 'interminable sex therapy,' " *Journal of Marital and Family Therapy* 2: 11–13

Regas, S., and D. H. Sprenkle (1984) "Functional family therapy and the treatment of inhibited sexual desire," *Journal of Marital and Family Therapy* 10: 63–72.

Zilbergeld, B., and C. R. Ellison (1980) "Desire discrepancies and arousal problems in sex therapy," in Leiblum and Pervin, *Principles and Practice of Sex Therapy*. New York: Guilford Press, 65–107.

Zilbergeld, B., and P. Kilman (1984) "The scope and effectiveness and sex therapy," *Psychotherapy* 21: 319–26.

CHAPTER SEVENTEEN

FAMILY THERAPY WITH BULIMIA AND OBESITY

Marvin Glassmann, Ed.D.

Abstract

Eating disorders have attained high public visibility in recent years. This phenomenon has been fueled in part, paradoxically, by the health or fitness craze. Women, because of society's pressure on them to be attractive, slim, and "perfect," have been most vulnerable to these disorders. Bulimia, the binge and purge syndrome, and obesity, or compulsive overeating, appear to be manifestations of the same disorder. Both are used as solutions to similar problems, as relief from stress and as manifestation of conflicts—such as the need to be nurtured versus the need to be independent—or a rebellion against demands of family and society, to be good, to conform, and to be attractive. Despite the reportedly high incidence of eating disorders among females, case studies presented here involve two obese married males who shared similar etiological characteristics, both dynamically and in their marital interactions. The need for a holistic approach to counsel is suggested to deal more successfully with obesity and compulsive overeating.

Introduction

Concern about weight, appearance, eating, and health have become national obsessions. The media has played its part through casting and advertising, and the fitness craze has done much to affect the public's perceptions. Problems associated with eating disorders appear more often in females, and are possibly a greater problem for the better-educated (Wooley and Wooley 1985). Anorexia nervosa, bulimia, and obesity (overeating), have discrete characteristics, but all share certain common elements beyond their classification as eating disorders. Essentially they represent solutions to emotionally based problems and, as such, are symptoms of these underlying difficulties. They encroach upon the social functioning of the individual and his/her family and peer group. Self-starvation, binge-purge behavior, and compulsive overeating constitute a continuum of eating behavior—e.g., anorexics deal with their conflicts by reducing food intake to achieve a sense of mastery in their lives; bulimics give in to their impulses, then attempt to regain control by purging; and at the other end of the continuum compulsive eaters surrender control and lose themselves in their addictive activity. It is conceivable, therefore, that etiological factors and treatment techniques may also share certain similarities.

This chapter explores two of these syndromes, bulimia and obesity, to demonstrate their similarities. Interventive strategies are also presented to be utilized in dealing with bulimia and also in treating obesity.

Compulsive overeating, or obesity, often occurs with individuals within a family or marital context, yet the disorder is commonly dealt with as an individual phenomenon. It is, therefore, hypothesized that, like other eating disorders, obesity is both a symptom of and a solution to other problems. Dealing with obesity's underlying causes is more effective than directly attempting to ameliorate the behavior. Since obesity generally occurs with individuals involved in intimate relationships, it is further hypothesized that these relationships must play a role in maintaining the symptom. It may be helpful to determine whether these relationships recapitulate early relationships, thereby keeping the conflicts and the solution to the conflicts active and viable.

Although less dramatic and unique than bulimia, obesity takes an overwhelming toll on modern society in terms of both medical costs (diabetes, cardiovascular disease, etc.), and mental anguish. Huge sums of money are spent on weight reduction programs, often with little success—as when weight that has been lost is regained for a total increase in body fat. Because bulimia and compulsive overeating (used synonymously with obesity for this paper) appear related, this writer will use the former to explain and supplement findings about the latter.

Bulimia

Bulimia is defined (American Psychiatric Association 1980) as "recurrent episodes of binge eating (rapid consumption of a large amount of food in a discrete period of time, usually less than two hours)." It also includes "consumption of high-calorie, easily ingested food, which is usually done in an inconspicuous manner. These episodes may be terminated by abdominal pain, sleep, social interruption or self induced vomiting." There may be further attempts to lose weight by "severely restricted diets, vomiting or the use of cathartics or diuretics." The weight may fluctuate by ten pounds because of binges and fasts. The individual knows that "the eating pattern is not normal and believes that he cannot stop eating of his own volition." There is a "depressed mood and self-deprecating thoughts after the binge."

Obesity, by contrast, is listed as a "Psychological factor affecting physical condition" (American Psychiatric Association 1980). "Psychological" is defined as the "meaning ascribed to environmental stimuli by the individual which could be sights and sounds arising in interpersonal transactions which have emotional factors associated with them"—e.g., arguments. There may be no awareness of the "meaning given to these stimuli or the relationship between these stimuli and the initiation and exacerbation of the physical condition." What stands out is the clear definition of bulimia and the more vague definition of obesity, which was previously classified as a psychosomatic disorder.

Foster (1966) sees bulimia as often manifesting in an intrapersonal context in a marital situation. He sees conflict in the bulimic couple as symbolic of the conflicts which evolve from family-of-origin separation-individuation issues. The identified patient attempts to assert autonomy, but feels ambivalent about it. He/she, therefore, submits resentfully to the demands of the spouse. The symptomatic partner's lack of autonomy and ego strength may be masked by apparent competence in caring for the needs of the family or pursuing a career. Unlike the anorexic couple who deal with conflict by denying it, the bulimic couple is likely to be overtly hostile and chaotic.

Schwartz, Barrett, and Saba (1985, p. 218) point out that bulimia can be viewed in many different ways. It can be seen as an addictive behavior maintained by high blood glucose levels and by tension reduction as a result of purging. It can be used to avoid feelings of depression, intimacy, or stress by providing a distraction and focusing on the bulimic symptoms. It can confront and nurture during periods of upset. It provides a rationalization for nonperformance or poor performance at work or a justification for unacceptable behavior in the family. It offers a means of passive rebellion against intrusive parents, particularly when eating has specific significance. The symptom can distract the family from more significant and/or threatening issues, such as anger. It can be a barometer of family problems and conflicts. Schwartz et al. also feel that bulimia can be both an attempt to control weight and a manifestation for women of the conflict between competing with and attracting men. And this is only a sample of the ways in which bulimia can be interpreted.

Minuchin, Rosman, and Baker (1978) characterize psychosomatic families as enmeshed, overprotective, rigid, unable to resolve conflict, and involving the client in parental conflict. Schwartz et al. (1985) add isolation, consciousness of appearance, and special meaning attached to food. They also believe that the most effective way to deal with the bulimic family is by combining the complementary aspects of structural and strategic family therapy. Thus, the therapist alternates two therapeutic positions: advocating change and warning against that change. The latter position is taken to minimize resistances and permit the family to explore the consequences that changes would entail. These families believe that their cohesion is so tenuous that they must organize against any change. The therapist in these situations must neither consider the symptom as the main problem nor attempt to eradicate it nor be overly concerned by increases or decreases in symptomatic manifestation. The therapist should focus instead on major factors, such as the family's patterns of interaction and orientation. He/she can then more sincerely introduce gradual symptom change, which is less threatening to the family. Once the symptom is ready to be dealt with directly, the goal is not abstinence from binging. It is a change in the "patient's relationship with and the attitude toward food and her weight" (p. 290).

For some bulimics the loss of the symptom means growing up, getting close to people, which may upset the family. The negative consequences of the loss of this symptom should always be explored. The symptom has served the client well; it has a positive function. To attempt to eliminate the symptom cannot only preclude therapeutic movement, but may lead to an expulsion of the therapist—i.e., premature termination.

Chelton and Bonne (1987) point out that psychogenic eating problems have an addictive aspect. They describe the addictive use of powerful sensations to stimulate and soothe in a "pattern or system on which the individual desperately attempts to rely to maintain cohesion and continuity in a fragile self" (p. 41). There is an observable euphoria produced by anorexia nervosa which occurs through both biochemical and psychological change. Bulimics and other overeaters apparently describe a similar sensation which seems to be related to fasting and purging. Chelton and Bonney (1987) believe that this euphoria reawakens earlier feelings of safety and stimulation in the parent-child relationship. These feelings give the individual a short-lived sense of self-cohesion and vitality. Addiction to eating disorders is ultimately a failure in enabling the individual to stay intact and grow; in fact, such addictions are attempts to return to an earlier state. These therapists believe that the main focus of treatment should be the same as with any addictive disorder: using the peer (self-help) group to make direct and current connections with other human beings. They also feel that family involvement is important.

White and White (1981) are convinced that group therapy can be effective in treating bulimic women. Their group was an experiential one, extending over a five-day period for five hours a day, led by a female therapist in the morning and by her and a male therapist in the afternoon. The group approach was utilized to help the women overcome their sense of isolation and shame. It was important to show the women how they had habitually failed to accept responsibility for their thoughts and actions. It was equally important for them to learn to explore alternatives to passivity and helplessness. These authors reported that of the fourteen women involved in the study, three had stopped binging, seven had binges of shorter duration and frequency, and none had engaged in purging. The four remaining women reported little change after six months. The latter were found to be particularly concerned with creating a favorable impression and focused on what others thought of them.

O'Connor (1984) points out that little is known about the efficacy of different treatments for bulimia. The family approach to treatment is rare, perhaps because bulimia's onset usually comes in late adolescence and early adulthood, when the young person may be living away from home at school or independently in her own residence. Just as success with anorexia can be quantifiably measured by weight increase, so too can bulimic symptom remission be assessed by decreases in frequency of vomiting. This may not be enough, however. There is also a need to determine what other problems, displaced by the symptom, were reduced.

O'Connor (1984) utilizes the Mental Research Institute model, which goes beyond the hierarchical model of Haley and Madanes, and the model of the Milan Group, which views the family context as the system in which the symptom is embedded and includes the individual's own system, which "can create, maintain and exacerbate the problem in a circular way" (p. 495). In an illustrative base study, O'Connor (1984) intervened, utilizing four steps. First he prescribed an obsession about food, to help the patient control her thoughts. Second he substituted compulsions such as masturbation for dealing with stress, because these were mutually exclusive of the symptom and would, therefore, interfere with the binge activity. Third, he helped the client develop a positive ritual for the first time, one that involved writing down what was to be eaten. Finally, he blocked the problem-maintaining solution with an aversive ritual—i.e., to binge after she vomited. This last strategy reversed the binge-purge sequence and its priorities. In the past, the patient vomited to regain control of her binging, and the directive had her using binging deliberately as a way of controlling the vomiting. It gave her more effective control.

O'Connor (1984) believes that the simple elimination of a symptom is not sufficient to maintain the gain. The individual needs to develop more functional coping strategies to supplant the "symptom as a solution," once the symptom is removed. Therefore, if the symptom is used as a way of asserting oneself, then other, more effective ways to do this must be found before the symptom will be permanently given up.

For strategic psychotherapy to be effective with the bulimic, the therapist must determine what, if any, purpose the symptom serves dysfunctionally, and conceptualize other methods for discharging these forces more effectively. Next, the therapist should issue a directive to block the symptom in the context of the family or couple. This directive should challenge or change the typical ways the family members relate to one another. While the symptom is being reduced, the client can develop other ways to deal with the conflict that originally led to the symptom. This is the significant therapeutic work. Termination can take place only when these alternative methods have been put into practice.

Another method for dealing with bulimia is to utilize the transgenerational (family) approach as described by Roberto (1986). This model provides a frame for specific belief systems transmitted in the form of family legacies over three or more generations. The treatment focuses on the role of the offspring's worry in the family history. Both the family and the therapist construct patterns linking self-defeating behavior to values, relationship patterns, and roles handed down through the generations. This is particularly noticeable with the tradition-bound, rigid families of bulimics.

These families place great value on appearance, success, eating, and filial loyalty. Rather than focusing on dysfunctional behaviors and trying to replace them, the therapeutic approach takes an intermediate position, reframing the behavior as a compliance with family legacies. This technique distinguishes it from structural, strategic, behavioral, and psychoeducational approaches and more closely resembles the philosophy of systemic family therapy. The transgenerational technique is particularly suited to the bulimic family because of its rigid boundaries and its tendency to view any attempt at structural change as an intrusion to be resisted in the interest of preserving the family organization. By urging the family not to change, the therapist "increases the experiential constriction which is already suffocating them" (p. 235).

Madanes (1981) points out that all couples deal with sharing power and determining a hierarchy in which control and responsibility are divided between the spouses. Power has to do not only with domination, but also with comforting each other. Couples may functionally divide responsibility for tasks in a complementary manner. Power can be balanced in several ways—for example, by using children, by becoming helpless, by using a symptom. The use of a symptom permits each spouse to be in both an inferior and superior position: the symptomatic spouse needs help but refuses to use it; the asymptomatic spouse provides help, but the help is not successfully utilized. If the "normal" spouse helps the symptomatic one, both lose—the former because he/she no longer holds the superior position of being the one without the problem, the latter because he/she has given up the power of being the helpless one who gets all the attention for being "sick."

In a case of binge eating and vomiting, the latter may be a metaphor for the wife's submissiveness and rebellion. She is overtly submissive and dependent, but she covertly rebels and undermines her husband. The symptom is a way to get back at her husband, so therapy must find a substitute way. The therapist's directive was to throw food into the garbage every day, whenever she had the urge to vomit. Her husband was told to monitor her by checking the garbage every day when he came home from work. The vomiting was then replaced by another behavior which served the same purpose—getting back at the husband—without being so destructive. It cost money and gave the husband an unpleasant task. The wife was also to stuff herself in her husband's presence if she vomited after she binged, and she, therefore, had to binge when she vomited. This was both an ordeal for the wife and a way for them to work together. Spending money on superfluous things was another metaphor to replace the throwing away of food. Directing the husband to order his wife to pretend to vomit created a paradox: The desire to vomit was an act of rebellion, yet if she complied with the husband's order, she was submitting to him. The result was that the frequency of vomiting was appreciably reduced and was sometimes eliminated. Madanes (1981, p. 634) concludes that symptomatic behavior is a dysfunctional solution "to the couple's difficulties in that it equalizes the power of the spouses providing a focus of interaction that stabilizes the marriage."

As to the treatment of choice with bulimia, Foster (1986) points out that there have been no controlled treatment studies to determine which treatment modality (individual, marital, family, or group therapy) is most effective. It is important to determine what technique is most effective with a specific individual, taking into consideration the wide diversity of individuals in this diagnostic category. It is not reasonable to believe that one method will be equally effective with all types of clients.

Positive indications for marital therapy include a manifestation of the symptoms during the early stages of the relationship or an increase of symptoms at crisis points in the relationship, failure in individual therapy while in a relationship, reporting marital conflict as a problem, and the ability to tolerate interpersonal change without decompensation. Contraindications are an unstable previous relationship caused by a character disorder, strong resistance, or evidence that the identified patient could benefit more from another treatment modality because of a major personality dysfunction. The latter patient might benefit from individual therapy, according to Foster (1986). She seems to feel that individual pathology is antithetical to effective marital therapy, although family therapy is often the treatment of choice with schizophrenics. What is more important, however, is the need to maintain a flexible approach and to utilize other treatment modalities and variations—e.g., the use of transgenerational family therapy with couples who have not separated sufficiently from their families of origin. The therapeutic aim with these eating-disordered couples is to help them disengage from focusing on the symptom, to explore other issues in the marital relationship, to help the couples decide if they want to work on change, and to offer the symptomatic spouse symptom-management aid.

Thus, an eating disorder can be symptomatic of an oppositional desire to cyclically lose and gain control, to conform and rebel, to dominate and to be helpless, and to play out the legacy of the extended family. It most frequently manifests itself in the late adolescence and early adulthood of females who are particularly subject to societal pressures of conformity and idealized appearance.

Overeating

Next follows a brief review of the literature exploring the etiology, dynamics, and therapeutic intervention of overeating.

Orbach (1978) proposes several reasons why women use compulsive eating as a solution to certain problems. Women are seen as sexual objects, based particularly upon their appearance. Being fat permits one to avoid rigid role stereotypes. The fashion industry places emphasis on the perfect female, yet this perfection is particularly difficult to achieve because the norms and expectations of how females should look are always changing. Being fat can feel liberating. Obesity can neutralize a woman's sexuality in the perception of those with whom she is intimately involved. The fat woman may feel she will be taken more seriously for her essential self and not seen as a frivolous, sexy, and therefore incompetent worker. Orbach points out that as the caretaker, the woman's needs come last, so food can represent a way to nurture herself. Providing a boundary for herself can militate against her sense of merging with and feeding others. It can also serve to maintain the mother-daughter connection. The appearance of the fat may tell the mother that the daughter does not know how to take care of herself or feed herself properly. The message from the daughter to the mother is, "You can still be my mother" (Orbach p. 182). The daughter's fat can represent a way for them to escape the conflict surrounding separation, a conflict which can be painful for mothers and daughters. Although Orbach primarily uses group and individual treatment modalities, this issue of overeating would appear an excellent opportunity for utilizing a mother-daughter "couple" treatment experience.

The compulsive eater knows two realities—control (abstinence) and total lack of control (binging). It is important for the compulsive eater to find out what special meaning the fat has for her. If, for example, it represents a way to say "no," she will need to learn to say it more directly. If it represents a way to stay connected to her family, she must find other ways to do this and give up her addiction. In order to break the addiction and lose the weight, the compulsive eater must accept her fat. Acceptance is achieved by examining and understanding the purpose the fat served. If this purpose is not explored, the loss of weight can become very frightening. There may be feelings of deprivation, so that in order to look "normal" the woman may feel a compulsive need to diet.

Orbach (1978) feels it is important to help this client withdraw from the mechanics of eating—such as calorie counting and weighing oneself. She focuses on the feelings and experiences associated with the behavior. She concludes that the goal of treatment, which utilizes body awareness and psychoanalytic and behavioral techniques, is not to lose weight, but rather to break the addictive relationship of the eater to the food. However, she feels that "weight loss is generally an important sign that the addiction is broken" (Orbach, p. 188).

Zitter and Fremouw (1978) indicate that although behavior modification is successful with short-term weight loss, clients have serious problems maintaining that loss. They report on several studies which indicate that in groups with husband involvement, or at least partial husband involvement, individuals lost more weight than did those in other groups without spousal involvement. Their study compared groups of individuals who were paired with overweight partners, to groups of individuals who were not so paired. Though both groups lost more weight than did a control group, only the individual group maintained the loss. One partner convincing the other to engage in appropriate eating behavior was a possible explanation. Not taking responsibility for one's own behavior, and the absence of emotional involvement with each other, could have been other confounding factors.

Using a case study approach, Matson (1977) found that when the husband acted as a social reinforcer, praising her, the overweight wife lost significantly more weight than she did when she received no reinforcement. This weight loss was maintained. Success was attributed to increased self-confidence created by the praise. More important, perhaps, the reinforcement also improved social interaction at home. There was mutual satisfaction with the weight loss and an increase of positive feelings toward each other. Though Matson did not elaborate on this (1977), the husband had been strongly encouraged to refrain from his customary abusive language regarding his wife's weight.

Wilson and Brownell (1978), however, found no significant difference in weight loss between a group of obese dieters with spouses present to give positive reinforcement and a group with no spouses present. There was, however, no attempt made to determine the extent to which these absent spouses cooperated with the program.

Supporting these findings, Weisz and Bucher (1980) report that the client group in which husbands were actively involved in treatment did not lose significantly more weight than did other groups. Short treatment periods of six to ten weeks did not "produce an enhanced weight loss effect for spouse inclusion" (p. 648). However, marital adjustment was significantly enhanced and there was decreased depression. They suggest that weight loss by itself will not produce changes in depression and marital adjustment. The purpose of including the husband was to increase the positive interaction between spouses. These authors report instances of noncooperation or sabotage from spouses in weigh-control programs.

In contrast, Pearce et al. (1981) found that their group including cooperative spouses lost significantly more weight than did the alternative group, based on a follow-up after twelve months. The spouses were asked to be supportive, entered into the treatment, and were asked not to sabotage the experimental condition. Pearce et al. (1981) did not focus so extensively on spousal involvement, yet the group with involved spouses showed the greatest loss. An important difference between these findings and those of Weisz and Bucher (1980) was the time period: Weisz and Bucher's study involved a treatment period of only six to ten weeks, while the Pearce group's study stayed with the subjects for one year.

One limitation of many of these studies is their failure to explore the quality of support and encouragement which the spouse received. Stuart and Jacobson (1987) point out that women often want emotional support and encouragement, while men may prefer practical advice and incentives, including action-oriented solutions. There can be negative consequences in asking for support, as well as the possibility of rejection. The overeater may no longer be able to use an uncooperative spouse to justify his/her inability to control food intake. Stuart and Jacobson also feel that the request for help should not be a demand, but should be made in a specific and positive manner. The symptomatic spouse can also try to find out what the symptom-free spouse thinks and feels about the weight loss and the request for help.

Sobol (1984) indicates that the quality of the marital relationship may inhibit weight-loss attempts. Such an attempt may be resisted because the slimmer partner feels that he/she will lose a bargaining position in arguments, or fears an increase of sexuality and promiscuity. Sobol further reports that there are more likely to be marital problems if the weight was gained during the marriage than if obesity was present during courtship or at the beginning of the marriage. Although this may be due to the difficulty the slimmer spouse has in accepting the change, Sobol presumes that it is a causal relationship rather than a circular one: Difficulties in the relationship can lead to obesity, which can further "heat up" the couple's problems. In an attempt to explore which techniques are best utilized in weight control programs, Franzini and Grimes (1981) point out that binge eaters are different from most individuals in treatment programs, and that conventional programs have been unsuccessful with the binging overweight person. Long-term psychotherapy is indicated as treatment for the binge eater. Lack of success in the treatment programs that utilize behavior modification techniques may be due to counterforces—for example, being obese provides the person with a justification for not competing socially or athletically; ethnic subcultures and advertising media offer cues for eating; eating can reduce anxiety; relinquishing immediate pleasure for long-term advantages is difficult. One technique that can be effective in weight loss is a signed contract promising an immediate commitment to change present eating habits for long-term benefits.

Prognostic factors which mitigate against success are "childhood obesity, overeating habits of many years and strong subcultural (i.e., ethnic) influences to overeat" (p. 87). Self-control techniques are most important in achieving success, and these require individual effort. Those individuals who were involved in group treatment regained weight after treatment terminated. The use of assertiveness training was found effective because it "increased autonomy and success in positively altering the social environment" (p. 88) which can be important to successful weight maintenance.

It seems important that success increases when behavioral changes are closely tied to cognitive modifications. Behavioral treatment programs sometimes apparently miss this point. A major force is on weight loss *per se*, which, though a demonstrable criterion, is obviously not enough unless actual behavior, perceptions, and interpretations are also modified and integrated.

Case Studies

Although most of the literature on eating disorders focuses on women, primarily because society places greater emphasis on their physical appearance, the author has had therapeutic involvement with two obese married men. Though they were from different backgrounds and were at different stages of their lives, there were significant similarities.

The Bs came for marital therapy because the wife, who was in her late fifties, was dissatisfied with her husband and was thinking of leaving him. She complained of his drinking and eating problems and of the intense anger she felt toward him. She was critical of his behavior and his appearance, and refused to engage in sex with him. He, though more intellectual, was more passive and looked to her for emotional support and encouragement, much as he said he had looked to his mother. He had supported her refusal to have sex for several years because of his weight. Positionally, he could not lie on his wife because of her "bad hip." When she was on top, he became impotent. Essentially, in their relationship, she was perceived as "on top" most of the time, except regarding the control of his drinking and eating. However, these symptoms gave her continual opportunity to criticize his habits and his physical appearance. This kept her in a "one up" position and permitted her to use him as a receptacle for much of her anxiety, frustration, and hostility. Needless to say, much of this had little to do with the husband directly, and was really a function of the wife's own insecurity. The weight problem had been with him since he was a youth, which was not prognostically favorable. Communication was a major problem for them. She was direct and critical; he was indirect, passive, and resentful. He dealt with his anger by withdrawal, by reading, by distancing emotionally, by using intellectualization, and physically, by singing in a quartet at night. His weight and his eating were a barrier against intimacy, a means of rebellion, and a substitute for the nurturance he craved. When he felt angry with her, he ate covertly. She was helpless to change him and he had the power to remain as he was, even though that kept him in a "down" position. He could not sacrifice his weight, for the loss could make him feel more vulnerable. Through therapy Mr. B learned to express his feelings more directly and closer to the times he experienced them. This was easier for him to do at work, where he was a supervisor, than at home. Mrs. B became more aware and accepting of his previously unexpressed feelings, and better able to express her own feelings less sharply and critically. Most important, Mr. B increased his ability to gain satisfaction and recognition through his own efforts, which made it less necessary to look to Mrs. B for acceptance and emotional feeding. As he became less needy, she felt fewer demands were placed upon her and, in turn, was able to give more. He gave up drinking, and their emotional distance decreased. Eventually they retired and moved out of state. He was able to gain some sense of functional power in his recognition of how he took care of many areas of reality which were frightening for her.

The Fs, a younger couple—he in his late forties, she in her early thirties—had young children living at home. Their seven-year marriage was his second and her first. He had been overweight since childhood, he was also asthmatic, and currently had gout. As a child he had been moved from his parental home to a residence for asthmatics. He described his mother as hostile and manipulating. By contrast, he described a particularly happy time in his life when a young, attractive nurse at the residence was nurturing toward him. He was essentially searching for a return to that blissful time through the use of drugs, food, and his young, attractive wife. The couple came on the wife's insistence because all other modalities—weight reduction programs, hypnosis, encounter groups, and a private trainer—had failed to solve his weight problem. He did not usually stay very long with any intervention, feeling he knew more than "the experts" and that only he could truly conquer his problem. He had once, a few years before he got married, overcome a drug problem. Both husband and wife felt uncomfortable with overweight people (he refused to have sex when she was pregnant) and he supported her lack of desire for sex with him now. Justification was based not only upon appearance, but also on the grounds that sex was too demanding for him physically. Both were defensive and supportive of each other, maintaining a barrier against intrusion by the therapist. He dominated the session with his high verbal flow, and she retreated because of her need to be a private person. He did not like seeking help and preferred to be in control. He exemplified what Buie (1987) describes as the addictive personality, facing help with distrust and fearing loss of control. Such people often have grandiose beliefs that they can handle anything. They avoid commitments to people or groups "which give them a sense of being trapped" or having "to submit to someone else's control" in order to deal with the symptom. Along with Mr. F's obesity offering a way for the couple to distance from each other, they slept in separate bedrooms because his asthma caused him to snore and disrupted her sleep. When he ate he often lost awareness of his surroundings. Because of his weight he was often too tired to do anything on weekends with the family; instead, he lay on his bed and watched football games on television. The weight and overeating, and now his dieting and exercise programs, provided a focus for their problems. Attention to his obesity also served as an effective means to avoid dealing with issues of intimacy and closeness. Dealing with these issues means exposing one's inner feelings. It requires a willingness to be vulnerable and to place oneself in a potentially weak and unsafe position. Neither of them felt secure enough to jeopardize their positions. The weight and binging served an important function by keeping Mr. F in a down position.

However, recent weight loss and involvement in a weight loss and exercise regimen have resulted in significant changes. He has become more overtly critical of his wife, moving from an idealization of her as the perfect person, to criticism of her as someone who is disorganized and not sufficiently giving to him. He has begun to recognize that food stifled many of his feelings and desires. Food was his friend as well as his tranquilizer. Communication at home was minimal, particularly concerning the exchange of feelings. Food blocked his feelings, which was comfortable for her because of her lack of trust and/or ease in exposing her own. In therapy sessions he would risk expressing his feelings, laughing to cover up his discomfort and jokingly indicating that he would be in trouble when he got home.

Her greatest pleasure was in being a "mom," a housekeeper, and finally a wife. This ex-nurse, who first met Mr. F in a weight reduction program, is a caretaker who does not feel comfortable with intimacy and emotional involvement emotionally, despite her ability to nurture.

Both Mrs. B and Mrs. F came of strict, conservative upbringings, and had difficulty enjoying pleasure. There was a certain cold, withholding quality in their interactions. They both took the parent role with their more pleasure-oriented, childlike men. Both couples dealt with conflict by attempting to avoid it and were able to use only their spouse's weight, eating, and drinking as focal points. As Mr. F pointed out in the early stages of therapy, with the exception of the issues around "weight and sex, we have a perfect marriage." The problem with sex is, of course, a result of the problem with weight. Both families maintained isolated positions which, along with the spouses' mutual protection pacts, made it difficult for the therapist to penetrate their problems.

The resolution of the Bs' therapy could not be considered successful. Several factors militated against success: His weight problem was chronic and his desire to be in therapy was minimal. Characterologically, he was well defended, rarely experienced stress, and, despite an ability to express feelings overtly in individual sessions, refused to do so in marital sessions. He was seen subsequently for a period of time on an individual basis to help build ego strength and autonomy (Foster 1986, p. 580). Despite minimal progress in this area, he was willing and able to risk dealing more directly with his wife. Although their relationship was strengthened somewhat, and his alcohol consumption was reduced, the primary symptom, obesity, remained intact. The functions it served outweighed the disadvantages of giving it up.

The Fs are currently in treatment, and because of the husband's weight loss, are coming into contact with the dissatisfaction and emptiness of their relationship. Their avoidance of conflict is less effective; at this time, the risks of change are being explored. The exchange of compulsive eating for compulsive dieting has not prevented the destabilization of the relationship. Their earlier resistance toward exploring the gains achieved in his symptom—e.g., avoidance of intimacy and his rushing into a diet-exercise program—has diminished, forcing a new scenario.

Implications for Treatment

Although there is obviously no one specific etiological factor which leads to the development of bulimia and compulsive overeating, there are several common themes. Among them are the pressures exerted by society, which are experienced primarily by women: The importance of appearance and the need to be helpless (e.g., the inability to lose weight, to be competent in athletic activity, to succeed when appearance is important) and yet to be in control. The manifestation of these factors is apparent in both the literature and the two cases reported here. These disorders are manifestations of conflict, intrapsychic and/or interpersonal. If one feels lonely, eating fills the emptiness, making it less necessary to find out why one is lonely and/or to deal with the loneliness by becoming involved in an intimate relationship. If one feels sexually frustrated, one can dull that feeling by eating, and thereby experience pleasure in another area. If this substitute behavior is engaged in often enough, sexual feelings can be denied or can become less attractive, diminishing the possibility that the individual will become involved in a sexually satisfying relationship. If one feels incompetent, eating can diminish that feeling. Ultimately the cause of feelings of incompetency can be placed upon one's appearance, or agility, or anaerobic capacity. As symptoms, these are convenient to focus on, to the exclusion of the underlying forces. What is patently clear in the literature is that, therapeutically, dealing directly with this symptomatic behavior generally fails—immediately or over the long term. However, dealing with it in a contextual manner, in a familial or marital relationship, provides an opportunity to reduce the impact of the reinforcing agents and to provide new support systems for the maintenance of modified behavior. This is based on learning theory.

From another perspective, the family and/or marital partner gains certain advantages from having the symptoms continue. He/she/they retain a power advantage, maintain a distance-intimacy balance, and have at his/her/their disposal a ready distraction from more threatening and possibly destructive conflicts. Loss of the symptom, without a complementary developing and strengthening of other mechanisms, can lead to a decompensation of the individual and/or to marital/familial relationship disruption.

However, both bulimia and compulsive overeating become self-maintaining or functionally autonomous, so that even when the cause or causes are ameliorated, the behavior may continue, perhaps due to the addictive qualities of the symptom: the high blood glucose levels achieved in binging or tension reduction from purging may continue to produce "highs" for the individual. Dealing more directly with the symptoms through behavior modification techniques may be necessary.

What is particularly important to note is that different therapeutic techniques can and should be utilized for different individuals and for clients at different stages of treatment. There is no one ideal approach for everyone; a multimodal treatment is necessary.

One possible effective approach to compulsive overeating is to link a psychotherapeutic approach (individual, marital, familial) to a weight reduction program. An assessment would be necessary to determine the past and current etiological factors having an impact upon the eating behavior, including physiological factors. Once an evaluation is completed, including not only the identified patient, but also the individuals involved in his/her current relationships, a determination can be made of the most effective form of therapy. Obviously the initial modality chosen need not be the final or only approach used. Marital therapy with individual sessions, followed by treatment with the extended family, and back to marital sessions is one possible sequence. Another possibility (the combinations are limited only by the practitioner's imagination, skill, and experience) is to see the couple sequentially, conducting an individual session with one spouse. The spouses alternate weekly therapy sessions, so the identified patient is not always the one receiving counseling.

At the point when a significant support structure has been developed to deal with the needs which the symptom serves, overeating can be dealt with as an addictive behavior. This can be accomplished through an organized weight reduction program that concentrates on individual behavior, rather than only on the caloric content of food ingested or on amount of weight lost. Both of these modalities would be used simultaneously to enhance and complement each other. This holistic approach appears to offer greater possibilities for dealing with compulsive overeating and for avoiding the destructive effects of "yo-yo dieting" (Brownell 1988).

References

American Psychiatric Association (1980) *Diagnostic and Statistical Manual for Mental Disorders,* 3rd ed. Washington, D.C.: American Psychiatric Association, 69–71.

Brownell, K. (1988) "Yo-yo dieting," *Psychology Today* (January): 20–23.

Buie, J. (1987) "12-step program can boost therapy," *APA Monitor* (November): 12.

Chelton, L. G., and W. C. Bonney (1987) "Addiction, affects and self-object theory," *Psychotherapy* 24: 40–46.

Foster, S. W. (1986) "Marital treatment of eating disorders," in N. S. Jacobson and A. S. Gurman, eds., *Clinical Handbook of Marital Therapy*. New York: Guilford Press, 575–93.

Franzini, L. R., and W. B. Grimes (1981) "Treatment strategies for therapists conducting weight control programs," *Psychotherapy: Theory, Research and Practice* 18: 81–93.

Madanes, C. (1981) *Strategic Family Therapy*. San Francisco: Jossey-Bass, 81–93.

Matson, J. L. (1977), "Social reinforcement by the spouse in weight control: A case study," *Journal of Behavior Treatment and Experimental Psychiatry* 8: 327–28.

Minuchin, S., B. Rosman, and L. Baker (1978) *Psychosomatic Families: Anorexia Nervosa in Context*. Cambridge, Mass.: Harvard University Press.

O'Connor, J. J. (1984) "Strategic individual psychotherapy with bulimic women," *Psychotherapy* 21: 491–99.

Orbach, S. (1978) "Social dimensions in compulsive eating in women," *Psychotherapy: Theory, Research and Practice* 15: 180–89.

Pearce, J., M. LeBon, and J. Orchard (1981) "The role of spouse involvement in the behavioral treatment of overweight women," *Journal of Consulting and Clinical Psychology* 49: 236–44.

Roberto, L. G. (1986) "Bulimia: the transgenerational view," *Journal of Marital and Family Therapy* 12: 231–40.

Schwartz, R., J. J. Barrett, and G. Saba (1985) "Family therapy for bulimia," in D. M. Garner and P. E. Garfinkle, eds., *Handbook of Psychotherapy for Anorexia and Bulimia*. New York: Guilford Press.

Sobol, J. (1984) "Marriage, obesity and dieting," in D. J. Kallen and M. B. Sussman, eds., *Obesity and the Family*. New York: Haworth Press.

Stuart, R. B., and B. Jacobson (1987) *Weight, Sex and Marriage*. New York: W. W. Norton.

Weisz, G., and B. Bucher (1980) "Involving husbands in treatment of obesity—effects on weight loss, depression and marital satisfaction," *Behavior Therapy* 11: 643–50.

White, W. C., and M. B. White (1981) "An experimental behavioral approach to the treatment of bulimarexia," *Psychotherapy: Theory, Research and Practice* 18: 501–507.

Wilson, G. T., and K. Brownell (1978) "Behavior therapy for obesity: Including family members in the treatment process," *Behavior Therapy* 9: 943–45.

Wooley, S., and O. W. Wooley (1985) "Intensive outpatient and residential treatment for bulimia," Garner and Garfinkle, *Handbook of Psychotherapy for Anorexia Nervosa and Bulimia*.

——— (1986) "Thinness Mania," *Psychology Today* (October): 68–74.

Zitter, R. E., and W. J. Fremouw (1978) "Individual versus partner consequation for weight loss," *Behavior Therapy* 9: 808–813.

CHAPTER EIGHTEEN

THE BOOK ABOUT DADDY DYING: A PREVENTIVE ART THERAPY TECHNIQUE

Maxine Borowsky Junge, Ph.D., L.C.S.W., A.T.R.

This paper presents a clinical art therapy technique to help a family cope with the death of one of its members. It describes the making of a book in which the whole family participates. A theoretical rationale about bereavement is proposed and two case examples described. The approach of the "Book About Dying" is presented as a technique and model for dealing with the feelings attendant on a death in the family. Perhaps its most important benefit to the family is its preventive mental health function. Also, the book's potential as a vehicle for family ritual to aid in the transition from one life stage to another is discussed.

Introduction and Theoretical Rationale

In the last ten years or so, we have experienced a virtual cultural revolution in our attitudes toward death and its vicissitudes, with a resulting proliferation of thought and literature on death and dying. Out of the pioneering work of Elizabeth Kubler-Ross (1969) and others we have gained important new insights into many of these areas, including the impact of death on those left behind.

The importance of the mourning process, and its role in the successful adaptation to separations and losses in later life has been emphasized in the psychological literature starting with Freud's seminal work, "Mourning and Melancholia" (1917). Further, it is well-known that failure to mourn or inadequate mourning by a parent may result in various pathological problems in parent-child relationships. Clearly, problems do not arise in all cases of death in a family, nor is there always resultant pathology or symptomatology, because a reaction to any crisis is strongly influenced by past and present life experiences, ego strengths, and coping mechanisms.

However, over the years the consistent and increasing presence in my clinical practice of families who need help in dealing with and communicating about the death of a family member leads me to believe that a reconsideration of the issues involved, and development of new effec-

Reprinted with permission of *Art Therapy*, published by the American Art Therapy Association.

tive interventions and strategies, are in order.

Studies on the level of stress's effect on the development of illness have found that the "death of a spouse is the life event associated with the greatest degree of stress" (Holmes and Masuda 1973). The parent whose spouse has died suddenly needs to cope with changed financial, emotional, and domestic roles and responsibilities, and faces an uncertain future at a time when she or he is least functional. Questions from children about the facts of the death, cremation or burial, may not be welcome or answered.

Sometimes the circumstances of death—e.g., violent death or suicide—may cause shame and make the subject of the death taboo. A surviving parent may also want to spare the children the pain of loss and may not share his or her own feelings with them. A parent overwhelmed with his or her own feelings of sadness, abandonment, and confusion finds it difficult at best to help the children grieve effectively. In any case, the surviving parent's silence conveys to the children that death is secret and frightening and cannot be openly discussed. After the intense reaction of the first few days or weeks, the loss may be covered over and becomes a taboo subject for the family, a hidden and uncommunicated reservoir of pain and secrecy which can cause grave family dysfunction and psychopathology.

The reaction of the child or children to a death in the family depends on many factors, including age, emotional and cognitive development, and emotional closeness to the dead family member. The death may result in loss of residence or change in schools. The child may have to cope not only with the primary loss, but also with his or her feelings of distance from and abandonment by the surviving parent, who, because of the situations noted above or others, is not emotionally available and withdraws from the child. Thus, the child experiences a second, perhaps even more devastating, loss and has no avenue of communication through which to question or understand. Family therapist Murray Bowen (1976) and others have found that "the most influential factor in the child's reaction to the loss of the parent appears to be the ability of the remaining parent to not allow his or her emotions to create distance from the child."

Herz, in Carter and McGoldrick (1980), cites four factors which she feels affect a family's reactions and adjustments to a death. These are: (1) the timing of the death in the life cycle of the family; (2) the nature of the death (Was it expected or unexpected? Was there a long term of caring for the dying family member or was it a sudden death?); (3) the family position of the dying or dead family member and his or her emotional significance to the family; and (4) the openness of the family system.

Herz feels that difficulties arise from a lack of openness in the family system and goes on to define openness as the "ability of each family member to stay nonreactive to the emotional intensity in the system and to be able to communicate thoughts and feelings to others without expecting others to act on them."

The book described in this paper is used as a technique to permit family expression and communication and to prevent the premature closing down of the family system.

Case Examples

The following two case examples show the process of making a book with two families. The first example describes the use of the book as intervention because of the clinical needs of a particular family. It describes an intact family with two young children undergoing the death of the father by suicide. The second case concerns a divorced family in which the 32-year-old father died of a melanoma, and is intended to underscore the flexibility of the book technique in its adaptability to use with various family constellations.

Case 1: The F Family

Ms. F came to the mental health clinic with her two young sons, Jimmy (four) and Mark (seven), two months after the suicide of her husband, Mr. F, a thirty-seven-year-old engineer, who had a history of depression. One month before his death he had been a patient in a psychiatric hospital where he was thought to be improved and no longer suicidal. Ms. F had disagreed with her husband's psychiatrist's assessment and asked that he be kept for a longer time at the hospital. The hospital refused. Three days after his release, Mr. F ingested an overdose of medication and died.

As presenting problems at the clinic, Ms. F cited her own intense and ongoing depression. She felt overcome with guilt for her inability to convince her husband's doctors of the seriousness of the situation and with intense anger at the mental health system. Both sons had been noted by their teachers as pervasively sad and unable to concentrate on their school work.

The F family was assigned to a staff psychologist for therapy. She saw them for four sessions, which she felt were of little help. Mother could do little more than cry through the sessions, and said she also cried at home whenever she thought of her husband. She was preoccupied with her loss and seemed unable to disconnect from her constant ruminations and to focus on her two sons and their grief. In the sessions, the psychologist observed that the boys made occasional bids for their mother's attention, but seemed to grow increasingly detached and withdrawn at her lack of response. The psychologist contacted me in her hope that a family art therapy task might serve to focus the family more productively.

As I thought about the F family system, it seemed to me that something more than the usual art therapy techniques were needed to symbolically contain all the overwhelming thoughts and feelings evoked by the father's suicide. Although there was clearly an overriding need for catharsis as a prelude to acceptance and support, Ms. F's inability to control her feelings had caused her to withdraw from her sons and them from her. Using a structural theoretical framework, it seemed necessary to help Ms. F reconnect with her sons, so that she could begin to help them with their loss, and perhaps gain some sustenance from them. Appropriate defenses would be supported and confrontation of fragile ones would be avoided. As I look back, however, the book idea may have emerged because I knew education was highly valued in this family and that Mr. F had read nightly to his sons.

The psychologist and I met with the family to suggest that they make a book about Mr. F. This would include their memories of him—both good and bad—family events before his death, their questions (and answers) about the death, and, of course, all their feelings. I asked the family to bring in photographs of Mr. F to include in the book.

We met weekly for six weeks, working together in the sessions on the book. During our work Ms. F became increasingly capable of concentrating and helping her sons to do so, resuming her nurturance of them. The distancing device of making the book and the focus on its pages seemed to dam up the previous overflow of the mother's feelings, giving her more control and more comfort and allowing more room for her sons' feelings. Sometimes the family worked individually, sometimes together, on one piece of paper around a central theme. The separate pages were kept in a folder by the therapist and we told the F family that when we finished the book, we would have it bound for them to take home.

In the sessions, family communication was emphasized and questions were asked, re-asked, and re-answered. This was my first experience working with very young children experiencing the death of a parent, and although many developmentalists emphasize the young child's lack of conceptual ability and inability to understand, I found that Jimmy was *trying* to understand. His repeated questions, as well as his ongoing involvement in the work of the book, convinced me of this. With Jimmy I came to believe that the young child must find some way to make sense out of his dramatically changed world in order to be able to go on.

At the end of the six weeks, family and therapists agreed that the book seemed finished. (The six weeks were not preplanned, and we would have continued work on the chapters for as long as seemed useful.) The therapists agreed to "get the book put together," and we arranged a last meeting. We mounted the newsprint pages on sturdier paper and put four notebook rings through the pages to hold them together. At the last meeting the family talked about its feelings about the book, and both family and therapists expressed the belief that they had shared a difficult but special experience. We recommended that the book be kept in a safe place at home where any family member could read it at will, but that the book be read by all three together at least once a week.

One year later, Ms. F called at the insistence of Jimmy who had told her "the book is falling apart and needs to go back to the clinic." We asked Ms. F to bring the boys and the book in for a reevaluation (what I like to call "a 2,000 mile checkup").

Indeed the book *was* falling apart—literally. We wondered: Was the family also? The family told us that they had read the book together almost every night all year. Ms. F stated that the book had given the family an avenue for communicating about Mr. F and a vehicle whereby they could continue to express feelings of all kinds. Each family member individually had read the book as needed in her or his own way, and it was the only thing in the house consistently returned to its "safe place" on the shelf.

In our reevaluation sessions, we created new pages for the book about what had been happening to the family in the year since Mr. F's death. Ms. F was now attending a widows' group. She had started graduate school with the goal of a career as a mathematics teacher. She had very recently had a few dates, and in the month before the call to the clinic, she had spent a weekend away skiing with friends. The boys had remained with a baby-sitter for the weekend. Jimmy and Mark had settled down in school and were doing well except for occasional spells of "moodiness." Mark was still ready to be overaggressive at times, and Jimmy had occasionally wet his bed. But generally all family members seemed to be progressing appropriately in their mourning process. Jimmy's urging that the Fs come to the clinic was seen as an anniversary reaction to Mr. F's death, probably exacerbated by Ms. F's ski trip.

We took the book, reinforced the binding with notebook "reinforcers," and sent the book and the family home with the recommendation that they call us as needed.

At the two-year point, we received no phone call, so we decided to follow up ourselves. Ms. F reported that all was well. She was still having trouble adjusting to her role as a single mother and felt overwhelmed and harried at times. She had finished her graduate work, acquired a teaching position which was very rewarding to her, was still attending the widows' group, and had recently begun a relationship that, she said, "might become very important." Both boys were doing well at school and with friends. Mark, the older, had begun to stay overnight at the houses of his friends. Jimmy, though invited, was not yet ready for this, but his incidences of bedwetting were down to practically nothing. Both boys had big brothers through the Big Brothers organization.

Ms. F said that in the second year, they had continued to read the book together, though not so often, and that she would sometimes find one or the other of the boys—usually Mark—engrossed in it. She said that they sometimes still cried when they read the book, but that the pain had diminished. The book stayed in its safe place on the shelf, for whichever family member might need it. Ms. F expressed her gratitude for the book and later wrote the director of the clinic a letter of thanks.

Case 2: The H Family

This family was in treatment for problems of stress and family disruption at the time of the divorced 32-year-old father's death from a malignant melanoma after a three-year illness. The family consisted of Ms. H, a single mother with two daughters, Ruthie (five) and Sharon (seven). Ms. H's live-in boyfriend Sam also periodically attended meetings. Because of the divorce (which had occurred four years earlier), this book was viewed as "belonging to the two children." However, the mother was included with Ruthie and Sharon in almost every session as a "therapeutic ally" in an attempt to help her help her children with their feelings of loss and to increase family cohesiveness.

Ms. H, as a self-supporting single mother with two young children, typically experienced role overload, and the family style tended toward chaos. However, after the divorce, when their daughters were very young, Mr. and Ms. H had managed to remain on good terms, and the girls had regular contact with their father. Ms. H had contributed financially to help her ex-husband with medical bills, and Mr. H had been included in several therapy sessions with his daughters. Mr. H's death was unexpected in spite of his long illness, and there had been little anticipatory grieving.

We met in the therapy room to begin the book soon after the family's brief memorial service, and the process continued for slightly more than three months. Ruthie and Sharon were invited to bring in photographs, and simple materials, such as markers, crayons, and collage pictures, were provided. At times the therapist gave specific directives. At other times free drawing was encouraged, so themes could emerge indirectly. Verbal exploration, discussion, and writing about the artwork were encouraged to extend communication. At times Ruthie and Sharon directed me or their mother about what to put on the picture, and we wrote it for them.

The weekly therapy sessions were often attended by Ms. H; occasionally the two girls met alone with the therapist, to offer information and feelings that might be difficult for them to say in front of their mother. Communication was enhanced when the girls shared these pages with their mother.

The artwork centered around typical issues of grieving, separation, and loss. The following are chronological, though not consecutive, examples of artwork from beginning, middle, and ending phases of the book. (*See* pp. 292–96 for figures)

Figure 18.1 shows the front cover of the book finished and bound by the therapist. Then the book begins with a page of Sharon's (7) writing:

> Daddy died Sunday. He was lying sick in bed when all of a sudden the door sprang open and two little girls came in. The nurse had to wake him up becuase (sic) right before they came, daddy had just had a shot. And right after they left he died.

Figures 18.2 and 18.3 by Sharon show the visit to the funeral home and the cremation. Pages in the first section of the book, along with feelings of grief, were often informational in tone. In the middle phase of the book, more ambivalent expressions prevailed. Figure 18.4 shows pleasant memories of past times and feelings of loss. Also in this section appropriate underlying anger surfaced.

In figure 18.5 "Daddy Lying Sick in Bed," a spontaneous drawing, Ruthie showed her vivid and mixed feelings. She told me about the picture and I wrote the words on another sheet of paper for her:

> Daddy's in pain. He feels sad and all Daddy said when we went to visit him was "Hi L," because L's my Grandpa and he is very tall. I wished he would say "Hi" to me. I felt mad that he didn't say "Hi" to me because I wasn't tall enough. I held his hand. My grandmother kissed him. I wanted to kiss him but right after she kissed him it was time to go because he fell back to sleep. I felt mad that I didn't get to kiss him. But there was another reason I didn't get to kiss him. I was scared cause he looked scarey. He had his mouth open and he was breathing hard and he was moaning.

Sharon's drawing of the aggressive "Packman (*sic*) Eating Daddy's Dreams" (figure 18.6) depicted her normal rage metaphorically. In the last month of making the book, Ruthie expressed a reunion fantasy and a wish to have a tangible part of her father—an ash (figure 18.7). Figure 18.8, by Sharon in a last session, "Daddy is as nice as a butterfly," shows Daddy floating away, smaller than the butterflies and in the distant top corner.

In her drawing at the end of the book, Sharon pictures one of her father's drawings. During his illness, Mr. H had been involved in a holistic cancer program which utilized techniques of guided imagery and drawing. After his death, the girls had asked for and been given his drawings. Both children often mentioned his drawings during the course of our therapy, as if their father's imagery on paper, now in their possession, had provided some tangible evidence of his presence in their lives. They often drew "his pictures" in their book.

For the last page of "The Book About Daddy Dying" Ruthie and Sharon each chose to render one of their father's drawings. Sharon drew three arches (figure 18.9) with a handwritten "I love you Daddy" covered by a paper flap (shaped

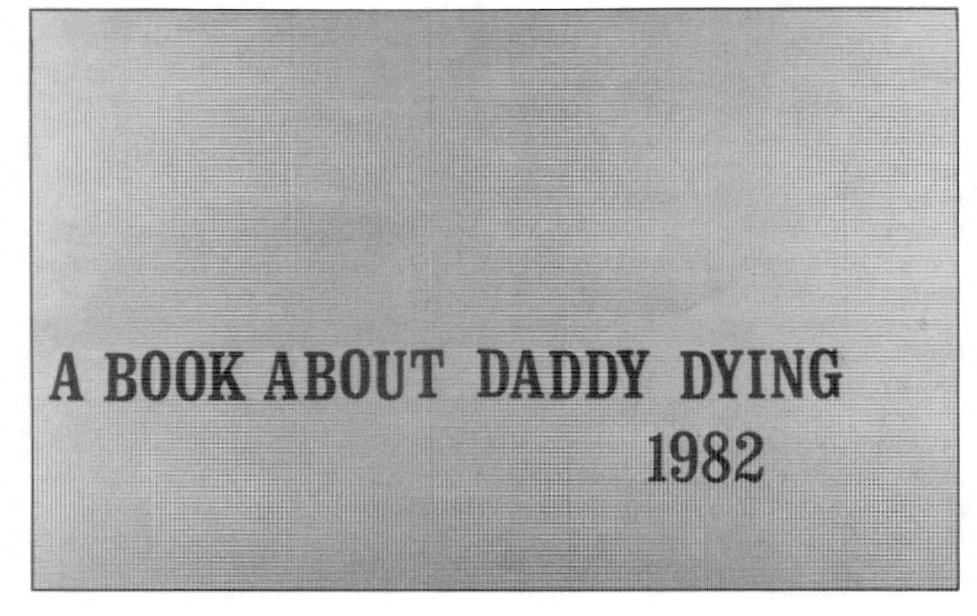

Figure 18.1

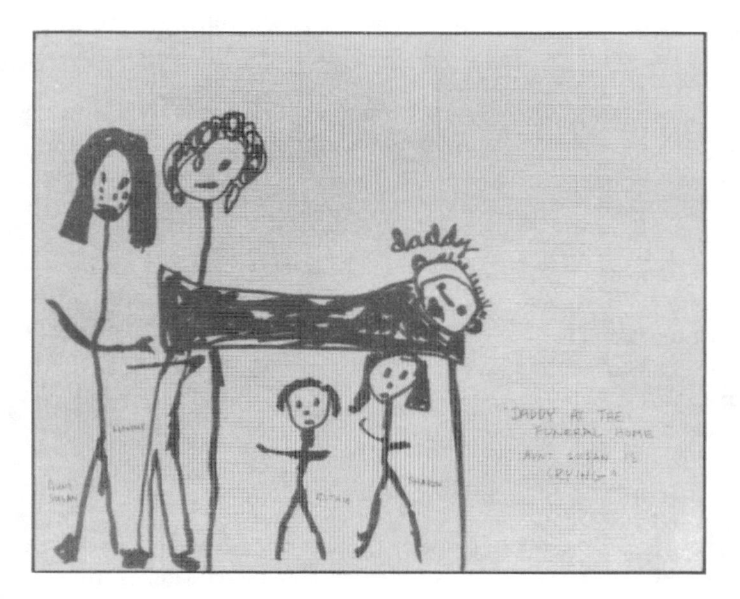

Figure 18.2

Figure 18.3

Figure 18.4

Figure 18.5

"ME (PACMAN) EATING UP
DADDY'S DREAMS BECAUSE
I'M MAD AT HIM"

Figure 18.6

Figure 18.7

Figure 18.8

Figure 18.9

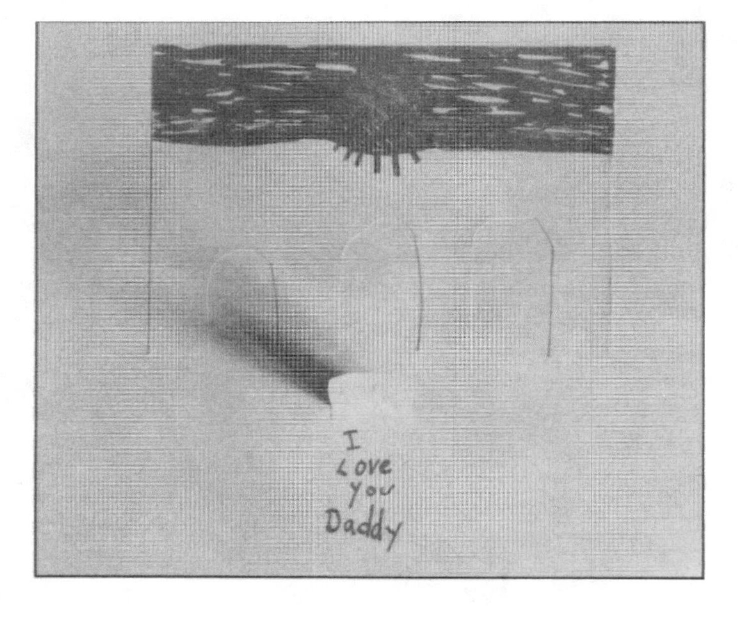

like a tombstone perhaps representing their lost father). Over the arches is a vibrant red sun setting into dark blue clouds. On the bottom the sun has spikey points reminiscent of the spikes of hair, typical of the girls' portrayals of their father's head, bald from chemotherapy. It is my speculation that the three arches represent the remaining family group, with Mr. H as the setting sun in the distance.

In the last session, we took the calendar and counted how long it had been since Mr. H's death. The girls wrote: "Daddy died May 3, 1982, on Sunday, 14 weeks and two days, three months and a week, 100 days ago today," and the book was finished.

Approximately a year later, I met Sharon and Ruthie in the waiting room where they were waiting for their mother, who was now participating in a group with a colleague in the office. Sharon's first words to me were, "We still have the book."

Conclusion

Each life transition in the developmental phases of a family requires more or less drastic changes by all family members, and death demands a uniquely difficult adjustment. The art therapy technique described here, based on a family systems approach, has as its goal the openness and flexibility of the system at a time of great family crisis and change. The book is seen as preventive as well as ameliorating, in that if grief is incompletely resolved by the premature closure of the system, family dysfunction and the development of psychopathology can result. This therapist believes that a book such as this can be an instrument of important family ritual to aid in a successful transition.

Grief rituals such as traditional funerals require the expression of different emotions within a context, and can thereby help stimulate both the mourning process and the restoration of normal life. In making the book, family members are given permission to express, communicate, and work on their feelings of grief within the safety of the therapeutic milieu.

Rituals are symbolic acts, and objects with symbolic value may be used. Being able to work with the symbolic act or object implies both a focus and a certain distance, and can free up psychic energy for real life activities. A book such as the ones described is a permanent, stable container of memories, feelings, and history. Like a life it has a beginning and an end and thus can provide a symbolic way of working through the sense of loss caused by a death. This may be particularly important in helping young children gain understanding and comfort.

We began and ended our sessions. We began to make and finished making the book. We began and ended our reading of the book, and we began and ended the first year and continued into the next. Throughout, the book remained in a "safe place" on the shelf to remind us of our beginnings, our endings, and our constancy in the face of them. A book made by those still living is representative of the acknowledgement and permanency of important feelings and memories and of the way that those we love live on in our memories and feelings. This acknowledgement can be crucial in the process of saying goodbye, for it is the beginning of letting go and going on.

References

Beecher, D., and F. Margolin (1967) "How Surviving Parents Handled Their Young Children's Adaptation to the Crisis of Loss," *American Journal of Orthopsychiatry* 37: 753–57.

Bowen, M. (1976) "Family Reaction to Death," in P. Guerin, ed., *Family Therapy: Theory and Practice*. New York: Gardner Press.

Bowlby, J. (1961) "Processes of Mourning," *The International Journal of Psychiatry* 42: 317–40.

Freud, S. (1917 [1915]) *The Standard Edition of the Complete Psychological Works of Sigmund Freud,* vol. 14. London: Hogarth Press.

Herz, F. (1980) "The Impact of Death and Serious Illness in the Family Life Cycle," in E. Carter and M. McGoldrick, eds., *The Family Life Cycle*. New York: Gardner Press.

Holmes, T., and M. Masuda (1973) "Life Change and Illness Susceptibility," *Separation and Depression Clinical and Research Aspects,* Pub. 94. Washington, D.C.: American Association for the Advancement of Science.

Kubler-Ross, E. (1969) *On Death and Dying*. New York: Macmillan.

Shneidman, E. S. (1976) *Death: Current Perspectives*. New York: Jason Aronson.

Solomon, M., and L. B. Hersch (1979) "Death in the Family, Implications for Family Development," *Journal of Marital and Family Therapy* 5 (2), April.

CHAPTER NINETEEN

FAMILY THERAPY AND BEREAVEMENT COUNSELING

Frank Genovese, Ph.D.

Mourning: From the Person to the Family

Introduction

Loss is the currency of therapy. It is the loss of love or nurturance or power or security or relationships which brings people to our offices. This list of losses can be expanded exponentially.

Dealing with loss well is not an inborn ability. "Coping and grieving are things we learn, we are taught, and we develop from the time we are infants. . . . By the time we are adults, we've all had a lot of experience with loss, starting with the rattle in our own crib, up through our baseball gloves, dolls, teddy bears, high school boyfriend or girlfriend, graduation from high school or college, moving away from friends, and deaths of grandparents" (Frantz 1984).

This last-mentioned loss, death, is one of life's few certainties. We shall all mourn. Some will do it well and be restored. Others will mourn poorly and compound their loss. Parkes and Weiss (1983) write, "Bereavement, the loss by death of someone loved, is the most severe psychological trauma most people will encounter in the course of their lives. Nor are its effects easily overcome. It has long been a topic of literary examination, philosophical speculation and psychological study; yet, as Shakespeare said, 'Everyone can cure a grief but he who has it.' "

Rando (1984) defines grief as the process of psychological, social, and somatic reactions to loss and to the perception of loss. She implies not only that grief has multiple manifestations, but also that it should be viewed as a developmental process. Rando further suggests that grief is a normal, expected occurrence. It is the reaction initiated by loss. The form it takes is based upon the unique fashion in which an individual mourner perceives the loss.

Rando (1984) understands the term *mourning* to have two meanings. The first refers to the wide variety of intrapsychic processes described by authors such as Freud (1917) and Bowlby (1980). The second describes the cultural response to grief. Americans do not grieve as do Chinese; Chinese grieve differently than do Eskimos. The implication is that there is no single correct way to mourn, but that reactions are socially and culturally influenced.

Rynearson's (1987) work is typical of a relatively new line of thinking which defines a typology of grief therapy predicated on combinations of pre-morbid behavior with specific forms of death. There is not only grief, therefore, but there are also various types of grief. Each may call for different therapeutic action.

While inquiry into the nature of the individual's reaction to the death of a loved one pre-dates even "Mourning and Melancholia" (Freud 1917), an understanding of grief from a system's perspective is elusive. Gelcer (1983) states, "Psychotherapy for unresolved grief reaction is still, by and large, based on Freudian psychoanalytic assumptions." Further, Frantz (1984), referring to his collection of systems-oriented articles on bereavement, writes, "(This volume) brings the experiences of those who work with death and grief to an audience of therapists who work with families. The volume reflects the early developmental state of grief counseling, in that most grief counselors work primarily with individuals and, more specifically with individuals in acute stages of dying or grieving . . . you will often need to make adaptations in applying the background, ideas and suggestions that are offered."

This paper attempts to make such adaptations. Based on the works of Breunlin (1983), Carter and Walsh (1980), Herz Brown (1988), Hoffmann (1988), Kerr and Bowen (1988), McGoldrick and Walsh (1983), and others, it is suggested that disruptions in the mourning processes may reveal themselves in (a) an intensification of the family's pre-morbid anxiety-reducing mechanisms, (b) a calcification of family structures which maintain symptoms in the identified patient, and (c) the appearance of emotional cut-offs engendered by communication distortions.

Part 1: Individual Reactions to Loss

Normal Bereavement: A Theoretical Sampler

Interest in individual reactions to the death of a loved one is intense. A volume entitled *Bereavement: Reactions, Consequences and Care* (Osterweis et al. 1984) was requested and funded by the Office of Prevention of the National Institute of Mental Health. A three-volume work has been published based on presentations at the First International Symposium on Grief and Bereavement held in Israel in 1985. This work, *Grief and Bereavement in Contemporary Society* (Chigier 1988), indicates that interest in the phenomenon of grief is not confined to researchers in the United States. Rando's (1984) work, based on research relevant to grief and dying, lists over four hundred references.

Freud (1917) presented one of the first discussions of the internal mechanisms employed by individuals faced with the death of a loved one. Freud's model suggests that even as reality demands that the person be buried, he or she is kept psychologically alive within the mourner who wishes to deny the reality of the loss: "A person never willingly abandons a libidinal, or non-reality based, position." Implicit in Freud's essay is the theme that bereavement will be difficult to the degree that the relationship between the mourner and the deceased has been ambivalent.

Lindemann (1944) studied the survivors of the Coconut Grove Fire, and concluded that most bereaved persons could be expected to resolve their losses within several weeks. While most current writers cite Lindemann's as a pioneering work, few agree with his conclusions. Both Bowlby (1961, 1980) and Parkes and Weiss (1983) believe that normal bereavement follows a developmental course.

Bowlby's (1980) view of bereavement is an extension of his attachment theory. This theory posits that the tendency to form attachment bonds is a trait of the human species which has been selected over evolutionary time. Beletsky and Jacobs (1986) succinctly summarize the highly articulated theory:

> . . . Bowlby . . . postulates that there is an instinctive propensity for human beings (as well as members of other species) to form strong and persistent affectional bonds. These are commonest between one or both parents and their off-spring . . . and between adults of the opposite sex. The essential feature of this attachment is the tendency of the bonded partners to remain in close proximity to one another and to elicit proximity keeping behavior. . . . Although the behavior is especially prominent during childhood, it remains active throughout adult life. Indeed attachment behavior is thought to be a normal and healthy part of man's instinctive makeup. Accordingly, separation anxiety and the activation of intense attachment behavior is seen as a natural and inevitable response to the loss of the attachment figure.

The anxiety and anger engendered by the threat of the loss of an attachment bond ensure that the bond remains unbroken. Consider this hypothetical scene: A young couple, intent on finishing their holiday shopping, is unaware that their seven-year-old son has wandered away. Some minutes later the mother asks, "Where is Matt?" When the couple realizes that the boy is missing, panic (separation anxiety) sets in. A Keystone Kops scenario ensues, with the parents rushing up and down aisles and calling for the boy. The store's security force is notified. Public address systems call out for the child. Finally a sobbing (anxiety-filled) boy and his frantic (anxiety-filled) parents are united. Hugs, kisses, and sighs of relief are followed shortly thereafter by a sharp slap on the behind! The slap represents the anger component of attachment behavior and is an example of that class of behaviors which evolved to decrease the probability of threats to the bond.

Stages of Mourning

Death, however, severs the bond beyond reparation. The inability to re-establish connection sets the stage for mourning. Bowlby (1980) describes the mourning process in four stages. The first stage—*numbing*—can last from a few hours to several days. In this stage, the mourner becomes intellectually aware of the loss but does not react emotionally. Bowlby understands this phenomenon as a defensive variation of normal information processing: the person needs to absorb the enormity of the event and to marshal resources to begin the work of mourning.

Yearning and Searching

The second stage is characterized by a *yearning* for the dead person. The central conflict at this point involves a realization of the permanence of loss versus an unconscious demand for reunion. The ebb and flow of the conflict is reflected in the bereaved. Sometimes the mourners behave realistically. At other times they behave irrationally, swayed by the fantasy of eventual reunion.

For example, John G. had never completed mourning his father, with whom he had had a highly conflicted relationship. The father had often behaved in an irrational, unpredictable, and highly punitive fashion. John's ambivalence took the form of hating what his father had been, while simultaneously loving and yearning for reunion with an idealized version of what his father might have been.

John was a very successful businessman, admired by his family, his peers, and his clientele. Yet at times he would be paralyzed by overwhelming guilt. At such times he would become highly agitated and depressed. Obsessive thoughts, of both his imagined misdeeds and his punitive father, would consume him. He could not work effectively. He would sit for hours, crying and immobilized, convinced of his "sinfulness."

John's malevolent father was surely alive within him during these recurring episodes. He could not bury the man because his need to resolve the ambivalent relationship was too great. Yet the ghost was frightening, angry, and powerful. Just as John had been unfairly punished as a child, so also would he be as an adult.

Behaving, feeling, and thinking as if the deceased were still alive may take more subtle forms than those that John manifested. Krupp (1965) describes how some mourners, through the process of identification, may adopt either the personality characteristics or the physical symptoms of the deceased.

The concept of identification assumes that an individual's personality is a mosaic of bits and pieces of the personalities of significant and introjected others. By taking on the characteristics of the lost loved one, mourners can deny the reality of the loss.

Krupp (1965) offers the example of a relatively open and outgoing young man whose father died unexpectedly of a heart attack. Within a year he had become as distrustful of others as his father had been. Although in perfect health, the young man often complained of chest pains.

Anger directed at the lost object, at the self, and at others believed to have caused the loss is common at this stage. Anyone who reminds the mourner of the loss is a potential target for anger.

When Mrs. M's twenty-year-old son returned home after withdrawing from college, she was furious at his "irresponsibility." She insisted that he support himself if he was not in school. The son died in an accident while working as a cab driver. Mrs. M was immensely angry with herself and with the taxi company. She was convinced that her insistence that the young man support himself was the distal cause of his death, and that the company's "negligence" was its proximal cause.

An automobile accident also took the life of fourteen-year-old Michael's brother. God bore the brunt of Michael's anger. "There cannot be a God; he would not have let this happen. And if there is a God, I hate him for this."

Sixteen-year-old Tommy's parents had been divorced for ten years when the mother died of lung cancer. The object of Tommy's anger was his father. Had he not divorced his mother, she would not have been anxious. If she had not been anxious, she would not have smoked. Had she not smoked, Tommy's mother would still be alive.

Disorganization

In the third stage, the mourner is *disorganized and depressed*. Many of his or her self-definitions may have been predicated on the existence of the now-dead person. The widower may still feel married; the orphan may still feel like a daughter. Until previous modes of feeling, thinking, and behaving are broken down and replaced by more adaptive affective, cognitive, and behavioral modes, the mourner may feel lost and disconnected.

Forty-two-year-old Linda had been a widow for seven years. She described her marriage as having been very happy. Unable to recover from the untimely loss of her husband, Linda felt as if she were still married. She considered herself to be part of an intimate dyad with her late spouse. She refused to date. Weiss (1975) defines loneliness as the continuance of attachment behavior when there is no longer an object for that behavior. Linda, then, was not only disorganized and depressed, but lonely as well.

The mourning-liberation process is complete when the mourner is free to function well and fully in the present, and to plan adequately for the future. As in any developmental process, the possibility is always present of becoming fixated at one of the stages. Bowlby (1980) believes that incomplete mourning is pathological.

Sanders (1989) suggests that, "The phases of disorganization and reorganization are set forth without clearcut division." This author has found it useful to view the work of Parkes and Weiss (1983) as a more complete delineation of the reorganization process. The combined works of Bowlby (1980) and Parkes and Weiss (1983) provide a stage which is termed "resolution."

Resolution

Parkes and Weiss (1983) conceive of the mourning process as comprised of three primary tasks: intellectual recognition and explanation of the loss, emotional acceptance, and formation of a new identity.

From an operational perspective, the first task requires the mourner to "feel that the world makes sense." The mourner must formulate an "account" which "explains" the loss. This story need not be factually true. What is important for recovery is that the mourner believes it and that it explains why the loss has occurred. "Without an account that settles the question of 'Why?' (mourners) can never relax their vigilance against the threat of new loss."

Emotional acceptance occurs when the mourner no longer fears being overwhelmed by grief, pain, or remorse. This state is accomplished through an "obsessive review." During the review, the mourner repeatedly goes over the same thoughts and memories. In healthy mourning, slowly the thoughts and memories change as the original ones become neutralized.

A new identity is attained when the mourner's self-definitions no longer involve the lost loved one. A spouse who reports, for example, "I still feel like her husband" continues to see himself in terms of the lost attachment bond. Parkes and Weiss (1983) observe that the maintenance of these other-directed self-images indicates that the mourner is ". . . being inattentive to possibilities for new satisfaction that would be entirely appropriate. . . ." He or she is dead to life.

Perhaps some of Linda's behaviors are understandable in these terms. If she has not settled the question of "Why?", she may feel that the establishment of a new relationship will leave her open to another future loss. If Linda can begin to believe, for example, that her husband's death was beneficial in that it relieved his pain, she might be able to get on with her obsessive review and begin to reestablish her identity.

Table 19.1 summarizes the work of

Table 19.1 Stages of Grief from Bowlby (1980) and Parkes and Weiss (1983)

Process Stage	Nature of Grief Work
Numbing	Allows time to absorb the enormity of the event and to begin the work of mourning through defensive information processing.
Yearning and Searching	Attempts to deny the permanence of loss.
Disorganization and Despair	Permits the breakdown of previous modes of feeling, thinking, and behaving, and the establishment of more adaptive ones.
Resolution	
Intellectual Recognition	Formulates a story, believed by the bereaved, which settles the question "Why?"
Emotional Acceptance	Diminishes the fear of being overwhelmed by grief, pain, or remorse. Begins and carries out the "obsessive review."
Identity Transformation	Creates new definitions of self in the present.

Bowlby (1980) and Parkes and Weiss (1983). The contribution of the latter authors is seen as an expansion of Bowlby's fourth stage.

Different Forms of Grief

Individuals and systems comprised of individuals are highly complex. The behavior of people and of family systems is rarely as predictable as theoretical discussions may imply. Theoreticians are aware of this incongruency. Sanders (1989) writes, ". . . it is important to keep in mind that the experience of loss is affected by many moderator variables, both situational and personal. While the stages of bereavement are set forth in a particular order, it does not mean that they represent an inflexible pattern. The griever unquestionably moves forward and backward, as circumstance or need requires, occasionally becoming stuck in one phase or another for some time."

The irregularity of a mourner's progress through the process of bereavement is not the only factor which complicates the translation from a theoretical position to a therapeutic approach.

Rynearson (1987), Raphael (1977), and Parkes and Weiss (1983) each describe interactions of various grief reactions, the quality of the relationship between the deceased and the mourner, and the nature of the death. Rynearson (1987) defines dependent grief syndrome, unexpected loss syndrome, and conflicted grief syndrome.

Dependent Grief

In dependent grief the attachment of the mourner to the deceased is characterized by a relationship

> of relative non-differentiation in which one's self-image is contingent upon the availability of another. This dependence demands continuing interchange as a requisite in maintaining an image of self as whole and acceptable. The death of the dependent figure initiates a pathogenic

> shift in self-image from that of being strong, caring and worthwhile to discrepant images of being weak, uncaring and incompetent. (Rynearson 1987)

Gaylin (1985) and Horowitz (1984) agree that dependency can strongly influence the course of mourning. Horowitz (1984) suggests that not only is the degree of dependence at the time of death an important variable, but so also are dependency-oriented dyadic images which may have arisen much earlier in the history of the relationship. Gaylin (1985) writes, "Ambivalence is most likely to lead to pathologic grief when it is accompanied by a strong psychological dependence on the person who had died."

Rynearson's (1987) position is that the self-images of weakness and incompetence become strong organizers of perception. The mourner interprets both internal and external reality in the light of these irrational beliefs of worthlessness. The negative self-images become cognitive structures (Beck et al. 1979), colored lenses which systematically distort reality. Even as Beck's depressed patients can understand and interpret their existence only in terms of self-loathing, the unfairness of the world, and the ugliness of the future, Rynearson's (1987) dependent grievers see the death as a result of their own weakness. They believe that if they had been better persons the loss would not have occurred.

These negative self-images often develop during the early stages of differentiation. The relationship served to block the emergence of the behavioral and cognitive manifestations of these self images. Death results not only in the loss of the loved one, but also in the loss of the palliative relationship.

Unexpected Grief

In another article Rynearson (1986) describes the clinical picture of bereavement following unexpected death. Mourners are seen as suffering from post-traumatic stress disorder. They show startle reactions, explosive outbursts of anger, flashbacks, and nightmares. These symptoms alternate with psychic numbing, constriction of affect, diminution of social interaction, and loss of a sense of control over one's destiny. These mourners feel victimized in the same way as does any individual who is deliberately harmed or coerced. They are preoccupied with grotesque images of how the body looked at the time of death. They lose their belief in protection from violence. Death is not fair, so it is not accepted. Society offers little in the way of explanation or of retribution.

Lehman et al. (1987) have studied the statistical effects of unexpected loss. Results indicate that mourning reactions are most likely to be severe when the loss is untimely or unexpected.

Rando (1984) reports that much of the literature suggests that there is adaptive value in having advanced warning. The warning allows anticipatory grief work to begin. She states, "In unanticipated grief, mourners are unable to grasp the full implications of the loss. Their adaptive capacities are severely assaulted and they suffer extreme feelings of bewilderment, anxiety, self-reproach and depression that render them unable to function normally in any area of their lives. There is difficulty in accepting the loss, despite intellectual recognition of the death, and the death may continue to seem inexplicable. Grief symptomatology persists much longer than usual."

Parkes and Weiss (1983) present statistical evidence that mourning, following unexpected death is different. Rather than going through an ultimately liberating process, persons grieve in a manner characterized by difficulties in acceptance, self-punitive tendencies, and alienation. These responses complicate grief work and are correlated with later psychiatric problems.

A possible explanation of this clinical picture is offered by Parkes and Weiss (1983). People can function in reality only because of the maintenance of internal, assumptive schema of that reality. People recognize and behave appropriately with chairs, tables, language, people, etc., because models have been formed to interpret perception and to guide behavior. Death of a loved one causes a permanent alteration in reality, but it takes time for the internal representation to assimilate the change. Those who have warning prior to the death do not go through anticipatory grief. Rather, they learn to discern the discrepancies between external and internal truth. Those who have suffered unanticipated loss have no such opportunity.

Unwarned mourners believe in the unpredictability of the world. Having been hurt by one unforeshadowed disaster, they feel at risk for future unexpected loss. They withdraw from the risk of new commitment, taking themselves away from family, friends, coworkers.

At the time of any loss, Parkes and Weiss (1983) continue, people turn to their attachment figures for solace. If the primary attachment is to the person who has died, the mourner is alone. In unanticipated death, the fear and loss of security can be overwhelming. That these mourners cling to the fantasy of a continuing relationship with the lost loved one is demonstrated by their marked inability to visit the grave or to socialize with persons who may evoke painful memories. The loss is experienced as special: It is more wrong; it is more unjustifiable; it is more outrageous.

Conflicted Grief

There may be some truth in Rynearson's (1987) assertion that conflicted grief syndrome has received more attention from researchers than other kinds of loss, but the problem of pathological grief reactions which stem from conflicted, ambivalent attachment to the deceased is a serious one. For example, Zisook et al. (1985) found that 17 percent of patients entering a psychiatric outpatient unit had difficulties with unresolved grief. To test the hypothesis that conflicted grief is often overlooked—although it is readily diagnosable—the authors studied all new patients over a four-month period. Those with unresolved grief had a higher incidence of multiple losses, a history of difficulty in getting along with their mothers, present complaints of depression, and physical problems. The authors caution clinicians evaluating new patients to be alert for the presence of unresolved grief.

Rando (1984) and Parkes and Weiss (1983) describe the clinical picture similarly. Conflicted grievers, unlike those who have suffered unexpected loss, seem to have no immediate problem in accepting the reality of the death. There is no prolonged numbing, and many experience a sort of relief that the angry, conflicted, and ambivalent relationship is over. Problems arise later in the course of mourning. Resolution is not achieved, and the mourners are full of anger, guilt, and self-reproach.

Parkes and Weiss (1983) cite several possible etiologies for the syndrome. The authors report that their subjects provide evidence for each of these explanations:

Table 19.2 Various Grief Syndromes (Rynearson 1987)

Syndrome	Clinical Picture	Treatment of Choice
Dependent Grief	Bereaved's self-image is contingent upon the availability of the deceased. Pathogenic shift in self-image from strong, caring, and worthwhile to weak, uncaring, and incompetent.	Cognitive-behavioral strategies aimed at restructuring distorted self-image.
Conflicted Grief	Immediate reaction to death appears healthy. No prolonged numbing. Many feel relief that the ambivalent relationship is over. Later become immobilized with anger, guilt, and self-reproach. Resolution unattained.	Insight-oriented psychotherapy to deal with issues such as autonomy and ambivalence.
Unexpected Grief	Mourner feels victimized. Often preoccupied with grotesque images of the body. Intense anger. Emotionally labile. Startle reactions. Nightmares.	Post-traumatic shock interventions.

the Freudian concept that anger is directed at the internalized object (the deceased); the cognitive concept that attachment figures do not cease to affect internal dialogues after death; the concept that continued grief can be a means of restitution for not having loved the deceased better during life; the concept that not only the dead person, but also an idealized version of the relationship that might have been, are mourned; the concept that the failure to attain early secure attachments makes conflicted mourners less capable than others of successful recovery from loss.

Dependent, unexpected, and conflicted griefs are not the only syndromes described in the literature. Sanders (1989) identifies "death of a child," "death of a spouse," and "death of a parent" as three other types of bereavement. In addition Rando (1984) defines different types of grief following stillbirth, miscarriage, neonatal death, and suicide. She also delineates some characteristics of children's grief.

The differences in the clinical pictures presented by dependent, unexpected, and conflicted grief alert the therapist to the likelihood that no two griefs are exactly the same. Any number of factors can have an impact upon the course of bereavement. Rando (1984) lists twenty "psychological" factors, four "social" factors, and five "physiological" factors. The individual qualities of the lost relationship, the individual's coping behavior, personality, mental health status, and past experiences with loss and death are psychological factors. The quality of the mourner's support systems and cultural, ethnic, and religious background are social factors. Physical state of health and possible use of drugs are physiological factors. It is beyond the scope of this paper to describe all these. However, one must agree with Rando's (1984) statement, "Each person's grief will be idiosyncratic, determined by a unique combination of psychological, social and physiological factors." Theory, therefore, serves to direct, not to dictate, the course of intervention.

Characteristics of Healthy Mourning

Successful mourning is a liberating process. Garfield (1982) writes, "The process must run its own course, not being interfered with or prevented from happening, so that its ultimate purpose can be accomplished: the freeing of the individual to reinvest emotional energies in purposeful activities and new relationships."

The term recovery usually implies a return to a previously healthy state, as when one recovers from an illness. Recovery from loss, however, does not imply a return to the state which existed prior to the loss.

Parkes and Weiss (1983) comment, "Those who recover from bereavement do not return to being the same people that they had been before their marriages or before their spouses' deaths. Nor do they forget the past and start a new life. Rather, they recognize that change has taken place, accept it, examine how their basic assumptions about themselves and their world must be changed and go on from there." Bowlby (1980), also referring to the final stages of successful mourning, writes, "Nevertheless, if all goes well, this previous phase may soon begin to alternate with a phase during which (the mourner) starts to examine the new situation he (sic) finds himself in and to consider ways of meeting it. . . . This redefinition of self and situation is as painful as it is crucial, if only because it means relinquishing finally all hope that the lost person can be recovered and the old situation reestablished."

Freud, in his classic "Mourning and Melancholia," first published in 1917, observes, "Reality passes its verdict—that the object no longer exists—upon each single one of the memories and hopes through which the libido was attached to the lost object, and the ego, confronted as it were, over a decision whether it will share this fate, is persuaded by the sum of its narcissistic satisfactions in being alive, to sever its attachment to the nonexistent object."

These descriptions of successful mourning each imply that a necessary step in recovery involves giving up the fantasy that the lost relationship can be recovered. It is the theoretical position of Bowlby (1980) (see also Herz Brown 1988; Parkes and Weiss 1983; and Rynearson 1987) that many who exhibit unresolved bereavement unconsciously act, think, and feel as if the dead were still alive.

Therapeutic Considerations

Two groups of people can benefit from grief counseling: those who know that they can and those who do not.

Everyone suffers loss, but as Parkes (1985) and Raphael (1984) point out, not all bereaved persons need psychotherapy. Sanders (1989) implies that those who need help will seek it, when she writes, "The bereaved usually know what their needs are."

However, many whose lives have become to some degree dysfunctional are unaware of the impact of incomplete mourning. Krupp et al. (1986) describe how individuals who suffer from a wide variety of cognitive, affective, and behavioral symptoms often cannot identify unresolved mourning of a previous loss as the unifying theme. In taking the history of a presenting problem, inquiry into the timing, number, and nature of losses should be routine.

Assessment and Intervention

Table 19.3 describes some behaviors, effects or cognitions typically encountered at the various stages.

The work of Bowlby (1980) and Parkes and Weiss (1983) provides the therapist with a tool for assessing the development of the grief process. Sanders's comments concerning the nature of grief therapy are germane to work done both with individuals who recognize the impact of the death on the state of their current functioning and those who do not. She writes,

> . . . because the grief process is supported by a number of theories, the type of psychotherapy used will depend on the particular training and orientation of the therapist. Yet with any of the theoretical foundations, the care giver must recognize that *grief is a process rather than a state*. [Emphasis mine.] It is not a linear process, however, because grief has so many cul de sacs, swoops, and pauses. In many cases the bereaved can be stuck in one phase or another for an extended period, feeling unable ever to move on. Nonetheless, the object of psychotherapy is to make the process as progressive as possible so that the bereaved moves in the desired direction, despite the regressions or delays encountered along the way.

An understanding of the nature of successful mourning and of the works of Bowlby (1980) and Parkes and Weiss (1983) provides the counselor with the essential therapeutic tasks: to make overt

Table 19.3 A Model for Assessment

Process Stage	Typical affective, cognitive-behavioral responses.
Numbing	Emotional denial. Aware of the death but no emotional acceptance.
Yearning and Searching	Anger. At times behaves as if the deceased were still alive: "hearing" his or her voice, expecting the deceased to return at the normal hour. Angry outbursts at the deceased, the self, the doctor, the hospital, well-wishers, God, etc.
Disorganization and Despair	Depression. Disorganized and confused. Still defines self in terms of relationship with the deceased. Feels lost and disconnected.
Resolution	
Intellectual Recognition	Unable to answer the question "Why?" Fearful of establishing new relationships lest they be lost for "no reason."
Emotional Acceptance	Fearful of being overwhelmed by grief, pain, or remorse. Goes over the same memories. No change in the "obsessive review."
Identity Transformation	Believes, e.g., "I can't be happy unless she is still alive." Inattentive to the possibility of new satisfactions. Fails to turn to the family for nurturant needs, friends for social needs, work or school for achievement needs.

any covert refusals to accept the permanence of loss, any ambivalent feelings toward the deceased, any sense of victimization, or any negative self-images, etc. Grief therapy also recognizes the importance of integrating the past with the present, as this integration helps the bereaved to reform his or her identity. In addition to the tasks of decathexis (Freud 1917; Rynearson 1987) and identity reformation (Bowlby 1980; Parkes and Weiss 1983), Rando (1984) suggests that a new, transformed relationship with the deceased should be considered a therapeutic goal.

Table 19.4 derived from the work of Parkes and Weiss (1983), offers a suggested course for counseling. The numerous injunctions warning against the assumption that any two griefs are identical are, of course, applicable.

Part II: Mourning in the Family System

Death, Mourning, and Linear Thinking

The dominance of psychoanalytic thinking in the formulation of theories about the nature of both normal and incomplete mourning is well documented (Frantz 1984; Herz Brown 1988). Gelcer (1983) concludes succinctly that "Psychotherapy for unresolved grief reaction is still, by and large, based on Freudian and psychoanalytic assumptions" (p. 502).

Psychoanalytic formulations, along with medical and behavioral ones, are based on linear logic. Nichols (1984) describes the application of linear thinking to problems of adjustment: "Before the advent of family therapy, explanations of psychopathology were based on linear

Table 19.4 A Suggested Course for Counseling

Stages of Counseling	Counseling Goal	Indicators of Growth	Contraindicators of Growth
Early	Intellectual recognition and understanding of the loss.	Formulation of a story, believed by the bereaved, which "settles" the question of "Why?"	Failure to establish new relationships for fear that these, too, will be lost.
Middle	Emotional Acceptance	Diminished fear of being overwhelmed by grief, pain or remorse. Does not avoid the "obsessive review."	No change in the content of the "obsessive review."
Late	Formulation of a new identity.	Creation of self-definitions in the present, which no longer involve the deceased.	Statements such as, "I can't be happy unless I feel she is still my wife." Inattentive to the possibility of new satisfactions. Failure to use family for nurturant needs, friends for social needs, work or school for achievement needs.

models—medical, psychodynamic, and behavioral. In all of these, etiology was conceived in terms of prior events—disease, emotional conflict, or learning history—which caused symptoms in the present. The patient is the locus of the problem in all of these models" (p. 83). Linear thinking is based then, on the traditional Western logic which suggests that A→B→C.

Perhaps there is something about the nature of death which promotes linear thinking. Death occurs at a discrete moment in time. Therapists and theorists trace its effects on individuals and families from that point in time. The underlying assumption seems linear. Death causes things to happen to people and their families.

Family Therapy and Circularity

The discipline of family therapy embraces many schools of thought. Some place great emphasis on prior events, some do not. Some emphasize the nature of the communication among family members, while others underscore the structural relationships among the various subsystems which comprise the family. Some focus on the presenting problem, while others see specific symptoms as indications of system-wide dysfunction.

The disparate schools, however, all share certain basic assumptions. Perhaps the core concept is that of circular causality. The position that complex systems behave in ways which transcend Western logic grew from a dissatisfaction with linear models. Hoffman (1981) writes,

> After decades of strict adherence to these (linear) models, a new conception began to emerge. Evidence . . . supported the growing disenchantment with the linear, historical view. If one saw a person with a psychiatric affliction in a clinician's office, it would be easy to assume that he or she suffered from an intrapsychic disorder arising from the past. But if one saw the same person with his or her family, in the context of current relationships, one began to see something quite different. One would see communications and behaviors from everybody present, composing many circular causal loops that played back and forth, with the behavior of the afflicted person only part of a larger, recursive dance. (p. 6–7)

Circularity, then, contends that the behaviors and communications of every individual and subsystem which comprise the system contribute to, and in turn, are affected by, the behaviors and communications of the other individuals and subsystems. Nuclear families also behave in a circular fashion with extended families and with certain social institutions such as schools or hospitals. The assumptions of circular thinking can be graphically represented as

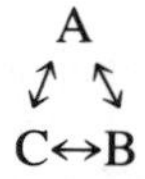

Bateson (1979) suggests that while the assumptions of linear thinking may allow for the making of good predictions in the study of physical objects, a circular view is more appropriate when living creatures interact. Hoffman (1981) provides an illustration:

> The classic example of this viewpoint is the difference between kicking a stone and kicking a dog. In the case of the stone, the energy transmitted by the kick will make the stone move a certain distance,

> which can be predicted by the heaviness of the stone, the force of the kick, and so forth. But if a man kicks a dog, the reaction of the dog does not depend wholly on the energy of the man, because the dog has its own source of energy, and the outcome is unpredictable. What is transmitted is news about the relationship—the relationship between the man and the dog. The dog will respond in one of a number of ways, depending upon the relationship and how it interprets the kick. It may cringe, run away, or try to lick the man. But the behavior of the dog in turn becomes news for the man, which may modify his own subsequent behavior. If for instance the man is bitten, he may think twice before kicking that particular dog again. (p. 7)

Grief and the Family Life Cycle

A second line of thinking which enjoys wide acceptance in the family therapy community and which appears to be of value in understanding mourning from a systems perspective is that of the family life cycle.

Life cycle theory suggests that both families and individuals develop through a predictable sequence of stages. Symptoms are reframed as developmental blocks which impede the transition from one stage of the cycle to the next. Transitions become necessary as the system's typical patterns of interaction grow increasingly incapable of dealing with pressures arising from the growth and development of its individual members and from the demand that their roles must conform to societal norms.

Although first presented by Haley (1973) and Solomon (1973), the names most closely associated with the theory are those of Carter and McGoldrick (1980, 1988). Families are plotted along three axes: the time dimension, the vertical dimension, and the horizontal dimension.

The Time Dimension

With respect to time, Carter and McGoldrick (1988) write, "Although family process is by no means linear, it exists in the linear dimension of time. From this we can never escape" (p. 7). Implicit in this statement is the imperative to view systems as evolving, developing, growing, and alive. To assume that the system today is the same as it was yesterday or that it will be the same tomorrow is to make a grave reductionistic error.

The temporal sequence of events in a family's history is considered by McGoldrick and Walsh (1983), who call for an "evolutionary" view of family processes. In their view, "recognition of historical influence does not necessarily imply a linear-causal assumption: that a particular past experience resulted in current behavior or dysfunction (A caused B), or even that a set of past experiences combined to produce current patterns (A+B caused C). It is an error to regard origin as determining outcome."

McGoldrick and Walsh (1983) suggest, however, that to completely ignore the influence of history is an error: "Family systems, their structural patterns, communication processes, and dynamics develop, are maintained, and are altered over time. . . . In no system can a behavior in the present be comprehended apart from its motion in time, which is history. No system is ever static. Only by some understanding of where it is coming from can one understand the direction in which it is heading. . . . Since human beings rarely operate only in relation to immediate circumstances, it is not surprising when their behavior is not comprehensible solely from observations of the present."

The Vertical Dimension

Carter and McGoldrick (1988) argue that while the past is not the cause of the present, it is an aid to understanding the family *in* the present. They believe that families approach developmental demands and nodal events with idiosyncratic patterns, that these patterns are transmitted over time and across generations, and that these patterns can become rigid and replicated.

A family, as described by these authors, "comprises the entire emotional system of at least three, and now frequently four generations" (p. 6). This multi-generational definition refers to the vertical dimension: "The vertical flow in a system includes patterns of relating and functioning that are transmitted down the generations of a family primarily through the mechanism of emotional triangling. . . . It includes all the family attitudes, taboos, expectations, labels, and loaded issues with which we grew up. One could say that these aspects of our lives are like the hand we are dealt: they are the given. What we do with them is the issue for us" (p. 8).

A nuclear family reflects the content of its vertical dimension. Adaptive as well as non-adaptive legacies have an impact on the system's functioning. A salient question for family therapists doing grief work is, "What is this family's inheritance with regard to dealing with death?" As Carter and McGoldrick (1988) point out, ". . . the tremendous life-shaping impact of one generation on those following is hard to overestimate" (p. 7).

The Horizontal Dimension

As families move through time with their transgenerational inheritance, they experience the stress associated with developing through the predictable life cycle stages: launching the young adult, marriage, having children, adolescence, launching the children, aging. These stages along with those unpredictable stressors such as firings, movings, and deaths, comprise the horizontal dimension.

Stress and the Life Cycle

Sufficient stress along either the vertical or the horizontal axis can render a family dysfunctional. The stage is set for major upheaval when, at some specific time, both vertical and horizontal stressors arise and intersect.

Of particular interest to therapists engaged in grief therapy are Eliot's (1955) observation that crisis often ensues when a family either gains or loses a member and Holmes and Rahe's (1967) finding that ten of the fourteen greatest stress-producers involve the gaining or losing of a family member.

Drawing from clinical experience and a review of the literature, Herz Brown (1988) assesses the impact of death at various stages of the life cycle. She found that, generally, the further along the cycle the death occurs, the less stress on the family. The death of a grandparent is "developmentally appropriate." If the aged person has become incapable of caring for him or herself prior to dying, the stress escalates dramatically. In addition, the death of a member of the older generation increases system stress in that it brings the next generations closer to its own demise.

Herz Brown (1988) writes,

> Whereas an elderly family member is viewed as having completed his/her life and has few remaining tasks and responsibilities, serious illness or death at another

> life cycle phase is considered to end an incomplete life; it does not follow the normative course of life. The timing is off, it is out of sync . . . those deaths or serious illnesses whose victims are in the prime of life are the most disruptive to the family. This can be partly understood by the fact that it is in this phase of the life cycle that the individual has the greatest responsibilities. The death . . . of the individual at this point in the life cycle leaves the family with a gap in function that is difficult, if not impossible to fill, and may therefore prevent the family from completing its life cycle tasks. (p. 464)

Difficulty in completing life cycle tasks after the death of a parent has special connotations if the children are adolescents. Herz Brown (1988) points out that the major task for families with adolescents is the mutual weaning of parents and children. Should the death cause the adolescent to adopt the role of parentified child, he or she will be bound tightly to the family. The usual rebellion and extra-familial focus employed to facilitate weaning will be unavailable (p. 465).

The death of a child is one of life's most tragic events. Yet from an instrumental point of view, children have few responsibilities; families do not need them to function. Herz Brown (1988) speculates that, "Since most parents view children as extensions of their hopes and dreams in life, the loss of the child is an existential wound of the worst kind. How does one get over watching the child one created and raised die?" (p. 466).

The answer to this question is: not very easily. The author points to statistics which indicate that in from 70 to 90 percent of cases in which the child died in a hospital, the separation or divorce of the parents ensued. Families fared better when the child died at home or in a hospice.

The death of a family member represents the loss to the family of functions, roles, and relationships.

A Systemic Perspective

After mentioning the preponderance of psychodynamic thinking around the question of grief, Herz Brown (1988) writes, "However, there is much clinical evidence from family therapy that death is a systemic process in which all members participate in mutually reinforcing ways, with the symptom bearer being just one of those directly or indirectly affected by the loss of a family member" (p. 457).

Frantz (1984) warns family therapists who do grief work that they must adapt the techniques and theories of individual psychotherapy. Any such adaptations will certainly involve the application of circular causality and life cycle considerations: What impact has the death had on individuals? How have the behaviors of individuals and subsystems mutually and reciprocally changed? Which redundant patterns maintain incomplete mourning? Which produce a symptom-bearer for the family? At what stage in the family life cycle does the death occur? What are the vertical legacies, the horizontal stressors?

At least three sorts of families may seek therapeutic help as a result of the death of a loved one: those who are in crisis just prior to, at the time of, or shortly following the death; those who have suffered interminable grief over a long period of time following a loss; and those who see no connection between their current difficulties and unresolved mourning. Herz Brown (1988) and Rando (1984) provide excellent outlines for intervention with the first type of family. Berman and Bufferd (1986), Black and Urbanowicz (1987), Soricelli and Utech (1985), Valeriote and Fine (1987) and Wood (1987) provide insight to and suggest interventions with them. Rosen's (1988) article on interminable grief provides an excellent theoretical discussion of the problem and outlines a course of treatment in great detail.

The therapist is presented with a far more difficult assessment-intervention problem by those families who do not relate current dysfunction to previous loss.

Unresolved Grief and the Family System

It was suggested earlier that the denial of the permanence of loss lies at the heart of unresolved grief reactions in the individual psyche. Herz Brown (1988) has described a similar phenomenon within families:

> Families (with unresolved mourning issues) do not generally seek treatment for issues relating to a recent or past death. Treatment is often sought for a problem or dysfunction in a family member or relationship. Although the symptoms are part of the emotional shock wave following the death, the family does not view the death as important to the current problem and so will not mention it. Unless the therapist routinely does a genogram and a chronology of important life events, he or she may not suspect that a death has occurred in the family. If the therapist mentions the relationship between the symptom development and the death, the family will deny it or say it is coincidence. Pushing the issues will only bring more denial, and possible withdrawal from treatment. (p. 479)

Rosen (1988) defines unresolved grief operationally as a reaction to one or more previous losses that have not been fully mourned. He adds, "Furthermore, the mourner will not connect the previous death with his or her present state of mind, having chosen to focus all emotion on (some other issue)" (p. 190). The author describes a family in treatment during four years of interminable grief over the death of a teenage member. Only after a detailed family history and genogram were taken did inquiry with the parents reveal that the current situation was directly related to the unresolved loss of a stillborn sixteen years earlier.

Gelcer (1983) describes the teenage daughter of a reconstituted family as the identified patient in a dysfunctional family system. The girl has been diagnosed as severely depressed and borderline psychotic. Family therapy indicated that her symptoms were metaphoric expressions of the family's inability to mourn the death of the biological mother seven years prior to the onset of the girl's current problems.

Fulmer (1983) reports an enmeshed mother-son dyad in a single-parent family system. The presenting problem was the son's academic underachievement. Using a structural analysis, the author reports that this problem, as well as the enmeshment and the mother's depression, were all related to the mother's unresolved mourning of the death of her parents and of the loss of her marriage.

Unresolved Mourning: Considerations for Family Therapists

Are the authors above, all systemic thinkers, approaching the question of unresolved mourning from a linear perspective? Do they believe that the death of a loved one begins a chain of events which may result in individual symptomology? Are they suggesting that the only contribution of a systemic approach to unresolved mourning is the observation that death may also begin a chain of events which can cause family dysfunction?

One answer to these rhetorical questions is found in the *Handbook of Family Therapy* (1981). In attempting to illustrate a theoretical point, H. J. Aponte and J. M. Van Deusen (1981) write, "Furthermore, if an adolescent son of this marriage were to begin acting out in a delinquent manner because of what was happening between his parents, the youngster's problems would be a derivative of the parents' difficulties" (p. 316).

The editors' note which follows this statement reads, "While the authors may appear to be speaking here about unidirectional causality ('because of what was happening between his parents'), this is not the case; indeed, such a position would be greatly at variance with the fundamental assumption in structural therapy of circular causality. Rather, in this illustration, the therapist may choose to *punctuate* a long string of interactions in this way for the purpose of intervening into the sustaining structure of the son's acting out" (p. 316).

Preexistence of Dysfunctional Family Patterns

Death may punctuate "a long string of interactions" with an exclamation point. Unresolved mourning within the individual is often the result of a conflicted or dependent relationship with the deceased: those who have lived poorly with the living will live poorly with the dead. These conflictual dyadic relationships will affect and be affected by the entire family system long before the death. Dysfunctional communications, incongruent hierarchies, and role confusions might ensue. Family secrets, loyalties, and rules concerning the "correct" way to deal with losses of all sorts may remain active but unspoken. One might find triangular relationships, deflection of anxiety onto children, spousal dysfunction, or marital conflict. It may be that families which are dysfunctional after the death of an ambivalently loved one were dysfunctional, or only marginally functional, prior to the death. The increase in systemic anxiety following loss may exaggerate or magnify family processes and/or structures which existed, perhaps latently, prior to the death.

Whether fully functional, at-risk, or dysfunctional, a system which loses a member is faced with a life cycle demand: to adapt. Here is the point of therapeutic intervention.

The Nature of Change

There is no agreement among theorists as to the nature of the change process. Within the family therapy community, the dominant position concerning the nature of life cycle transitions is that they are the results of discontinuous, irreversible second-order changes: Once a family makes a leap to a new organization, it cannot return to its previous state. For example, a family which has learned to function well and to be happy following the father's death will be unable to behave as if it wished that he were still alive.

This is the position taken by Hoffman (1988). She proposes a "natural history" for discontinuous change:

> First the patterns that have kept the family system in a steady state relative to its environment begin to work badly. New conditions arise for which these patterns were not designed. Ad hoc solutions are tried, and sometimes work, but usually have to

> be abandoned. Irritation grows over small but persisting difficulties. The accumulation of dissonance eventually forces the entire system over an edge, into a state of crisis, as the homeostatic tendency brings on ever intensifying corrective sweeps that get out of control. The end point of what cybernetic engineers call a 'runaway' is either that the system breaks down, that it creates a new way to monitor the same homeostasis, or that it simultaneously takes a leap to an integration that will deal better with the changed field. (p. 93–94)

Therapists who view change in this way conduct therapy in order to trigger second-order change through a discontinuous leap. They rely heavily on the use of paradoxical intervention.

Breunlin (1983) views change differently—as continuous rather than discontinuous. This theoretical view gives rise to a different therapeutic approach. The four stages of therapy mirror the changes which the family is going through: engaging the family, unbalancing the family, dealing with the consequences of change, and normalizing family functioning.

Unlike those theorists who view transitional change as discontinuous, Breunlin (1983) takes the position that no change occurs without some negative consequences and that these consequences can lead to the undoing of the change: the family without Father may return to being the family who wants Father alive. Regret, anger, fear, and denial of the loss of the previous relationship are some of these negative forces. Successful therapy must address these: ". . . it is not enough to say that the benefit of change will be self-reinforcing or that change itself is permanent because it is irreversible" (p. 7).

Any family therapist engaged in grief therapy (any therapist engaged in any form of therapy, for that matter) would be wise to take a position on the nature of change. Is it discontinuous, continuous, or both? How one conducts therapy derives from this basic position. It is interesting to note the similarities between the nature of systemic change and the individual's reaction to loss. The immediate tendency is to deny the reality of the loss; recovery involves evolution to a new state, not a return to an old one.

Crystallization of Symptom-Maintaining Structure

Herz Brown's (1988) admonition—families may be so resistant to the suggestion that previous loss affects current problems that they leave treatment—should be taken seriously. She writes, "The family therapist must remain relevant to the problem presented by the family, coaching the family in that area and beginning to ask questions about the dead family member's relationships. Frequently, after the initial problem has been relieved to some extent, the focus of the sessions begins to shift. The goal of treatment becomes a resolution of the past relationship" (p. 479).

If the family therapist is faced with the problem of unresolved mourning that is not mentioned at the beginning of therapy, one answer may be found in Minuchin's (1974) work on structural therapy. The unresolved mourning will have had its effects on family and subsystem boundaries, hierarchy incongruities, alliances, and cross-generational coalitions. These structures in turn will have helped to maintain the unresolved mourning. Modifications in structure, which in a circular fashion maintain both the incomplete mourning and the presenting problems, can be altered through therapy even without the family's recognition of the impact of its previous loss on its current functioning. Working to achieve this move should help the therapist avoid resistance that might arise if the family were forced to directly confront that previous loss.

This therapeutic ploy is used by Fulmer (1988) and Hare-Mustin (1979). Although addressing a somewhat different therapeutic dilemma than the one discussed here, Hare-Mustin's comments are important to the therapist who must deal with a family which is invested in denying the importance of previous loss. She writes, "The family members were not articulate or used to self-examination and self-disclosure. It became apparent in early sessions that the family could respond to a structural approach that focused on behavioral aspects of daily living, clarifying generational boundaries, and assigning tasks to improve family functioning" (p. 51).

Fulmer (1983) contends that much of the enmeshment found in dysfunctional single-parent families is understandable in terms of repetitive recursive patterns which maintain the enmeshment, the symptoms, and the incomplete mourning. He calls for the use of joining, framing and reframing the mourning process, enactment of the mourning, boundary making, and reframing. Reframing the sadness associated with mourning and the protracted length of the process as normal may bring the family relief. Feelings of hopelessness, anger, depression, and disorganization—reframed as incomplete mourning—may empower a family and allow its members to see the conceptual unity which runs through the entire dysfunctional mass. Reframing a child's acting-out as loyalty in the service of keeping the parent from becoming depressed may also serve the system well.

Fulmer (1983) believes that the rules of the system become overt and open to change through the enactment of mourning. By insisting that the family dwell on its loss, the therapist exceeds the family's threshold for pain. Implicit rules and patterns become explicit: "Mother must not be allowed to cry." "We children will act up in order to deflect her sadness." "When the kids act up, I, Mother, will direct my attention outward to them and away from my own grief; I will label them as bad, not sad."

The therapist may find other effective structural moves. Herz Brown's (1988) observation that the autonomy of adolescents may be threatened when death occurs during that life cycle phase raises the question of boundaries. The formation of appropriate boundaries is a life cycle task for all families with adolescents. If death has occurred, the system's need for a parentified child may make the developmental task more difficult. In those families in which an enmeshment between the adolescent and parental holons arises after the loss of a loved one, the therapist may employ some of the boundary-making techniques suggested by Minuchin and Fishman (1981).

Closing Off Communication Flow

At some point in the therapy, the question of the system's openness must be confronted. In discussing the myriad forms in which family dysfunction can become manifest as a result of loss by death, McGoldrick and Walsh (1983) speculate that communication difficulties are common to all. They write, "Distorting and obscuring communication processes, more than the death per se, are the prime pathogenic elements in the loss of a family member. In our view it is the cutoff and emotional isolation, which follow such distorted communication, that have the most devastating effects on the future evolution of the system." In light of this significant clinical observation, the therapist should attempt to identify, make overt, and correct such distorted communications. Gelcer (1983) reports that in her work the most common striking paradox to be found in families with unresolved grief is that the dead are regarded as living and the living regarded as dead. The "ghost" is involved in all triangular relationships, and there is a close connection between the behavior of the identified patient and the role of the dead member in the family life cycle. So long as the "deceased member's role is maintained alive in the family, other members' roles are rendered dead or inactive; progress in the accomplishment of the family life cycle tasks is arrested." Families, as well as individuals, can think, feel, and behave as if the dead were alive.

Gelcer (1983) suggests that the family be given assignments which symbolize the finality of death. For example, one couple whose child had died was told to build a "new home" for themselves without the input of grandparents or children. They were to check every room, every piece of furniture. What they both liked was to remain. What either objected to was to be discarded or sold.

Herz Brown (1988) notes that the dead family member is often viewed unfairly, either idealized or calumniated. The facts surrounding the death are often confused and not well recalled. The family may never speak of the dead person, or may overfocus on him or her as if the dead were still alive. Herz Brown (1988) summarizes her position on family therapy for unresolved mourning in this way:

> The first [task] is to help the family members obtain a clear view of the details around the death, and a balanced view of the person who has died. Often accomplishing these goals means that the therapist must coach the individual to make the "dead person" and the death real; visits to the grave site and to relatives and friends of the deceased are often helpful in this endeavor. It is also extremely important for the family therapist to take time to deal with the intensity of the feelings that these tasks engender in the individual and to respect the pacing and timing necessary to accomplish these goals. (p. 480)

Perhaps it is at the point of "taking time to deal with the intensity of the feelings that these tasks engender in the individual" that the interaction between the therapist's knowledge or both individual grief and family grief is most powerful.

Conclusions

After outlining some core concepts of individual reactions to loss, this paper has tried to frame mourning in terms of circular causality, the family life cycle, and the basic aspects of systemic thinking. Emphasis has been placed on the assessment and treatment of unresolved mourning. As such, the interplay between the mourning process and the family roles, rules, structures, and subsystems which combine to produce family dysfunction have been highlighted. Obviously, family interactions can also encourage healthy mourning and allow the further growth of both the individual and the larger system.

This is an essay based mainly on other essays and on case studies. Empirical research is called for, to transform the opinions stated and cited here into testable hypotheses. Sound research design utilizing both individual families and groups of families will not only add to the body of knowledge concerning the nature of the grief experience, it will also foster the growth of family therapy as a science.

References

Aponte, H. J., and J. M. Van Deusen (1981) "Structural family therapy," in A. Gurman and D. Kniskern, eds., *Handbook of Family Therapy*. New York: Brunner/Mazel.

Bateson, G. (1979) *Mind and Nature*. New York: Holt, Rinehart and Winston.

Beck, A. T., et al. (1979) *Cognitive Therapy of Depression*. New York: Guilford Press.

Beletsky, R., and S. Jacobs (1986) "Bereavement, attachment theory and mental disorders," *Psychiatric Annals* 16 (5): 276–80.

Berman, L. C., and R. K. Bufferd (1986) "Family treatment to address loss of adoptive families," *Social Casework* 67 (1): 3–11.

Black, D., and M. A. Urbanowicz (1987) "Family intervention with bereaved children," *Journal of Child Psychology and Psychiatry and Allied Studies* 28 (3): 467–76.

Bowlby, J. (1961). "Childhood mourning and its implications for psychiatry," *American Journal of Psychiatry* 118: 481–98.

——— (1980). *Attachment and Loss,* vol. 3—*Loss*. New York: Basic Books.

Breunlin, D. C. (1983) "Therapy in stages: A life cycle view," in H. Liddle, ed., *Clinical Implications of the Family Life Cycle,* in J. Hansen, ed., *The Family Therapy Collections*. Rockville, Md: Aspen Systems.

Carter, B., and M. McGoldrick, eds. (1980) *The Changing Family Life Cycle: A Framework for Family Therapy*. New York: Gardner Press.

——— (1988) *The Changing Family Life Cycle: A Framework for Family Therapy,* 2nd ed. New York: Gardner Press.

Chigier, E., ed. (1988). *Grief and Bereavement in Contemporary Society*. London: Freund Publishing House.

Eliot, T. D. (1955) "Handling family strains and shocks," in H. Becker and R. Hill, *Family, Marriage and Parenthood*. Boston: Heath.

Frantz, T. T. (1984) "Helping parents whose child has died," in T. Frantz, ed., *Death and Grief in the Family,* in Hansen, *The Family Therapy Collections*.

Freud, S. (1937 [1917]) "Mourning and melancholia," in *The Standard Edition of the Complete Psychological Works of Sigmund Freud,* vol. 14, London: Hogarth Press—*1914–1916*.

Fulmer, R. H. (1983). "A structural approach to unresolved mourning in single parent family systems," *Journal of Marital and Family Therapy* 9 (3): 259–69.

Garfield, R. (1982). "Mourning and its resolution for spouses in marital separation," in L. Messinger, ed., *Therapy with Remarriage Families,* in Hansen, *The Family Therapy Collections*.

Gaylin, W. (1985) "Mourning: New research affirms its benefits," *The New York Times,* 5 February.

Gelcer, C. (1983) "Mourning is a family affair," *Family Process* 22: 501–516.

Gurman, A. S., and D. P. Kniskern (1981) *Handbook of Family Therapy*. New York: Brunner/Mazel.

Haley, J. (1973) *Uncommon Therapy: The Psychiatric Techniques of Milton Erikson*. New York: W. W. Norton.

Hare-Mustin, R. T. (1979) "Family therapy following the death of a child," *Journal of Marital and Family Therapy* 5 (2): 51–59.

Herz Brown, F. (1988) "The impact of death and serious illness on the family life cycle," in Carter and McGoldrick, *The Changing Family Life Cycle*.

Hoffman, L. (1981) *Foundations of Family Therapy: A Conceptual Framework for Change*. New York: Basic Books.

——— (1988) "The family life cycle and discontinuous change," in Carter and McGoldrick, *The Changing Family Life Cycle*.

Holmes, T. H., and R. H. Rahe (1967) "The social readjustive rating scale," *Journal of Psychosomatic Research* 11: 213–18.

Horowitz, J. (1984) *Personality Styles and Brief Psychotherapy*. New York: Basic Books.

Kerr, M. E., and M. Bowen (1988) *Family Evaluation*. New York: W. W. Norton.

Krupp, G. (1965) "Identification as a defense against anxiety in coping with loss," *International Journal of Psychoanalysis* 46: 303–314.

Krupp, G., F. Genovese, and T. Krupp (1986) "To have and have not: Multiple identifications in pathological bereavement," *Journal of the American Academy of Psychoanalysis* 14 (3): 337–48.

Lehman, D. R., C. B. Wortman, and A. F. Williams (1987). Long-term effects of losing a spouse or child in a motor vehicle crash," *Journal of Personality and Social Psychology* 52 (1): 218–31.

Lindemann, E. (1944). "Symptomatology and management of acute grief," *American Journal of Psychiatry* 101: 141–48.

McGoldrick, M., and F. A. Walsh (1983). "A systemic view of family history and loss," in L. Wolberg and M. Aronson, eds., *Group and Family Therapy, 1983*. New York: Brunner/Mazel.

Meichenbaum, D. (1977) *Cognitive Behavior Modification: An Integrative Approach*. New York: Plenum Press.

Minuchin, S. (1974) *Families and Family Therapy*. Cambridge, Mass.: Harvard University Press.

Minuchin, S., and H. C. Fishman (1981) *Family Therapy Techniques*. Cambridge, Mass.: Harvard University Press.

Nichols, M. (1984) *Family Therapy: Concepts and Methods*. New York: Gardner Press.

Osterweis, M., F. Solomon, and M. Green, eds. (1984) *Bereavement: Reactions, Consequences and Care*. Washington, D.C.: National Academy Press.

Parkes, C. M., and R. S. Weiss (1983). *Recovery from Bereavement*. New York: Basic Books.

Rando, T. A. (1984) *Grief, Dying and Death: Clinical Interventions for Caregivers*. Champaign, Ill.: Research Press.

Raphael, B. (1977) "Preventive intervention with the recently bereaved, "*Archives of General Psychiatry* 34: 1450–54.

——— (1984) *The Anatomy of Bereavement*. London: Hutchinson.

Rosen, E. J. (1988) "Family therapy in cases of interminable grief for the loss of a child," *Omega: Journal of Death and Dying* 19 (3): 187–202.

Rynearson, E. K. (1986) "Psychological effects of unnatural dying on bereavement," *Psychiatric Annals* 16 (5): 272–75.

——— (1987) "Psychotherapy of pathologic grief: Revisions and limitations," *Psychiatric Clinics of North America* 10 (3): 487–99.

Sanders, (1987) *Grief: The Mourning After*. New York: John Wiley.

Solomon, M. (1973) "A developmental conceptual premise for family therapy," *Family Process* 12: 179–88.

Soricelli, B. A., and C. L. Utech (1985) "Mourning the death of a child: The family and group process," *Social Work* 30 (5): 429–34.

Valeriote, S., and M. Fine (1987) "Bereavement following the death of a child: Implications for family therapy," *Contemporary Family Therapy* 9 (3): 202–217.

Weiss, R. S. (1975) *Marital Separation*. New York: Basic Books.

Wood, B. (1987) "Survival kit for the holidays: A grief workshop approach," *Journal of Applied Family and Child Studies* 36 (3): 237–41.

Zisook, S., S. Schuchter, and M. Schuckit (1985) "Factors in the persistence of unresolved grief among psychiatric outpatients," *Psychosomatics* 26 (6): 497–503.

CHAPTER TWENTY

DISCOVERING MEANING WITH FAMILIES

John Mince, Ph.D.

"Meaning, understanding, and language never remain static in dialogue. They are always becoming history on the way to change."

Anderson and Goolishian (1988)

"We are picturing the family as an active initiator: a historian of its past, an interpreter of its present, and a designer of its future."

Reiss (1981)

Introduction

This chapter will take the reader through the processes of a paradigm shift in family therapy. A paradigm shift always represents a type of revolution in our way of thinking and conceptualizing a problem and its solutions (Kuhn 1970). The present paradigm shift moves the practice and theory of family therapy from a cybernetic base to a linguistic base. This does not mean that systemic metaphors are no longer useful for conceptualizing family transactions, but rather that the new paradigm operates from a different underlying premise. We will demonstrate how the new paradigm actually brings together the cognitive and systemic domains under the overarching concept of self-reference.

This new premise views humans as participants in the construction of their own realities and their own meanings about those realities. The paradigm is characterized by a move away from cybernetic explanations and toward constructivism.

Constructivism is an epistemological explanation of how we come to know what we know. This domain of knowing is of concern and interest to therapists. If therapists can learn more about the nature of knowing, they can learn to design therapies to help families know more about themselves and thus know about change in themselves.

Throughout the last decade, family therapists in particular have raised questions about how a therapist can know a family's problems and how a family can come to know itself differently (Anderson and Goolishian 1988; Boscolo et al. 1987; Tomm 1987, 1988; Dell 1985; and Hoffman 1990).

Constructivism as a way of thinking in family therapy has some distinct advantages over other models. It offers a rigorous biological explanation about how human beings operate internally and socially. While a constructivist-oriented therapy is not informed by a cybernetic logic *per se*, it tends to shift our emphasis in therapy from a first cybernetic to a second cybernetic stance. The constructivist sees the therapist as an integral part of the therapeutic dialogue, not simply as someone who operates upon the family system in a deterministic manner. Constructivism also offers us the opportunity to develop therapeutic methods less invasive to the family and the individual than some other models. That is, it may find ways to help families without having to fit the family into a previously held conceptual schema about its functioning.

Certainly with regard to the present text, constructivism may be seen as an *epistemological explanation*—i.e., an explanation which attempts to clarify how we know what we know about families and change. It is an explanation about the processes of knowing. Constructivism thus brings together the cognitive and the systemic. In this chapter constructivism demonstrates a view of cognition as the fundamental activity of living. Yet it views this cognitive activity as socially participatory, recursive, and self-forming—i.e., as a *systemic* activity.

Background

The background of this paradigm shift from cybernetics to language is particularly rich. As with most paradigm shifts, the actual transition follows slowly from a series of shifts among different thinkers in different fields.

The background offered here presents a series of comments on some of those works which helped the transition to a language-based family therapy. We will look specifically at the fields of philosophy, physics, mathematics, communication, sociology, biology, and family therapy.

Philosophy

In 1855 Emmanuel Kant published *The Critique of Pure Reason*. This major philosophical work was compelling in its refutation of the possibility of directly observing or contacting reality, and thus the impossibility of knowing it directly. Kant (Jahn and Dunne 1987, p. 218) states, "The possibility of experience is, then, that which gives objective reality to all our *a priori* cognitions." Note that he does not state that we can know objective reality, but that experience "gives," or creates, objective reality for the experiencer.

D. P. Dryer clarifies this in his analysis of Kant (Harper and Meerbote 1984), when he describes Kant's central argument: "No one knows the existence of a certain state without observing it, yet observing a certain state does not suffice to enable someone to know that it has come about."

This theme regarding whether or not we can ever directly discover or contact objective reality is taken up by other leading philosophers. In more recent times Ludwig Wittgenstein moved further and further from his original explorations in math and logic toward a philosophy which sought to understand *language* and the logic of *meaning* embedded in language. He thus moved from a concern about the things of the world to a concern about the human construction of the world through language.

Consider the following two quotes from Wittgenstein's *Notebooks 1914–1916* (von Wright and Anscombe 1979). He wrote, "All that we can describe at all could also be otherwise" (p. 80), and "What cannot be imagined cannot even be talked about" (p. 84).

Even though he did not begin to elaborate on his mature philosophy of language until years later, we can see that he was very concerned with *description* and *speech* as acts which somehow filter or create perceived reality. These purely philosophical quotes have surprising applicability to the therapy done by constructivist family therapists today.

Physics

Constructivism in its modern form emerges logically out of a major paradigmatic shift in physics. The newly emergent paradigm uses new methods, new language, and ultimately evokes a new world in place of the old.

The paradigmatic shift from Isaac Newton's predictable and determinable universe to Einstein's relativity and quantum mechanics Uncertainty Principle has marked this as a dramatic century for physicists. The realization that human observation at the quantum level could actually change physical outcomes in measurement launched a wellspring of philosophical writings about the nature of reality, our relationship to nature, and other metaphysical concerns. Fritjof Capra (1982) and Gary Zukav (1979) each wrote works inviting us to understand the beauty of the new physics and of our emerging dialogue with nature.

Ilya Prigogine and Isabelle Stengers, in *Order out of Chaos* (1984), explain that the universe is not simply running down, dying a slow death of increasing entropy (disorder) as the Second Law of Thermodynamics dictates, but rather that information is increasing as disorder increases. Information as an aspect of human consciousness is increasing in complexity even as physical order and organization are decreasing. This insight shifts our view of the universe as a deterministically ending system, to a view of it as a system in the process of becoming. It is becoming through the increase and exchange of information among sentient beings who inhabit it.

By demonstrating for us how dynamic systems move from equilibrium to chaos, and how chaos itself may be seen as a different level of order, these authors help us appreciate the limitations of linear equations in physics and, metaphorically, of linear thinking in human affairs. Chaos from this point of view is not something unnatural, out of control, and to be avoided. Chaos theory offers a new way of seeing the world and developing methods for understanding order where we previously thought none existed. We living beings are involved in chaos at all times and at all levels. Chaos theory (Gleick, 1987) demonstrates far more lifelike forms than linear models can represent. Physicists and biologists have come to understand how generative these non-linear systems actually are. Some chaotic systems have been graphically described on computers (Lorenz 1961). The forms generated demonstrate the new level of order implicit in the previous chaos.

These discoveries and writings shift our thinking away from a family therapy paradigm of information as control in a cybernetic model. While utilizing chaos for therapy may sound strange, it is actually very comforting as a way of thinking about families and their movements through time. Even "chaotically" organized families are in the process of becoming, whether or not they enter into a therapeutic dialogue.

Mathematics

One might not think that the field of mathematics could undergo revolutions. Mathematics and number theory have been developed over millennia and thus appear to be stable. An example of this apparent stability would be the Pythagorean Theorem: A (squared) + B (squared) = C (squared). This theorem was developed at the height of ancient Greek civilization. Its logic and usefulness has held ever since. Indeed, it is taught throughout the world as one of the axioms of plane geometry.

In the second decade of this century, Bertrand Russell and Alfred North Whitehead published a major work on number theory, *Principia Mathematica* (1913). These logician-philosophers considered this their finest work. Indeed, the work was received as a central philosophical work of the British School for nearly twenty years following its publication. However, an Austrian named Kurt Godel wrote a paper in 1931 which has since become famous for its refutation of some of the basic logic in the *Principia*. Godel made a leap of intuition and used mathematical reasoning to explore mathematical reasoning itself (Hofstadter 1979). Thus Godel introduced the notion of self-reference into mathematics.

A translation of Godel's famous theorem states, "All consistent axiomatic formulations of number theory include undecideable propositions" (Hofstadter 1979, p. 17). At first this phrase appears daunting, but its implications for a family therapy of constructivism are apparent. That is, Godel's Theorem represents one more step away from a scientifically and mathematically determinable world of absolute hierarchical categories and toward a world which is regularly self-referential (i.e., the observer is part of what is being observed). It further delineates a world which emerges in a recursive, informing manner. This has not been lost on the new family theorists and therapists. They have begun developing therapeutic methods which emphasize and take advantage of self-reference logic.

Communication

The twentieth century has seen this field also move away from the idea of clear representation between people of some external reality and toward a view that communication is the ongoing construction of realities *by* social interaction among people. Cronen, Johnson, and Lannamann (1982) wrote an article which encompassed the new view of communication and augmented it through new methods of analysis of human communication episodes. Their methods are summed up in their description of a theory entitled the Coordinated Management of Meaning (Cronen, Pearce, and Harris 1979). This theory assumes that meanings are reflexively organized. They describe a six-level hierarchical idealization (classification) which can be thought of as contexts. In ascending order they are:

1. Content
2. Speech Acts
3. Speech Episodes
4. Relationships
5. Life Scripts
6. Cultural Patterns

The authors stress that this is an idealization. Although there may be a hierarchy of contexts within any given communicative contact the hierarchy is reflexive and thus we cannot know how each one contextualizes the other. Consider, for example, the case of two brothers from the same Irish-Catholic family. Both are raised by the same parents, sent to the same parochial schools, and given essentially the same set of parental values. One decides in late adolescence to enter the priesthood and becomes the pride of the family. The other, during his adolescent years, gets into more and more trouble at school and in the neighborhood. Ultimately, he commits several crimes, is caught, convicted, and sent to jail.

Although this scenario is plausible, it is not predictable. Both boys were reared in the same family (Life Script Context) and given the same values (Cultural Patterns), but their processes as a system within a system within yet another system could not be predicted. As one boy grew closer to the family values, the other boy may well have compensated by moving further away from the family values. In this sense, their very siblingship presented a context which operated on both of them. The siblingship context may have been more powerful in terms of outcomes than either the family or the cultural context within which they were raised.

Since there is a tendency in highly religious families to think and speak in terms of "good" and "bad," a natural dialectic was set up which created polar opposite responses in the two boys.

It is patently impossible, therefore, to precisely predict the meaning of any given communicational sequence prior to its enactment.

According to Cronen et al. (1982, p. 101), "meaning at one level of abstraction counts as meaning at another level in light of a context higher than both."

This propensity of communication specialists to see meaning as context-dependent and contexts as reflexively organized in a recursively changing hierarchy is especially relevant for family therapists. If reality is constructed by social interaction, and if the meaning evoked in any communication depends upon contexts which themselves are recursively organized, then families must evoke and maintain their own meaningful realities through self-referential internal communications within an external context.

An aphorism coined by Bandler and Grinder (1975) makes a cogent point with regard to human dyadic communication. It is paraphrased here as follows: The *meaning* of the message we send *is the response* of the person we send it to. This is a powerful way to say that meaning given communicational sequence is constructed by the receiver, not by the sender. The senders can only give the messages they intend to give. They cannot simultaneously know how that message will be constructed by the receiver, because they cannot control the internal, physical, emotional, and contextual variations of the receiver as they give their message. Nor can they control the external contexts within which the message is given. They have only limited control over the sending of the message and an awareness of their own intent. In this sense, intent alone counts for very little. Meaning is what counts for human beings. We construct meanings as we communicate. And finally, these constructed meanings are co-developed within an ecology of contexts which are recursively evoked.

Rommetveit and his associates (1971) researched the activity of people in the process of communicating and concluded that social action could be viewed "as a process of tacking back-and-forth between higher and lower levels of meaning" (Cronen, Johnson and Lannamann, 1979, p. 96). The idea that social meaning is constructed by people operating as context-shapers is also helpful for organizing a family therapy. The therapist comes to understand that he or she is a participant in the evocation of meaning, and that meaning can only be evoked through shifts in context.

This is quite different from the earlier notion that a context should be held constant over the course of therapy. The notion of shifting contexts and levels of meaning also undermines the use of static diagnostic categories and of static hypotheses for therapeutic purposes.

Sociology and Social Psychology

The 20th century scholars who construct and inform this field have been keenly aware of the concept of reality as a social construction. Berger and Luckmann (1966), Gergen (1985), and Reiss (1981) have each contributed to our understanding of the social construction of reality. They have emphasized that what we call our reality is an evoked effect. It is the product of social operations among participants in the maintenance of our society.

A well-known example of the social construction of reality is the adage about our concept of snow in the United States and the words we use to explain and describe snow. When our words and constructions are compared to those of Eskimo societies, we find that Eskimos use more than three times our number of descriptions for snow. They are thus capable of far finer discriminations, offering them a wider gradation of experiences with regard to snow. These finer linguistic distinctions enable the Eskimos more choices with regard to their references. Through social interactions and languages the two societies literally construct different realities about snow.

David Reiss (1981) carried out a series of intriguing experiments regarding the processes by which families construct their own realities. Reiss and his associates worked from the premise that a family operates very much as does a group of scholars with regard to a paradigm. Paradigm shifts follow crises in a scholarly field, when the crisis requires new conceptualizations. They hypothesized that families, too, may utilize crisis for change.

In the concluding section of *The Family's Construction of Reality* (1981, p. 377) Reiss states:

> First the family's shared conception of the world in which it lives plays a central regulatory role in family life. Second, crisis plays a mutative and generative role in family life: in particular it initiates change and development in the family's shared concepts of its world. Third, intimate social groups conserve their shared conceptions of the outside world not through individual memory—the agency familiar to psychologists—but through regular patterns of their own interaction behavior.

Social scientists studying these phenomena have concluded, as have others in this chapter, that one's experience of reality is dependent not so much upon the actual objective state of reality which surrounds a person, but rather upon the social and linguistic constructions with which he or she constructs a personally perceived reality. What becomes immediately apparent is the recursive and systemic aspect of that reality construction. Reality is created as two or more people communicate, and this communication is contextualized by the society within which it occurs.

The implications for family therapists could hardly be more clear. These conceptualizations fly in the face of a therapy which seeks to discover an objective pathology or an objective truth about a family. These are simply not available to us as observer-participants. We are participant observers in the construction of reality as social actors with the family in the process we call therapy.

This represents a dramatic departure

from the past therapeutic stances and postures. Diagnoses, unearthing truths and secrets, searching for the "real" cause of the family's problem become patently impossible to a constructivist way of thinking.

Biology and the New Biology

Biology has traditionally been concerned with the classification of life forms into species, varieties, etc. It was concerned with evolution and thus quite naturally defined life as that which could grow and reproduce itself. More recently biology has focused on understanding how the gene pool changes over time and on the intricacies of the subtle chemical processes of life.

The new biology derives from a different search entirely. Maturana (1970), McCulloch (1988), Varela (1979), and von Foerster (1981) focused their formidable minds on the internal logic of living organization. That is, they sought to describe the processes of living with the rigor of logicians. Their work was so unusual and innovative that they came to be described as epistemological biologists, which implies that they were researching some fundamental biological activities of knowing, of cognition itself.

The special place of the new biology in the recent paradigm shift deserves more expansive presentation.

The New Biology

Maturana and Varela in *Autopoiesis and Cognition* (1980) focused on the formal characteristics of what it means to be alive. These researchers were neurobiologists at the University of Santiago, Chile. Subsequently, their prominence in the field brought them to Harvard where they continued their work, and in 1959, Lettvin, Maturana, McCulloch and Pitts published a seminal though unheralded paper entitled "What the Frog's Eye Tells the Frog's Brain" (McCulloch 1988).

By carefully researching the various roles of nerve cells, ganglia, effectors, and receptors which make up the visual apparatus of the frog, they learned that it was the frog's structure as a living organism which determined what it could see, not what was actually external to the frog. The frog's visual apparatus is so specifically structured to see small moving objects such as insects and worms that it would literally starve if its prey stood absolutely still. The only thing the food-seeking frog responds to is movement. This is because the organization of the retinal rods, cones, and attached neural networks can perceive only movement. The perception of movement reasonably ensures that the frog will catch food and avoid predators.

Experiments such as these led to changes in these biologists' thoughts about living entities. The new biologists eventually realized that the nervous system of living things operates in its connections to the organism's receptors and effectors as a closed system. That is, the structure of the nervous system is such that it cannot know about external reality in any direct manner. It is a closed system which operates through a series of electrochemical structural changes to inform itself about the outside world. The closing of the nervous system was necessary for the eventual development of constructivist theory, and provided a scientific rigor for concepts which had long been discussed in the philosophical community.

From experiments which followed this one, Maturana and his associates began to describe a biology of *structure determinism*. Structure determinism is a theoretical concept which states that a living entity can only perceive, respond, think, believe, and act according to the limits of its own structure as a physical being.

This may seem obvious at first, but such an idea has important implications for our understanding of how life itself works, and more specifically, of how we live, think, and communicate as human beings in this world.

Structure determinism led these biologists inevitably to a philosophy of constructivism.

It is essential for the reader to understand that constructivism has evolved as an epistemological explanation of how we know what we know about families, and how families come to know that which they speak of in therapy. It certainly makes sense for family therapists to study its implications, since they are working with families of human beings, i.e., biological entities who dwell in language.

Essential Concepts of the New Biology

Autopoiesis

This term, coined by Maturana (1979), means essentially the self-organizing capacity of a system. The term grew out of Maturana's insistence that life and the living organization be described and explained in mechanistic ways. That is, autopoietic explanation derives from purely physical events around physical components in a physical universe. There is no necessity to posit other than purely physical causes for a description of living processes.

This being the premise, autopoiesis describes those systems whose organization in the physical domain is made up of component parts. These component parts operate in relation to each other in such a way that their "output" function maintains both the relationship between the component parts and the parts themselves.

While this definition is highly circular, it is a superb leap of intuition on Maturana's part. He understands that living is organization among component parts of an entity in such a way that through its own internal operations, it continues to produce its own component parts, and maintains the relation between those parts.

Imagine the processes of your own body. It is not enough to describe the continuation of your life as the beating of your heart, or the inhalation-exhalation of your lungs. Living insists that these activities continue in order that the relationship between heart and lungs be maintained. It is the relationship between the parts, not the parts in isolation, which gives rise to living. Living is a relation-static operation. Thus, the heart pumping maintains the kidneys filtering, which maintains the lungs respiring, which maintains the stomach digesting, which maintains the brain neurons firing, which maintains the limbs moving, which maintains, etc. Living organization may be seen as a huge circular concatenation of events which close upon themselves in a unifying manner. This is autopoiesis.

A distinctly different type of organization is that of *allopoiesis*. Allopoiesis is the process whereby a group of component parts are systemically related in such a way that their operation of productions yields an outcome which has external utility. Your family car, for example, is an allopoietic machine. Its parts produce motion through their reciprocal relation to each other. That same car cannot produce or maintain its own component parts nor the relation between them. It can only produce motion as its product.

Autopoiesis is the characteristic organization which yields life. Autopoiesis, not growth or reproduction, as the traditional biology has held, is *the* characteristic of living things.

This great insight of the new biologists has become central to all the explanations and descriptions of living which follow from this logic. It is central also to understanding the position of those who consider themselves *radical constructivists*. These are scholars who see autopoiesis and its natural consequences not as an interesting metaphor, but as a physical and mechanistic explanation of the processes of living.

The Closing of the Nervous System

Following the research conducted on numerous organisms, Maturana and his associates realized that the nervous system is organized through its neurons, effectors, and receptors, to coordinate its activities in a series of transactional loops. That is, each perturbation from the outside sets off a chain of actual structural changes within the nervous system. The net effect of the sum total of all the changes is a return to the stability and internal organization held prior to the perturbation.

What became clear to researchers was that the entire nervous system operates as a closed system. It is impossible for that system ever to know anything objectively about the external world which surrounds it. At best it can only generate internal correlations to that world through these looping, internally consistent changes within itself.

They concluded that reality is literally constructed by the organism itself, and that the reality so constructed is determined by that organism's particular structure. Thus, a frog, horse, butterfly, or human generates different realities, even though all share approximately the same "outside world."

Perturbations

All actions, verbal or nonverbal, may be seen as *perturbations*. That is, each statement, action, or omission of an expected action or statement perturbs the nervous system of the receiver in some way. That is, people are literally changed by any perturbation. This is so fundamental that it is easy to miss the point. Any message from the outside literally changes the nervous system. There are clear and detectable structural changes in the nervous system following any perturbation. When Person A uses words or languaging, changes may occur in the linguistic domain of Person B, because human beings dwell in language. A perturbation by Person A may elicit a compensation which changes the linguistic construction of Person B. The second individual automatically undergoes a structural change in his/her nervous system.

Compensation

This *compensation* within the nervous system is the structural change resulting from a perturbation. The automatic compensation then becomes an action, languaging, or other message which forms a new perturbation for Person A, who then automatically compensates with a structural change in his/her nervous system. Thus two or more individuals in interaction are living entities, coupled by a medium of exchange, structurally changing and being changed by each other, in an ongoing recursive sequence.

Mutual Perturbation-Compensation Process

This automatic, reflexive, and recursive process is called the mutual *perturbation-compensation process*. Persons in a conversation or an ongoing relationship can maintain this interaction as long as the degree of compensation required by perturbation is not beyond either one's ability to maintain the logic of the dialogue. For example, consider a man and woman having a conversation in which they begin by expressing the usual social niceties. Their conversation continues. The man begins to speak more and more stridently about aspects of their relationship. Initially, the woman compensates by maintaining the conversation, hoping that it will return to its original tone of social nicety. However, the man becomes caustic in both his verbal remarks and his kinesic expressions. At some point the woman decides to end the dialogue and simply walks away. In effect, her method of compensating finally reached a point at which she broke off that particular speech episode with the man. Be aware that this in no way signals an end to their entire relationship; indeed, the relationship may weather—and even welcome—such storms.

This example illustrates the fact that a verbal mutual perturbation/compensation process (i.e., a dialogue) can reach a point at which it goes beyond the limits which were agreed upon at the outset of the sequence. The woman, therefore, dismissed the man and broke the sequence. The dialogue may begin again at another time.

This rapid and unending spiral of interaction, the perturbation-compensation process, is our key to understanding the notion of a family's co-construction of its reality.

Structural Coupling

In order to survive and maintain themselves in the world, each organism is *structurally coupled* to the medium within which it lives. We humans are structurally coupled to the biosphere: we breathe the air, need a certain amount of heat and light, need food and water, etc. We are coupled to that medium at the deepest levels through our own organic structure. We are also structurally coupled in the domain of social interaction through languaging.

Languaging

The term *language* is a noun form in, for example, Spanish, English, or French. These are culture-specific, interactional forms with their own phonemic, syntactic and semantic regularities. *Languaging* is the action which includes not only words, but all sounds, all messages, all signs, and the omission of any of these. Actions or the omission of actions in a relationship are within the domain of languaging, since they may all be utilized by any participant to construct meanings. Since human beings dwell in language (Maturana 1980; Maturana and Varela 1987) by interacting through languaging, and since human beings internally generate correlations to the external world through the circular processes of a closed nervous system, we conclude that they utilize languaging as the primary process by which to construct their individual and family realities.

This notion of constructing, through languaging, the realities by which we live is particularly meaningful for family therapists. Adopting such a notion, we are struck by the realization that there are no absolute truths available to families or therapists, nor is there any direct contact with objective reality, even though the family and the therapist will construct realities which appear absolutely objective. There can be no true family story in an objective sense. Families dwell in their collective and individual constructions—i.e., domains of actions and languaging—by which they both maintain and change themselves. Thus, the stories, the myths, the legends, the tragedies, and the comedies of life also undergo change.

Structural Coupling and Languaging

As organisms structurally coupled to a biological medium, we know that we would not survive were it not for the structural coupling of two entities: (1) the biological components, and their specific organization of these, which render us human; and (2) the biosphere with its specific component parts and organization.

If there were changes in the component parts or organization of either of these two entities, structural coupling could fail and the human might die. We are just beginning to understand that the inverse of this is also true, that the manner in which human beings treat the biosphere may well decide whether it survives or dies. In either case, we now understand that the fundamental union between the organism and its medium is structural. This coupling is the foundation of life itself.

We are also structurally coupled to a domain of interaction called languaging. Human beings dwell in language as well as in biology. We are not only biological entities, but also social entities. We depend for the maintenance of our own living organization on the continuance of media to which we are structurally coupled.

The structural coupling with language has important implications for the full functioning of human beings. Languaging (the action of using language in transaction with others and with ourselves) can lead to the most intense physical (biological) responses. Consider, for example, being told, "Good riddance!" by an especially beloved person in your life, or simply failing to get an expected telephone call from someone you love. These are both purely linguistic phenomena. They occur in the domain of languaging, yet your response to them will probably be powerful and experienced somatically—i.e., physically. This is an example of languaging and *emotioning* as actions of the human organism within a medium—a social medium to which it is structurally coupled.

Conversely, a person may wake up one morning with a mild virus or flu which leaves him/her "under the weather." S/he may not realize s/he has contracted a mild flu. Often when the symptoms are not yet fully developed, the person cannot find a rational (linguistic) cause for his/her discomfort. Under such circumstances people will language things differently in reference to themselves. They may say they "are depressed," or "Things don't seem to be going right," or they "feel angry toward someone," or they are "suffering from low self-esteem."

They will seek a causal link between their internal discomfort and some linguistically constructed cause. They will transform their early physical symptoms of the flu into linguistic phenomena. This can be observed in their comments about their lives, their internal emotional states, or other people, which may have little or nothing to do with the flu virus and the discomforts they are experiencing.

Construction and Co-construction

Biological events inform our languaging, and linguistic events inform our biology. Both are wound around each other in recursive loops. *We are bio-linguistic beings.*

Precisely because we are bio-linguistic organisms, we are continually in the internal process of constructing our world through a closed nervous system and of co-constructing a world through dialogic interaction with others. It is through structural coupling and co-construction that we maintain or create certain aspects of those conditions necessary to life. One of these necessities for humans is the co-construction of meaning. Maturana's aphorism tells us, "All things stated are stated by an observer" (1980). Our first operation as cognizant beings is to draw a distinction; we literally distinguish some thing (a unity) from all the possible things we observe. The distinction we draw is the first part of the operation by which we evoke or construct a reality.

It should be noted here that the new biologists agree completely with G. S. Brown, whose conclusion in *Laws of Form* (1970) is that the first law of form is to draw a distinction. Brown was a logician, not a biologist, yet there is complete agreement on the fundamental operation of an observer in these two separate fields of inquiry.

Description

We linguistically distinguish our observations through *descriptions*. That is, we transform an observation into a linguistic phenomenon in order to participate in languaging as our primary social operation.

Explanation

After transforming our observations into a linguistic form which we call descriptions, we then explain those descriptions in interactions with others. An *explanation* could be considered the description of our internal descriptions to others. This may appear strange at first, but it makes sense when we consider that we do not directly contact reality, we distinguish something, we language it, and we offer it through languaging to another person.

We do this through those repetitive actions and communications, differentiations and couplings necessary to the maintenance of our organization as living entities. Through these processes we participate in the construction and maintenance of a society which then operates as a medium through which we can continue to live. Beyond this, we continue to maintain the relationships of our component parts—that is, the internal parts of the living unity (our physical bodies) as well as the external parts (our families and social systems)—in such a way that the parts themselves will function to maintain the relationships between them. This process insures their continuation.

This is precisely the point with the most demanding and chaotically organized families: They are simply attempting to survive by the routes and mechanisms best known to them, given the context, interactional history, and meaning that they know (because they have co-constructed it) and to which they are coupled.

Meaning

This entire process of observation, distinction, description, explanation, construction, and co-construction occurs in a belief system which contextualizes it and offers a *meaning* to any persons in interaction. This process is further contextualized by people living within a sociocultural exchange medium in which their co-constructed meaning is reified by interaction with other individuals, families, and institutions—all of whom cooperate to qualify the co-construction as real and objective.

What is real and has meaning thus becomes that which is co-constructed linguistically and interactionally by the human participants in continued interplay with the surrounding sociocultural, linguistic, and interactional environment.

Reality and Objectivity

As each action, word, and communicational episode is co-constructed by the participants through these perpetual processes, individuals are left to believe absolutely in the realities they co-construct. Interactional episodes become their beliefs, values, loyalties, and mythology. In a word, these define the logic of their life as a people.

As family therapists fully appreciate this process—a process which is highly systemic and operationally cognitive at the bio-linguistic level—they can see that any problem or symptom is a part of this continual co-construction of the family. The meaning the family constructs is absolutely real to its members, and that meaning contextualizes all they say and do.

It is this aspect of the constructivist stance which offers trained family therapists the greatest encouragement for linguistic and meaningful change, since the therapists' perturbations through languaging will elicit compensations in the family so that the pain, problem, or symptom may no longer be part of the family's co-construction. That is, it enables the family to co-construct new meanings.

We should emphasize here that the therapist, from a constructivist point of view, will also change, since any participant in the dialogue undergoes structural changes in order to language. This follows naturally from the earlier biological analysis of the processes of living and cognition as a single unified operation.

These changes in internal structure, languaging, and meaning as co-constructed by the family-therapist system may yield observable changes on levels other than the linguistic/meaning level. For instance, the shifts in languaging and meaning may involve shifts (1) at the individual level: attitudes, beliefs, emotions, behaviors, and somatics; (2) at the structural level: boundaries, alliances, and coalitions; and finally (3) at the family narrative level through which meaning is construed and maintained.

Generating linguistic perturbations in the hope of eliciting compensations to change a family's customary transactional patterns and the co-constructed beliefs about those transactions—this is the work of the family therapist. The following section amplifies this theme by presenting the views of family therapists and theorists who work from a constructivist stance.

Family Therapy

This field has undergone fundamental shifts in its concept of families and methods for helping families ameliorate their pain through processes of change. Among these shifts has been the change from a neo-Freudian or psychodynamic position to a behavioral one; from a first cybernetic stance, which saw behavior as circularly organized in a system with rules of operation, to a second cybernetics stance. In the second cybernetic stance, family therapists recognized their own participation in a larger family-therapist system with its own rules of operation including both family and therapist, the therapist still attempting to change the family through interventions, reframings, etc. The present shift is to the constructivist perspective, which deemphasizes the family as a social system with predictable regulatory mechanisms and sees the family as a creator of its own reality through operations of its members' nervous systems and as through those social actions by which they co-construct family meanings within a social milieu.

Lest there be misunderstanding about these shifts in viewpoint, we underscore that there is no firm agreement among family therapists regarding the efficacy of any particular viewpoint. There are today a wide variety of stances, each with its mentors, its creative protagonists, its protectors, and its practitioners. While this essay obviously focuses upon the constructivist stance, it does not in any way promote the notion that only one stance is beneficial.

Indeed, it may be that the maintenance of a multiplicity of stances is a positive factor in the rich growth of the field itself. Over-unification of thought might produce orthodoxy, which nearly always strikes the death knell for creative ideas and actions.

Family therapy has thrived on paradigm shifts and on critique of these shifts within a community of observer-participants. This intellectual interaction is one of our greatest strengths as a field of professional inquiry and action. Octavio Paz, a recent Nobel Prize winner in poetry, convincingly promotes intellectual criticism as a necessary foundation upon which schools of literature are fully recognized and edified (Paz 1983). This seems to be the case for schools of family therapy as well.

The paradigm shifts in the field of family therapy indicate a rich and varied intellectual search for viewpoints and methods which will be most helpful to families. They also represent a continual struggle to understand ourselves as therapists, since we are, after all, members of families and of a society of families. In the broadest sense, these paradigm shifts represent an ongoing search for human meaning in a universe we strive to understand.

Constructivist Concepts in Family Therapy

The Milan Approach

The original Milan Team developed in the early 1970s consisted of Mara Selvini-Palazzoli, Juliana Prata, Luigi Boscolo, and Gianfranco Cecchin. Their first publication, *Paradox and Counterparadox* (1978), was considered a tour de force of finding therapeutic methods that closely fit Batesonian systemic ideals regarding families.

However, this team split up in the early 1980s and diverged with regard to its philosophical orientations. Selvini-Palazzoli and her team continued their search for the most potent interventions to "unwind" psychotically transacting families. This led her to conclude that "the invariant prescription" (1988) could be a single, most powerful intervention for such families. Although she saw the family as a system, she saw the therapist as someone who operates upon the system from an expert perspective. The therapist designs specific interventions for specific purposes. Although these interventions follow from the team's hypotheses, this is a deterministic approach which differs widely from the perspective of Boscolo and Cecchin.

During approximately this same period, Boscolo and Cecchin were utilizing the thinking of the new biologists, Maturana, Varela, and von Foerster, to inform their therapy. They began developing a therapeutic model that was far less instrumental than that of their former Milan team members.

This new Milan Team, composed only of Boscolo and Cecchin, has been most diligent in carrying out the ideals of a constructivist stance and developing a model of therapy to fit those ideas—although their concepts have recently been challenged by the Galveston and Norwegian Teams (Tjersland 1990).

The methods developed by Boscolo and Cecchin arose from years of working toward a congruent therapeutic model. These same years have been punctuated by the team's travels around the globe, demonstrating and being openly critiqued about the model they were developing. This Milan Team openly encourages such dialogue since, as constructivists, they are convinced that the finest solutions will arise as new realities, new meanings, and new concepts are co-constructed in an ongoing dialogue among peers.

The following concepts and methods have evolved directly from the ongoing narrative of the Milan Team and the community of observer-participants with whom it is structurally coupled.

Circular Questioning

This is a style of questioning by which relationships, as well as the constructed meanings within those relationships, are made clear. Its form is deceptively simple. One simply asks one member of the family to comment upon another member's thinking, statement, action, or belief. Circular questioning encourages members to talk about one another in the other's presence.

However, the method makes this a far more intriguing operation. The therapist has previously developed a hypothesis about the family and the problems it presents. This hypothesis represents the therapist's own belief about the family. It is important that the therapist's own beliefs be brought directly into the linguistic aspect of the therapy, since a basic premise of this work involves co-construction of meaning. Therapists who do not entertain their own beliefs may implicitly understand their beliefs to be "facts," while the family's beliefs are its "story." It is this self-searching aspect of constructivist therapy which is regarded as self-referential. The circularity of the questions includes not only the family members' beliefs, but the therapist's thinking as well (Tomm 1988).

In asking the circular questions, the therapist begins to work concentrically, from the inside out, so to speak. He will ask the family first about the immediate situation: What brought them to therapy? Who referred them? What do they hope to get out of it? Who is most hopeful? Who is least hopeful?

In this questioning there is a conscious attempt to elicit the greatest possible number of differences from the family's responses. This notion derives directly from the Batesonian belief that only difference can inform. The therapist encourages almost any response. If a child says, "I don't know," the therapist encourages the child to guess, or to try to answer on a scale of 1 to 10. These questions elicit a great deal of information. They demonstrate the internal politics of the family, the manner in which different members construct their individual belief systems, the family's constructions as a system of meaning, and the levels of intensity regarding certain beliefs of the members. For an excellent guideline on how to proceed with circular questioning, see Fleuridas et al. (1986).

In the early days of their new work, Boscolo and Cecchin Family Studies (Workshop Presentation, Huntington, N.Y. 1985) almost invariably offered a positive connotation at the end of a therapy session and sometimes prescribed a ritual to be performed in the week between sessions. In recent years they have discovered that the circular questions alone were interventions. That is, changes were taking place in the families even though no specific interventions were being given (Tomm 1988).

Boscolo and Cecchin came to believe that the interventions *per se* were not necessary, but that the questioning of the family elicited the co-construction of new meanings about the dilemma and the generation of novel solutions to the dilemma.

Keeney and Ross's (1985) analysis of the Milan Team's method is interesting and helpful. They state,

> A Milan therapeutic reality moves from stabilizing the client's semantic definition of the situation to stabilizing the therapist's semantic frame or "systemic hypothesis" while prescribing change in how so-called problems are viewed. (p. 253)

Clearly this is a therapy which focuses on beliefs and systems of belief, on meanings and systems of meaning. It does not attempt to shift behavior in the hope that belief will change. Rather, it works directly with the commonly held beliefs and attempts to enrich or shift them, enabling the entire system to reestablish the behaviors and interactions that flow from the altered beliefs.

In this way the therapy seeks to avoid invasive methods on the part of the therapist. It relies on the ability of families to rearrange themselves when the basic premises or contexts of their lives have been shifted to allow for more possibilities. It is a narrative therapy in which the therapist seeks the family "story." In so doing the therapist includes questions, comments, and context shifts in a manner that the family can utilize to free themselves in its own ongoing narrative.

The Milan Team and other constructivist therapists see families as stuck not so much in habitual transactional patterns or secret alliances as in its beliefs about life and the meanings it co-constructs about itself. This stuckness can only be understood when considered in relation to the narrative tradition of the family. That is, each family is in the ongoing production and creation of the story of its life. Its members cannot know directly or objectively about life, about themselves, or about others, but they know their life through the story they have been actively co-constructing. This story has no real beginning. Members are born into it and it carries on after they are gone. But its power to sway, to free, to bind, to pathologize, or to enrich is enormous.

Since all meanings occur within contexts, these family stories are rich with the contexts that support the meanings held by the participants. Yet contexts are constantly changing and external contextual change has enormous narrative impact on a family's story and on its ability to generate solutions. This is key to understanding the premises of constructivist therapy.

Perpetual Hypothesizing

Another important posture taken by the Milan Team is its insistence that hypotheses are never correct. They are never accurate diagnostic statements about family functioning. At best they are working hypotheses about the family and what is happening in it. Boscolo and Cecchin (1987) believe it is necessary to listen to one's own hypotheses and be able to state them when working with a family, since these hypotheses will inform the manner of questioning and the direction of eliciting responses. But they insist that no hypothesis, no matter how clever, no matter how apparently obvious, is to be taken as a statement of objective truth about the family. These two therapists are considered "radical constructivists" in that they regard objective truth as impossible. Thus, terms such as "objective" and "truth" are always couched in quotation marks to indicate that the speaker is aware of the innate subjectivity of all linguistic constructions.

A "New" Family Each Session

This posture follows quite naturally from perpetual hypothesizing. The team sees the family as essentially "different" at each session. That is, whatever it discovered about the family in previous sessions is remembered, but is not allowed to petrify into a static entity. By accepting the premise that the same family may come in and present itself differently each time, the team allows the greatest flexibility of perception. It is all too easy for a therapist to arrive at an early perception of a family and then work each session so as to fit the family back into his original perception. After all, it is less draining on the creativity of the therapist if he can decide what kind of family this "really" is and then note how it fails because of his pronouncement about its pathology as a state, rather than as an aspect of its narrative and tradition. Staying open to the possibility that the family can change at any time takes a perpetual wish to stay alive with the family and to continue being curious about it in a humble way (Cecchin 1987).

This way of thinking is far afield from the notions of discrete categorization and taxonomic thinking implicit in the psychiatric model as delineated in the DSM III-R. Yet Boscolo and Cecchin would be eager to point out that since the psychiatric model is the prevailing mental health model, it sets up basic premises and contexts for the family. They never advise a therapist to go directly against this model, but to find ways to re-contextualize the family's story to fit the psychiatric context and still yield change. One way to do this is through circular questioning, perhaps asking what the psychiatrist believed was best, which family member agreed with the psychiatrist, which felt he was partly right, etc. In this way the therapist allows the family's beliefs about the psychiatrist's beliefs to enter the linguistic domain of the therapy and to enrich the story.

A poignant example of this kind of work can be seen in Boscolo's treatment of a schizophrenic woman in a psychiatric hospital (taped presentation, 1987, Huntington, N.Y.). He not only shifted the beliefs the woman held, but also shifted the beliefs held by the team of psychiatrists and social workers who attended to her. Since constructivism is a therapy of context, meaning, and belief, he could shift the co-constructed beliefs of the woman-plus-psychiatric team so as to let her return home and reestablish a productive new life with the continued narrative support of the hospitals' psychiatric team. This was essential to her therapy, since any pressure from the team could easily have re-contextualized her situation as a need to return to the hospital.

An Agreement Not to Know Outcome

Boscolo and Cecchin's work proceeds in a manner which does not insist on their knowing the outcomes. They have come to understand, by watching families change over many years, that the therapist's need to watch change occur can tempt the therapist to act too instrumentally. If the therapist must always know the outcomes, she may not be able to make the context changes which can help change occur.

Often Boscolo and Cecchin will follow up to find out how the therapy went. They usually work in consultation with a therapist-plus-family system of meaning. Since they work with beliefs, they carefully question the therapist to learn how her beliefs may bind her, as well as how the family member's beliefs bind them. Often it is the interaction of these belief systems—i.e., the co-construction of meanings by therapist and family—that gets the therapy stuck.

Since their consultations take them all over the globe, their work with families is often a matter of follow-up calls or letters to therapists. As consultants they had to find a way to work to ensure that the family and the therapist would continue creating new perspectives after the consultation.

Again, such a stance follows naturally from the constructivist acceptance that objective reality cannot be learned. This being so, the therapist listens for the story told by the family following consultation to learn whether the change has occurred.

There are other aspects of the new Milan Team's work which are pertinent to therapy but which would take us outside the scope of this chapter. For a more complete account, see *Milan Systemic Therapy* (Boscolo et al. 1987).

Other Constructivist Methods in Therapy

Hypothetical Futuring

This is a questioning method which generates future possibilities and solutions in a purely hypothetical manner. It encourages families to imagine different future scenarios under different conditions. In this way it languages an ecology of changes and their results in the safety of the present. Since it is a languaging of the future, no direct action is required now, nor are any present risks involved. If risks and difficulties arise in the hypothetical conversation, the therapist can turn the questioning to hypothetical ways the families might handle such risks, keeping the entire conversation in the hypothetical domain (Penn 1985).

This technique is perhaps one of the clearest demonstrations of the constructivist stance, since there is no attempt to pin down the family or the individual to making a choice in the present. The therapist helps the family generate an assortment of possibilities and an assortment of family adjustments to those possibilities, all within a frame of "could happen" or "might happen."

The technique also enables families to safely imagine different patterns of relations at different times in the future. Since such shifts in the family relational pattern are often difficult to bring about in the present, hypothetical and future questions can introduce the possibility of change in a narrative, imaginary way.

For example, one might ask the family these questions: What do you believe would happen if Michele moved out of the house? Who do you think would most worry about her? What would be the hardest part of this for the family? Who would be most helpful to the family after she left? Would anyone take Michele's place in the family if she were to leave? Do you think you would miss her more in the first month, the second month, after one year, after five years? How old will each of you be in five years? What did you hope life would be like for you at that age? Et cetera.

These are very easy questions to generate, but the finest line of hypothetical and future questions will naturally follow from an ongoing conversation with the family. These questions will "fit" more naturally within a conversation and will allow the family to be more exploratory than if the questions are prearranged outside the dialogue.

The Reflecting Team

This concept has grown out of the work of Anderson (1987). In this approach a clinical team is utilized, but not in the usual strategic sense. Rather, the team may be in the room with the therapist and family, simply listening carefully to the conversation that develops between them. At a certain juncture the therapist may ask the family if they would like to hear from the team, or the therapist himself may want to hear from the team.

In either case the therapist and family stop conversing and the team has a dialogue about what it has been listening to in the therapeutic conversation. Generally the frame or context is a positive one which enables the team to conjecture in an open, unthreatening manner about what is happening in the family, what might occur if the family saw things differently, what might happen if a change occurred, whether the family will still see things this way in the future, etc. The reflecting team actually carries on a conversation "meta" to the family-therapist conversation. It is a conversation about the family's conversation. This is an extraordinarily gentle way to introduce novelty into the dialogue precisely because it does not insist on a response. The therapist and/or family may respond to what they heard or may go right on conversing with each other where they left off. One can see in the development of such a technique how carefully these constructivist therapists try not to be directly instrumental in requesting change or implying blame. Since the entire process involves a series of interlocking conversational loops, and each loop simply contextualizes the other loops in a series of reflexive recursions, there can be no real end, or "correct" thing for the family to do. This author believes that the reflecting team approach comes closer to the stated ideals of constructivism than does any other method developed to date. For a comparison of three constructivist team approaches, see Tjersland (1990).

Is a Constructivist Stance an "Improvement" in Therapy?

This question is difficult precisely because many systemically based therapies see themselves as having partially adopted constructivist themes. It could be argued that even Haley's work, which strategically makes clients conform to his intended behavioral shifts, eventually leads to clients' and families' new constructions of reality and beliefs. Is this constructivism or instrumentalism? Can any set of changes be considered constructivist if the client or family eventually undergoes changes in their story or their beliefs about themselves?

The pure constructivists believe that only a therapy based on human language and dialogue can meet the requirements of a constructivist stance. That is, constructivists look for a change in the languaging and meanings co-constructed as the goal of therapy, not in behavioral shifts in the family stimulated by a therapist who remains unchanged. They argue that any other initial premise, such as "homeostatic system" or "object relations theory," simply locks the therapist into a predetermined belief to which the family must be fitted if therapy is to take place.

Their argument makes good sense if one considers that the therapist-and-family, not the family alone, comprise the actual therapeutic system.

Critics of constructivism have wondered whether enough change takes place during and between sessions to enable a constructivist to help families. Accounts of constructivist teams and consultations indicate that they achieve change at least as often as do other forms of family therapy, but that their posture with regard to the family is more humble and more curious. The constructivists allow the ongoing narrative flow to inform them, rather than follow a predetermined hypothesis about how all systems function. Indeed, one would probably not hear the word "function" in a constructivist dialogue, since it invalidates and disqualifies the constant creation of actions, interactions, and beliefs as an ongoing aspect of family dialogue within a tradition (Hoffman 1990).

Feminist theory and feminist family therapists have taken on both systems theory as well as constructivism for their failures to address the inequalities that regularly persist in families. These inequalities are primarily gender issues, but they also relate to abuse and neglect of children. Feminists argue persuasively that there is still no comprehensive therapeutic theory which can handle these painful and pervasive political problems (Hare-Mustin 1987; Miller and MacKinnon 1987).

Erickson (1988) takes on the entire systemic paradigm in much the same way as do the feminists, although he arrives at some interesting conclusions.

He writes (1988, p. 233):

> With respect to this, there seems little alternative to adopting a social network perspective. Such a perspective offers the advantages of generating three kinds of information: (a) about persons, (b) about relationships, and (c) about the structure of relationships and how structures, persons and relationships have changed over time in particular social contexts.

I hold, as does Octavio Paz (1983), that criticism such as Erickson's, Hare-Mustin's, and Miller's are essential if our field is to grow and improve. The critical vigilance that such authors demonstrate represents perhaps the greatest validation that these theories and models are having an impact, and that they can be improved upon.

This dialogic approach to families, to individuals, to oneself, and to the entire field is the essence of the constructivist stance. It is an overarching idea of how to look at what we believe and at how we operate from those beliefs. Constructivism as a way of thinking will continue to encourage the penetrating and insightful criticism necessary for its development.

Conclusions

This chapter presents highlights of a way of thinking, a paradigm called *constructivism*. It presents the evolution of this stance from philosophy to the practice of family therapy.

This excursion has taken us from a world of concrete objects, things, and relationships that are clearly known, to a world of internally generated correlations to reality, a world devoid of objectivity but filled with "objectivity," a world wherein there are no fast and easy truths or correct answers. The therapy that has been developing from this new way of thinking has become increasingly language-based, since for constructivism, languaging is the action which evokes a world to believe in rather than a world to "understand." Therefore we might conjecture, as Hoffman (1990) recently has, about the forms that may emerge from this ongoing search within a linguistic tradition.

Future Directions

Consider that we do not always speak in simple dialogues to construct our beliefs; sometimes we use a far richer and more subtle languaging. Human beings have extended languaging and its formal expressions into a wide variety of forms, each with its own manner of meaning. Prose, poetry, epic, drama, prayer, blessing, riddle, paradox, non-sequitur, palindrome, and joke are just a few linguistic forms used for constructing meaning among persons.

I believe that we have just begun to think in linguistic terms with regard to therapy. For example, we can be moved to tears or joy by the wonder of how a poem means. A poem evokes meanings from its reader precisely because it does not clearly spell out its narrative content. Its beauty and elicitation of new worlds emerge as aspects of its semantic "thickness" (Swanger 1974). This thickness of meaning may be something for the field of family therapy to consider as its next area of serious inquiry.

For me, the key questions at this juncture are, How can we find ways to enrich, to thicken, the experience of meaning for our client families? How do we construct linguistic space/time experiences for them in therapy, by which they can safely, yet more fully imagine hypothetical changes?

Could we make better use of phonemic variety and similarity? This would involve listening attentively to how our words actually sound and to how they construct meanings. Do the words' sounds in some way support the meaning? Aren't we suffused with meaning when we read Edgar Allen Poe's "Quoth the raven, nevermore," because we intuitively understand the tragedy conveyed by the very sound of the line? The line falls back upon itself in a sort of phonemic recursion while we are understanding its content at the narrative level (Jacobson 1987).

We will probably not become poets for our clients, but the search and analysis of beauty in linguistic forms may offer possibilities for change that will take us far from the instrumentalism of our previous paradigms. We may create a therapy of ethical aesthetics. Perhaps the term "therapy" will fall away entirely and we will learn to converse with beauty, intelligence, and benevolence in changing a family's ongoing narrative.

The reader who has read this far has no doubt begun to agree or disagree with certain of its aspects, has recognized regularities and irregularities in its presentation, and has at least initially begun to dialogue internally with the author regarding these constructivist concepts.

If in so doing the reader has been encouraged to wonder about the nature of reality and objectivity in family therapy—if he or she is somewhat concerned about an overly instrumental approach, if he or she now openly speculates about the creation of his or her own beliefs and helps client families to do the same, this article itself has created a perturbation, a linguistic disturbance, which could someday be felicitously utilized in the therapeutic conversation.

References

Anderson, H., and H. Goolishian (1990) "Beyond cybernetics: Comments on Atkinson and Heath's 'Further Thoughts on Second

Order Family Therapy,' " *Family Process* 29: 157–63.

Anderson, T. (1987) "The reflecting team: Dialogue and meta-dialogue in clinical work," *Family Process* 26: 415–28.

——— (1988) "Human systems as linguistic systems: Preliminary and evolving ideas about the implications for clinical theory," *Family Process* 27: 371–93.

Bandler, R., and J. Grinder (1976) *The Structure of Magic, II*. Palo Alto, Calif.: Science and Behavior Books.

Berger, P., and T. Luckmann (1966) *The Social Construction of Reality*. Garden City, N.Y.: Doubleday.

Bogdan, J. (1984) "Family organization as an ecology of ideas: An alternative of the reification of family systems," *Family Process* 23: 375–88.

Boscolo, L. (1986, 1987, 1988, 1989) Workshop presentations and conversations with the author in Huntington and Westhampton Beach, New York.

Boscolo, L., et al. (1987) *Milan Systemic Therapy*. New York: Basic Books.

Byng-Hall, J. (1988) "Scripts and legends in families and family therapy," *Family Process* 27 (2): 167–80.

Capra, F. (1982) *The Turning Point*. New York: Simon and Schuster.

Cecchin, G. (1987) "Hypothesizing, circularity, and neutrality revisited: An invitation to curiosity," *Family Process 26* (4): 405–414.

Coyne, J. (1985) "Towards a theory of frames and reframing: The social nature of frames," *Journal of Marital and Family Therapy* 11 (4): 337–44.

Cronen, V., K. Johnson, and J. Lannamann (1982) "Paradoxes, double binds, and reflective loops: An alternative theoretical perspective," *Family Process* 21: 91–112.

Cronen, V., W. Pearce, and L. Harris (1979) "The coordinated management of meaning: A theory of communication," in F. Dance, ed., *Comparative Communication Theory*. New York: Harper and Row.

Dell, P. (1985) "Understanding Bareson and Maturana: Toward a biological foundation for the social sciences," *Journal of Marital and Family Therapy* 11: 1–20.

Efran, J., M. Lukens, and R. Lukens (1990) *Language, Structure, and Change: Frameworks of Meaning in Psychotherapy*. New York; W. W. Norton.

Efran, J., and M. Lukens (1985) "The world according to Humberto Maturana," *Networker* 9 (3): 22–28.

Erickson, G. (1988) "Against the grain: Decentering family therapy," *Family Process* 14: 225–36.

Fleuridas, C., T. Nelson, and D. Rosenthal (1986) "The evolution of circular questions: Training family therapists," *Journal of Marital and Family Therapy* 12 (2): 13–128.

Foerster, H. von (1981) *Observing Systems*. Seaside, Calif.: Intersystems.

Furman, B., and T. Ahola (1988) "The return to the question, 'Why?': Advantages of exploring pre-existing explanations," *Family Process* 27 (4): 395–410.

Gergen, K. (1985) "The social constructionist movement in modern psychology," *American Psychology* 40: 266–75.

Glasersfeld, E. von (1987) *The Construction of Knowledge*. Salinas, Calif.: Intersystems.

Gleick, J. (1987) *Chaos*. New York: Viking Press.

Hare-Mustin, R. (1987) "The problem of gender in family theory," *Family Process* 26: 15–28.

Harper, W., and R. Meerbote (1984) *Kant on Causality, Freedom, and Objectivity*. Minneapolis: University of Minnesota Press.

Held, B. (1990) "What's in a name? Some confusions and concerns about constructivism," *Journal of Marital and Family Therapy* 16 (2): 179–86.

Hoffman, L. (1990) "Constructing reality: An art of lenses," *Family Process* 29: 1–12.

Hofstadter, D. (1979) *Godel, Escher, Bach: An Eternal Golden Braid*. New York: Vintage Books.

Jacobson, R. (1987) *Language in Literature*.

Cambridge, Mass.: Harvard University Press.

Jahn, R. and B. Dunne (1987) *Margins of Reality: The Role of Consciousness in the Physical World*. New York: Harcourt Brace Jovanovich.

Kuhn, T. (1970) *The Structure of Scientific Revolution*. Chicago: The University of Chicago Press.

Lorenz, E. (1961) "Deterministic non-period flow," in Gleick, *Chaos*.

Maturana, U. (1970) "Biology of cognition," *Boston Studies on the Philosophy of Science,* vol. 100. Boston: Boston University Press.

Maturana, U., and F. Varela (1980) "Autopoesis: The organization of the Living," *Boston Studies in the Philosophy of Science,* vol. 100.

——— (1987) *The Tree of Knowledge: The Biological Roots of Human Understanding*. Boston: New Science Library.

McCulloch, W. (1988) *Embodiments of Mind*. Cambridge, Mass.: MIT Press.

Miller, D., and L. MacKinnon (1987) "The new epistemology and the Milan approach: Feminist and sociopolitical considerations," *Journal of Marital and Family Therapy* 13 (2): 139–56.

Palazzoli, M. S., et al. (1989) *Family Games: General Models of Psychotic Processes in the Family*. New York: W. W. Norton.

Paz, O. (1983) "On criticism," *Alternating Currents*. New York: Seaver.

Penn, P. (1985) "Feed-forward: Future questions, future maps," *Family Process* 24 (3): 299–310.

Prest, L., E. Darden, and J. Keller, (1990) "The fly on the wall: Reflecting team supervision," *Journal of Marital and Family Therapy* 16 (3): 265–74.

Prigogine, I., and I. Stengers (1984) *Order Out of Chaos*. New York: Bantam Books.

Reiss, D. (1981) *The Family's Construction of Reality*. Cambridge, Mass.: Harvard University Press.

Rommetveit, R., et al. (1971) "Processing utterances in context," in R. Rommetveit and E. Carswell, eds. New York: Academic Press.

Russell, B., and A. Whitehead (1927) *Principia Mathematica*. Cambridge: Cambridge University Press.

Selvini-Palazzoli, M., et al. (1978) *Paradox and Counterparadox*. New York: Jason Aronson.

Swanger, D. (1974) *The Poem as Process*. New York: Harcourt Brace Jovanovich.

Swann, B. (1988) "Who is the East? The riddle in literature and life," *Parabola* 13 (3): 70–75.

Tjersland, O. (1990) "From universe to multiverse—and back again," *Family Process* 29 (4): 285–98.

Tomm, K. (1988) "Interventive interviewing: Part III. Intending to ask circular, strategic, or reflexive questions?" *Family Process* 27 (1): 1–16.

——— (1987) "Interventive interviewing: Part II. Reflexive questioning as a means to enable self-healing," *Family Process* 26 (2): 167–84.

Varela, F. (1979). *Principles of Biological Autonomy*. New York: North Holland Press.

Wright, G. von, and G. Abscombe, eds. (1979) *Ludwig Wittgenstein: Notebooks 1914–1916,* 2nd ed. Chicago: University of Chicago Press.

Zukav, G. (1979) *The Dancing Wu Li Masters: An Overview of the New Physics*. New York: William Morrow.

Contributors

Joan D. Atwood, Ph.D., C.S.W., coordinator of the graduate programs in marriage and family counseling and director of the Marital and Family Clinic at Hofstra University. Is a New York State board member and approved supervisor of the American Association of Marriage and Family Therapy. She is also a clinical supervisor and diplomate of the American Board of Sexology.

Vita Bollman, M.S.W., is a special education teacher of the learning disabled and emotionally disturbed and a certified social worker in private practice in Massapequa, New York.

Frank Genovese, Ph.D., a school psychologist at Xaverian High School, is a clinical member of the American Association for Marriage and Family Therapists. He is the clinical supervisor at the Hofstra University Marriage and Family Counseling Clinic.

Marvin Glassmann, Ed.D., is the co-director of Parkway Consultation Center, a New York Board Member, and a Clinical Member of the American Association of Marriage and Family Therapists. He is in private practice in Queens, New York.

Maxine Borowsky Junge, Ph.D., L.C.S.W., A.T.R., is an associate professor of marriage and family studies at Loyola Marymount University, Los Angeles, California.

Leonard Marlow, Esq., is an attorney and divorce mediator in Garden City, New York.

George Meyer, Ed.D., is a professor of psychology at Suffolk County Community College, a New York State board member, and an approved supervisor of the American Association of Marriage and Family Therapists.

John Mince, Ph.D., is a guidance director in the Three Village School System, an adjunct assistant professor in the graduate programs in marriage and family counseling, Hofstra University, and the clinical supervisor at Family Studies, Huntington, New York.

Shirley Riley, M.A., A.T.R., M.F.C.C., is an assistant professor in the graduate school of marriage and family studies, Loyola Marymount University, Los Angeles, California.

Ethan Roberts, M.A., is a family therapist and supervisor at Youth Environmental Services. He specializes in work with families of acting-out adolescents and has extensive experience counseling families of handicapped children.

Richard Sheaman, Ph.D., is a school psychologist in the secondary school system in Massapequa, New York. He has also worked in army drug and alcohol programs in Germany and in mental health and children's clinics in Hawaii.

Efrem Rosen, Ph.D., is the coordinator of interdisciplinary studies of human sexuality, and the coordinator of the Human Sciences Program, Hofstra University.

Estelle Weinstein, Ph.D., is coordinator of the programs in health at Hofstra University and is a clinical member of the American Association of Marriage and Family Therapists.

Barrie Zucal, M.S., is a clinical member of the American Association of Marriage and Family Therapists and is in private practice in New York.

Index